Fodor's 2003

Las Vegas

The Guide
for All Budgets

Completely
Updated

Where to Stay, Eat,
and Explore

On and Off
the Beaten Path

When to Go,
What to Pack

Maps, Travel Tips,
and Web Sites

Fodor's Travel Publications • New York, Toronto, London, Sydney, Auckland
www.fodors.com

Fodor's Las Vegas 2003

EDITOR: Mary Beth Bohman

Editorial Contributors: Bill Burton, Geoff Carter, Fred Couzens, Lenore Greiner, Satu Hummasti, M. Elizabeth Leong, Haas Mroue, Heidi Knapp Rinella, Mike Weatherford

Editorial Production: Taryn Luciani

Maps: David Lindroth, *cartographer*; Bob Blake and Rebecca Baer, *map editors*

Design: Fabrizio La Rocca, *creative director*; Guido Caroti, *art director*; Jolie Novak, *senior picture editor*; Melanie Marin, *photo editor*

Cover Design: Pentagram

Production/Manufacturing: Angela L. McLean

Cover Photo: Bill Ross/Corbis *(Walking Mall on Fremont Street)*

Copyright

Important Tip

Although all prices, opening times, and other details in this book are based on information supplied to us at press time, changes occur all the time in the travel world, and Fodor's cannot accept responsibility for facts that become outdated or for inadvertent errors or omissions. So **always confirm information when it matters,** especially if you're making a detour to visit a specific place.

Special Sales

Fodor's Travel Publications are available at special discounts for bulk purchases for sales promotions or premiums. Special editions, including personalized covers, excerpts of existing guides, and corporate imprints, can be created in large quantities for special needs. For more information, contact your local bookseller or write to Special Markets, Fodor's Travel Publications, 1745 Broadway, New York, NY 10019. Inquiries from Canada should be directed to your local Canadian bookseller or sent to Random House of Canada, Ltd., Marketing Department, 2775 Matheson Boulevard East, Mississauga, Ontario L4W 4P7. Inquiries from the United Kingdom should be sent to Fodor's Travel Publications, 20 Vauxhall Bridge Road, London SW1V 2SA, England.

PRINTED IN THE UNITED STATES OF AMERICA

10 9 8 7 6 5 4 3 2 1

CONTENTS

Maps and Charts

ON THE ROAD WITH FODOR'S

A TRIP TAKES YOU OUT OF YOURSELF. Concerns of life at home completely disappear, driven away by more immediate thoughts—about, say, what marvels will beguile the next day, or where you'll have dinner. That's where Fodor's comes in. We make sure that you know all your options, so that you don't miss something that's around the next bend just because you didn't know it was there. Mindful that the best memories of your trip might have nothing to do with what you came to Las Vegas to see, we guide you to sights large and small all over town. You might set out to gamble away your bankroll on the Strip, but back at home you find yourself unable to forget hiking in Red Rock Canyon at sunrise or attending a performance by Cirque de Soleil. With Fodor's at your side, serendipitous discoveries are never far away.

About Our Writers

Our success in showing you every corner of Las Vegas is a credit to our extraordinary writers. Although there's no substitute for travel advice from a good friend who knows your style, our contributors are the next best thing—the kind of people you would poll for travel advice if you knew them.

Bill Burton is the Casino Gambling Guide for About.com and is our gambling tutor. He writes for several national gaming publications, including *Chance & Circumstance* magazine and two newsletters, *The Crapshooter* and *Viva Las Vegas*. His book *Getting The Edge at Low Limit Texas Hold'em* was published in January 2002.

Geoff Carter reflects on anything and everything in Vegas, from casino carpets to the myth of Elvis, in his "Tourists for Breakfast" column in *Las Vegas Weekly*. He is the film columnist for the *Las Vegas Sun* and writes lifestyle pieces for *Las Vegas Life* magazine. Though he's lived in Vegas 11 years, he claims to have only gambled maybe $50, tops.

Fred Couzens clocked some serious car time while updating the Side Trips chapter. A Las Vegas resident, Fred has experience roaming the state as a freelance writer

for the *Las Vegas Mercury* and for the *Nevada Business Journal*—not to mention all of the trips taken with golf clubs or his camera in the back seat.

Lenore Greiner frequently crosses the Mojave from her home in San Diego to visit the excellent shops and spas of Las Vegas. Sometimes she does gamble but considers it just a waste of valuable shopping time. Besides contributing to Fodor's guides, she has written for *Newsday*, the *San Francisco Examiner*, and *Healing Retreats and Spas*, among others.

M. Elizabeth Leong hones her gambling skills on frequent trips to Vegas. New to Fodor's this year, she circled the tables and sized up the slots while updating the Casinos chapter.

Haas Mroue started coming to Las Vegas when he lived in Southern California, and he keeps coming back. Covering hotels from Bangkok to Monte Carlo for travel guides and magazines, Haas still feels that when it comes to opulence and grandeur without stuffy attitude, Las Vegas resorts can't be beat. He also focused his keen eye for details on our Smart Travel Tips.

Heidi Knapp Rinella has been reviewing restaurants for the better part of 20 years and currently is the restaurant critic for the *Las Vegas Review-Journal*, which gives her a front-row seat to observe the explosion of the Las Vegas culinary scene.

Mike Weatherford came to us well prepared for the task of revising the Nightlife and the Arts chapter of this book. He is an entertainment reporter for the *Las Vegas Review-Journal*, so he sees all the shows and visits all the clubs. This year Mike also layered on the sunscreen to cover Outdoor Activities and Sports. He has lived in Las Vegas since 1987.

You can rest assured that you're in good hands—and that no property mentioned in the book has paid to be included. Each has been selected strictly on its merits, as the best of its type in its price range.

How to Use This Book

Up front is Smart Travel Tips A to Z, arranged alphabetically by topic and loaded with tips, Web sites, and contact information. Destination: Las Vegas helps get you in the mood for your trip. The Exploring chapter is divided into neighborhood sections arranged in logical geographical order; each recommends a good tour and lists local sights alphabetically. The chapters that follow Exploring are arranged alphabetically. At the end of the book you'll find the Books and Movies section which suggests enriching reading and viewing.

Icons and Symbols

★	Our special recommendations
✕	Restaurant
🏠	Lodging establishment
✕🏠	Lodging establishment whose restaurant warrants a special trip
⚠	Campgrounds
⏱	Good for kids (rubber duck)
☞	Sends you to another section of the guide for more information
✉	Address
☎	Telephone number
◷	Opening and closing times

☒   Admission prices (those we give apply to adults; substantially reduced fees are almost always available for children, students, and senior citizens)

Numbers in white and black circles ③ ❸ that appear on the maps, in the margins, and within the tours correspond to one another.

Don't Forget to Write

Your experiences—positive and negative—matter to us. If we have missed or misstated something, we want to hear about it. We follow up on all suggestions. Contact the Las Vegas editor at editors@fodors.com or c/o Fodor's, 1745 Broadway, New York, New York 10019. And have a fabulous trip!

Karen Cure

Karen Cure
Editorial Director

The Western United States

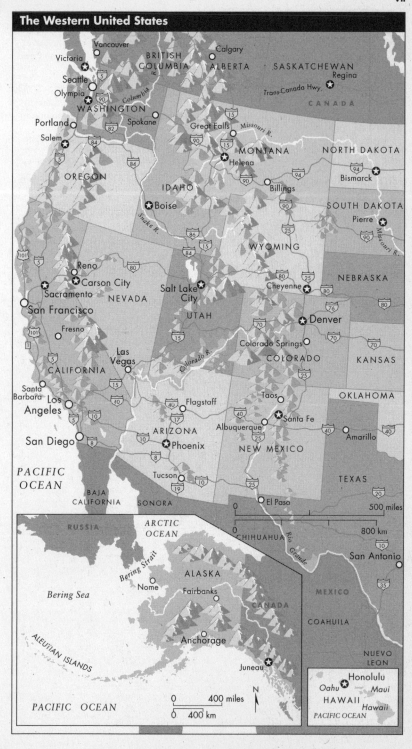

Vancouver
Victoria
BRITISH
COLUMBIA
Calgary
ALBERTA
SASKATCHEWAN
Regina
Seattle
Olympia
WASHINGTON
Columbia
Trans-Canada Hwy.
CANADA
Portland
Salem
Spokane
Great Falls
Missouri R.
MONTANA
Helena
NORTH DAKOTA
Bismarck
OREGON
IDAHO
Billings
Boise
Snake R.
SOUTH DAKOTA
Pierre
Missouri R.
Reno
Carson City
Sacramento
San Francisco
NEVADA
Salt Lake
City
UTAH
WYOMING
Cheyenne
NEBRASKA
Denver
Fresno
Las
Vegas
CALIFORNIA
Colorado R.
Colorado Springs
COLORADO
KANSAS
Santa
Barbara
Los
Angeles
San Diego
Flagstaff
ARIZONA
Phoenix
Taos
Santa Fe
Albuquerque
NEW MEXICO
Amarillo
OKLAHOMA
PACIFIC
OCEAN
Tucson
BAJA
CALIFORNIA
SONORA
El Paso
TEXAS
CHIHUAHUA
Rio Grande
San Antonio
MEXICO
COAHUILA
NUEVO
LEON

0   500 miles
0   800 km

RUSSIA
ARCTIC
OCEAN
Bering Strait
ALASKA
Nome
Bering Sea
Fairbanks
CANADA
ALEUTIAN ISLANDS
Anchorage
Juneau
PACIFIC OCEAN
0   400 miles
0   400 km
N

Honolulu
Oahu
Maui
HAWAII
Hawaii
PACIFIC OCEAN

Nevada

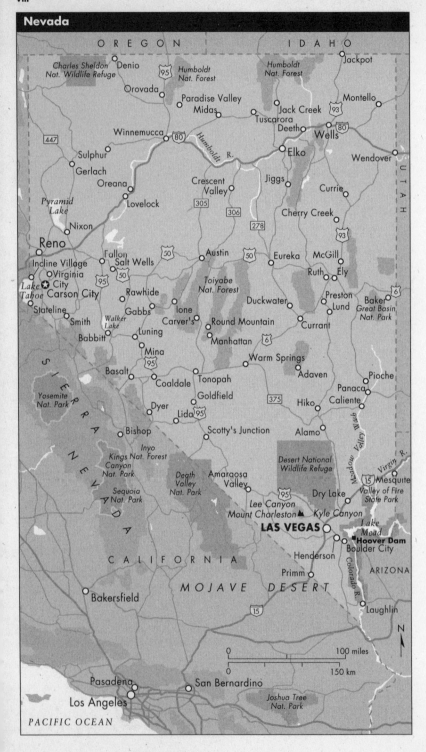

Greater Las Vegas

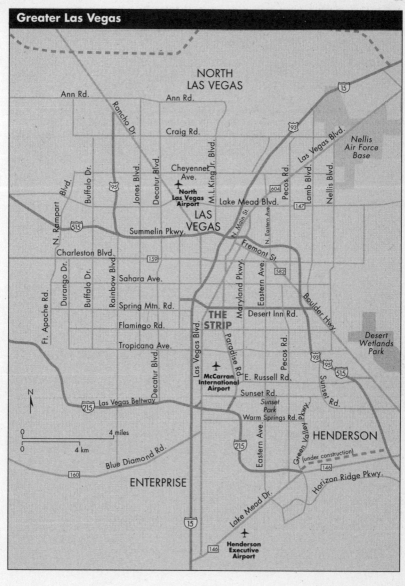

Las Vegas

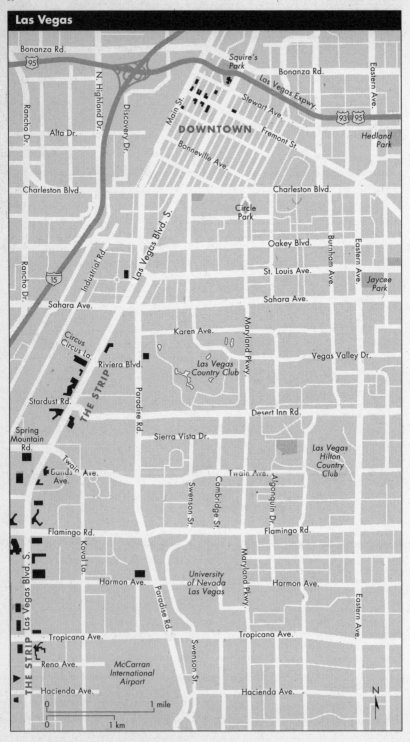

Bonanza Rd.
95
N. Highland Dr.
Discovery Dr.
Rancho Dr.
Alta Dr.
Squire's Park
Bonanza Rd.
Las Vegas Expwy.
Stewart Ave.
Eastern Ave.
DOWNTOWN
Main St.
Fremont St.
93 95
Hedland Park
Bonneville Ave.
Charleston Blvd.
Charleston Blvd.
Circle Park
Las Vegas Blvd. S.
Oakey Blvd.
Burnham Ave.
Eastern Ave.
Rancho Dr.
15
Industrial Rd.
St. Louis Ave.
Jaycee Park
Sahara Ave.
Sahara Ave.
Circus Circus La.
Karen Ave.
Maryland Pkwy.
Vegas Valley Dr.
Riviera Blvd.
THE STRIP
Paradise Rd.
Las Vegas Country Club
Stardust Rd.
Desert Inn Rd.
Spring Mountain Rd.
Sierra Vista Dr.
Las Vegas Hilton Country Club
Sands Ave.
Twain Ave.
Twain Ave.
Algonquin Dr.
Swenson St.
Cambridge St.
Flamingo Rd.
Flamingo Rd.
Koval La.
Maryland Pkwy.
Harmon Ave.
University of Nevada Las Vegas
Harmon Ave.
Eastern Ave.
Paradise Rd.
THE STRIP
S. Las Vegas Blvd.
Tropicana Ave.
Tropicana Ave.
Reno Ave.
McCarran International Airport
Swenson St.
Hacienda Ave.
Hacienda Ave.

N

0   1 mile
0   1 km

ESSENTIAL INFORMATION

ADDRESSES

The Greater Las Vegas area is located in Clark County Nevada and encompasses four cities: Las Vegas, North Las Vegas, Henderson, and Boulder City.

AIR TRAVEL TO AND FROM LAS VEGAS

Las Vegas McCarran International Airport (LAS) is well served by many nonstop and direct flights. All theairlines operate frequent service from their hub cities and between them offer one-stop connecting flights from virtually every city in the country. In addition to the "usual" hub cities (i.e., Atlanta, Chicago, Dallas, Denver, Houston, Minneapolis, St. Louis, Salt Lake City), some smaller airlines offer nonstop service from other destinations. Las Vegas's own National Airlines flies 16 brand-new Boeing 757s nonstop from 10 major U.S. cities (including New York–JFK, Newark, Miami, and Philadelphia). Southwest remains the dominant airline (with highest number of passengers carried), and it offers frequent flights to many cities in the south and west, including San Diego, Los Angeles, Oakland, Seattle, and Phoenix. Many international carriers serve Las Vegas as well, including direct flights from Canada and the UK.

BOOKING

When you book **look for nonstop flights** and **remember that "direct" flights stop at least once.** Try to avoid connecting flights, which require a change of plane. Two airlines may operate a connecting flight jointly, so ask if your airline operates every segment of the trip; you may find that the carrier you prefer flies you only part of the way. To find more booking tips and to check prices and make on-line flight reservations, log on to www.fodors.com.

CARRIERS

➤ MAJOR AIRLINES: **American** (☎ 800/433–7300, WEB www.aa.com). **America West** (☎ 800/235–9292, WEB www.americawest.com). **Continental** (☎ 800/523–3273, WEB www.continental.com). **Delta** (☎ 800/221–1212, WEB www.delta.com). **Northwest** (☎ 800/225–2525, WEB www.nwa.com). **Southwest** (☎ 800/435–9792, WEB www.southwest.com). **United** (☎ 800/241–6522, WEB www.united.com). **US Airways** (☎ 800/428–4322, WEB www.usairways.com).

➤ SMALLER AIRLINES: **Alaska Airlines** (☎ 800/426–0333, WEB www.alaskaairlines.com). **Allegiant Air** (☎ 877/202–6444, WEB www.allegiant-air.com). **Aloha** (☎ 800/367–5250, WEB www.alohaairlines.com). **American Trans Air/ATA** (☎ 800/435–9282, WEB www.ata.com). **Frontier Airlines** (☎ 800/432–1359, WEB www.frontierairlines.com). **Hawaiian Airlines** (☎ 800/367–5320, WEB www.hawaiianair.com). **Midwest Express** (☎ 800/452–2022, WEB www.midwestexpress.com). **National Airlines** (☎ 888/757–5387, WEB www.nationalairlines.com). **Skywest** (☎ 800/453–9417, WEB www.skywest.com). **Sun Country Air** (☎ 800/752–1218, WEB www.suncountry.com). **Vanguard** (☎ 800/826–4827, WEB www.flyvanguard.com). **Worry-Free Vacations** (☎ 800/328–0025, WEB www.worryfreevacations.com).

CHECK-IN AND BOARDING

Always **ask your carrier about its check-in policy.** Plan to arrive at the airport about two hours before your scheduled departure time for domestic flights and 2½ to 3 hours before international flights.

Las Vegas used to be the premiere destination for remote check-in facilities, a service that allowed passengers to check-in for flights at various hotels on the Strip and head straight for the departure gate with seat assignment and boarding pass. At press time, however, all non-airport check-in was suspended until further notice due to heightened airport security measures. National Airlines' remote check-in facility at Harrah's is also closed until further notice.

Assuming that not everyone with a ticket will show up, airlines routinely overbook planes. When everyone does show, airlines ask for volunteers to give up their seats. In return, these volunteers usually get a certificate for a free flight and are rebooked on the next flight out. If there are not enough volunteers, the airline must choose who will be denied boarding. The first to get bumped are passengers who checked in late and those flying on discounted tickets, so **get to the gate and check in as early as possible,** especially during peak periods.

Always **bring a government-issued photo I.D. to the airport;** even when it's not required, a passport is best.

CUTTING COSTS

Always ask for package rates as these tend to be the best bargains to Las Vegas—airfare that includes hotel and sometimes car rental. It's smart to **call a number of airlines,** and when you are quoted a good price, **book it on the spot**—the same fare may not be available the next day. Always **check different routings** and look into using alternate airports. Also, price off-peak flights, which may be significantly less expensive than others. Saturday afternoon flights are usually the best flights for bargain fares. Travel agents, especially low-fare specialists (☞ Discounts and Deals), are helpful.

Consolidators are another good source. They buy tickets for scheduled international flights at reduced rates from the airlines, then sell them at prices that beat the best fare available

directly from the airlines. Sometimes you can even get your money back if you need to return the ticket. Carefully read the fine print detailing penalties for changes and cancellations, purchase the ticket with a credit card, and **confirm your consolidator reservation with the airline.**

➤ CONSOLIDATORS: **Cheap Tickets** (☎ 800/377–1000 or 888/922–8849, WEB www.cheaptickets.com). **Discount Airline Ticket Service** (☎ 800/576–1600). **Unitravel** (☎ 800/325–2222, WEB www.unitravel.com). **Up & Away Travel** (☎ 212/889–2345, WEB www.upandaway.com). **World Travel Network** (☎ 800/409–6753).

ENJOYING THE FLIGHT

State your seat preference when purchasing your ticket, and then repeat it when you confirm and when you check in. For more legroom, you can request one of the few emergency-aisle seats at check-in, if you are capable of lifting at least 50 pounds—a Federal Aviation Administration requirement of passengers in these seats. Seats behind a bulkhead also offer more legroom, but they don't have under-seat storage. Don't sit in the row in front of the emergency aisle or in front of a bulkhead, where seats may not recline.

Ask the airline whether a snack or meal is served on the flight. If you have dietary concerns, **request special meals when booking.** These can be vegetarian, low-cholesterol, or kosher, for example. It's a good idea to pack some healthy snacks and a small (plastic) bottle of water in your carry-on bag. On long flights, try to maintain a normal routine, to help fight jet lag. At night, **get some sleep.** By day, **eat light meals, drink water** (not alcohol), and **move around the cabin** to stretch your legs. For additional jet-lag tips consult *Fodor's FYI: Travel Fit & Healthy* (available at bookstores everywhere).

All airlines flying into Las Vegas prohibit smoking.

FLYING TIMES

To Las Vegas: From New York, 5 hours; from Dallas, 2 hours; from Chicago, 4 hours; from Los Angeles, 1 hour; from San Francisco, 1½ hours; from London, 11 hours; from Sydney, 18 hours.

HOW TO COMPLAIN

If your baggage goes astray or your flight goes awry, complain right away. Most carriers require that you **file a claim immediately.** The Aviation Consumer Protection Division of the Department of Transportation publishes *Fly-Rights,* which discusses airlines and consumer issues and is available on-line. At PassengerRights. com, a Web site, you can compose a letter of complaint and distribute it electronically.

➤ AIRLINE COMPLAINTS: **Aviation Consumer Protection Division** (✉ U.S. Department of Transportation, Room 4107, C-75, Washington, DC 20590, ☎ 202/366–2220, WEB www. dot.gov/airconsumer). **Federal Aviation Administration Consumer Hotline** (☎ 800/322–7873).

RECONFIRMING

Check the status of your flight before you leave for the airport. You can do this on your carrier's Web site, by linking to a flight-status checker (many Web booking services offer these), or by calling your carrier or travel agent.

AIRPORTS AND TRANSFERS

The gateway to Las Vegas is McCarran International Airport (LAS), 5 mi south of the business district and immediately east of the southern end of the Strip. Some people choose to fly into Los Angeles International (LAX), rent a car, and drive the five hours to Las Vegas. Fares are usually lower into LAX but after adding the car rental it averages to about the same.

➤ AIRPORT INFORMATION: **McCarran International Airport** (☎ 702/261–5733, WEB www.mccarran.com).

AIRPORT TRANSFERS

By shuttle van: this is the cheapest way from McCarran to your hotel. The service is shared with other riders, and costs $5–$7 per person to the Strip, $6–$8 to downtown, and $8–$12 to outlying "locals" casinos. The vans wait for passengers outside the terminal in a marked area, near the cabs. Since the vans stop at many of the major hotels, it's not the best means of transportation if you're in a hurry.

By taxi: the metered cabs awaiting your arrival at McCarran are the quickest way of getting to your destination. The fare is $2.30 on the meter when you get in, plus $1.80 for every mile. The trip to most hotels on the Strip should cost less than $11–$18; the trip downtown should be about $20–$25.

➤ TAXIS AND SHUTTLES: **Bell Trans** (☎ 702/739–7990, WEB www. bell-trans.com). **Checker, Star,** and **Yellow Cab** (☎ 702/873–2000). **Gray Line** (☎ 702/739–5700, WEB www. grayline.com).

BUSINESS HOURS

Las Vegas is a 24-hour city, 365 days a year. Casinos, bars, supermarkets, almost all gas stations, even some health clubs and video stores cater to customers at all hours of the day and night (many people work odd hours here).

MUSEUMS AND SIGHTS

Most museums and attractions are open seven days a week.

PHARMACIES

Most pharmacies are open seven days a week from 9–7.

➤ 24-HOUR PHARMACIES: **Walgreens** (✉ 3765 Las Vegas Blvd. S, ☎ 702/ 739–9645).

SHOPS

Most stores are open weekdays 10–9, Saturday 9–6, and Sunday 11–6. The souvenir shops on the Strip and downtown remain open until midnight and some are open 24 hours. Grocery stores are open around the clock.

BUS TRAVEL TO AND FROM LAS VEGAS

Greyhound runs bus service in and out of Las Vegas; the bus terminal is downtown.

FARES AND SCHEDULES

Call Greyhound or visit their Web site for fare and schedule information.

PAYING

Cash, travelers checks, and credit cards are accepted.

RESERVATIONS

Reservations are not accepted on Greyhound. Seating is on a first-come, first-served basis. The most frequently plowed route out of Las Vegas is the one to Los Angeles, with departures approximately every two hours around the clock. Arriving at the bus station 30 to 45 minutes before your bus departs to purchase tickets nearly always ensures you a seat. On Sunday evening and Monday morning, arriving an hour or more before departure is recommended as buses fill up quickly on those days.

➤ BUS INFORMATION: **Greyhound** (✉ 200 S. Main St., Las Vegas, ☎ 800/231–2222, ⓦⓔⓑ www.greyhound.com).

BUS TRAVEL WITHIN LAS VEGAS

The municipally operated Citizen Area Transit (CAT) runs local buses throughout the city and to most corners of the sprawling Las Vegas Valley. The overall quality of bus service along the main thoroughfares is decent.

Most visitors only ride CAT buses up and down the Strip, between Mandalay Bay and the Stratosphere. Some continue on to the Downtown Transportation Center. The Strip buses stop on the street in front of all the major hotels every 15 minutes (in a perfect world) 24 hours a day. The fare is $2 (exact change required, but one-dollar bills are accepted). If you plan to get on and off the bus, **buy a discounted commuter card** from the driver. Other routes serve the Meadows and Boulevard shopping malls and Sam's Town Hotel and Casino on Boulder Highway. The schedule for all buses other than those along the Strip is 5:30 AM–1:30 AM daily; the fare is $1.25.

Bus service in Las Vegas is not perfect. If you're not traveling up and down the Strip, you may need to change buses downtown if you're heading to outlying areas. Mornings and afternoons the buses are frequently crowded with standing-room only. Since traffic is quite haphazard along the Strip, delays are frequent. Buses supposedly running every 15 minutes can take 25 to 30 minutes to show up.

From 9:30 AM to 1:30 AM, the Las Vegas Strip Trolley travels every 15 to 20 minutes among Strip hotels, with stops at Fashion Show Mall and Wet 'n Wild. An exact fare of $1.65 is required.

➤ BUS INFORMATION: **Citizens Area Transit** (☎ 702/228–7433). **Las Vegas Strip Trolley** (☎ 702/382–1404).

CAMERAS AND PHOTOGRAPHY

Only a few casinos allow people to photograph or videotape the games or machines. This is a holdover from the bad old days, when gambling was considered a vice and people were ashamed to be caught doing it. Some players are still sensitive about having their picture taken while gambling, so the casinos generally prohibit it, though you may take pictures at Harrah's, Excalibur, and the Four Queens.

The *Kodak Guide to Shooting Great Travel Pictures* (available at bookstores everywhere) is loaded with tips.

➤ PHOTO HELP: **Kodak Information Center** (☎ 800/242–2424, ⓦⓔⓑ www.kodak.com).

EQUIPMENT PRECAUTIONS

Don't pack film and equipment in checked luggage, where it is much more susceptible to damage. X-ray machines used to view checked luggage are becoming much more powerful and therefore are much more likely to ruin your film. Try to **ask for hand inspection of film,** which becomes clouded after repeated exposure to airport X-ray machines, and **keep videotapes and computer disks away from metal detectors.** Carry an extra supply of batteries, and **be prepared to turn on your camera, camcorder, or laptop** to prove to airport security personnel that the device is real. Always **keep film, tape, and computer disks out of the sun.**

Windy and dusty conditions are not infrequent in Las Vegas where your photo lenses will be quickly covered with a layer of sand. Always carry your equipment tightly sealed in protective covering and bring extra lens cleaner solution to wipe off lenses.

CAR RENTAL

Rates in Las Vegas begin at $23 a day and $115 a week for an economy car with unlimited mileage. This does not include the 7.25% state sales tax and a 6% "license tag" fee; also, if you rent your car at the airport an additional 10% tax applies.

➤ MAJOR AGENCIES: **Alamo** (☎ 800/327–9633; WEB www.alamo.com). **Avis** (☎ 800/331–1212; 800/879–2847 in Canada; 02/9353–9000 in Australia; 09/526–2847 in New Zealand; 0870/606–0100 in the U.K.; WEB www.avis.com). **Budget** (☎ 800/527–0700; 0870/156–5656 in the U.K.; WEB www.budget.com). **Dollar** (☎ 800/800–4000; 0124/622–0111 in the U.K., where it's affiliated with Sixt; 02/9223–1444 in Australia; WEB www.dollar.com). **Hertz** (☎ 800/654–3131; 800/263–0600 in Canada; 020/8897–2072 in the U.K.; 02/9669–2444 in Australia; 09/256–8690 in New Zealand; WEB www.hertz.com). **National Car Rental** (☎ 800/227–7368; 020/8680–4800 in the U.K.; WEB www.nationalcar.com).

CUTTING COSTS

For a good deal, **book through a travel agent who will shop around.** Also, **price local car-rental companies**— whose prices may be lower still, although their service and maintenance

may not be as good as those of major rental agencies—and **research rates on-line.** Remember to ask about required deposits, cancellation penalties, and drop-off charges if you're planning to pick up the car in one city and leave it in another. If you're traveling during a holiday period, also make sure that a confirmed reservation guarantees you a car.

Owing to the large number of visitors who rent cars, there are many deals to be had at the airport for car rentals. During special events and conventions rates frequently go up as supply dwindles, but during other times bargains are to be had in Las Vegas. Although there are several local car rental companies along the Strip, they tend to be more expensive than those at the airport.

➤ LOCAL AGENCIES: **Allstate/Payless** (☎ 702/736–6147). **Brooks Rent-A-Car** (☎ 702/735–3344 or 800/634–6186). **Dream Car Rentals** (☎ 702/731–6452 or 877/373–2601). **Rent-A-Vette** (☎ 800/372–1981).

INSURANCE

When driving a rented car you are generally responsible for any damage to or loss of the vehicle. You may also be liable for any property damage or personal injury that you may cause while driving. Before you rent, see what coverage you already have under the terms of your personal auto-insurance policy and credit cards.

For about $15 to $20 a day, rental companies sell protection, known as a collision- or loss-damage waiver (CDW or LDW), that eliminates your liability for damage to the car; it's always optional and should never be automatically added to your bill. In most states you don't need a CDW if you have personal auto insurance or other liability insurance.Some states, including Nevada, have capped the price of the CDW and LDW. However, **make sure you have enough coverage to pay for the car.** If you do not have auto insurance or an umbrella policy that covers damage to third parties, purchasing liability insurance and a CDW or LDW is highly recommended.

REQUIREMENTS AND RESTRICTIONS

In Nevada you must be 21 to rent a car, and several of the major car rental agencies (such as Hertz) have a minimum age of 25. Those agencies that do rent to those under 25 may charge you higher rates. There is no upper age limit for car rental. Non-U.S. residents will need a reservation voucher, a passport, a driver's license, and a travel policy that covers each driver, when picking up a car.

SURCHARGES

Before you pick up a car in one city and leave it in another, **ask about drop-off charges or one-way service fees,** which can be substantial. Note, too, that some rental agencies charge extra if you return the car before the time specified in your contract. To avoid a hefty refueling fee, **fill the tank just before you turn in the car,** but be aware that gas stations near the rental outlet may overcharge. It's almost never a deal to buy the tank of gas in the car when you rent it; the understanding is that you'll return it empty, but some fuel usually remains. Surcharges may apply if you're under 25. You'll pay extra for child seats (about $6 a day), which are compulsory for children under five, and for additional drivers (about $5 per day).

CAR TRAVEL

Las Vegas is an easy city to navigate. The principal north–south artery is Las Vegas Boulevard (I–15 runs roughly parallel to it, less than a mile to the west). A 3½-mi stretch of Las Vegas Boulevard South is the Strip, where a majority of the city's hotels and casinos are clustered. Many of the major streets running east–west (Tropicana Avenue, Flamingo Road, Desert Inn Road, Sahara Avenue) are named for the casinos built at their intersections with the Strip.

Because the capacity of the streets of Las Vegas has not kept pace with the city's incredible growth, traffic can be slow in the late afternoon, in the evening, and on the weekend. At those times, you may prefer to drive the streets that parallel Las Vegas Boulevard: Paradise Road to the east, and Industrial Road to the west. The Industrial Road shortcut (from Tropi-cana Avenue almost all the way to downtown) will save you an enormous amount of time. You can enter the parking lots at Caesars Palace, the Mirage, Treasure Island, the Stardust, the New Frontier, and Circus Circus from Industrial Road.

EMERGENCY SERVICES

You can call 911 from most locations in Nevada to reach police, fire, or ambulance assistance. Otherwise, dial the operator. If you have a cellular or digital phone, dial *647 to reach the Nevada Highway Patrol.

PARKING

Free parking is available at virtually every hotel, although you may have to hunt for a space and you can wind up in the far reaches of immense parking lots. To avoid this, simply **make use of valet parking.** You can't park anywhere on the Strip itself, and parking spaces on Fremont Street downtown are nearly always taken. Parking in the high-rise structures downtown is free, as long as you **validate your parking ticket at the casino cashier.** Street parking regulations are strictly enforced in Las Vegas, and meters are continuously monitored, so whenever possible it's a good idea to leave your car in a parking lot.

ROAD CONDITIONS

It might seem as if every road in Las Vegas is in a continuous state of expansion or repair. Orange highway cones, road-building equipment, and detours are ubiquitous. But once the roads are widened and repaved, they're efficient and comfortable. The city's traffic-light system is state-of-the-art, and you can often drive for miles on major thoroughfares, hitting green lights all the way. Signage is excellent, both on surface arteries and freeways. The local driving style is fast.

For information on weather conditions, highway construction, and road closures call the **Department of Transportation** for the state you're traveling in.

➤ AGENCIES: **Arizona Department of Transportation** (☎ 888/411–7623). **California Department of Transportation** (☎ 800/427–7623). **Northern Nevada Department of Transportation**

(☎ 775/793–1313). **Southern Nevada Department of Transportation** (☎ 702/486–3116). **Utah Department of Transportation** (☎ 800/492–2400).

RULES OF THE ROAD

The speed limit on residential streets is 25 mph. On major thoroughfares it's 45 mph, though drivers often get impatient with people who obey the speed limit and pass on either side. On the interstate and other divided highways within the city the speed limit is a fast 65 mph; outside the city, the speed limit on I–15 is 70 and 75 mph. California's speed limit is 70 mph. Right turns are permitted on red lights after coming to a full stop in Arizona, California, Nevada, and Utah.

Always **strap children under age five or under 40 pounds into approved child-safety seats.** In Nevada, children must wear seat belts regardless of where they're seated.

CHILDREN IN LAS VEGAS

Las Vegas, with all its oddities and entertainment, actually can be a good family destination. Other than in the casinos, children are welcome everywhere.

Las Vegas Kids is a monthly periodical for keeping up with events of interest to parents and children; single issues are $5.

If you are renting a car, don't forget to **arrange for a car seat** when you reserve. For general advice about traveling with children, consult *Fodor's FYI: Travel with Your Baby* (available in bookstores everywhere).

➤ LOCAL INFORMATION: **Las Vegas Kids** (☎ 702/233–8388).

BABY-SITTING

One reliable independent local agency is Nanny's and Granny's, which charges a variable rate depending on the number of children (fees for one child begin with a minimum $50 for the first four hours). Baby-sitters are cleared through the FBI and local sheriff's department.

Several casinos also provide child care services, but they tend to be those that appeal to locals. The facilities at Castaways, Sam's Town, and Gold Coast are free for casino patrons, two-hour maximum; you must stay in the building. At the Gold Coast and Sam's Town, children must be potty-trained. There's an hourly rate and a 3½-hr limit at Kids' Quest, the mega play areas at Texas Station, Boulder Station, Palace Station, and Sunset Station.

➤ AGENCIES: **Nanny's and Granny's** (✉ 6440 W. Coley Ave., Las Vegas, NV 89117, ☎ 702/364–4700, WEB www.nanny4u.com).

➤ CASINOS: **Boulder Station** (✉ 4111 Boulder Hwy., Boulder Strip, ☎ 702/432–7569). **Castaways** (✉ 2800 Fremont St., Boulder Strip, ☎ 702/385–9123). **Gold Coast** (✉ 4000 W. Flamingo Rd., West Side, ☎ 702/367–7111). **Orleans** (✉ 4500 W. Tropicana Ave., West Side, ☎ 702/365–7111). **Palace Station** (✉ 2411 W. Sahara Ave., West Side, ☎ 702/367–2411). **Sam's Town** (✉ 5111 Boulder Hwy., Boulder Strip, ☎ 702/456–7777). **Sunset Station** (✉ 1301 W. Sunset Rd., Henderson, ☎ 702/547–7773). **Texas Station** (✉ 2101 Texas Star La., Rancho Strip, ☎ 702/631–8355).

FLYING

If your children are two or older, **ask about children's airfares.** As a general rule, infants under two not occupying a seat fly at greatly reduced fares or even for free. When booking, **confirm carry-on allowances** if you're traveling with infants. In general, for babies charged 10% of the adult fare you are allowed one carry-on bag and a collapsible stroller; if the flight is full, the stroller may have to be checked or you may be limited to less.

Experts agree that it's a good idea to use safety seats aloft for children weighing less than 40 pounds. Airlines set their own policies: U.S. carriers usually require that the child be ticketed, even if he or she is young enough to ride free, since the seats must be strapped into regular seats. Do **check your airline's policy about using safety seats during takeoff and landing.** Safety seats are not allowed everywhere in the plane, so get your seat assignments as early as possible.

When reserving, **request children's meals or a freestanding bassinet** (not available at all airlines) if you need them. But note that bulkhead seats, where you must sit to use the bassinet, may lack an overhead bin or storage space on the floor.

LODGING

Most hotels in Las Vegas allow children under a certain age to stay in their parents' room at no extra charge, but others charge for them as extra adults; be sure to **find out the cutoff age for children's discounts.** Hotels will usually provide cribs for babies and "rollaways" (cots) for children. Children are actively discouraged at the Bellagio, and they are allowed on the property only if they are accompanied by their parents and staying at the hotel.

Most major Las Vegas hotels provide extensive video-game arcades for their underage guests (though leaving children under the age of 14 or 15 alone in arcades and game rooms is not recommended). The Orleans is the casino closest to the Strip with a commercial child-care facility, Kids Tyme. An especially comprehensive child-care program can be found at MGM Grand's Youth Center. Guests of the Grand take precedence, but guests at any hotel can take advantage of this large day-care facility if space is available. Children ages 3–12 play, snack, and eat meals from 11 AM until 11 PM (midnight Friday and Saturday), starting at $8 an hour per child (up to $10.50 an hour for nonguests). Activities include basketball, Foosball, Nintendo, arts and crafts, and air hockey; there are also two six-hour supervised amusement-park excursions a day.

➤ BEST CHOICES: **Orleans Hotel and Casino** (⊠ 4500 W. Tropicana Ave., ☎ 800/675–3267). **MGM Grand's King Looey's Youth Center** (☎ 702/891–1111).

SIGHTS AND ATTRACTIONS

The free spectacles, the thrill rides (both big and small, actual and virtual), the many movie theaters, bowling alleys, video-game arcades, amusement and water parks, children's museums, and other activities make Las Vegas a fun place for youngsters. Places that are especially appealing to children are indicated by a rubber-duckie icon (🦆) in the margin.

CONCIERGES

Concierges, found in many hotels, can help you with theater tickets and dinner reservations: a good one with connections may be able to get you seats for a hot show or prime-time dinner reservations at the restaurant of the moment. You can also turn to your hotel's concierge for help with travel arrangements, sightseeing plans, services ranging from aromatherapy to zipper repair, and emergencies. Always, **always tip** a concierge who has been of assistance (☞ Tipping).

CONSUMER PROTECTION

Whether you're shopping for gifts or purchasing travel services, **pay with a major credit card** whenever possible, so you can cancel payment or get reimbursed if there's a problem (and you can provide documentation). If you're doing business with a particular company for the first time, **contact your local Better Business Bureau and the attorney general's offices** in your state and (for U.S. businesses) the company's home state as well. Have any complaints been filed? Finally, if you're buying a package or tour, always **consider travel insurance** that includes default coverage (☞ Insurance).

➤ BBBs: **Council of Better Business Bureaus** (⊠ 4200 Wilson Blvd., Suite 800, Arlington, VA 22203, ☎ 703/276–0100, FAX 703/525–8277, WEB www.bbb.org). **Better Business Bureau of Southern Nevada** (⊠ 2301 Palomino La., Las Vegas, NV 89107, ☎ 702/320–4500, FAX 702/320–4560, WEB www.vegasbbb.org).

CUSTOMS AND DUTIES

IN AUSTRALIA

Australian residents who are 18 or older may bring home A$400 worth of souvenirs and gifts (including jewelry), 250 cigarettes or 250 grams of tobacco, and 1,125 ml of alcohol (including wine, beer, and spirits). Residents under 18 may bring back A$200 worth of goods. Prohibited items include meat products. Seeds, plants, and fruits need to be declared upon arrival.

➤ INFORMATION: **Australian Customs Service** (Regional Director, ⊠ Box 8, Sydney, NSW 2001, ☎ 02/9213–

2000 or 1300/363263; 1800/020504 quarantine-inquiry line, FAX 02/9213–4043, WEB www.customs.gov.au).

IN CANADA

Canadian residents who have been out of Canada for at least seven days may bring in C$750 worth of goods duty-free. If you've been away fewer than seven days but more than 48 hours, the duty-free allowance drops to C$200; if your trip lasts 24 to 48 hours, the allowance is C$50. You may not pool allowances with family members. Goods claimed under the C$750 exemption may follow you by mail; those claimed under the lesser exemptions must accompany you. Alcohol and tobacco products may be included in the seven-day and 48-hour exemptions but not in the 24-hour exemption. If you meet the age requirements of the province or territory through which you reenter Canada, you may bring in, duty-free, 1.5 liters of wine *or* 1.14 liters (40 imperial ounces) of liquor *or* 24 12-ounce cans or bottles of beer or ale. If you are 19 or older you may bring in, duty-free, 200 cigarettes and 50 cigars. Check ahead of time with the Canada Customs and Revenue Agency or the Department of Agriculture for policies regarding meat products, seeds, plants, and fruits.

You may send an unlimited number of gifts (only one gift per recipient, however) worth up to C$60 each duty-free to Canada. Label the package UNSO-LICITED GIFT—VALUE UNDER $60. Alcohol and tobacco are excluded.

➤ INFORMATION: **Canada Customs and Revenue Agency** (✉ 2265 St. Laurent Blvd. S, Ottawa, Ontario K1G 4K3, ☎ 204/983–3500, 506/636–5064, or 800/461–9999, WEB www.ccra-adrc.gc.ca/).

IN NEW ZEALAND

All homeward-bound residents may bring back NZ$700 worth of souvenirs and gifts; passengers may not pool their allowances, and children can claim only the concession on goods intended for their own use. For those 17 or older, the duty-free allowance also includes 4.5 liters of wine or beer; one 1,125-ml bottle of

spirits; and either 200 cigarettes, 250 grams of tobacco, 50 cigars, *or* a combination of the three up to 250 grams. Meat products, seeds, plants, and fruits must be declared upon arrival to the Agricultural Services Department.

➤ INFORMATION: **New Zealand Customs** (✉ Head Office, The Customhouse, 17–21 Whitmore St., Box 2218, Wellington, ☎ 09/300–5399, WEB www.customs.govt.nz).

IN THE U.K.

From countries outside the European Union, including the United States, you may bring home, duty-free, 200 cigarettes or 50 cigars; 1 liter of spirits or 2 liters of fortified or sparkling wine or liqueurs; 2 liters of still table wine; 60 ml of perfume; 250 ml of toilet water; plus £145 worth of other goods, including gifts and souvenirs. Prohibited items include meat products, seeds, plants, and fruits.

➤ INFORMATION: **HM Customs and Excise** (✉ Portcullis House, 21 Cowbridge Rd. E, Cardiff CF11 9SS, ☎ 029/2038–6423 or 0845/010–9000, WEB www.hmce.gov.uk).

DINING

The restaurants we list are the cream of the crop in each price category. Properties indicated by an ✕🔲 are lodging establishments whose restaurant warrants a special trip.

In general, when you order a regular coffee, you get coffee with milk and sugar.

RESERVATIONS AND DRESS

Reservations are always a good idea; we mention them only when they're essential or not accepted. Book as far ahead as you can, and reconfirm as soon as you arrive. (Large parties should always call ahead to check the reservations policy.) We mention dress only when men are required to wear a jacket or a jacket and tie.

WINE, BEER, AND SPIRITS

You must be 21 years of age to purchase alcoholic beverages in Nevada and California. Alcohol is available for purchase 24 hours a day in Nevada, and until 2 AM in California.

DISABILITIES AND ACCESSIBILITY

Las Vegas gets a B-plus when it comes to accommodating travelers with disabilities. It's not perfect, but because so much major construction—from sidewalks to megaresorts—is recent, accessibility is very good for most places. Also, Las Vegas is well laid out for people who use wheelchairs: flat, wide sidewalks (especially in the tourist areas) and curb cuts, ramps, and wheelchair elevators and lifts are almost everywhere. Only the crowds make it at all difficult for people in wheelchairs to get around efficiently.

HELP of Southern Nevada refers callers to the proper social agency, and the Nevada Association for the Handicapped refers callers to agencies serving people with disabilities. The Southern Nevada Sightless provides general information and transportation assistance.

➤ LOCAL RESOURCES: **HELP of Southern Nevada** (☎ 702/369–4357). **Nevada Association for the Handicapped** (✉ 6200 W. Oakey Blvd., Las Vegas 89102, ☎ 702/870–7050). **Southern Nevada Sightless** (✉ 1001 N. Bruce St., Las Vegas 89101, ☎ 702/642–0100).

LODGING

Generally, the layouts of most Las Vegas hotels and casinos are such that you have to cross long distances to get from one place to another. These resort-casinos are so big—3,000 rooms, a dozen restaurants, extensive retail areas, and huge gambling halls—that they're no less than minicities under one roof. Whether you're walking or moving around in a wheelchair, you have to cover a lot of ground.

The Imperial Palace has the most facilities accommodating people with disabilities, including a hydraulic lift at the pool, an Amigo chair in the pit, and more than 100 accessible rooms, many of which feature roll-in showers and transfer chairs. Most hotels have some rooms that are accessible to travelers in wheelchairs.

Despite the Americans with Disabilities Act, the definition of accessibility seems to differ from hotel to hotel. Some properties may be accessible by ADA standards for people with mobility problems but not for people with hearing or vision impairments, for example.

If you have mobility problems, ask for the lowest floor on which accessible services are offered. If you have a hearing impairment, check whether the hotel has devices to alert you visually to the ring of the telephone, a knock at the door, and a fire/emergency alarm. Some hotels provide these devices without charge. Discuss your needs with hotel personnel if this equipment isn't available, so that a staff member can personally alert you in the event of an emergency.

If you're bringing a guide dog, get authorization ahead of time and write down the name of the person you spoke with.

➤ WHEELCHAIR-ACCESSIBLE ACCOMMODATIONS: **Aladdin Hotel and Casino** (✉ 3667 Las Vegas Blvd. S, ☎ 702/736–0111). **Caesars Palace** (✉ 3570 Las Vegas Blvd. S, ☎ 702/731–7110). **Excalibur Hotel and Casino** (✉ 3850 Las Vegas Blvd. S, ☎ 702/597–7777). **Lady Luck Casino and Hotel** (✉ 206 N. 3rd St., ☎ 702/477–3000). **Luxor Hotel-Casino** (✉ 3900 Las Vegas Blvd. S, ☎ 702/262–4452). **Mandalay Bay Resort and Casino** (✉ 3950 Las Vegas Blvd. S, ☎ 702/632–7777). **MGM Grand Hotel Casino and Theme Park** (✉ 3805 Las Vegas Blvd. S, ☎ 702/891–1111). **Mirage Hotel and Casino** (✉ 3400 Las Vegas Blvd. S, ☎ 702/791–7111). **Riviera Hotel and Casino** (✉ 2901 Las Vegas Blvd. S, ☎ 702/794–9451).

RESERVATIONS

When discussing accessibility with an operator or reservations agent, **ask hard questions.** Are there any stairs, inside *or* out? Are there grab bars next to the toilet *and* in the shower/tub? How wide is the doorway to the room? To the bathroom? For the most extensive facilities meeting the latest legal specifications, **opt for newer accommodations.** If you reserve through a toll-free number, consider also calling the hotel's local number to confirm the information from the central reservations office. Get confirmation in writing when you can.

SIGHTS AND ATTRACTIONS

All major attractions in Las Vegas are accessible for persons with physical disabilities, in accordance with the Americans with Disabilities Act. Call ahead for specific information.

TRANSPORTATION

Citizens Area Transit in Las Vegas (☎ 702/455–4481) operates buses that accommodate persons with disabilities.

➤ COMPLAINTS: **Aviation Consumer Protection Division** (☞ Air Travel) for airline-related problems. **Departmental Office of Civil Rights** (for general inquiries, ✉ U.S. Department of Transportation, S-30, 400 7th St. SW, Room 10215, Washington, DC 20590, ☎ 202/366–4648, FAX 202/366–9371, WEB www.dot.gov/ost/docr/index.htm). **Disability Rights Section** (✉ NYAV, U.S. Department of Justice, Civil Rights Division, 950 Pennsylvania Ave. NW, Washington, DC 20530, ☎ ADA information line 202/514–0301; 800/514–0301; 202/514–0383 TTY; 800/514–0383 TTY, WEB www. usdoj.gov/crt/ada/adahom1.htm).

TRAVEL AGENCIES

In the United States, the Americans with Disabilities Act requires that travel firms serve the needs of all travelers. Some agencies specialize in working with people with disabilities.

➤ TRAVELERS WITH MOBILITY PROBLEMS: **Access Adventures** (✉ 206 Chestnut Ridge Rd., Scottsville, NY 14624, ☎ 716/889–9096, dltravel@ prodigy.net), run by a former physical-rehabilitation counselor. **Accessible Vans of America** (✉ 9 Spielman Rd., Fairfield, NJ 07004, ☎ 877/282–8267; 888/282–8267 reservations, FAX 973/808–9713, WEB www.accessiblevans.com).**Care-Vacations** (✉ No. 5, 5110–50 Ave., Leduc, Alberta T9E 6V4, Canada, ☎ 780/986–6404 or 877/478–7827, FAX 780/986–8332, WEB www. carevacations.com), for group tours and cruise vacations. **Flying Wheels Travel** (✉ 143 W. Bridge St., Box 382, Owatonna, MN 55060, ☎ 507/451–5005, FAX 507/451–1685, WEB www.flyingwheelstravel.com).

➤ TRAVELERS WITH DEVELOPMENTAL DISABILITIES: **New Directions** (✉ 5276 Hollister Ave., Suite 207, Santa Barbara, CA 93111, ☎ 805/967–2841 or 888/967–2841, FAX 805/964–7344, WEB www.newdirectionstravel.com).

DISCOUNTS AND DEALS

Some hotels offer "funbooks" with gambling coupons (bet $5 and win $7 on an even-money wager, for example) and discounts for food and attractions. Inquire at the front desk when you check in. The **Las Vegas Convention and Visitors Authority** has coupon books for discounts and deals at hotels, restaurants, and casinos.

Be a smart shopper and **compare all your options** before making decisions. A plane ticket bought with a promotional coupon from travel clubs, coupon books, and direct-mail offers or purchased on the Internet may not be cheaper than the least expensive fare from a discount ticket agency. And always keep in mind that what you get is just as important as what you save.

DISCOUNT RESERVATIONS

To save money, **look into discount reservations services** with Web sites and toll-free numbers, which use their buying power to get a better price on hotels, airline tickets, even car rentals. When booking a room, always **call the hotel's local toll-free number** (if one is available) rather than the central reservations number—you'll often get a better price. Always ask about special packages or corporate rates.

➤ AIRLINE TICKETS: ☎ 800/AIR–4LESS.

➤ HOTEL ROOMS: **Accommodations Express** (☎ 800/444–7666, WEB www. accommodationsexpress.com). **Hotel Reservations Network** (☎ 800/964–6835, WEB www.hoteldiscount.com). **Quikbook** (☎ 800/789–9887, WEB www.quikbook.com). **RMC Travel** (☎ 800/245–5738, WEB www. rmcwebtravel.com). **Turbotrip. com** (☎ 800/473–7829, WEB www. turbotrip.com).

PACKAGE DEALS

Don't confuse packages and guided tours. When you buy a package, you travel on your own, just as though you had planned the trip yourself. Fly/drive packages, which combine airfare and car rental, are often a good deal. In cities, ask the local visitor's bureau about hotel packages that include tickets to major museum exhibits or other special events.

DIVERS' ALERT

Do not fly within 24 hours of scuba diving.

GAY AND LESBIAN TRAVEL

Las Vegas has a growing gay community; contact the Gay and Lesbian Community Center of Southern Nevada for information on local services and events. For details about the gay and lesbian scene, consult *Fodor's Gay Guide to the USA* (available in bookstores everywhere). *The Las Vegas Bugle* is a local gay publication.

➤ GAY- AND LESBIAN-FRIENDLY TRAVEL AGENCIES: **Different Roads Travel** (✉ 8383 Wilshire Blvd., Suite 902, Beverly Hills, CA 90211, ☎ 323/651–5557 or 800/429–8747, FAX 323/651–3678, lgernert@tzell.com). **Kennedy Travel** (✉ 314 Jericho Tpke., Floral Park, NY 11001, ☎ 516/352–4888 or 800/237–7433, FAX 516/354–8849, WEB www.kennedytravel.com). **Now, Voyager** (✉ 4406 18th St., San Francisco, CA 94114, ☎ 415/626–1169 or 800/255–6951, FAX 415/626–8626, WEB www.nowvoyager.com). **Skylink Travel and Tour** (✉ 1006 Mendocino Ave., Santa Rosa, CA 95401, ☎ 707/546–9888 or 800/225–5759, FAX 707/546–9891), serving lesbian travelers.

➤ RESOURCES: **Gay and Lesbian Community Center of Southern Nevada** (✉ 912 E. Sahara Rd., ☎ 702/733–9800). *Las Vegas Bugle* (☎ 702/369–6260).

GUIDEBOOKS

Plan well and you won't be sorry. Guidebooks are excellent tools—and you can take them with you. You may want to check out color-photo-illustrated *Compass American Guide: Las Vegas,* which is thorough on culture and history and is available at on-line retailers and bookstores everywhere.

HEALTH

The dry desert air in Las Vegas means that your body will need extra fluids, especially during the punishing summer months. Always drink lots of water even if you're not outside very much. When you're outdoors wear sunscreen in summer and always carry water with you if you plan a long walk.

HOLIDAYS

Major national holidays include New Year's Day (Jan. 1); Martin Luther King, Jr., Day (3rd Mon. in Jan.); President's Day (3rd Mon. in Feb.); Memorial Day (last Mon. in May); Independence Day (July 4); Labor Day (1st Mon. in Sept.); Thanksgiving Day (4th Thurs. in Nov.); Christmas Eve and Christmas Day (Dec. 24 and 25); and New Year's Eve (Dec. 31).

INSURANCE

The most useful travel-insurance plan is a comprehensive policy that includes coverage for trip cancellation and interruption, default, trip delay, and medical expenses (with a waiver for pre-existing conditions).

Without insurance you will lose all or most of your money if you cancel your trip, regardless of the reason. Default insurance covers you if your tour operator, airline, or cruise line goes out of business. Trip-delay covers expenses that arise because of bad weather or mechanical delays. Study the fine print when comparing policies.

U.K. residents can buy a travel-insurance policy valid for most vacations taken during the year in which it's purchased (but check pre-existing-condition coverage).

Always **buy travel policies directly from the insurance company**; if you buy them from a cruise line, airline, or tour operator that goes out of business you probably will not be covered for the agency or operator's default, a major risk. Before making any purchase, **review your existing health and home-owner's policies** to find what they cover away from home.

➤ TRAVEL INSURERS: In the U.S.: **Access America** (✉ 6600 W. Broad St., Richmond, VA 23230, ☎ 800/284–8300, FAX 804/673–1491 or 800/346–9265, WEB www.accessamerica.com). **Travel Guard International** (✉ 1145 Clark St., Stevens Point, WI 54481, ☎ 800/826–1300, FAX 800/955–8785, WEB www.travelguard.com).

FOR INTERNATIONAL TRAVELERS

For information on customs restrictions, *see* Customs and Duties.

CAR RENTAL

When picking up a rental car, non-U.S. residents need a reservation voucher for any prepaid reservations that were made in the traveler's home country, a passport, a driver's license, and a travel policy that covers each driver.

CAR TRAVEL

In Las Vegas gasoline costs $1.50 a gallon at press time. Stations are plentiful. Most stay open late (24 hours along large highways and in big cities), except in rural areas, where Sunday hours are limited and where you may drive long stretches without a refueling opportunity. Be sure to fill your tank when an opportunity arises. Highways are well paved. Interstate highways—limited-access, multilane highways whose numbers are prefixed by "I–"—are the fastest routes. Interstates with three-digit numbers encircle urban areas, which may have other limited-access expressways, freeways, and parkways as well. Tolls may be levied on limited-access highways. So-called U.S. highways and state highways are not necessarily limited-access but may have several lanes.

Along larger highways, roadside stops with rest rooms, fast-food restaurants, and sundries stores are well spaced. State police and tow trucks patrol major highways and lend assistance. If your car breaks down on an interstate, pull onto the shoulder and wait for help, or have your passengers wait while you walk to an emergency phone. If you carry a cell phone, dial *647, noting your location on the small green roadside mileage markers.

Driving in the United States is on the right. Do **obey speed limits** posted along roads and highways. Watch for lower limits in small towns and on back roads. Nevada requires front-seat passengers to wear seat belts. On weekdays between 6 and 10 AM and again between 4 and 7 PM **expect heavy traffic.** To encourage carpooling, some freeways have special lanes for so-called high-occupancy vehicles (HOV)—cars carrying more than one passenger.

Bookstores, gas stations, convenience stores, and rest stops sell maps (about $3) and multiregion road atlases (about $10).

CONSULATES AND EMBASSIES

The following all have consulates in Los Angeles.

➤ AUSTRALIA: **Australian Consulate-General** (✉ Century Plaza Towers, 19th floor, 2049 Century Park E, Los Angeles, CA 90067, ☎ 310/229–4800, FAX 310/277–2258).

➤ CANADA: **Canadian Consulate General** (✉ 550 South Hope St., 9th floor, Los Angeles, CA 90071, ☎ 213/346–2700, FAX 213/620–8827).

➤ NEW ZEALAND: **New Zealand Consulate-General** (✉ 12400 Wilshire Blvd., Suite 1150, Los Angeles, CA 90025, ☎ 310/207–1605, FAX 310/207–3605).

➤ UNITED KINGDOM: **British Consulate-General** (✉ 11766 Wilshire Blvd., Suite 400, Los Angeles, CA 90025, ☎ 310/477–3322, FAX 310/575–1450).

CURRENCY

The dollar is the basic unit of U.S. currency. It has 100 cents. Coins include the copper penny (1¢); the silvery nickel (5¢), dime (10¢), quarter (25¢), and half-dollar (50¢); and the golden $1 coin, replacing a now-rare silver dollar. Bills are denominated $1, $5, $10, $20, $50, and $100, all green and identical in size; designs vary. The exchange rate at press time was 93¢ to the Euro, US$1.45 per British pound, 64¢ per Canadian dollar, 52¢ per Australian dollar, and 43¢ per New Zealand dollar.

ELECTRICITY

The U.S. standard is AC, 110 volts/60 cycles. Plugs have two flat pins set parallel to each other.

EMERGENCIES

For police, fire, or ambulance, **dial 911** (0 in rural areas).

INSURANCE

Britons and Australians need extra medical coverage when traveling overseas.

➤ INSURANCE INFORMATION: In the U.K.: **Association of British Insurers** (✉ 51 Gresham St., London EC2V 7HQ, ☎ 020/7600–3333, FAX 020/7696–8999, WEB www.abi.org.uk). In Australia: **Insurance Council of Australia** (✉ Level 3, 56 Pitt St., Sydney, NSW 2000, ☎ 02/9253–5100, FAX 02/9253–5111, WEB www.ica.com.au). In Canada: **RBC Insurance** (✉ 6880 Financial Dr., Mississauga, Ontario L5N 7Y5, ☎ 905/816–2400 or 800/668–4342, FAX 905/813–4704, WEB www.rbcinsurance.com). In New Zealand: **Insurance Council of New Zealand** (✉ Level 7, 111–115 Customhouse Quay, Box 474, Wellington, ☎ 04/472–5230, FAX 04/473–3011, WEB www.icnz.org.nz).

MAIL AND SHIPPING

You can buy stamps and aerograms and send letters and parcels in post offices. Stamp-dispensing machines can occasionally be found in airports, bus and train stations, office buildings, drugstores, and the like. You can also deposit mail in the stout, dark blue, steel bins at strategic locations everywhere and in the mail chutes of large buildings; pickup schedules are posted.

For mail sent within the United States, you need a 37¢ stamp for first-class letters weighing up to 1 ounce (23¢ for each additional ounce) and 23¢ for domestic postcards. For overseas mail, you pay 80¢ for 1-ounce airmail letters, 70¢ for airmail postcards, and 35¢ for surface-rate postcards. For Canada and Mexico you need a 60¢ stamp for a 1-ounce letter and 50¢ for a postcard. For 70¢ you can buy an aerogram—a single sheet of lightweight blue paper that folds into its own envelope, stamped for overseas airmail.

To receive mail on the road, have it sent c/o General Delivery at your destination's main post office (use the correct five-digit ZIP code). You must pick up mail in person within 30 days and show a driver's license or passport.

PASSPORTS AND VISAS

When traveling internationally, **carry your passport** even if you don't need one (it's always the best form of I.D.) and **make two photocopies of the data page** (one for someone at home and another for you, carried separately from your passport). If you lose your passport, promptly call the nearest embassy or consulate and the local police.

Visitor visas are not necessary for Canadian citizens, or for citizens of Australia and the United Kingdom who are staying fewer than 90 days.

➤ AUSTRALIAN CITIZENS: **Australian State Passport Office** (☎ 131–232, WEB www.passports.gov.au). **United States Consulate General** (✉ MLC Centre, 19–29 Martin Pl., 59th floor, Sydney, NSW 2000, ☎ 02/9373–9200; 1902/941–641 fee-based visa-inquiry line, WEB www.usis-australia.gov/index.html).

➤ CANADIAN CITIZENS: **Passport Office** (☎ 819/994–3500; 800/567–6868 in Canada).

➤ NEW ZEALAND CITIZENS: **New Zealand Passport Office** (☎ 04/474–8100 or 0800/22–5050, WEB www.passports.govt.nz). **Embassy of the United States** (✉ 29 Fitzherbert Terr., Thorndon, Wellington, ☎ 04/462–6000 WEB usembassy.org.nz). **U.S. Consulate General** (✉ Citibank Center, 3rd floor, 23 Customs St. E, Auckland, ☎ 09/303–2724, WEB usembassy.org.nz).

➤ U.K. CITIZENS: **London Passport Office** (☎ 0870/521–0410, WEB www.passport.gov.uk), for application procedures and emergency passports). **U.S. Consulate General** (✉ Queen's House, 14 Queen St., Belfast BT1 6EQ, Northern Ireland, ☎ 028/9032–8239; WEB www.usembassy.org.uk). **U.S. Embassy** (enclose a SASE to ✉ Consular Information Unit, 24 Grosvenor Sq., London W1 1AE, for general information; ✉ Visa Branch, 5 Upper Grosvenor St.,

London W1A 2JB, to submit an application via mail; ☎ 09068/200–290 recorded visa information or 09055/444–546 operator service, both with per-minute charges; WEB www.usembassy.org.uk).

TELEPHONES

All U.S. telephone numbers consist of a three-digit area code and a seven-digit local number. Within most local calling areas, you dial only the seven-digit number. To call between area-code regions, dial "1" then all 10 digits; the same goes for calls to numbers prefixed by "800," "888," and "877"—all toll-free. For calls to numbers preceded by "900" you must pay—usually dearly.

For international calls, dial "011" followed by the country code and the local number. For help, dial "0" and ask for an overseas operator. The country code is 61 for Australia, 64 for New Zealand, 44 for the United Kingdom. Calling Canada is the same as calling within the United States. Most local phone books list country codes and U.S. area codes. The country code for the United States is 1.

For operator assistance, dial "0". To obtain someone's phone number, call directory assistance, 555–1212 or occasionally 411 (free at public phones). To have the person you're calling foot the bill, phone collect; dial "0" instead of "1" before the 10-digit number.

At pay phones, instructions are usually posted. Usually you insert coins in a slot (10¢–50¢ for local calls) and wait for a steady tone before dialing. When you call long-distance, the operator tells you how much to insert; prepaid phone cards, widely available in various denominations, are easier. Call the number on the back, punch in the card's personal identification number when prompted, then dial your number.

LODGING

In the larger hotels in Las Vegas, it's generally not possible to haggle over room rates, as in, "Well, will you take sixty dollars for the room, instead of seventy-five?" However, because many of the Las Vegas megaresorts use yield-management models to determine room rates, prices change continuously. You can always ask for a lower-priced room; you can also call the same hotel several times within a short span and be quoted several different rates.

The lodgings we list are the cream of the crop in each price category. We always list the facilities that are available—but we don't specify whether they cost extra: when pricing accommodations, always ask what's included and what costs extra. Properties marked ✗▥ are lodging establishments whose restaurants warrant a special trip.

Assume that hotels operate on the **European Plan** (EP, with no meals) unless we specify that they use the **Continental Plan** (CP, with a Continental breakfast), **Breakfast Plan** (BP, with a full breakfast), **Modified American Plan** (MAP, with breakfast and dinner), or the **Full American Plan** (FAP, with all meals).

APARTMENT RENTALS

If you're staying in Las Vegas for a week or more, you might want to book a motel suite with a kitchenette at a weekly rate. The savings over a daily rate can be as high as 50%, and with a refrigerator, stove, and microwave, you can also save plenty on meals. Some "snowbirds" stay in these suites throughout the winter and pay monthly rates. **Budget Suites of America** has seven locations—and nearly 4,000 such two-room suites with full kitchen—around the city.

Vacation rentals in Las Vegas are not very common since the abundance of inexpensive hotel rooms and all-suite hotels eliminates the demand. But www.vacationrentals.com does list several Las Vegas vacation home rentals.

➤ BEST CHOICES: **Budget Suites of America** (☎ 888/391–0539).

➤ LOCAL AGENTS: **Worldwide Travel Exchange** (☎ 800/445–5527) handles rentals in Las Vegas, Reno, and Tahoe.

HOME EXCHANGES

If you would like to exchange your home for someone else's, **join a**

home-exchange organization, which will send you its updated listings of available exchanges for a year and will include your own listing in at least one of them. It's up to you to make specific arrangements.

➤ EXCHANGE CLUBS: **HomeLink International** (✉ Box 47747, Tampa, FL 33647, ☎ 813/975–9825 or 800/638–3841, FAX 813/910–8144, WEB www.homelink.org; $106 per year). **Intervac U.S.** (✉ 30 Corte San Fernando, Tiburon, CA 94920, ☎ 800/756–4663, FAX 415/435–7440, WEB www.intervacus.com; $90 yearly fee for a listing, on-line access, and a catalog; $50 without catalog).

HOSTELS

No matter what your age, you can **save on lodging costs by staying at hostels.** There is only one hostel in Las Vegas. Located on Las Vegas Boulevard South between downtown and the Strip, it's easily accessible, although the neighborhood is not the safest at night. It has 55 beds in men's and women's dorms (six beds per dorm room), a handful of very basic private rooms, shared baths (that could use some sprucing up), and a communal kitchen and lounge.

In some 4,500 locations in more than 70 countries around the world, Hostelling International (HI), the umbrella group for a number of national youth-hostel associations, offers single-sex, dorm-style beds and, at many hostels, rooms for couples and family accommodations. Membership in any HI national hostel association, open to travelers of all ages, allows you to stay in HI-affiliated hostels at member rates; one-year membership is about $25 for adults (C$35 for a two-year minimum membership in Canada, £13 in the U.K., A$52 in Australia, and NZ$40 in New Zealand); hostels run about $10–$30 per night. Members have priority if the hostel is full; they're also eligible for discounts around the world, even on rail and bus travel in some countries.

➤ BEST OPTIONS: **Las Vegas International Hostel** (✉ 1208 Las Vegas Blvd. S, ☎ 702/385–9955).

➤ ORGANIZATIONS: **Hostelling International—American Youth Hostels** (✉ 733 15th St. NW, Suite 840, Washington, DC 20005, ☎ 202/783–6161, FAX 202/783–6171, WEB www.hiayh.org). **Hostelling International—Canada** (✉ 400–205 Catherine St., Ottawa, Ontario K2P 1C3, ☎ 613/237–7884 or 800/663–5777, FAX 613/237–7868, WEB www.hihostels.ca). **Youth Hostel Association of England and Wales** (✉ Trevelyan House, Dimple Rd., Matlock, Derbyshire DE4 3YH, U.K., ☎ 0870/870–8808, FAX 0169/592–702, WEB www.yha.org.uk). **Youth Hostel Association Australia** (✉ 10 Mallett St., Camperdown, NSW 2050, ☎ 02/9565–1699, FAX 02/9565–1325, WEB www.yha.com.au). **Youth Hostels Association of New Zealand** (✉ Level 3, 193 Cashel St., Box 436, Christchurch, ☎ 03/379–9970, FAX 03/365–4476, WEB www.yha.org.nz).

HOTELS

Hotels book up quickly in Las Vegas. The city is filled with people every weekend, and there are even more visitors during holiday weekends, big conventions, and when prizefights and other major sporting events are held here. **Make your hotel reservations as far in advance as possible.** Overbooking is not common; if you have a reservation, you'll get a room. Noise-sensitive travelers should bring earplugs. All hotels listed have private bath unless otherwise noted.

➤ TOLL-FREE NUMBERS: **Best Western** (☎ 800/528–1234, WEB www.bestwestern.com). **Choice** (☎ 800/424–6423, WEB www.choicehotels.com). **Comfort Inn** (☎ 800/228–5150, WEB www.comfortinn.com). **Days Inn** (☎ 800/325–2525, WEB www.daysinn.com). **Doubletree and Red Lion Hotels** (☎ 800/222–8733, WEB www.hilton.com). **Embassy Suites** (☎ 800/362–2779, WEB www.embassysuites.com). **Fairfield Inn** (☎ 800/228–2800, WEB www.marriott.com). **Four Seasons** (☎ 800/332–3442, WEB www.fourseasons.com). **Hilton** (☎ 800/445–8667, WEB www.hilton.com). **Holiday Inn** (☎ 800/465–4329, WEB www.sixcontinentshotels.com). **Howard Johnson** (☎ 800/654–4656, WEB www.hojo.com). **Hyatt Hotels & Resorts** (☎ 800/233–1234, WEB www.hyatt.com). **La**

Quinta (☎ 800/531–5900, WEB www. laquinta.com). **Marriott** (☎ 800/ 228–9290, WEB www.marriott.com). **Quality Inn** (☎ 800/424–6423, WEB www.choicehotels.com). **Radisson** (☎ 800/333–3333, WEB www. radisson.com). **Ramada** (☎ 800/ 228–2828; 800/854–7854 international reservations, WEB www. ramada.com or www.ramadahotels. com). **Sheraton** (☎ 800/325–3535, WEB www.starwood.com/sheraton). **Sleep Inn** (☎ 800/424–6423, WEB www.choicehotels.com). **Westin Hotels & Resorts** (☎ 800/228–3000, WEB www.starwood.com/ westin).

MAIL AND SHIPPING

The main post office is open weekdays 9–4. Lines are often long. There are drop boxes for overnight delivery services all over town and **Let Us Mail** offices in every strip mall.

➤ POST OFFICES: **Main post office** (300 Las Vegas Blvd. S, Las Vegas 89101).

➤ MAJOR SERVICES: **Federal Express** (5870 S. Eastern Ave., ☎ 800/238–5355). **UPS** (☎ 800/742–5877).

MARRIAGE LICENSES

You can **obtain a marriage license at the Clark County Marriage License Bureau.** The cost is $50, and both applicants must apply in person. Those ages 16–18 need the consent of their parents or legal guardians. Blood tests are not required, and there is no waiting period. The bureau is open from Monday through Thursday 8 AM–midnight and from Friday at 8 AM to Sunday at midnight.

➤ INFORMATION: **Clark County Marriage License Bureau** (✉ 200 S. 3rd St., ☎ 702/455–3156; 702/455–4415 after 5 PM weekends and holidays, WEB www.co.clark.nv.us).

MEDIA

NEWSPAPERS AND MAGAZINES

The morning *Las Vegas Review-Journal* is the largest daily newspaper in Nevada; its Friday entertainment section is called "Neon." The *Las Vegas Sun* is an afternoon daily. It is small, but has good local coverage.

Published bi-monthly, *Las Vegas Magazine* offers fashion, food, entertainment, and news articles for locals and visitors. The monthly *Las Vegas Style Magazine* focuses primarily on the hotel-casino business and features gossip and articles on food and entertainment. Published by the state, the bi-monthly *Nevada Magazine* is one of the oldest magazines in the west (since 1936); it has a large section covering Las Vegas events. *Nevada Woman* is a bi-monthly glossy regional magazine geared toward southern Nevada women over 25. The monthly *Nevada Business Journal* offers coverage of business news and profiles of businesses and executives.

RADIO AND TELEVISION

Local AM radio stations include KDWN 720 (talk, big band, news, sports), KXNT 840 (talk), KBAD 920 (sports), KNUU 970 (news, talk, sports), and KENO 1460 (CNN and sports).

The local FM radio stations are KNPR 89.5 (National Public Radio), KOMP 92.3 (adult-oriented rock), KWNR 95.5 (new country), KKLZ 96.3 (classic rock), KLUC 98.5 (Top 40), KFMS 101.5 (contemporary country), KJUL 104.3 (soft nostalgia), KVBC 105.1 (news, sports, weather), and KQOL 105.5 (oldies).

The network television stations are KVBC (3, NBC), KVUU (5, Fox), KLAS (8, CBS), and KTNV (13, ABC). The public TV station is KLVX (10).

MONEY MATTERS

The prices of typical items range from gratis to outrageous. For example, you can get a good deli sandwich at one of the rock-bottom casino snack bars (Riviera, Westward Ho) for $2–$3, or you can spend $12 for a skyscraper special at the Stage Deli in the Forum Shops at Caesars. A cup of coffee in a casino coffee shop will set you back $1–$1.50, while that same cuppa is free if you happen to be sitting at a nickel slot machine when the cocktail waitress comes by. A taxi from the airport to the MGM Grand goes as low as $10 if you tell the driver to take Tropicana Avenue and there's no traffic, or runs as high as

$25 if you take the Airport Connector and there's a wreck on the freeway. The more you know about Vegas, the less it'll cost you.

The Strip is expensive and if you're on a budget then consider having meals at the buffets in downtown Las Vegas which are generally more of a bargain. For shopping, the locals save money by driving 5 mi south of the Strip to the **Las Vegas Factory Outlet** (⌧ 9115 Las Vegas Blvd. S, ☎ 702/897–9090), where you'll find 50 shops where you can purchase designer wear at reduced prices.

Prices throughout this guide are given for adults. Substantially reduced fees are almost always available for children, students, and senior citizens. For information on taxes, *see* Taxes.

ATMS

ATMs are widely available in Las Vegas; they're at every bank and at most minimarts, convenience stores, and gas stations as well. In addition, all casinos have cash-advance machines, which take credit cards. You just indicate how large a cash advance you want, and when the transaction is approved you pick up the cash at the casino cashier. But beware: you'll pay up to a 12% fee in addition to the usual cash-advance charges and interest rate for this convenience; in most cases, the credit card company begins charging interest the moment the advance is taken, so you will not have the usual grace period to pay your balance in full before interest begins to accrue.

CREDIT CARDS

Throughout this guide, the following abbreviations are used: **AE,** American Express; **D,** Discover; **DC,** Diners Club; **MC,** MasterCard; and **V,** Visa.

➤ REPORTING LOST CARDS: **American Express** (☎ 800/441–0519); **Discover Card** (☎ 800/347–2683); **Diners Club** (☎ 800/234–6377); **MasterCard** (☎ 800/622–7747); and **Visa** (☎ 800/847–2911).

NATIONAL PARKS

Look into discount passes to save money on park entrance fees. For $50, the National Parks Pass admits you (and any passengers in your private vehicle) to all national parks, monuments, and recreation areas, as well as other sites run by the National Park Service, for a year. (In parks that charge per person, the pass admits you, your spouse and children, and your parents, when you arrive together.) Camping and parking are extra. The $15 Golden Eagle Pass, a hologram you affix to your National Parks Pass, functions as an upgrade, granting entry to all sites run by the NPS, the U.S. Fish and Wildlife Service, the U.S. Forest Service, and the Bureau of Land Management (BLM). The upgrade, which expires with the parks pass, is sold by most national-park, Fish-and-Wildlife, and BLM fee stations. A percentage of the proceeds from pass sales funds National Parks projects.

Both the Golden Age Passport ($10), for U.S. citizens or permanent residents who are 62 and older, and the Golden Access Passport (free), for those with disabilities, entitle holders (and any passengers in their private vehicles) to lifetime free entry to all national parks, plus 50% off fees for the use of many park facilities and services. (The discount doesn't always apply to companions.) To obtain them, you must show proof of age and of U.S. citizenship or permanent residency—such as a U.S. passport, driver's license, or birth certificate—and, if requesting Golden Access, proof of disability. The Golden Age and Golden Access passes, as well as the National Parks Pass, are available at any NPS-run site that charges an entrance fee. The National Parks Pass is also available by mail and via the Internet.

➤ INFORMATION: **National Park Foundation** (⌧ 1101 17th St. NW, Suite 1102, Washington, DC 20036, ☎ 202/785–4500, WEB www.nationalparks.org). **National Park Service** (⌧ National Park Service/Department of Interior, 1849 C St. NW, Washington, DC 20240, ☎ 202/208–4747, WEB www.nps.gov). **National Parks Conservation Association** (⌧ 1300 19th St. NW, Suite 300, Washington, DC 20036, ☎ 202/223–6722, WEB www.npca.org.)

➤ PASSES BY MAIL AND ON-LINE: **National Park Foundation** (WEB www.

nationalparks.org). **National Parks Pass** (✉ 27540 Ave. Mentry, Valencia, CA 91355, ☎ 888/GO–PARKS or 888/467–2757, WEB www. nationalparks.org); include a check or money order payable to the National Park Service for the pass, plus $3.95 for shipping and handling.

PACKING

Ever since the original Frontier Casino opened on the Los Angeles Highway (now the Strip), visitors to Las Vegas have been invited to "Come as You Are." The warm weather and informal character of Las Vegas render casual clothing appropriate day and night.

Always wear comfortable shoes; no matter what your intentions may be, you'll find yourself covering a lot of ground on foot.

In your carry-on luggage, **pack an extra pair of eyeglasses or contact lenses and enough of any medication** you take to last the entire trip. You may also ask your doctor to write a spare prescription using the drug's generic name, since brand names may vary from country to country. In luggage to be checked, **never pack prescription drugs or valuables.** And don't forget to carry with you the addresses of offices that handle refunds of lost traveler's checks. Check *Fodor's How to Pack* (available in bookstores everywhere) for more tips.

To avoid customs and security delays, carry medications in their original packaging. Don't pack any sharp objects in your carry-on luggage, including knives of any size or material, scissors, manicure tools, and corkscrews, or anything else that might arouse suspicion.

CHECKING LUGGAGE

You are allowed one carry-on bag and one personal article, such as a purse or a laptop computer. Make sure that everything you carry aboard will fit under your seat or in the overhead bin. Get to the gate early, so you can board as soon as possible, before the overhead bins fill up.

If you are flying internationally, note that baggage allowances may be determined not by piece but by weight—generally 88 pounds (40 kilograms) in first class, 66 pounds (30 kilograms) in business class, and 44 pounds (20 kilograms) in economy.

Airline liability for baggage is limited to $2,500 per person on flights within the United States. On international flights it amounts to $9.07 per pound or $20 per kilogram for checked baggage (roughly $640 per 70-pound bag) and $400 per passenger for unchecked baggage. You can buy additional coverage at check-in for about $10 per $1,000 of coverage, but it excludes a rather extensive list of items, shown on your airline ticket.

Before departure, **itemize your bags' contents** and their worth, and label the bags with your name, address, and phone number. (If you use your home address, cover it so potential thieves can't see it readily.) Inside each bag, **pack a copy of your itinerary.** At check-in, **make sure that each bag is correctly tagged** with the destination airport's three-letter code. If your bags arrive damaged or fail to arrive at all, file a written report with the airline before leaving the airport.

REST ROOMS

Free rest rooms can be found in every casino.

SAFETY

The well-known areas of Las Vegas are among the safest places for visitors in the world. With so many people carrying so much cash, security is tight inside and out. The casinos have visitors under constant surveillance, and hotel security guards are never more than a few seconds away. Outside, police are highly visible, on foot and bicycles and in cruisers. But this doesn't mean you can throw all safety consciousness to the wind. You should take the same precautions you would in any city—be aware of what's going on around you, stick to well-lighted areas, and quickly move away from any situation or people that might be threatening—especially if you're carrying some gambling cash. It's wise not to stray too far off the three main streets downtown: Fremont, Ogden, and Carson between Main and Las Vegas Boulevard.

Be especially careful with your purse and change buckets around slot machines. Grab-and-run thieves are always looking for easy pickings, especially downtown.

WOMEN IN LAS VEGAS

Apart from their everyday vulnerability to aggressive men, women should have few problems with unwanted attention in Las Vegas. If something does happen inside a casino, simply go to any pit and ask a boss to call security. The problem will disappear in seconds. Outside, crowds are almost always thick on the Strip and downtown, and there's safety in numbers.

Men in Las Vegas need to be on guard against predatory women. "Trick roller" is the name of a particularly nasty breed of female con artist. These women are expert at meeting single men by "chance." After getting friendly in the casino, the woman joins the man in his hotel room, where she slips powerful knockout drugs into his drink and robs him blind. Some men don't wake up.

SENIOR-CITIZEN TRAVEL

Las Vegas is such a bargain town in general that special subsidies and discounts for seniors are uncommon. Some casinos—Four Queens, Boulder Station—give seniors special deals through their slot clubs; ask when you join.

To qualify for age-related discounts, **mention your senior-citizen status up front** when booking hotel reservations (not when checking out) and before you're seated in restaurants (not when paying the bill). Be sure to have identification on hand. When renting a car, ask about promotional car-rental discounts, which can be cheaper than senior-citizen rates.

➤ EDUCATIONAL PROGRAMS: **Elder-hostel** (⊠ 11 Ave. de Lafayette, Boston, MA 02111-1746, ☎ 877/426–8056, FAX 877/426–2166, WEB www.elderhostel.org).

SIGHTSEEING TOURS

BOAT TOURS

The *Desert Princess*, a 250-passenger Mississippi River–style stern-wheeler, cruises Lake Mead. Tours include 90-minute sightseeing cruises, two-hour dinner cruises, and three-hour dinner and dancing excursions.

➤ FEES AND SCHEDULES: *Desert Princess* (⊠ Lake Mead marina, ☎ 702/293–6180).

BUS TOURS

Gray Line offers city tours, trips to Red Rock Canyon, Lake Mead, and Valley of Fire, and longer trips to the Grand Canyon and Death Valley.

➤ FEES AND SCHEDULES: **Gray Line Tours** (⊠ 4020 E. Lone Mountain Rd., Las Vegas 89031, ☎ 702/384–1234 or 800/634–6579).

HELICOPTER TOURS

Helicopters do two basic tours in and around Las Vegas: a 20-minute fly-over of the Strip and a several-hour trip out to the Grand Canyon and back.

➤ FEES AND SCHEDULES: **Sundance Helicopters** (⊠ 265 E. Tropicana Ave., Las Vegas 89119, ☎ 702/736–0606, WEB www.helicoptour.com).

STUDENTS IN LAS VEGAS

No special discounts or considerations are offered students in Las Vegas. No one under 21 is allowed in the casinos.

➤ I.D.s AND SERVICES: **STA Travel** (☎ 212/627–3111 or 800/781–4040, FAX 212/627–3387, WEB www.sta.com). **Travel Cuts** (⊠ 187 College St., Toronto, Ontario M5T 1P7, Canada, ☎ 416/979–2406 or 888/838–2887, FAX 416/979–8167, WEB www.travelcuts.com).

TAXES

Las Vegas and Reno-Tahoe international airports assess a $3 departure tax, or passenger facility charge. The hotel room tax is 10% in Las Vegas.

SALES TAX

The sales tax rates for the areas covered in this guide are: Las Vegas, 7.25%; Arizona, 5%; and Utah, 4.75%.

TAXIS

Las Vegas is heavily covered by taxi-cabs. You'll find cabs waiting at the airport and at every hotel in town. If you dine at a restaurant off the Strip, the restaurant will call a taxi to take you home.

The fare is $2.30 on the meter when you get in, plus $1.80 for every mile. Taxis are limited by law to carrying a maximum of four passengers, and there is no additional charge per person. No fees are assessed for luggage, but taxis leaving the airport are allowed to add an airport sur-charge of $1.30.

➤ TAXI COMPANIES: **Desert Cab** (☎ 702/376–2687). **Whittlesea Blue Cab** (☎ 702/384–6111). **Yellow** and **Checker Cab** (☎ 702/873–2000).

TIME

The states of Nevada and California are in the Pacific time zone. Arizona and Utah are in the Mountain time zone. Arizona does not observe day-light saving time.

TIPPING

More so than in other U.S. destinations, workers in Las Vegas are paid a minimum wage and rely on tips to make up the primary part of their income. At restaurants, a 15% tip is standard for waiters; up to 20% may be expected at more expensive estab-lishments. The same goes for taxi drivers, bartenders, and hairdressers. Coat-check operators usually expect $1; bellhops and porters should get 50¢ to $1 per bag. Maids should receive at least 4%–5% of the room-rate total, before taxes, for rooms that cost $100 a night or more. If the room is less than $100 per night, then 3%–4%. If the hotel charges a service fee, be sure to ask what it covers, as it may include this gratuity. A 50¢ or $1 tip per drink is appropriate for cock-tail waitresses, even when they bring you a free drink at a slot machine or casino table. On package tours, conductors and drivers usually get $10 per day from the group as a whole; check whether this has already been figured into your cost. For local sightseeing tours, you may individu-ally tip the driver-guide $1 if he or she has been helpful or informative. Tip dealers with the equivalent of your average bet once or twice an hour if you're winning; slot-machine change personnel and keno runners are accustomed to a buck or two. Ushers in showrooms may be able to get you better seats for performances for a gratuity of $5 or more. Tip the con-cierge 10%–20% of the cost for a ticket to a hot show. Tip $5–$10 for making dinner reservations or ar-rangements for other attractions.

TOURS AND PACKAGES

Because everything is prearranged on a prepackaged tour or indepen-dent vacation, you spend less time planning—and often get it all at a good price.

BOOKING WITH AN AGENT

Travel agents are excellent resources. But it's a good idea to collect brochures from several agencies, as some agents' suggestions may be influenced by relationships with tour and package firms that reward them for volume sales. If you have a special interest, **find an agent with expertise in that area**; the American Society of Travel Agents (ASTA; ☞ Travel Agencies) has a database of specialists worldwide.

Make sure your travel agent knows the accommodations and other services of the place being recommended. Ask about the hotel's location, room size, beds, and whether it has a pool, room service, or programs for children, if you care about these. Has your agent been there in person or sent others whom you can contact?

Do some homework on your own, too: local tourism boards can provide information about lesser-known and small-niche operators, some of which may sell only direct.

BUYER BEWARE

Each year consumers are stranded or lose their money when tour operators—even large ones with excellent reputations—go out of business. So **check out the operator.** Ask several travel agents about its reputation, and try to **book with a company that has a consumer-protection program.** (Look for infor-mation in the company's brochure.)

In the United States, members of the National Tour Association and the United States Tour Operators Association are required to set aside funds to cover your payments and travel arrangements in the event that the company defaults. It's also a good idea to choose a company that participates in the American Society of Travel Agents' Tour Operator Program (TOP); ASTA will act as mediator in any disputes between you and your tour operator.

Remember that the more your package or tour includes the better you can predict the ultimate cost of your vacation. Make sure you know exactly what is covered, and **beware of hidden costs.** Are taxes, tips, and transfers included? Entertainment and excursions? These can add up.

➤ TOUR-OPERATOR RECOMMENDATIONS: **American Society of Travel Agents** (☞ Travel Agencies). **National Tour Association** (NTA; ✉ 546 E. Main St., Lexington, KY 40508, ☎ 859/226–4444 or 800/682–8886, WEB www.ntaonline.com). **United States Tour Operators Association** (USTOA; ✉ 275 Madison Ave., Suite 2014, New York, NY 10016, ☎ 212/599–6599 or 800/468–7862, FAX 212/599–6744, WEB www.ustoa.com).

TRAIN TRAVEL

You can't take a train to Las Vegas, but **Amtrak** can get you there via a Thruway bus from Los Angeles. You can also pick up a timetable at any Amtrak station or request one by mail. Amtrak accepts all major credit cards and personal checks. You can purchase tickets aboard trains; however, an additional charge applies if the ticket office is open at your time of departure.

➤ TRAIN INFORMATION: **Amtrak** (☎ 800/872–7245, WEB www.amtrak.com).

TRANSPORTATION AROUND LAS VEGAS

Though you can get around Las Vegas fine without a car, the best way to experience the city may be to drive it. A car gives you easy access to all the casinos and attractions, lets you make excursions to Lake Mead and elsewhere at your leisure, and gives you the chance to cruise the Strip and bask in its neon glow.

Parking on and around the Strip, although free, is not so easy. You'll have to brave some rather immense parking structures and walk up and down stairs or escalators. Valet parking is available if you're willing to wait your turn and tip the valets. Taxis are an easy way to go door to door, although the downside is that you can't hail one off the street, so waiting in line at hotels is the only way to get a cab. During busy weekends, the wait can run anywhere from 10 to 30 minutes. Buses don't always run on time and they're frequently crowded. If you're not covering great distances, and when the weather is decent, the best way to get around Las Vegas is on foot.

TRAVEL AGENCIES

A good travel agent puts your needs first. Look for an agency that has been in business at least five years, emphasizes customer service, and has someone on staff who specializes in your destination. In addition, **make sure the agency belongs to a professional trade organization.** The American Society of Travel Agents (ASTA)—the largest and most influential in the field with more than 24,000 members in some 140 countries—maintains and enforces a strict code of ethics and will step in to help mediate any agent-client disputes involving ASTA members if necessary. ASTA (whose motto is "Without a travel agent, you're on your own") also maintains a Web site that includes a directory of agents. (If a travel agency is also acting as your tour operator, *see* Buyer Beware *in* Tours and Packages.)

➤ LOCAL AGENT REFERRALS: **American Society of Travel Agents** (ASTA; ✉ 1101 King St., Suite 200, Alexandria, VA 22314, ☎ 800/965–2782 24-hr hot line, FAX 703/739–7642, WEB www.astanet.com). **Association of British Travel Agents** (✉ 68–71 Newman St., London W1T 3AH, ☎ 020/7637–2444, FAX 020/7637–0713, WEB www.abtanet.com). **Association of Canadian Travel Agents** (✉ 130 Albert St., Suite 1705, Ottawa, Ontario K1P 5G4, ☎ 613/237–3657,

FAX 613/237–7052, WEB www.acta.ca).
**Australian Federation of Travel
Agents** (✉ Level 3, 309 Pitt St.,
Sydney, NSW 2000, ☎ 02/9264–
3299, FAX 02/9264–1085, WEB www.
afta.com.au). **Travel Agents' Association of New Zealand** (✉ Level 5,
Tourism and Travel House, 79 Boul-
cott St., Box 1888, Wellington 6001,
☎ 04/499–0104, FAX 04/499–0827,
WEB www.taanz.org.nz).

VISITOR INFORMATION

Before you go, contact the city and
state tourism offices for general information. When you get there, visit the
Las Vegas Convention and Visitors
Authority, next door to the Las Vegas
Hilton, for brochures and general
information. Hotels and gift shops on
the Strip have maps, brochures, pam-
phlets, and free events magazines—
*What's On in Las Vegas, Las Vegas
Today,* and *Tourguide*—that list shows
and buffets and offer discounts to area
attractions.

The *Las Vegas Advisor,* a 12-page
monthly newsletter, keeps up-to-the-
minute track of the constantly changing Las Vegas landscapes of gambling,
accommodations, dining, entertainment, Top Ten Values, complimentaries, and more, and is an indispensable
resource for any Las Vegas visitor.
Send $5 for a sample issue.

➤ CITY TOURIST INFORMATION: **Las
Vegas Convention and Visitors Authority** (✉ 3150 Paradise Rd., Las
Vegas, NV 89109, ☎ 702/892–0711,
FAX 702/892–2824). **Las Vegas Chamber of Commerce** (✉ 3720 Howard
Hughes Pkwy., Las Vegas, NV 89109,
☎ 702/735–1616, FAX 702/735–
2011). **Las Vegas Advisor** (✉ 3687 S.
Procyon Ave., Las Vegas, NV 89103,
☎ 702/252–0655 or 800/244–2224).

➤ STATE TOURIST INFORMATION:
Nevada Commission on Tourism (✉
Capitol Complex, 5151 S. Carson St.,
Carson City, NV 89710, ☎ 702/687–
4322; 800/237–0774; 800/638–2328
for brochures; FAX 702/687–6779).

WEB SITES

Do check out the World Wide Web
when planning your trip. You'll find
everything from weather forecasts to
virtual tours of famous cities. Be sure
to **visit Fodors.com** (www.fodors.

com), a complete travel-planning site.
You can research prices and book
plane tickets, hotel rooms, rental cars,
vacation packages, and more. In
addition, you can post your pressing
questions in the Travel Talk section.
Other planning tools include a currency converter and weather reports,
and there are loads of links to travel
resources.

The Web site of the **Las Vegas Convention and Visitors Authority** has travel
tips, events calendars, and other resources, as well as links to other
visitor-oriented Nevada-based Web
sites at WEB www.lasvegas24hours.com.
The **Las Vegas Chamber of Commerce**
has lots of useful information at WEB
www.lvchamber.com, including visitor
tips, local businesses, even relocation
advice. One of the biggest sites is **Las
Vegas Leisure Guide,** at WEB www.
pcap.com, full of hotel, restaurant, and
nightlife info. **Las Vegas Online Entertainment Guide** is at WEB www.lvol.
com; it has listings for hotels and
an online reservations system, plus
local history, restaurants, a business
directory, and even some gambling
instruction.

WHEN TO GO

Las Vegas is a year-round destination.
Except for the first three weeks in
December and weekdays during July,
you can assume that Las Vegas will be
running at full speed. Weekends,
always crowded, are especially jam-
packed for the Super Bowl, Valentine's
Day, President's Day, the NCAA Final
Four, Easter, Cinco de Mayo, Memorial Day, July 4, and Labor Day. The
week between Christmas and New
Year's is the most crowded week of
the year. In addition, nearly 50 conventions of more than 10,000 participants are held here every year; prices
skyrocket, availability plummets, and
the hordes fill every open space.
Sporting events, such as boxing
matches, golf tournaments, the National Finals Rodeo and the NASCAR
Winston Cup Las Vegas 400, also
have a major impact on the crowd
situation. It's a good idea to **call the
Las Vegas Convention and Visitors
Authority** (☞ Visitor Information) to
find out who or what will be in town
at the time you're planning to visit.

During a "normal" week—that fairly rare time of no conventions, holidays, title fights, or local events—you can count on Sunday through Thursday being less crowded, less expensive, and less stressful than the weekend. During even a routine weekend, however, traffic jams—along with competition for room, restaurant, and show reservations, as well as spots at the slots or tables—can be ferocious.

CLIMATE

Weather-wise, the most comfortable times to be in Las Vegas are the spring and fall. In April and May, daytime temperatures are delightful, in the 70s and 80s F. In September and October, the summer heat has abated, and the pools remain open.

Winter is a distinctly different season, with snowcapped mountains in the distance, windy and chilly days, and surprisingly cold nights. The three weeks before Christmas find Las Vegas nearly deserted, with rooms going for bargain rates and hardly a traffic jam on the Strip.

Summer is a time of dry, uncomfortably hot weather (sometimes literally 110°F in the shade), when lounging at an outdoor pool requires protection from the relentless desert sun. You'll probably find yourself continuously thirsty. At the height of the heat, however, hotels offer their lowest rates.

What follows are the average daily maximum and minimum temperatures for Las Vegas.

➤ FORECASTS: **Weather Channel Connection** (☎ 900/932–8437), 95¢ per minute from a Touch-Tone phone.

CLIMATE IN LAS VEGAS

Jan.	60F	16C	May	89F	32C	Sept.	95F	35C
	28	–2		51	11		57	14
Feb.	66F	19C	June	98F	37C	Oct.	84F	29C
	33	1		60	16		46	8
Mar.	71F	22C	July	102F	39C	Nov.	71F	22C
	39	4		68	20		35	2
Apr.	80F	27C	Aug.	102F	39C	Dec.	60F	16C
	44	7		66	19		30	–1

FESTIVALS AND SEASONAL EVENTS

Las Vegas is not known for specific celebrations—the Strip is the venue for a never-ending parade. Still, a number of annual events do attract wide attention. They are listed below, along with the major conventions that take place annually in Las Vegas, which affect everything from room rates and rental car availability to lines at buffets and crowds at the crap tables.

➤ EARLY DEC.: **CineVegas Film Festival** is a six-day event featuring works by local filmmakers (including film students at UNLV) as well as movies about Las Vegas. Films are shown in theaters around town. ☎ 702/946–7000.

➤ EARLY DEC.: **National Finals Rodeo**, the Super Bowl of rodeos, brings together 15 finalists to compete in each of seven events; there are 10 performances in nine days at the Thomas and Mack Center. When the rodeo comes to town, the showrooms all feature country music, and it seems as though everyone on the street is wearing jeans, boots, and a cowboy hat. ☎ 702/731–2115.

➤ MID DEC.: In the **Parade of Lights**, boats large and small, all decked out in holiday lights, come together in a flotilla of illumination on Lake Mead. It's most fun to be on a boat, but it's also exciting to watch from the shoreline along Lakeshore Drive. ☎ 702/293–2034.

➤ DEC. 31: **New Year's Eve** is celebrated with fireworks over Fremont Street in downtown Las Vegas. ☎ 702/382–6397.

➤ EARLY JAN.: The **Consumer Electronics Show** is a convention that attracts upwards of 125,000 participants.

➤ MID-FEB.: The early spring **Men's Apparel Guild Convention,** a.k.a. MAGIC, attracts some 100,000 participants.

➤ MID-FEB.: The **Las Vegas International Marathon** draws more than 5,000 runners. The starting line changes from year to year, but the finish line of the 5K race is Vacation Village, 2 mi south of Mandalay Bay. ☎ *702/876–3870.*

➤ EARLY MAR.: The **NASCAR Winston Cup Race** is the largest sporting event of the year in Nevada. Some 135,000 racing fans converge on Las Vegas to watch the grueling 400-mi race on the 1½-mi track, with top national drivers competing for $3 million in prize money. ☎ *702/644–4443.*

➤ MID-MAR: The **Conexpo** trade show is the largest show of its kind in the western hemisphere, focusing on construction products (e.g. cement) and drawing over 150,000 attendees over four days.

➤ MAR. 17: **St. Patrick's Day** in Las Vegas is a festive occasion, with many of the casinos decorated in green and serving bargain corned-beef-and-cabbage dinners.

➤ MAR.: The **LPGA Invitational golf tournament** draws top women golfers. ☎ *702/382–6616.*

➤ EARLY APR.: **NHRA Drag Racing** is new to Las Vegas. The Las Vegas Motor Speedway completed a ¼-mi drag strip and 80,000-seat grandstand in 2000, just in time for a large National Hot Rod Association race. A major NHRA race will take place here each April. ☎ *702/644–4444.*

➤ MID-APR.: The **National Association of Broadcasters** convention fills the town with 125,000 attendees, including a bevy of major TV and movie celebrities.

➤ APR.: The **Clark County Fair** takes place 60 mi north of Las Vegas in Logandale. ☎ *702/398–3247.*

➤ APR.–MAY: The **World Series of Poker** draws crowds to the Binion's Horseshoe casino to watch the poker faces of players from around the world. This monthlong tournament culminates in a four-day final round in which nearly 300 players each invest $10,000 in the hope of winning first prize: $1 million. ☎ *702/366–7397.*

➤ MAR., APR., OR MAY: The **Gay Pride Parade** in Sunset Park is a large festival featuring a picnic, entertainment, and seminars. ☎ *702/733–9800.*

➤ MAY OR JUNE: **Helldorado Days and Rodeo** celebrates the Old West with parades, contests, Western costumes, and a championship rodeo at the Thomas and Mack Center. ☎ *702/870–1221.*

➤ EARLY JULY: **Damboree Days** is a weekend-long festival in Boulder City that coincides with the July Fourth holiday. It culminates in the largest fireworks event in the area. ☎ *702/293–2034.*

➤ LATE AUG.: The early fall **Men's Apparel Guild Convention,** a.k.a. MAGIC, attracts 100,000 participants.

➤ MID-SEPT.: **Football season** begins at the University of Nevada–Las Vegas. ☎ *702/895–3900.*

➤ MID-SEPT.: The **World Gaming Congress and Expo** only attracts 25,000–30,000 attendees, so it barely makes a dent in hotel occupancy rates. But all the new-generation slot and video-poker machines, table games, and casino paraphernalia are on display at the Las Vegas Convention and Visitors Authority. ☎ *702/892–0711.*

➤ OCT.: The **Pro Bull Riders Finals** is the two-day Super Bowl of the bull-riders circuit. The top 50 bull-riders compete for a $1-million purse. ☎ *702/891–7272 or 800/929–1111.*

➤ EARLY OCT.: **Art in the Park,** one of the largest events of the year in Boulder City, is an early Christmas crafts fair, with artists and craftsmen displaying their wares in Bicentennial Park in downtown Boulder City. ☎ *702/294–1611.*

➤ MID-OCT.: The **Las Vegas Invitational golf tournament,** a five-day event, is played on three courses, with television coverage. ☎ *702/382–6616.*

➤ MID-OCT.: The **U.S. Triathlon Series national championships and**

world invitational draws top competitors from around the globe. ☎ *702/731–2115.*

➤ LATE OCT.: Masses of hot-air balloons take to the sky for the **Las Vegas Balloon Classic.** ☎ *702/434–0848.*

➤ EARLY NOV.: The **AAPEX/Automotive After-market Products** is a huge trade show bringing in over 90,000 participants.

➤ MID-NOV.: The **Comdex** computer hardware, software, and electronics convention, held the week before Thanksgiving, is the largest convention of the year in Las Vegas. It attracts 250,000 participants and fills the town to the gills. Avoid Las Vegas like the plague during Comdex week.

➤ NOV.–MAR.: **Basketball season** at the University of Nevada–Las Vegas. ☎ *702/895–3900.*

1 DESTINATION: LAS VEGAS

Bright Lights, Gambling, Growth

What's Where

Pleasures and Pastimes

Fodor's Choice

Great Itineraries

BRIGHT LIGHTS, GAMBLING, GROWTH

ILLUSION IS EVERYWHERE in Las Vegas. A 50-story Eiffel Tower looms over the Strip, gondoliers "o sole mio" their way down an ersatz Grand Canal, and acres of neon turn night into multicolored day. Gamblers defy reason (and the considerable odds against winning) in their attempts to seduce the goddess of chance, while onstage extravaganzas manipulate reality with mind-bending special effects. Even a meal can be an adventure, whether at an over-the-top, all-you-can-eat buffet or in a house of haute cuisine that you wouldn't expect to find in the Nevada desert. Head out of town and you'll come across otherworldly landscapes that nature has etched over the years. Yes, a trip to Las Vegas offers a chance to surrender to fantasy—and you'll have the time of your life doing it.

The Las Vegas of the Strip and downtown is Siegfried & Roy, the Rockettes, and Cirque du Soleil. It's cards, dice, roulette wheels, and slots. It's harried keno runners and leggy cocktail waitresses, grizzled pit bosses and nervous break-in dealers. It's cab and limo drivers, valet attendants, and bellmen. Las Vegas is showgirls with smiles as white as spotlights and head wear as big and bright as fireworks. It's a place where thousands of people earn their living counting billions in chips, change, bills, checks, and markers.

Gimmicks, glitz, and gigawatts of electrical power are what keep Las Vegas humming day and night, not to mention the more than 36 million casino-bound visitors who arrive every year and bed down in some of the world's largest, showiest hotels (the city has 18 of the 21 biggest in the world). Vegas Vic and Vicky, the 50-ft-tall ambassadors of Glitter Gulch, are forever duded up in high western style to give gamblers a flashy welcome. Locals aren't spinning yarns when they say you can hear the buzz of Las Vegas neon in the quiet of the Mojave Desert, as far as 10 mi beyond the city limits.

While the Strip and downtown are the best known and principal tourist areas of the city, more than 1 million people live—and lead "normal" lives—within 10 mi of them. Endless subdivisions enclose rows and rows of pink-stucco and red-tile, three-bedroom-two-bath houses, most of them fewer than five years old and occupied by transplants hoping to cash in on the boom. "Lost Wages" is a city of dreamers: gamblers hoping to beat the odds and get rich; dancers, singers, magicians, acrobats, and comedians praying to make it in the Entertainment Capital of the World; and increasingly realtors, supermarket cashiers, computer techs, credit card accounting clerks, shoe salesmen, and librarians seeking a better way of life.

For all the local talk about Las Vegas citizens being average people who just happen to live and work in an unusual city, living here is undeniably different. The town is full of people whose jobs involve catering to strangers 24 hours a day, 365 days a year. Las Vegas probably has the largest graveyard shift in the world. And the notion that locals never gamble and rarely see a show or eat at a buffet is also largely a myth—residents are a large and active part of the total market that relishes 99¢ breakfasts and $5 prime ribs, slot clubs, casino paycheck-cashing promotions, and free lounge entertainment. Indeed, the casinos that cater primarily to locals (Palace Station, Boulder Station, Texas Station, the Rio, Gold Coast, Orleans, Santa Fe, Arizona Charlie's, and Fiesta) are among the most successful in town. Surprisingly, Las Vegas is also a religious town—about a third of the 450 congregations here are Mormon—which adds a somewhat incongruous conservative dimension to local politics and morals.

GAMBLING AND TOURISM are not the only games in town. Nellis Air Force Base employs thousands of people. The construction industry is huge. Large corporations and small manufacturing firms frequently relocate to southern Nevada, which offers tax incentives as well as a lower cost of living. But local life is merely a curiosity to the tens of millions of tourists whose primary concern is choosing among over 60 major hotel-casinos, dozens of shows, a mind-boggling list of gambling options, limitless dining, and spectacular day trips.

The largest city in Nevada, Las Vegas is 2,030 ft above sea level. It's one of the most remote large cities in the country: the nearest major population center to the west is Barstow, California, 2½ hours away; St. George, Utah, is two hours to the east. Through the years Las Vegas has wrested the political and economic power of Nevada away from Reno, 448 mi to the northwest, the city where legalized gambling first became popular and where the early casinos were built.

Las Vegas is surrounded by the Mojave Desert, and Las Vegas Valley is flanked by mountain ranges. Among them are the Spring Mountains, including Mount Charleston (11,918 ft), which has downhill skiing, and Red Rock Canyon, characterized by stunning Southwest sandstone. The Las Vegas Wash drains the valley to the southeast into Lake Mead and the Colorado River system.

Average high temperatures in Las Vegas rise to 105°F in July and August; lows drop to 30°F in January and February. The heat is saunalike throughout the summer, except during electrical storms that can dump an inch of rain an hour and cause dangerous flash floods. Heavy rains any time of year exacerbate two of Las Vegas's major problems: a lack of water drainage and a surplus of traffic. The summer blaze often makes it very uncomfortable to be outside for any length of time. Winters can be surprisingly chilly during the day and especially cold after the sun goes down. But in September and October and April and May it doesn't get any better.

Las Vegas is the largest U.S. city founded in the 20th century—1905 to be exact. Some might argue that the significant year was 1946, when Bugsy Siegel's Fabulous Flamingo opened for business. But the beginnings of modern Las Vegas can be traced back to 1829, when Antonio Armijo led a party of 60 on the Old Spanish Trail between Santa Fe and Los Angeles. While his caravan camped about 100 mi northeast of the present site of Las Vegas, an advance party set out to look for water. Rafael Rivera, a young Mexican scout, left the main party, headed due west over the

unexplored desert, and discovered an oasis. The abundance of artesian spring water here shortened the Spanish Trail to Los Angeles by allowing travelers to go directly through, rather than around, the desert and eased the rigors of travel for the Spanish traders who used the route. They named the oasis Las Vegas, Spanish for "the meadows."

The next major visitor to the Las Vegas Springs was John C. Fremont, who in 1844 led one of his many explorations of the Far West. Today he is remembered in the name of the principal downtown thoroughfare—Fremont Street.

Ten years later a group of Mormon settlers were sent by Brigham Young from Salt Lake City to colonize the valley. They built a large stockade; a small remnant of it—a 150-square-ft, adobe-brick fort—still stands today. The old fort is the oldest building in Las Vegas. The Mormons spent two years growing crops, mining lead, and converting the local Paiute natives, but the climate and isolation defeated their ambitions and by 1857 the fort was abandoned.

THINGS DIDN'T START HOPPING here until 1904, when the San Pedro, Los Angeles, and Salt Lake Railroad laid its tracks through Las Vegas Valley, purchased the prime land and water rights from the handful of homesteaders, and surveyed a town site for its railroad servicing and repair facilities. In May 1905 the railroad held an auction and sold 700 lots. Las Vegas became a dusty railroad watering stop with a few downtown hotels and stores, a saloon and red-light district known as Block 16, and a few thousand residents. It remained just that until 1928, when the Boulder Canyon Project Act was signed into law, in which $165 million was appropriated for the building of the world's largest antigravity dam, 40 mi from Las Vegas.

Construction of Hoover Dam began in 1931, a historic year for Nevada. In that year Governor Fred Balzar approved the "wide-open" gambling bill that had been introduced by a Winnemucca rancher, Assemblyman Phil Tobin. Gambling had been outlawed several times since Nevada became a state in 1864, but it had never been completely eliminated. Tobin maintained that controlled gaming would be good for tourism and the state's economy; people were going to gamble anyway, so why shouldn't the state tax the profits? Thus, he was able to convince lawmakers to make gambling permanently legal. Also in 1931, the Legislature reduced the residency requirement for divorce to a scandalous six weeks, immediately turning Nevada into a "divorce colony."

The early 1930s marked the height of the Great Depression and Prohibition. The construction of the dam on the Colorado River (bridging the gap between Arizona and Nevada) brought thousands of job seekers to southern Nevada. Because the federal government didn't want dam workers to be distracted by the temptations of Las Vegas, it created a separate government town, Boulder City—still the only community in the state where gambling is illegal.

At this time Nevada's political and economic power resided in the northern part of the state: the capital in Carson City and the major casinos (notably Harold's Club and Harrah's) in Reno. But the completion of the dam in 1935 turned southern Nevada into a magnet for federal appropriations, thousands of tourists and new residents, and a seemingly inexhaustible supply of electricity and water. In addition, as the country mobilized for World War II, tens of thousands of pilots and gunners trained at the Las Vegas Aerial Gunnery School, opened by the federal government on 3 million acres north of town. Today this property is Nellis Air Force Base and the Nevada Test Site.

By the early 1940s downtown Las Vegas boasted several luxury hotels and a dozen small but successful gambling clubs. In 1941, Thomas Hull, who owned a chain of California motor inns, decided to build a place in the desert just outside the city limits on Highway 91, the road from Los Angeles. El Rancho Vegas opened with 100 motel rooms, a western-motif casino, and, right off the highway, a large parking lot with an inviting swimming pool in the middle. El Rancho's quick success led to the opening a year later of the Last Frontier Hotel, a mile down the road. Thus, the Las Vegas Strip was established.

Benjamin "Bugsy" Siegel, who ran the New York mob's activities on the West Coast, began to see the incredible potential of a remote oasis where land was cheap and gambling was legal. He struggled for two years to build his Fabulous Flamingo, managing to alienate his local partners and silent investors with his lavish overspending. He opened the joint prematurely, on a rainy night, the day after Christmas 1946. Although movie stars attended and headliners Jimmy Durante, Xavier Cugat, and Rose Marie performed, the Flamingo flopped; the casino paid out more money than it took in. This made Siegel's partners not only unhappy but also suspicious, and six months later Bugsy was dead. Once he had been bumped off, business at the Flamingo boomed—Siegel's gangland assassination had made front-page news across the country, and people flocked to see the house that Bugsy built.

The success of the Flamingo paved the way for gamblers and gangsters from all over the country to invest in Las Vegas hotel-casinos, one after another. The Desert Inn, Horseshoe, Sands, Sahara, Riviera, Dunes, Fremont, Tropicana, and Stardust were all built in the 1950s, financed with mob money. Every new hotel came on like a theme park opening for the summer with a new ride. Each was bigger, better, more unusual than the last. The Sahara had the tallest freestanding neon sign. The Riviera was the first high-rise building in town. The Stardust had 1,000 rooms and the world's largest swimming pool.

That the underworld owned and ran the big joints only added to the allure of Las Vegas. And the town's great boom in the 1950s couldn't have happened without the mob's access to millions of dollars in cash. Under the circumstances, no bank, corporation, or legitimate investor would have touched the gambling business.

In time, however, the state began to take steps to weed out the most visible undesirables. The federal government assisted in the crackdown, using its considerable resources to hound the gangsters out of business. And, finally, an eccentric man arrived on a train and soon revolutionized the nation's image of Las Vegas.

Howard Hughes had just sold Trans World Airlines for $546 million, and he either had to spend half the money or turn it in as taxes. During a three-year stay in Las Vegas he bought the Desert Inn, Frontier, Sands, Landmark, and Silver Slipper hotels, a television station, an airfield, and millions of dollars' worth of real estate. His presence in Las Vegas gave gambling its first positive image: As a former pilot and aviation pioneer, Hollywood mogul, and American folk hero, Hughes could in no way be connected with gangsters.

Hughes's presence also opened the door to corporate ownership of hotel-casinos. In 1971, Hilton Corporation purchased the International (now the Las Vegas Hilton) and the Flamingo, becoming the first major publicly traded hotel chain to step onto the Las Vegas playing field. Ramada, Holiday Inn, Hyatt, Sheraton, and others have since followed suit.

L AS VEGAS FELT THE EFFECTS of both the legalization of gambling in Atlantic City in the late 1970s and of the national recession of the early 1980s—but not for very long. Through the years the city has carved a secure niche for itself as a destination for national and international tourists, a winter sojourn for snowbirds from the north; a weekend getaway for gamblers and families from California, Arizona, and Utah; and convention central. Las Vegas has expanded at a ferocious pace for the past 10 years, during which more than 65,000 hotel rooms have been added and more than a half million people have moved to the area, many of them fleeing California.

And why not? Though inching up, room rates are lower than in any other major U.S. city. There are lavish gourmet spots, but the inexpensive restaurants and buffet dining here can be cheaper than preparing a meal at home. Entertainment is abundant and reasonably priced. Las Vegas is possibly the easiest place in the world to receive freebies—the ubiquitous "comps." And best of all, gambling promotions such as coupons, slot clubs, paycheck bonuses, and drawings provide a fighting chance to win in the casino. In the back of everyone's mind is the idea that a trip to Las Vegas can be free or even a money-making vacation. That kind of thinking keeps the corporations smiling as they add a few more finishing touches to their $2-billion hotels.

WHAT'S WHERE

Las Vegas Hot Spots

The Strip
Officially titled Las Vegas Boulevard South, the Strip runs north–south through the city. Without leaving this street you could sample all that's best in Vegas: the food, the shows, and of course the gambling. Almost all the major casinos are either on or just off the Strip. In fact, there's so much to see and do on the Strip that we've broken it down into South, Center, and North to help you navigate through the options.

New Four Corners
Vegas is all about newer, bigger and brighter, and you'll find all three at the junction of Las Vegas Boulevard and Tropicana Avenue. One of the newest megaresorts on the South Strip, Mandalay Bay, is just a short tram ride away; the world's biggest hotel—the MGM Grand—is within walking distance of the corner; and one of the brightest beams of light in the world tops the Luxor pyramid just to the south. The centerpiece of the South Strip, this intersection is fast becoming the prime tourist crossroads in the country.

Old Four Corners
The intersection of Las Vegas Boulevard and Flamingo Road has set the standards for excess ever since Bugsy Siegal first set up shop here with his Fabulous Flamingo in 1946. Caesars, the Mirage, and now Bellagio have upped the stakes in their turn, and, as of yet, there appears to be no betting maximum at the hub of the Center Strip.

Fremont Street
You'll find the heart of downtown Vegas where Fremont Street meets Las Vegas Boulevard. It's also the epicenter of the Fremont Street Experience, the world's greatest collection of neon signs, covered by the world's largest electric sign. The hotels and casinos on Fremont tend to be older and a lot less expensive than those on the Strip.

Side Trips from Vegas

Red Rock Canyon

You have probably seen Red Rock in the movies; this 13-mi scenic loop road through the red rock formations and unusual high-desert scenery of southern Nevada is a very popular location spot for Hollywood. And it's only 20 minutes from the heart of the city.

Mt. Charleston

The eighth-highest peak in Nevada, Mt. Charleston is the perfect retreat for a day or two away from the madness of Vegas. In wintertime it's a local ski haven, and in the summer hikers, mountain bikers, and campers hit the slopes.

Hoover Dam, Lake Mead, and Boulder City

About 35 mi east of Vegas lies one of the seven man-made wonders of the world, the monster Hoover Dam. This 4.4-million-cubic-yard concrete beast dams the Colorado River, creating the 229 square mi of Lake Mead, the largest man-made lake in the country. This is your destination for water sports if your ambitions extend beyond swim-up blackjack. Nearby Boulder City, built in the early 1930s to house workers who were constructing Hoover Dam, is the only community in Nevada where gambling is illegal.

Valley of Fire State Park

Nevada's first state park is about 55 mi northeast of Las Vegas. The name comes from the distinctive coloration of its rock formations, which range from lavender to tangerine to bright red. The lights of Vegas pale in comparison to the rays of sunset on this fantastic natural backdrop.

Laughlin

This is a major gambling center, about 90 mi south of Vegas on the Arizona state line. If the pace of Vegas gets to you, you might try the low-pressure, low-minimum tables, and low-cost rooms of this Colorado River town.

St. George

Only 100 mi north of Las Vegas is the picturesque town of St. George, Utah. Its Victorian-style streets offer low-price lodging and dining, as well as a number of Mormon historical sites and some magnificent red rocks.

Zion National Park

When the Mormons first saw this area they believed they had found God's country. Drive through 6 mi of monstrous red rocks and stunning vistas, and you might be tempted to agree with them.

Bryce Canyon National Park

A hike through Bryce is like a trip back to a prehistoric age. As with much of this area, red is the dominant natural color here, but reds like you've never seen them before, dancing and glinting in the desert sun.

PLEASURES AND PASTIMES

Downtown Neon

It is a simple (and free) pleasure in Las Vegas to stand in the middle of the pedestrian mall in the evening and behold a testament to the extraordinary powers of electricity, which has turned night into day. The area has a collection of neon signs that only downtown Tokyo can claim to match. The 50-ft-tall neon cowboy (Vegas Vic) and cowgirl (Vegas Vicky) are perhaps the most famous signs. Once an hour, after dark, the modern-day wizards of odds fire up the Fremont Street Experience, all 2 million lightbulbs and 500,000 watts and four blocks of it, for a light-and-sound show unequaled anywhere on (and possibly off) the planet.

The High Rollers

If you get a chance—that is, if it happens in one of the casinos' public rooms—just stand (in Vegas, chairs are for gamblers only) and watch one of the bigger players or high rollers take on the tables at Vegas. You have nothing to lose, but if the player hits a big streak and those chips start piling up, you can ride his or her adrenaline rush for free.

The Las Vegas Buzz

Besides the renowned enticements of Las Vegas, there are other, more subtle ones. There's the twisting of time, noticeable, for example, in coffee shops, when at any hour some people are having breakfast, others lunch or dinner, and still others snacks or coffee. There's the unmistakable air—sounds, smells, sights—of a casino. And there's the phenomenon of a city that never closes or seems to sleep, that galvanizes and emblazons the familiar activities of daily life.

Magic and Song
Nobody ever came to Vegas to see Shakespeare. The city has made famous a certain brand of entertainment based on big name entertainers, spectacular production values, sex, and illusion. Siegfried and Roy remain the biggest draw here, old reliable Wayne Newton packs them in, and you can still catch a scantily dressed chorus line if you want. But a new breed of show, the high-tech spectacular, is popping up in some of the major hotels and each one is competing with the other for even more amazing special effects. "EFX" at the MGM, Bally's "Jubilee," "O" at Bellagio, and "Mystère" at Treasure Island fit into this new category.

Wining and Dining
Dining out in Las Vegas is an adventure in variety. The fun lies in choosing from the vast array of styles and price ranges, from cheap prime rib to hip and happening eateries to big-name-chef restaurants. Every major hotel has at least four or five eating places, and independent restaurants are scattered about town. The fabulous buffets are a traditional treat, where you find yourself, plate in hand, standing before a mountain of all-you-can-eat food—some for as little as $4.99. But the big news in Las Vegas is the arrival of excellent—albeit expensive—new restaurants offering everything from the latest California fusion to the best aged steaks.

Winning and Losing
Times may change, but gambling is still the thing to do in Las Vegas. The first-timer is faced with a terrifying choice of possible bets, what seems like 1,001 different ways to part with your hard-earned dollars. But once you know your way around the casino, you'll quickly settle on your wagering thrill of choice. Blackjack and video poker offer the best odds for winning in a Vegas casino. The average bankroll of a Vegas gambler is $500, but you can experience either the excitement of winning or the frustration of losing for a lot less. The smaller casinos off the Strip are often the best bet for the amateur gambler; the pressure is less intense, the minimums are reasonable, and the staff is friendlier.

FODOR'S CHOICE

Dining
Eiffel Tower Restaurant. If you can't make it to Paris, you can still enjoy an impressive view and elegant cuisine in the half-scale replica of the real Eiffel Tower in the Paris Las Vegas. *$$$$*

Picasso. The Bellagio's top restaurant offers prix-fixe menus featuring innovative takes on the regional cuisines of France and Spain in a room adorned with Picasso originals. *$$$$*

Renoir. Chef Alessandro Stratta, known for his artistic shellfish creations, offers his culinary treasures in this elaborate restaurant in the Mirage, complete with paintings from the Impressionist master. *$$$$*

Lawry's The Prime Rib. This Los Angeles institution puts $3.99 prime rib specials to shame with a decidedly upscale atmosphere and consistently excellent, perfectly prepared meat. *$$$*

Rosemary's. Michael and Wendy Jordan have created an outstanding restaurant off the crowded Strip with a varied, contemporary menu but without atmospheric prices. *$$$*

Le Village Buffet. The buffet at Paris Las Vegas has a novel spin: the serving stations each offer a different regional French cuisine. Also atypical is the beautiful, elaborately themed room. *$$*

Extravaganzas and Other Excitement
Big Shot. Strap yourself into this gravity ride atop the Stratosphere Tower—if you dare. Riders are flung 160 ft up the tower's needle (which starts on the 112th floor), then dropped like a rock. Your knees will wobble for the rest of the day.

Jubilee! Bally's over-the-top spectacle is the last true old-style Las Vegas show, complete with gargantuan sets and props (the sinking of the Titanic is recreated), and the largest display of feathers and bare breasts you'll ever see.

O. Cirque du Soleil's show is the most expensive in history. At the Bellagio, acrobats, trapeze artists, swimmers, and contortionists perform above, below, and even on the surface of a stage made of water.

Race for Atlantis. The animatronic show at The Forum Shops at Caesars re-creates the sinking of the fabled continent with state-of-the-art talking statues, wraparound video, and special effects.

Speed–The Ride. The Strip's newest roller coaster, at the Sahara, uses magnetic thrust to send riders on a 70-mph trip.

Treasure Island Pirate Show. Watch the show at Buccaneer Bay from the safety of the boardwalk, as the pirate schooner *Hispaniola* sinks the Navy frigate HMS *Britannia* six times a day.

Lodging

Bellagio. Offering a level of luxury not found in other giant Las Vegas resorts, this hotel brings Lake Como to the Nevada desert, along with dancing fountains and upscale boutiques. *$$$$*

Four Seasons. This hotel within a hotel atop the Mandalay Bay resort provides perhaps the city's most civilized accommodations. With nary a slot machine in sight, it's a cushy retreat from the mayhem. *$$$$*

Mandalay Bay. Hip and fun, one of the city's most popular mega-resorts has a wave pool with 8-ft swells, a walk-through aquarium, a 12,000-seat arena, and a House of Blues restaurant and concert hall. *$$$*

The Mirage. This South Seas–theme resort includes a rain forest, a tiger habitat, a 53-ft long aquarium, the largest saltwater pool in the world (complete with seven dolphins), and a 50-ft waterfall that becomes an exploding volcano after dark. *$$$*

Treasure Island. The pirate theme (and the famous pirate show) is still in full force, but the resort has grown up. A tropical pool and a relaxing spa add to the grown-up ambience. *$$$*

Only in Las Vegas

Bikini blackjack. Check out the grotto pool at the Tropicana, where you swim up and ante up. Wet cash is dehydrated in the bill dryer.

Bonanza. Looking for a life-size Wayne Newton blow-up doll? Look no further than what claims to be the biggest souvenir shop on earth. Stock up on the Las Vegas T-shirts and snow globes you can't live without.

Liberace Museum. Costumes, cars, pianos, and even mannequins of the late entertainer make this the campiest place in town. Check out the gift shop for items you'll find nowhere else.

Little Church of the West. Anyone can attend a ceremony at this town's busiest wedding chapel. Just walk in, take a seat, and enjoy the minidrama that unfolds.

Shrimp cocktail at the Golden Gate. The Las Vegas bargain icon for more than 40 years gives you 6 full ounces of crustaceans in a tulip glass, with tangy cocktail sauce, a lemon wedge, and a package of crackers, all for 99¢.

World's largest gold nugget. Catch a glimpse of this wonder in the lobby of the Golden Nugget Hotel and Casino downtown. It weighs 62 pounds and is valued at about $1 million.

GREAT ITINERARIES

Las Vegas in 5 Days

You could easily spend a lifetime taking advantage of all Las Vegas has to offer in attractions, meal deals, and gambling, and many locals do just that. But if you're here for a short period, you'll need to wade through the seemingly limitless ways to spend your time (and money). The following suggested itinerary will help you structure your visit efficiently.

Day One. Today is your day to cruise the Strip. Start at the South Strip with a look around Mandalay Bay and Luxor, then make your way north up Las Vegas Boulevard. You'll want to peek into the Tropicana and traipse through New York–New York and Monte Carlo before heading back down to MGM Grand. From there, take the free monorail behind MGM Grand for a quick ride up to Bally's and the Center Strip.

The Center Strip has a dozen different casinos; the must-sees include Bellagio, the Flamingo Las Vegas, Caesars Palace, the Mirage, Paris, Aladdin, and the Venetian (don't miss The Forum Shops at Caesars or the Desert Passage at the Aladdin). Walk off a buffet lunch on your way to the North Strip, where you'll want to visit the Fashion Show Mall, Circus Circus, and the Sahara.

Be sure to catch the sunset at the top of Stratosphere Tower; with dinner reservations at the Top of the World restaurant you ride the high-speed elevators for free. After dark, head downtown for the Fremont Street Experience sound-and-light show, a drink at the top of the Horseshoe, and your choice of shows, lounge acts, gaming tables, or slot machines.

☉ *Works any day, though a weekday will be less crowded.*

Day Two. Take a quick morning break from casino madness in the awesome scenery of Red Rock, then fling yourself back into the fray in the afternoon by experiencing an "only in Vegas" attraction. Rise early and take Charleston Boulevard west to Red Rock Canyon and hike the desert or scramble up the sandstone. On the way back, stop off at the Rio to check out the "Masquerade Show in the Sky" and have lunch at its popular buffets. In the afternoon, take your pick of Vegas attractions—ride the Manhattan Express roller coaster at New York–New York, visit Adventuredome at Circus Circus, or get face to fin with ocean creatures at Mandalay Bay's Shark Reef. If museums are more to your taste, take in the Liberace Museum, Elvis-A-Rama Museum, Guggenheim Museum, or the Imperial Palace Auto Collection. Dine at any one of the recommended restaurants, then settle back for an extravaganza such as *EFX Alive, Siegfried and Roy, Blue Man Group,* or Cirque du Soleil's *O.*

☉ Plan this day around the availability of the show you plan to see. The rest of the items on the agenda work any day of the week.

Day Three. Today you can marvel at the civil engineering masterpiece that makes Las Vegas possible, and then gamble like a local. Begin by heading out to Boulder City and Hoover Dam. Tour the visitors center and dam, and maybe drive over to Lake Mead Marina, where you can hop on the *Desert Princess* paddle wheeler for a cruise on Lake Mead. Then head to either of the "other" casino strips to mingle with the locals. You can see the parklike atrium and laser–dancing water show at Sam's Town on the Boulder Strip or you might choose to sample the sumptuous buffet at either Texas Station or Fiesta (or both!) on the Rancho Strip. Wind up the evening with a showroom seat at *Mystère, Lance Burton: Master Magician,* or *Danny Gans,* or a seat at a blackjack table or video-poker machine.

☉ *If your plans include a visit to a showroom, plan this day around your tickets. The other stops work any day of the week.*

Day Four. Expand your horizons a bit by taking Northshore Drive along the north shore of Lake Mead to Valley of Fire State Park and the Lost City Museum in Overton. Return to town for the usual dinner, show, or gambling.

☉ *Works any day.*

Day Five. On your fifth day, you can head up to Mt. Charleston for a mountain (skiing or hiking) experience, hop a flightseeing tour to the Grand Canyon, drive down to Laughlin for a taste of gambling that's qualitatively different from Las Vegas, or, if you're willing to spend a couple of hours on the road, drive out to Death Valley. Works any day.

☉ *So that you don't show up somewhere and find the doors locked, shuffle the itinerary segments with closing days in mind.*

If You Have More Time

If you're in Las Vegas for a week, you should consider renting a weekly room with a kitchenette, and you can save money in two ways: with a good discount over the daily rate, and by buying groceries at the supermarket and having some meals in your room. You'll save on a weekly car rental, too.

2 EXPLORING LAS VEGAS

The Las Vegas you knew no longer exists.
This holds true even if you last visited
America's most dynamic city a week ago.
Even longtime residents have a difficult time
of keeping up with Vegas' rapid growth,
and it's quite likely that you'll see something
new—and better—every time you come to
town. A whole new world of casinos,
attractions, museums, souvenir stands, and
historical landmarks is out there, waiting to
be explored. See it now—it'll be completely
different next time.

Revised and
updated by
Geoff Carter

FOR 50 YEARS, up until the early 1990s, the name Las Vegas was synonymous with adult entertainment, a place that existed for one reason and one reason only: gambling. Then the city attempted to remake itself as a family destination, adding roller coasters, animal attractions and arcades to its predominantly adult makeup; the strategy didn't really take, as a recent explosion in topless shows and after-hours nightclubs would seem to indicate. But the legacy of Vegas' family "experiment" lingers on: fabulous theme hotels such as the Luxor, New York–New York, the Venetian, the Aladdin, and the Paris, as well as amusement parks such as Wet 'n Wild and Grand Slam Canyon all provide a minivacation's worth of excitement—without ever stepping up to a slot machine or blackjack table.

The reasons for Vegas' turn against the family policy continue to affect business. Today one out of every eight visitors is under the age of 21 and therefore can't gamble. Adults who travel with children spend less time—and less money—in casinos. Underage gambling has been a highly visible problem. And Bellagio won't allow children on premises unless they're guests of the hotel and accompanied by an adult at all times.

Despite its on-again, off-again attention to families, Las Vegas has never—and probably will never—become a family destination in the sense that Orlando or Cape Cod are. Every year, tens of millions of people still come to Las Vegas for the traditional reason—to gamble, plain and simple. There are no supermarkets, post offices, video-rental stores, or other conveniences of everyday life on the Strip—just casinos, wedding chapels, gift stores, strip clubs, and discotheques. Vegas is a fantasyland—a very adult fantasyland.

The Strip, the 3½-mi stretch of Las Vegas Boulevard South between Russell Road and Sahara Avenue, is the heart of Las Vegas. Its soul is the downtown area north of the Strip, whose core is Fremont Street. By exploring these two areas, you'll experience both the commercial lifeblood and pioneer spirit of this most flamboyant of American cities.

It's easy to get around Las Vegas by car. Note, however, that driving up and down the Strip to get to where you're going might take only five minutes on a Tuesday morning but could take almost an hour on a Friday or a Saturday night. Parking at the hotel garages on the Strip and downtown is free if you have your ticket validated by a casino cashier.

Getting around on foot can be a challenge, as distances are deceiving in Las Vegas. Although all the casinos at Center Strip, for example, may be within a mile of each other, when you add walking from the street to and around the hotels, especially the large ones, you can easily triple that distance. Some of the newer casinos have moving sidewalks, trams, and elevated crosswalks to make it easier to get around on foot. The Strip Trolley, which runs every thirty minutes, is the most convenient means of hotel-hopping, because it picks up and drops off passengers at hotel front doors. The local buses are more frequent, though less convenient to the actual hotels, and usually crowded to overflowing.

We've organized the Strip exploration into three good walks: south, center, and north. A fourth walk covers downtown. Most of the sights in Las Vegas are casinos, so you can start exploring any time of the day or night. But the earlier you set out, the fewer crowds and the less heat (in the summer) you'll face along the way. To see the museums and historical sights, you'll have to coordinate your tour with hours of operation.

SOUTH STRIP

The South Strip has been the beneficiary of the lion's share of Las Vegas's family boom. In 1989 the only hotel-casino to anchor the South Strip was the Tropicana, which had stood alone for more than 30 years. But then came the San Remo and Excalibur (1990), Luxor and MGM Grand (1993), Monte Carlo (1996), New York–New York (1997), and Mandalay Bay (1999). To better manage the expected millions of tourists, these properties joined forces with the county in 1994 to install four overhead pedestrian walkways, complete with escalators and elevators, at a cost of $10 million. For tourists these walkways not only facilitate exploring, they provide good views (through a protective wire mesh). The South Strip's "New Four Corners"—the intersection of Las Vegas Boulevard and Tropicana Avenue—is one of the most magnetic tourist intersections in the world.

Numbers in the text correspond to numbers in the margin and on the Las Vegas Strip map.

A Good Walk

If the glitz and neon lights don't scream loud enough that you're in Vegas, the WELCOME TO LAS VEGAS sign ①—at the southern end of Las Vegas Boulevard—will take away all doubts. Be advised—it's difficult to snap photos in front of it without jaywalking.

From the sign, you'll probably want to drive up the Strip and park in the gigantic garage at **Mandalay Bay Resort and Casino** ②, the latest and greatest megaresort by former Circus Circus Enterprises (now Mandalay Resort Group). Parking your car in Mandalay's garage keeps it out of the brutal summer sun and enables you to take in all the South Strip sights. Because this walk winds up about a mile north, you might want to hop on a Strip bus or trolley, or into a cab, to get back to your car. Next door to Mandalay Bay is the **Luxor Hotel-Casino** ③, a perfect pyramid with some 2,500 rooms (plus close to 2,000 more in the step towers next to it) and the largest atrium in the world. And next to that is **Excalibur Hotel and Casino** ④, the pink-and-blue, turreted-and-towered, 4,032-room "castle."

Across the Strip from Excalibur is the **Tropicana Resort and Casino** ⑤, featuring a large, lush swimming pool with rock waterfalls; a water slide; exotic fish, birds, and vegetation; and swim-up blackjack. The **Casino Legends Hall of Fame** museum of Nevada memorabilia has Vegas memorabilia ranging from over five decades. For a break from all the hotel fluff, visit UNLV's **James R. Dickinson Library** ⑥ on Maryland Parkway or the **Liberace Museum** ⑦, 2 mi east on Tropicana Avenue. (These two destinations are a bit out of the way. You'll definitely want to take a cab, especially in summer.) Across the avenue from the Trop is the **MGM Grand** ⑧—with 5,005 rooms, a 171,000-square-ft casino, and a lions' habitat.

The children might want to make a stop at the **Showcase Mall** ⑨, next door to the MGM, for **M&M's World** and **Gameworks,** one of the largest arcades in the city. Across the Strip is **New York–New York Hotel and Casino** ⑩, with such exact replicas of famous Big Apple landmarks that copyright lawyers had to argue the legality of it all. Next door is **Monte Carlo Resort and Casino** ⑪, a joint venture between Mandalay Resort Group and Mirage Resorts; check out the stunning lobby and European-style casino.

A mile or so east, on Paradise Road, is the **Hard Rock Hotel and Casino** ⑫, which is billed as the "world's only rock 'n' roll casino."

It's best to drive from the Strip to the Hard Rock, especially at night, when Harmon Avenue is very dark.

TIMING

The South Strip walk has the largest casinos; a stroll to see them all will take almost a full day. Add another hour each for the side trip over to the Hard Rock Hotel and Casino or the Liberace Museum.

Sights to See

④ Excalibur Hotel and Casino. Before they opened this spectacular property in 1990, the executives of the Circus Circus Resort Group—now the Mandalay Resort Group—visited castles in England, Scotland, and Germany in search of inspiration. The result might be described as "King Arthur does Las Vegas." The pseudo-Bavarian castle, which has been called "the greatest hole in God's own miniature golf course," has plenty of turrets, spires, belfries, a moat, and a 265-ft bell tower. The over-the-top medieval theme is continued inside, with staff members in elaborate royal-court costumes and such place names as the Court Jester's Stage and Sir Galahad's Prime Rib House.

Downstairs from the 100,000-square-ft casino is **Fantasy Faire,** a midway of carnival games and international gifts. The main attractions here are the carnival midway games and **Merlin's Magic Motion Film Rides,** which last about 5 to 10 minutes each; there are six different movie and motion simulators including a virtual roller coaster.

Upstairs from the casino is the **Renaissance Village,** which has shops, theme restaurants, a huge buffet, and an open stage where jugglers, puppeteers, and magicians perform.

Families enjoy the *Tournament of Kings* extravaganza in the showroom. The Excalibur also offers more than 4,000 guest rooms (making it the third-largest hotel in town) and plenty of ways to win (or lose) a buck. ⊠ *3850 Las Vegas Blvd. S, South Strip,* ☎ *702/597–7777 or 800/937–7777,* WEB *www.excaliburlasvegas.com.* ☜ *Film Rides: $4 per ride.* ☉ *Fantasy Faire open daily 10–10.*

⑫ Hard Rock Hotel and Casino. A haven for the young and hip, the Hard Rock is a high-class rock 'n' roll museum, with memorabilia from every rock decade adorning its walls. The multimillion-dollar collection is undoubtedly one of the best on display in the country—you can see everything from Kurt Cobain's guitar to one of Britney Spears' many outfits. And since the Hard Rock is a favorite hiding spot for many of the music and film stars of today, you've got a pretty good chance of bumping into one. Navigating the property is simple: it's completely circular. On the inside of the circle is the small but accommodating gaming floor, and on the outside, various shops, restaurants, and the Hard Rock's intimate concert venue, The Joint. Down one hallway is the Hard Rock's pool area, a tropical beach–inspired oasis featuring a floating bar, private cabanas, and poolside blackjack. In recent years it's become a favorite filming location for MTV. The logo shop is large, so you won't have to wait in Hard Rock's signature long, slow-moving line to buy a T-shirt. ⊠ *4455 Paradise Rd., Paradise Road,* ☎ *702/693–5000 or 800/693–7625,* WEB *www.hardrockhotel.com.*

⑥ James R. Dickinson Library. The special-collections department of this library of the University of Nevada–Las Vegas has the best collection of materials about Las Vegas and gambling that you'll find anywhere. ⊠ *4505 Maryland Pkwy., University District,* ☎ *702/895–3285.* ☜ *Free.* ☉ *Weekdays 9–5.*

★ ⑦ Liberace Museum. Costumes, cars, photographs, even mannequins of the late entertainer make this museum the kitschiest place in town. In

14

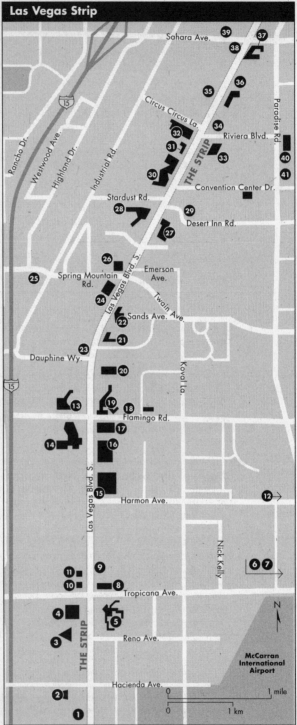

Las Vegas Strip

addition to Lee's collection of pianos (one of them was played by Chopin; another, a concert grand, was owned by George Gershwin), you can see his Czar Nicholas uniform and a blue‑velvet cape styled after the coronation robes of King George V. Be sure to check out the gift shop—where else can you find Liberace soap, ashtrays, and other novelties? ⊠ *1775 E. Tropicana Ave., East Side,* ☎ *702/798–5595,* WEB *www.liberace.com.* ✆ *$8.* ☉ *Mon.–Sat. 10–5, Sun. 1–5.*

❸ Luxor Hotel-Casino. In Luxor, the folks at Mandalay Resort Group have built one of the modern wonders of the world—and made sure it could be seen from anywhere in the valley at night. Luxor, a 36-story black glass and bronze pyramid, is made with 13 acres of black glass and topped with a beam that burns brighter than any other in the world. It's composed of 45 xenon lights, and it projects enough light to be visible from space. Standing right at the base of one of the exterior walls and looking up, you'll get a glimpse of infinity. Inside is the world's largest atrium, with 29 million cubic ft of open space soaring to the building's apex. You get the full impact of the space from the second floor, also known as the Attractions Level.

The "Passport to Adventure" for the entertainment attractions in the Luxor's **Pharaoh's Pavilion** is all-inclusive—it gets you an IMAX movie; the "Search for the Obelisk" ridefilm; entry into the reproduction of King Tutankhamen's tomb; and your choice of a virtual roller coaster ride or AE's movie *The Great Pharaohs.* Stop by the vast two-story video arcade, too.

Luxor has 4,476 guest rooms. The rooms in the pyramid building (there are two hotel towers as well) are reached by four "inclinators," elevators that travel along the 39-degree incline of the pyramid. ⊠ *3900 Las Vegas Blvd. S, South Strip,* ☎ *702/262–4000 or 800/288–1000,* WEB *www.luxor.com.* ✆ *Pharaoh's Pavilion attractions $4–$8.95; Passport to Adventure $23.95.* ☉ *Pharoah's Pavilion open Sun.–Thurs. 9 AM–11 PM, Fri.–Sat. 9 AM–midnight.*

❷ Mandalay Bay Resort and Casino. The 43-story, $950-million Mandalay Bay Resort has 3,700 rooms, including a 400-room **Four Seasons Hotel** on the 36th through 39th floors (with its own parking, entrance, pool, health club, express elevators, restaurants, and meeting area). The name is a curious one—Mandalay is an ancient inland temple city in Myanmar, the country formerly known as Burma, which has no bay. And while the real Mandalay is in Southeast Asia, the hotel-casino is decked out like a South Seas beach resort, complete with the scent of coconut oil drifting through the casino. In fact, there's a 10-acre lagoon complete with a huge wave pool (8-ft waves, roughest waters on the Strip) and a ¾-mi-long "lazy river" pool. Also check out Treasures of Mandalay, a small museum displaying rare coins and currency. The **House of Blues,** an 1,800-seat theater and a 600-seat restaurant, is also here; the restaurant walls are covered with Louisiana Delta folk art.

The most distinctive attraction at Mandalay Bay is **Shark Reef.** The 105,000-square-ft facility holds some 2 million gallons of seawater housing exotic creatures large and small. The journey begins in temple ruins, where the humid, hot atmosphere may be uncomfortable for the humans but quite nice for the golden crocodiles, tree pythons, water monitors, and tropical fish. Two glass "hallways" allow you to get up close and personal with sea life. Other notable exhibits: A shallow pool offers you a chance to give a one-finger pet to small stingrays, small sharks, and starfish; and jellyfish swim a rhythmic dance in a specially designed environment. The tour saves the best for last—from the bowels of a sunken galleon, watch sharks swim below, above, and around the skeleton ship. Shark Reef offers a wondrous look into the ecology of the ocean—and all without getting wet.

Other features of this megaresort include a 12,000-seat arena complex that hosts major sporting contests, superstar concerts, and special events; a 1,700-seat showroom; the Coral Reef Lounge, surrounded by virtual vegetation, rock waterfalls, and lily ponds; the elegant China Grill featuring dishes such as Shanghai lobster and wasabi mashed potatoes; Rock Lobster, with a rubber conveyor belt circling the centerpiece bar and carrying plates of appetizers; the four-story "wine tower" at the signature restaurant Aureole; and rumjungle, one of the hottest nightspots in town. Plans are in the works for a 1.2-million-square-ft shopping mall that will link Mandalay Bay and sister property, Luxor. ⊠ *3950 Las Vegas Blvd. S, South Strip,* ☎ *702/632–7777 or 877/632–7400,* WEB *www.mandalaybay.com.* ⊠ *Shark Reef: $13.95.* ☉ *Daily 10 AM–11 PM.*

⟳ ❽ **MGM Grand.** With over 5,000 rooms, the MGM Grand is the largest hotel in the world, a self-proclaimed "City of Entertainment" sprawling over 112 acres. The front of the property is adorned with a 100,000-pound bronze lion statue that stands 45 ft tall and sits atop a 25-ft pedestal, making it the largest bronze statue in the United States. Inside you'll find a full half-mile of restaurants, ballrooms, nightclubs, and shops—even a research center for CBS Television, where you can screen potential new shows for parent company Viacom's networks, which also include Nickelodeon and MTV.

Well worth seeing is the MGM Grand's $9-million, 3,000-square-ft **Lion Habitat.** More than 12,000 visitors a day see the lions owned by feline expert and exotic-animal trainer Keith Evans. A see-through tunnel runs through the habitat, allowing you to watch the big cats prowl above and below. The enclosure was designed to replicate the lions' natural habitat as closely as possible and has stone, trees and foliage, four waterfalls, and a pond. The lions are trucked in each day; they really live 12 mi from the MGM Grand on an 8½-acre ranch. Admission is free. ⊠ *3799 Las Vegas Blvd. S, South Strip,* ☎ *702/891–1111 or 800/929–1111,* WEB *www.mgmgrand.com.* ☉ *Lion Habitat: daily 11–10.*

⓫ **Monte Carlo Resort and Casino.** This elegant megaresort is modeled after the *real* Monte Carlo—the Place du Casino in Monaco. The $350-million hotel-casino is like a sumptuous palace, filled with arches, chandeliers, marble, statuary, and fountains. Note the Gothic glass registration area overlooking the lush pool area—a touch that resort cocreator Steve Wynn dubbed "popular elegance."

In addition to the massive gaming floor and 3,000-plus rooms, the property includes an avenue-style shopping mall dubbed **The Street of Dreams.** There you can find everything from Monte Carlo logo wear to fine jewelry, as well as a number of eateries. Perhaps the most popular restaurant here is the Monte Carlo Brew Pub, which features live nightly entertainment, decent pub-style food, and six specialty ales made on the premises. Sports fans will especially love the 35 big-screen TVs regularly broadcasting various athletic events and the state-of-the-art sound system. Also along the Street of Dreams is a high-tech arcade with more than 60 games.

The resort's most popular attraction—world-class illusionist Lance Burton—performs five nights a week in an opulent, 1,200-seat, $27-million custom-built theater modeled after the opera houses of Europe. ⊠ *3770 Las Vegas Blvd. S, South Strip,* ☎ *702/730–7777 or 800/311–8999,* WEB *www.monte-carlo.com.*

⓾ New York–New York Hotel and Casino. Rome might not have been built in a day, but New York–New York, the $460-million, 2,000-plus-room megaresort on the corner of the Las Vegas Strip and Tropicana Avenue, took just under two years. When it opened in 1997, the stunning complex raised the bar for theme hotels, in Vegas and worldwide. The exterior is a mini-Manhattan skyline, complete with a 48-story Empire State Building; a 150-ft Statue of Liberty; and smaller versions of the Chrysler, Seagram, and CBS buildings and the New York Public Library, Grand Central Terminal, and the Brooklyn Bridge. A Coney Island–style roller coaster, the Manhattan Express, encircles the property. The Big Apple theme continues inside, with an art deco lobby, a casino pit themed after Central Park, a Coney Island-theme arcade, and a food court patterned after Greenwich Village. A bank of self-operated massage chairs is available to soothe weary bones. And last but not least, New York–New York is also home to ESPN Zone, the mother of all sports cafés, with plush seats for armchair quarterbacks and an arcade filled with sports games.

Roller-coaster aficionados take note: the **Manhattan Express** is a real rocker. While being whisked past great views of the faux New York skyline, you climb 15 stories, dive 75 ft, climb then dive 144 ft, do a 360-degree somersault, do a "heartline twist" (that simulates the sensation one gets in a jet doing a barrel roll), rocket over a dizzying succession of high-banked turns and camel-back hills, and finally zip along a 540-degree spiral before you pull back into the station. ⊠ *3790 Las Vegas Blvd. S, South Strip,* ☎ *702/740–6969 or 800/693–6763,* WEB *www.nynyhotelcasino.com.* ⊠ *Roller coaster: $10.* ☉ *Roller coaster: daily 10 AM–11 PM (weather permitting).*

⓽ Showcase Mall. This mall has several specialty shops, a movie theater, and Gameworks, a multi-level young-adult arcade.

M&M's World is four stories of fun that will melt in your mouth, not in your hand. The store offers plenty of candy-coated treats (including an **Ethel M. Chocolates** outlet for more upscale sweet tooths) plus everything from T-shirts to limited-edition lithographs. There's also the **M&M Academy,** featuring interactive exhibits and a free 3-D movie, "I Lost My M in Las Vegas."

Gameworks, a joint venture between Steven Spielberg and Sega, more than lives up to its hype—it's the biggest, most boisterous arcade in town. Gameworks has more than 300 arcade-style games, a 21-and-over bar with pool tables and live entertainment, a casual fast-food eatery, and the world's largest free-standing rock-climbing structure. ⊠ *3785 Las Vegas Blvd. S, South Strip,* ☎ *702/736—7611; 702/736–7611 M&M's World; 702/432–4263 Gameworks.* ⊠ *M&M Academy free entry; Gameworks free entry, $25 per 2 hrs of play.* ☉ *Showcase Mall, Gameworks, and M&M's World: Sun.–Thurs. 10 AM–midnight, Fri.–Sat. 10 AM–1 AM. M&M Academy: Sun., Mon., Thurs. 11–6, Fri.–Sat. 10:40–8.*

⓹ Tropicana Resort and Casino. The most eye-popping sight here is the 4,000-square-ft stained-glass dome that glows above the casino tables. Be sure to stroll through the property's ¼-mi Wildlife Walk, with flocks of tropical birds and aquariums filled with colorful fish. Also take a peek at the lush 5-acre pool area, where the famous swim-up blackjack game is played. The Tropicana hosts Las Vegas's longest-running show, the *Folies Bergère,* as well as a great comedy club featuring well-known and up-and-coming comedians.

A "must-see" at the Trop is the **Casino Legends Hall of Fame.** Portions of the world's largest collection of Nevada casino memorabilia have been displayed at several casinos through the years, but the collection has finally found a permanent home here. Thousands of items are on display, including Las Vegas chips, photographs, movie posters, postcards, slot machines, entertainer contracts and paychecks, menus, album covers, and more. There's a mock-up of a showgirl's dressing room and numerous video monitors run documentaries about the casino implosions, celebrities, hotel fires, and onetime association with organized crime figures—all the iconic people and events that shaped this town's legend. ⊠ *3801 Las Vegas Blvd. S, South Strip,* ☎ *702/ 739–2222 or 800/634–4000,* WEB *www.tropicanalv.com.* ⊠ *Hall of Fame $4, $3 for seniors (look for free-entry coupons throughout the casino).* ☉ *Hall of Fame: Sun.–Thurs. 8 AM–9 PM, Fri.–Sat. 8 AM–midnight.*

❶ **WELCOME TO LAS VEGAS.** Two blocks south of Hacienda Avenue, at the south end of the South Strip, is this welcome sign, a familiar part of the landscape since the early 1950s and quite possibly Vegas's most-photographed element. It makes a great photo or video backdrop, but wait for an ebb in the traffic: the sign is on an island in the middle of the boulevard. Also of note: nearby is the Glass Pool Inn, whose signature elevated swimming pool has appeared in dozens of television shows and movies.

CENTER STRIP

This entire part of the Strip is historic. Here you'll find the Flamingo Las Vegas, which stands on the site of Bugsy Siegel's original Flamingo, as well as Caesars Palace, whose name has been synonymous with opulence and excess for years. Casino mogul Steve Wynn raised even Caesars's high stakes with the 1989 opening of the lush Mirage, but it was another Wynn creation, the $1.8-billion Bellagio, that set a standard that has yet to be equalled. With its European elegance and gorgeous fountains, it is the true heart of the Center Strip.

A Good Walk

Park in the easily-accessible garage of **Caesars Palace** ⑬. It is centrally located and completely covered—just the thing to keep your vehicle's interior from turning into an oven.

From one of Caesars's exits, walk back to the Strip, turn right (south), head to the intersection of Las Vegas Boulevard and Flamingo Road, and use the pedestrian bridges to cross Flamingo. Here, **Bellagio Las Vegas** ⑭ awaits; don't miss its breathtaking botanical conservatory, high-end shops, and fine art gallery. The true gems of the Bellagio, however, are its gorgeous fountains and O, a nearly indescribable show by the peerless avant-garde performance troupe Cirque de Soleil.

Now cross to the east side of the Strip to the **Aladdin Hotel and Casino** ⑮. Its Desert Passage mall, a fanciful Middle Eastern marketplace, is a must-see. Next to it is **Paris Las Vegas** ⑯, with its 50-story, half-size Eiffel Tower. Its sister hotel-casino **Bally's Casino Resort** ⑰ is also right here; visitors enter on a long, moving sidewalk lit by colorful lights and surrounded by fountains.

Across Flamingo Road from Bally's is the **Barbary Coast Hotel and Casino** ⑱, a small, attractive joint wedged between giants, with a stunning stained-glass mural and Drai's, a popular restaurant and after-hours nightclub. Next is the venerable **Flamingo Las Vegas** ⑲, for which Bugsy Siegel gave his life. Its 15-acre water park is the one of the nicer pools in town. Next door is the Flamingo's casino annex for low rollers, O'Shea's.

BUGSY SIEGEL

T'S A COMMON MISCONCEPTION that Bugsy Siegel introduced gambling to Las Vegas: Siegel no more invented gambling and Las Vegas than Bugs Bunny invented cartoons and Warner Bros. But the gangster was instrumental in paving the way for his business partners from around the country to capitalize on the casino business. Gambling had been legal in Nevada and thriving in Las Vegas for more than 10 years by the time Siegel arrived on the scene.

Benjamin Siegel and Las Vegas were both born in May 1905, Las Vegas in the cruel desert of southern Nevada, and Benny on the mean streets of south Brooklyn. In his early teens Siegel met a street tough named Meyer Lansky, and by the time he was 20 he was a hardened criminal, a shooter in the bootlegging wars that raged in New York during Prohibition. A fearless and reckless soldier, Siegel earned the nickname "Bugsy," which he always hated; no one, not even underworld boss Lansky, called him "Bugsy" to his face.

Throughout the 1920s and '30s, Lansky, Siegel, Charles "Lucky" Luciano, and Frank Costello forged a nationwide coalition of gangsters into an organized-crime syndicate variously known as the Mob, the Mafia, and La Cosa Nostra. Siegel took control of the Mob's gambling, bookmaking, and narcotics-smuggling operations in southern California. When he extended his sphere of influence to Las Vegas, muscling into several downtown casinos in the early 1940s, Siegel instantly recognized the vast potential of the Nevada gambling business.

Siegel's dream was to build and run the classiest resort-casino in the world, and he recruited Mob investors to back him. The project quickly turned into a nightmare, as cost overruns on the Fabulous Flamingo Hotel spiraled out of control, reaching a healthy (or unhealthy, as it turned out) $5 million. Siegel's investors roundly suspected him of skimming a million or two from the construction costs. And in those days, with that bunch, if you were suspected of dipping into investment capital you weren't served with a subpoena. If you couldn't make the interest payments on corporate paper, you weren't protected by Chapter 11.

Siegel managed to open the Flamingo on the day after Christmas 1946, even though it wasn't ready (inaugurating a Las Vegas tradition that continues to this day). A magnet for every "crossroader" (casino cheat), "mechanic" (card sharp), and scam artist in town, the casino sustained heavy losses, which Siegel's investors took as further evidence of his embezzlement. The Flamingo closed less than three weeks after it opened, ostensibly to complete construction, but also to make a few adjustments in management.

In June 1947, in the Beverly Hills mansion of Virginia Hill, known as the "Mistress to the Mob," Siegel was shot through a window. He took two slugs, one in the eye, and died as he had lived. He was 42 years old. The murder of Bugsy Siegel remains unsolved to this day.

— Deke Castleman

Heading north on the Strip, stop by the **Imperial Palace Hotel and Casino** ⑳, with the **Automobile Museum**. Next door is **Harrah's Las Vegas Casino & Hotel** ㉑, with the Carnaval Court, an outdoor entertainment zone with shops, a bar, and live music. Beyond Harrah's is the **Venetian Resort-Hotel-Casino** ㉒, a meticulously crafted tribute to its namesake city, right down to the 1,800-ft-long Canalozzo running down the middle of the **Grand Canal Shops**. The Venetian is also the proud home of the **Guggenheim Las Vegas** and **Guggenheim Hermitage** museums, as well as a branch of **Madame Tussaud's** famous wax museum.

Across the Strip from the Venetian is **Treasure Island Las Vegas** ㉔, themed like a Disneyland-esque seaside village centered around Buccaneer Bay, where a pyrotechnic pirate battle is performed six times a night. Here you'll also find another Cirque du Soleil show, the incomparable *Mystère* which takes place twice nightly. Next door is the **Mirage Hotel and Casino** ㉓, the $650-million joint that in 1989 kicked off a multibillion-dollar casino construction frenzy that has yet to abate. At the Mirage, volcanoes, rain forests, dolphins, and tigers are found right alongside rows of $100 blackjack tables and $500 slot machines.

You can exit the Mirage at the south end (near the white tiger habitat) and pick up Caesars' people mover at its north end; wander through **The Forum Shops at Caesars**, one of the most upscale and unique malls in the country, and you'll emerge in Caesars's Olympic Casino, right by the elevators to the parking garage.

TIMING

The Center Strip walk is the shortest in terms of outside distance but has the most casinos; the whole circuit can be done in four hours if you're moving right along, five hours at a leisurely pace, and six hours if you take in the auto collection at the Imperial Palace or one of the Guggenheim museums.

Sights to See

🕒 **Aladdin Hotel and Casino.** It took Queen Scheherazade 1,001 nights to woo her husband with tales of Ali Baba, Sinbad the Sailor, and the Enchanted Garden before he learned how to love again—nearly five months longer than it took to build the $1.4-billion, 2,567-room Aladdin. The *Arabian Nights* motif is immediately evident in the 50-ft waterfall cascading down a sandstone cliff fronting the property. You walk directly inside from the Strip—one of the many elements of the Aladdin designed for convenience—but not into the casino, rather into a shopping mall.

The **Desert Passage** is a $300-million complex of 135 shops ensconced in minarets, onion domes, and other Moorish architecture. Merchants' Harbor, a North African village with a huge anchored steamer ship, treats mall-goers to regularly scheduled thunderstorms. Among the many restaurants in the mall and hotel are a branch of New Orleans's famous Commander's Palace and popular "California Chinese" joint P. F. Chang's.

Cocktail waitresses in harem garb glide through the 100,000-square-ft casino, which is bedecked with a 36-ft-long Aladdin's lamp. London Clubs International operates a separate casino-within-a-casino, a luxurious hideaway for high rollers. At night, Broadway shows and headliner concerts fill the 7,000-seat Aladdin Theatre for the Performing Arts. ✉ *3667 Las Vegas Blvd. S, Center Strip,* ☎ *702/736–0111 or 877/333–9474,* WEB *www.aladdincasino.com.*

🕒 **Bally's Casino Resort.** During the day it doesn't look like much, but at night Bally's facade is one of Vegas's most colorful—lights projected from below bathe the hotel in shades of green, red, purple, and blue. A plus for the foot-sore are the four 200-ft moving walkways that ferry people from the Strip to the casino, entertaining them on the three-minute ride with a series of special effects. The shopping arcade on the lower level sells everything from fine furs to ice cream. Bally's also hosts the $10-million showgirl spectacular *Jubilee!*. A mile-long monorail connects the resort to the MGM Grand. ⊠ *3645 Las Vegas Blvd. S, Center Strip,* ☎ *702/739–4111 or 800/644–0777,* WEB *www.ballyslv.com.*

⑱ Barbary Coast Hotel and Casino. Decorated with dark woods, stained glass, brass, and crystal, the Barbary Coast evokes turn-of-the-20th-century San Francisco. A stained-glass mural depicts *The Garden of Earthly Delights;* measuring 30 ft long and 5 ft high, it's the world's largest, and it took more than 8,000 man-hours to complete. One of the smallest hotels on the Strip, with only 200 rooms, the Barbary Coast is nonetheless a popular place to stay because of its central location and affordable rates. ⊠ *3595 Las Vegas Blvd. S, Center Strip,* ☎ *702/ 737–7111 or 888/227–2279,* WEB *www.barbarycoastcasino.com.*

★ ⑭ Bellagio Las Vegas. The $1.8-billion, 3,000-room Bellagio is one of the most opulent and expensive hotel-casinos ever built. Scores of full-grown evergreen and deciduous trees line the "shore" (actually, the Strip sidewalk) of the 12-acre lake that fronts the hotel and reflects its Tuscan village architecture.

Walking into the lobby, you're confronted with a fantastic and colorful, 2,000-square-ft glass sculpture called *Fiori di Como,* by famed artist Dale Chiluly. It's composed of more than 2,000 individually blown glass pieces and cost upwards of $10 million.

Beyond the lobby is a 12,500-square-ft conservatory, the **Bellagio Botanical Gardens,** full of living flowers, shrubs, trees, and other plants. All the horticulture in the conservatory and throughout the hotel is fresh and live, grown in Bellagio's 5-acre greenhouse, and changes with the seasons.

Through the conservatory is the **Gallery of Fine Art.** Although MGM has sold off most of the gallery's permanent collection (the pieces in the restaurants remain), the gallery remains operational, displaying rotating exhibits arranged with museums, other galleries, and private collectors. Recent exhibits have included the works of Alexander Calder and the private collection of Steve Martin.

Stretching 900 ft across Bellagio's lake is a signature outdoor spectacle: the $30-million **Fountains of Bellagio** water ballet, made famous by an appearance in the 2001 remake of "Ocean's Eleven." More than 1,000 fountain nozzles, 4,500 lights, and 27 million gallons of water combine to dazzle audiences with dancing waters choreographed to popular music. Some jets launch spray nearly 250 ft in the air. There's a show every 30 minutes from 2 PM to midnight; the best view is from the observation deck of the Eiffel Tower, directly across the street.

The resort also includes a $75-million showroom, where Cirque de Soleil performs its spectacular *O.* As elegant as the decor and entertainment in this resort are, the shops nearly outdo them. Bellagio has some of the most exclusive and beautiful stores in the world, including Giorgio Armani, Chanel, Gucci, Prada, and Tiffany & Co. Note: no one under 18 is allowed in Bellagio unless they are staying at the hotel. ⊠ *3600 Las Vegas Blvd. S, Center Strip,* ☎ *702/693–7111 or 888/744– 7687,* WEB *www.bellagio.com.* ▨ *Gallery of Fine Art: $12.* ☉ *Sun.– Thurs. 10–6, Fri.–Sat. 10–9.*

☾ 🖐 **⓭** **Caesars Palace.** A 20-ft statue of Caesar, which stands in front of the driveway to the main entrance, greets visitors to this iconic hotel-casino. Behind him, 18 fountains and 50-ft-high cypress trees adorn the approach to the door. Nearby is a replica of one of Thailand's most popular shrines, with a 4-ton, gold-plated Brahma (the gift of a Thai tycoon). Among the other sculptures that adorn the palatial property is a full-size reproduction of Michelangelo's *David*. Two people-movers transport you from the Strip into the hotel-casino complex. One is on the south end of the property, one is on the north. (You can step from Mirage's south-end people-mover right onto Caesars's north conveyor.) Having undergone major expansions in its 35-year history, the complex covers a vast area, including two casinos, **Cleopatra's Barge** lounge (which actually sits on water), the **Garden of the Gods** pool area, and numerous restaurants and entertainment venues.

A particular highlight is the ultra-exclusive **Forum Shops at Caesars,** a shopping mall/entertainment complex designed to resemble an ancient Roman streetscape. It houses roughly 100 retailers and eateries, including Abercrombie & Fitch, Emporio Armani, Gucci, Hugo Boss, Louis Vuitton, Virgin Megastore, FAO Schwartz, Spago, and the Cheesecake Factory. Overhead is a painted sky that changes throughout the day from airy clouds to stunning sunsets to star-studded nights. The mall also has a number of entertainment options, including two pretty astounding animatronic statue shows. Every hour on the hour, the Festival Fountain and the Atlantis shows spring into action; the former features robotic statues of Bacchus, Pluto, Venus, and Apollo, the latter the royal family of the doomed kingdom of Atlantis.

Race for Atlantis is the most sophisticated digital thrill ride in Las Vegas, combining motion simulation, computer-generated 3-D graphics, and a dome-shape IMAX film format. An electronic headset comes with a personal sound system and state-of-the-art 3-D goggles. If you can only experience one virtual ride, this is the one. ✉ *3570 Las Vegas Blvd. S, Center Strip,* ☎ *702/733–7900 or 800/223–7277,* ᴡᴇʙ *www. caesarspalace.com.* ✍ *Race for Atlantis $10.* ☾ *Forum Shops and Race for Atlantis: Sun.–Thurs. 10 AM–11 PM, Fri.–Sat. 10 AM–midnight.*

⓳ **Flamingo Las Vegas.** Prior to 1946, when Benjamin (Bugsy) Siegel imported Miami luxury to the desert, Las Vegas was still trying to keep alive the last little sliver of the Wild West. But Bugsy was intent on introducing a class joint to the new casino town, a place where his Hollywood buddies and Manhattan partners could gamble legally, where the lure of big-time entertainment would bring the beautiful people to play, and where the ordinary Joe would show up because he wanted to feel like a big shot. Although things didn't work out exactly as Bugsy planned (☞ Close-Up: Bugsy Siegel), the Flamingo of today is the classy joint that he dreamed of, glitzy and elegant—if relentlessly pink. A highlight of the property is the lovely 15-acre pool park, with pools connected by water slides. The park also includes a wild-animal habitat with a flock of live Chilean flamingos, African penguins, swans, ducks, koi, goldfish, and turtles. All of the animals live on islands and in streams surrounded by sparkling waterfalls and lush foliage. The last remnant of the complex originally built by Bugsy Siegel was torn down, but a monument in the pool park pays respect to the Flamingo's notorious founder. ✉ *3555 Las Vegas Blvd. S, Center Strip,* ☎ *702/733–3111 or 800/732–2111,* ᴡᴇʙ *www.flamingolv.com.*

㉑ **Harrah's Las Vegas Casino & Hotel.** A Carnival theme pervades Harrah's. The festive motif is carried throughout to the outdoor Carnaval Court entertainment and shopping area, which occupies a patio near the front entrance. Carnaval Court includes Carnival Corner, an international food mart; Legends, which sells sports and entertainment memorabilia; Ragin' Cajun, a Cajun country-inspired gift shop; and the Ghirardelli Chocolate Company. During the summer months, live bands play almost continuously, well into the night. ⊠ *3475 Las Vegas Blvd. S, Center Strip,* ☎ *702/369–5000 or 800/427–7247,* WEB *www. harrahsvegas.com.*

★ Ⓒ ⑳ **Imperial Palace Hotel and Casino.** The Imperial Palace is festooned with carved dragons and wind-chime chandeliers and has a distinctly Asian feel. It rests on a postage-stamp-size parcel, so the facilities rise instead of sprawl. On the first floor are the casino and shopping plaza. On the second are the coffee shop and buffet. The third houses the showroom, race and sports book, and meeting rooms. And on the fifth floor are the hotel restaurants.

On the fifth level of the hotel's parking garage (catch the elevator at the back of the casino) is the **Imperial Palace Automobile Museum,** a collection of more than 200 antique, classic, and special-interest vehicles. Among the cars, trucks, and motorcycles on view is a 1976 Cadillac Eldorado owned by Elvis Presley, and the world's largest Deusenberg collection, comprising 25 vehicles built between 1925 and 1937.

Imperial Palace also offers unique entertainment, including *Legends in Concert,* a multimillion-dollar stage production featuring look-and-sound-alike performers portraying stars such as Cher, Neil Diamond, Madonna, and Elvis. ⊠ *3535 Las Vegas Blvd. S, Center Strip,* ☎ *702/ 731–3311 or 800/634–6441,* WEB *www.imperialpalace.com.* 🖼 *Museum: $6.95; coupons for free admission are usually handed out in front of the hotel-casino.* ☉ *Museum daily 9:30 AM–11:30 PM.*

Ⓒ ㉓ **Mirage Hotel and Casino.** When it opened in November 1989, the Mirage launched a decade-long (and counting) building boom the likes of which the world has rarely seen. The place is pretty spectacular. Every 15 minutes from dusk to midnight the signature volcano in front of the Mirage erupts, shooting flames and smoke 100 ft above the water below. Just inside the resort's front entrance is a lush rain forest. Palm trees, cascading waterfalls, meandering lagoons, and exotic tropical flora are housed under a 100-ft-high dome and a 20,000-gallon aquarium provides a stunning backdrop to the front desk.

Behind the Mirage, seven Atlantic bottlenose dolphins live in a 2.5-million-gallon saltwater **Dolphin Habitat,** the largest in the world. The 15-minute tour, which leaves from the large and lush pool area, passes through an underwater observation area and winds up in a video room where you can watch tapes of two dolphin births at the habitat. A gift shop sells dolphin souvenirs, and there's a snack bar next door.

A major attraction at the Mirage is the **Secret Garden of Siegfried and Roy,** a palm-shaded sanctuary for a collection of the planet's rarest and most exotic creatures, including snow-white tigers, white lions, and an Asian elephant, all of which appear in the Siegfried and Roy illusion extravaganza in the showroom. Both attractions are free for children under 11. Danny Gans, a impressionist par excellence, also performs here. ⊠ *3400 Las Vegas Blvd. S, Center Strip,* ☎ *702/791–7111 or 800/ 627–6667,* WEB *www.mirage.com.* 🖼 *Secret Garden and Dolphin Habitat $10; Dolphin Habitat alone $5 on Wed. and daily after 3:30.* ☉ *Secret Garden Mon.–Tues. and Thurs.–Fri. 11–5, weekends 10–5; Dolphin Habitat weekdays 11–7, weekends 10–7. Secret Garden closed Wed.*

⑯ **Paris Las Vegas.** This $785-million homage to the City of Lights tries to reproduce all the charm of the French capital. Outside are replicas of the Arc de Triomphe, the Paris Opera House, the Hôtel de Ville, and the Louvre, along with an *Around the World in Eighty Days* balloon marquee. Also out front is the Mon Ami Gabi café, offering the only alfresco dining right on the Strip. The main gaming area sits on Monet-style floral carpeting beneath a perfect recreation of Paris's wrought-iron art nouveau Metro arches. Even the sinks in the rest rooms are French porcelain. Be sure to check out the dozen original LeRoy Neiman paintings that grace the walls of the high-roller pit. Paris Las Vegas offers several entertainment venues, including Le Théatre des Arts, a 1,200-seat Parisian-style theater that has hosted everything from French hip-hop groups to a musical version of The Hunchback of Notre Dame.

The 50-story **Eiffel Tower,** built almost exactly to a half-size scale, rises above it all; the Eiffel Restaurant is on the 11th floor, and three legs of the tower come right through the casino roof, resting heavily on its floor. A glass elevator ascends to the tower's small observation deck (a small caged catwalk) at the 460-ft level. While you can catch a better, bigger view of the Vegas Valley and have more walk-around room at the top of the Stratosphere, the Eiffel Tower offers an incomparable view of mid-Strip. After dark, hang around long enough to catch the dancing-waters show at Bellagio directly across the street.

Cobblestone "streets" meander through **Le Boulevard** shopping district, where you can purchase everything from fine jewelry to freshly baked breads and pastries; bread delivery men ride through on bicycles, singing "Alouette" in operatic voices. One shop, the Re Galeria Atelier, prints replica vintage posters on an 8-ton, 100-year-old French lithography press. ⊠ *3655 Las Vegas Blvd. S, Center Strip,* ☎ *702/739–4111 or 888/226–5687,* WEB *www.parislasvegas.com.* ☎ *Eiffel Tower $9.* ◷ *Eiffel Tower daily 10 AM–1 AM.*

☝ **㉔ Treasure Island Las Vegas.** Treasure Island appeals to a younger and more family-oriented clientele than its sister hotel the Mirage. The buccaneer theme is well-rendered throughout, from the pirate-show spectacle out front and the skull-and-crossbones door handles to the bone chandeliers. The pool area is large and lush, and sits next to a tropical-theme restaurant and bar, Margaritaville. A short tram connects the hotel to the Mirage next door. Treasure Island hosts the Cirque du Soleil production *Mystère,* a spectacular display of strength, dance, acrobatics, and singing.

The free **Treasure Island Pirate Show,** performed six times a night (weather cooperating) is simply amazing. It's a must-see, one of the top attractions in Las Vegas. The British Navy frigate HMS *Britannia* sails around the corner from its parking place on Spring Mountain Road to Buccaneer Bay on the Strip. There it encounters the pirate schooner *Hispaniola,* and a live battle ensues. The show rages with spectacular pyrotechnics, an impressive sound system, and major stunts. The pirates score the knockout blow and the frigate sinks, captain on board, but be sure to linger to see him come back up with the ship, a full three minutes later, through the magic of hydraulics. You'll want to see this show twice: in the daylight (to see the details) and after dark (to get the full effect of the explosions). ⊠ *3300 Las Vegas Blvd. S, Center Strip,* ☎ *702/894–7111 or 800/944–7444,* WEB *www.treasureisland.com.* ☎ *Pirate Battle free.* ◷ *Pirate Battle performances begin at 5:30 and run every 90 minutes until 10 (11:30 Friday and Saturday).*

★ ☝ **㉒ Venetian Resort-Hotel-Casino.** The 44-year-old Sands was imploded in 1996 to make room for this $1.2-billion resort complex. This meticulously themed hotel re-creates Italy's most romantic city with reproductions of various Venetian landmarks. From the Strip, you enter through a reproduction of the Doge's Palace, set on a walkway over a 585,000-gallon lagoon. Inside, reproductions of famous paintings with gilded frames adorn a 65-ft dome ceiling above the casino lobby. Hanging behind the front desk is a giant pictorial overview of 17th-century Venice; behind the guest services desk in the lobby is a wall mural with a detailed enlargement of one small panel of the pictorial map. The geometric design of the flat-marble floor provides an M. C. Escher-like optical illusion of climbing stairs. Renaissance characters roam the public areas, singing opera, performing mime, jesting, even kissing hands.

The centerpiece of the **Grand Canal Shops,** a 90-store mall, is the 1,200-ft-long reproduction of Venice's Canalozzo enclosed by brick walls and wrought-iron fencing, and cobbled with small change. Gondolas (ride for $10 per person, same-day reservations usually required) ply the waterway, steered by serenading gondoliers. The canal ends at a colossal reproduction of St. Mark's Square, authentic right down to the colors of the facades. The complex also includes **C2K** (Carnevale 2000), a four-level dining/performance venue with seating for 1,400, which, after midnight on the weekends, turns into a nightclub, and **Warner Brothers Stage 16,** a dining, retail, and entertainment complex. And it's also worth noting that the Venetian houses Venus—the first new Tiki Bar to be built in Vegas since the Stardust's classic Aku-Aku closed in the early 1980s.

Madame Tussaud's Wax Museum features more than 100 wax figures, many celebrating Sin City's past—classic Vegas crooners such as Tom Jones, Frank Sinatra, and Tony Bennett are among those replicated here.

The **Guggenheim Las Vegas Museum** and its sister space, the intimate **Guggenheim-Hermitage Museum,** are absolute must-sees. The larger of the two museums, a 64,000-square-ft "big box," hosts large multimedia shows such as its debut show, The Art of the Motorcycle. Across the hotel, the smaller, 7,660-square-ft "jewel box" displays masterworks from the Guggenheim and Hermitage collections. Both spaces were designed by Dutch architect Rem Koolhas, and would be worth seeing even if completely bereft of art. Guided tours are available for both spaces, and periodically the tour guides will linger and give mini-tours for free. The Guggenheim is next to the parking garage, and the Guggenheim-Hermitage near check-in. ⊠ *3355 Las Vegas Blvd. S, Center Strip,* ☎ *702/733–5000; 702/642–6440 wax museum; 800/494–3556,* WEB *www.venetian.com.* ⊠ *Wax museum $12.50; Guggenheim Las Vegas $15; Hermitage-Guggenheim Museum $15; combined ticket for both Guggenheim spaces $25.* ☉ *Wax museum daily 11–7, 10–10; Guggenheim Las Vegas and Hermitage-Guggenheim museums daily 9:30–8:30.*

NORTH STRIP

The North Strip hasn't kept pace with the latest developments of the South and Center Strips. In fact, the only large vacant lots on the Strip are in this area. But when the Stratosphere Tower opened in 1996, things started to happen.

Plans are currently being realized that will make the North Strip as busy and packed as the South. Luxury condominiums are being built next to, and across the street from, the venerable Sahara hotel. Former Mirage Resorts mogul Steve Wynn is building a 3,000-room resort, La Reve, on the former Desert Inn property; his long-range plans call for multiple resorts on its golf course. For now, he seems content to build just one hotel, and display his breathtaking art collection in a preserved wing of the Desert Inn.

A Good Tour

Park at the **Stardust Hotel and Casino** ③⓪. There's no parking garage at the Stardust, so your wheels will have to bake in the sun. An alternative: park in the Riviera's garage across the street and start and end your tour there.

This is a major trek, with greater distances between the casinos at either end. If you're not up for shin splints or if it's just too hot, consider driving and walking: hit the New Frontier, Fashion Show Mall, and Guardian Angel Cathedral, then the Stardust, Riviera, and Circus Circus on foot; drive to the Convention Center area and then to the Sahara, Bonanza Gift Shop, and Stratosphere.

From the Stardust, which has one of the most impressive neon signs and facades in town, walk south on the Strip down to the **New Frontier Hotel and Gambling Hall** ②⑧, which lures a bustling crowd with good, cheap food, low minimums, and minisuites. Next door to the New Frontier is the **Fashion Show Mall** ②⑥, one of four Strip shopping attractions, which has 140 specialty shops, boutiques, and major department stores. A short detour off Fashion Show Drive to Industrial Road (behind the mall) will take you to the **Elvis-A-Rama Museum** ②⑤. Return to the Strip via Spring Mountain Drive; across from the Fashion Show Mall is the former site of the Desert Inn, and the temporary home of the **Wynn Collection** ②⑦. East of the Strip on Desert Inn Road is the **Guardian Angel Cathedral** ②⑨, a Catholic church that serves the religious needs of many weekend visitors.

The next cross street north of Desert Inn Road is Convention Center Drive, which leads east to Paradise Road. At the corner of Paradise Road and Convention Center Drive is, logically enough, the **Las Vegas Convention Center** ④①, one of the largest and busiest convention centers in the country. North of the convention center stands the monumental **Las Vegas Hilton** ④⓪. Be sure to check out Star Trek: The Experience. Your best bets for parking are the garages at the Hilton or the Riviera. The walk from the latter isn't unreasonably long, but may be less advisable in summer.

If you head back to the Strip on Riviera Boulevard you'll come to the **Riviera Hotel and Casino** ③③, with its fast-food court and snack bar, three production shows, a comedy club, and one of the world's largest casinos. Continuing north on Las Vegas Boulevard, you'll pass **Candlelight Wedding Chapel** ③④, the busiest hitching post in town; and the **Wet 'n Wild Water Park** ③⑥ before coming to the northern terminus of the Las Vegas Strip at Sahara Avenue. There stands the **Sahara Hotel and Casino** ③⑦, a venerable joint which opened in 1952. You can park in the Sahara's garage or in the oversized lot across the street; there's a covered bridge leading from the lot to the hotel.

Across the Strip from the Sahara is **Bonanza Gift Shop** ③⑧, the "world's largest gift shop." North of Sahara Avenue starts Las Vegas city proper (south of it is Clark County); ½ mi up the street is the megalithic **Stratosphere Hotel Tower and Casino** ③⑨, the tallest building west of the Mississippi, with its two high-altitude thrill rides, 1,500 hotel rooms, giant casino, and extensive retail area.

Back down on the Strip is the **Guinness World of Records Museum** ③⑤, which is next door to **Circus Circus** ③②, where the pink-and-white big top covers an almost always crazy scene. Behind Circus Circus is **Adventuredome**, the world's largest indoor amusement park, with a rough roller coaster, flume ride, and kiddie attractions. The small casino next to Circus Circus is **Slots A Fun**, which has the least expensive snack-bar food on the Strip, some of the lowest minimums, and—what else?—lotsa slots.

Finally, continue heading south on the Strip to the **Westward Ho** ㉛, which has been billed as the largest motel in the country. Then you'll be back at the Stardust, several hours older but many times wiser in the ways of the gambling capital of the known universe.

TIMING

The North Strip is the longest of the suggested walks, even without the side trip to the Las Vegas Hilton (a leg we recommend you drive). It'll take four–five hours to see everything on the Strip; add another couple of hours to take in the sights on Paradise Road. If you like to shop, you could spend all day taking the tour, browsing in the Fashion Show Mall on one end and the Bonanza Gift Shop and Stratosphere on the other.

Sights to See

㊳ **Bonanza Gift Shop.** Those who are determined to visit only one gift shop in Las Vegas will want to make it this one, which bills itself as the world's largest. If it's not really the largest, it is the biggest and best in town, with an impressive collection of Las Vegas kitsch (this is where you'll find your life-size Wayne Newton blow-up doll), the most extensive selection of Las Vegas T-shirts and postcards, along with jewelry, gambling supplies, Western memorabilia, film, fudge, and aspirin. ⊠ *2460 Las Vegas Blvd. S, North Strip,* ☎ *702/385–7359.* ☉ *Daily 8 AM–midnight.*

㉞ **Candlelight Wedding Chapel.** Its central location helps to make this the town's busiest wedding chapel. There are often couples lined up here waiting to tie the knot (Saturday is especially busy). Anyone can watch a Las Vegas wedding ceremony; just walk in and take a seat. Some weddings take place in the gazebo outside the chapel. ⊠ *2855 Las Vegas Blvd. S, North Strip,* ☎ *702/735–4179,* WEB *www.nos.net/candlelight.*

㉜ **Circus Circus.** Circus Circus opened in 1968, with the then unique idea of appealing to the families that showed up in the adult fantasy land of Las Vegas. To this day, Circus Circus remains family central in Las Vegas—enticing to children, surreal to parents weaned on Hunter S. Thompson's "Fear and Loathing in Las Vegas." Under the pink-and-white big top, the clowns, trapeze stars, high-wire artists, unicyclists, and aerial dancers perform daily every 30 minutes from 11 AM to midnight. Also for the family market, Circus Circus has the only RV park on the Strip.

A **carnival midway** has old-time fair games (dime toss, milk can, bushel basket) along with clown-face painting, a video arcade with more than 200 games, fun-house mirrors, corn dogs, and pizza. Many parents park their teens on the midway while they go off to gamble, pull handles, and press buttons downstairs.

Behind the hotel-casino is the **Adventuredome**, a 5-acre indoor amusement park covered by a pink dome. Inside are the world's largest indoor roller coaster (the double-loop, double-corkscrew Canyon Blaster), a flume ride, a laser-tag room, bumper cars, four kiddie rides, a carnival midway, an arcade, and a snack bar. The roller coaster has two 360-degree loops and a corkscrew; it's a rough 105-second ride, but quite a thrill. If thrill rides are your thing, also check out the Inverter, 360 degrees of constant G force, and the Fun House Express, an IMAX motion-simulator experience. Designed exclusively for Circus Circus, the Fun House Express uses computer-generated images to portray a fast-paced roller coaster ride through a spooky world called Clown

GETTING HITCHED IN VEGAS

WHEN WIDE-OPEN GAMBLING was legalized in 1931, Nevada also adopted liberal divorce and marriage laws as part of the strategy to attract tourists. The rules haven't changed in seven decades: a divorce can still be obtained after only six weeks of residency and a wedding can be arranged without a blood test or a waiting period; once you have a license, a justice of the peace can unite you in marital bliss in five minutes.

Weddings are big business here, to the tune of more than $4 million in marriage licenses alone. To be among the 123,000-plus couples who tie the knot in Las Vegas every year, simply appear at the **Clark County Marriage License Bureau** (✉ 200 S. 3rd St., Downtown, ☎ 702/455–4415) with $50, some identification, and your beloved. It's open between 8 AM and midnight from Monday through Thursday and 24 hours Friday, Saturday, and holidays. New Year's Eve and Valentine's Day are the most popular wedding dates. Even celebrities (including Jon Bon Jovi, Bette Midler, Joan Collins, Michael Jordan, and Richard Gere) have found it handy to pop into a chapel for a quick ceremony.

For a no-frills, justice-of-the-peace nuptial ceremony, visit the **Commissioner of Civil Marriages** (✉ 309 S. 3rd St., Downtown), where a surrogate-J.P. deputy commissioner will unite you in holy matrimony for $35. For a more traditional ambience—flowers, organ music, photos—head to one of Vegas's renowned wedding chapels, where the average nuptials cost $200 to $700 (though you can spend a lot more or a bit less); hotel chapels tend to cost more.

The **Candlelight Wedding Chapel** (✉ 2855 Las Vegas Blvd. S, North Strip, ☎ 702/735–4179 or 800/962–1818, WEB www.nos.net/candlelight) opened its doors in 1967; it's small, elegant, and churchlike.

Weddings are reasonably priced; the most expensive package comes in at $500. The **Little Church of the West** (✉ 4617 Las Vegas Blvd. S, South Strip, ☎ 702/739–7971 or 800/821–2452) is listed on the National Register of Historic Places; the cedar and redwood chapel is one of the most famous chapels in Vegas, sitting on an acre of land at the south end of the Strip. The **Little White Chapel** (✉ 1301 Las Vegas Blvd. S, North Strip, ☎ 702/382–3546 or 800/545–8111, WEB www.littlewhitechapel.com), one mi north of the Sahara hotel, is where you can get married in a pink Cadillac while an Elvis impersonator croons. The world-renowned chapel is one of only two chapels that offer drive-through weddings (the other is A Special Memory).

Weddings at **Star Trek: The Experience** (✉ 3000 S. Paradise Blvd., North Strip, ☎ 702/697–8750 or 800/774–1500, WEB www.startrekexp.com) are held on the bridge of the Enterprise-D from Star Trek: The Next Generation; costumed characters, from Federation officers to Klingon warriors, bear witness to the proceedings.

The **Venetian** (✉ 3355 Las Vegas Blvd. S, Center Strip, ☎ 702/414–4280 or 800/883–6423, WEB www.venetian.com) offers weddings in a recreation of St. Mark's Square, on a replica of the Rialto Bridge or on the Venetian's canal in a gold-and-white gondola. The gondolier sings and passersby applaud loudly, dimming the lines between a real wedding in Venice and this fanciful interpretation.

The **Viva Las Vegas Wedding Chapel** (✉ 1205 Las Vegas Blvd. S, North Strip, ☎ 702/384–0771 or 800/574–4450, WEB www.vivalasvegasweddings.com) offers a wide variety of theme weddings, from Elvis's Blue Hawaii to Egyptian to Fairy Tale. Ever dream of a wedding themed for Charo? Here's where you'll find it.

town, it's still a sight to see—best of all by standing at its foot and staring up at the 29-story three-wing tower.

The biggest attraction at the Hilton is **Star Trek: The Experience** (WEB www.startrekexp.com), a $70-million museum and interactive theater/motion-simulator ride. Trekkies will go nuts over the museum, which has a Star Trek timeline of future history, costumes and props, and video loops from the shows. During the theater/ride, the audience is kidnapped by the Klingons and beamed into the 24th century and onto the bridge of the Starship *Enterprise*; it's up to the crew to get everyone safely back to the 21st-century Hilton. ✉ *3000 W. Paradise Rd., North Strip,* ☎ *702/732–5111 or 800/774–1500,* WEB *www.lv-hilton.com.* ✉ *Star Trek $24.99 (all-day pass).* ☯ *Star Trek daily 11–11.*

🔘 **28** **New Frontier Hotel and Gambling Hall.** The New Frontier is the oldest hotel-casino on the Las Vegas Strip, beating out the Flamingo by a full five years. In 1942, Hollywood producer D. W. Griffith opened the Last Frontier, the second hotel on the Los Angeles Highway (soon to be known as the Las Vegas Strip). It was sold in 1951 and renamed Last Frontier Village. The original building was torn down and replaced in 1955; the new hotel-casino was named the New Frontier. That structure was torn down and replaced again in 1967 and the property was named simply the Frontier. In 1998 it was sold again and renamed the New Frontier. The property is themeless and nondescript, though the vestibule of the Atrium (all-suite) Tower is gardenlike, with a waterfall, creek, and pools. ✉ *3120 Las Vegas Blvd. S, North Strip,* ☎ *702/794–8200 or 800/634–6966,* WEB *www.frontierhotelcasino.com.*

🔘 **33** **Riviera Hotel and Casino.** Other than being huge and a bit of a maze (after being expanded countless times in the past 45 years), there's little that distinguishes The Riviera in terms of decor and atmosphere. It has a good fast-food court at one end and an excellent snack bar at the other; in between is a sprawling, adult-oriented casino that's been a backdrop to dozens of Vegas films, including "Go," "Casino," "Diamonds are Forever," and "Austin Powers: International Man of Mystery." Its three house shows—*Crazy Girls, Splash,* and *An Evening at La Cage*—feature topless women, suggestive material, and a troupe of female impersonators, respectively. There's also a popular comedy club. ✉ *2901 Las Vegas Blvd. S, North Strip,* ☎ *702/734–5110 or 800/ 634–6753,* WEB *www.theriviera.com/theriv.html.*

🔘 **37** **Sahara Hotel and Casino.** The line between old Las Vegas and new is clear at the Sahara. The former Rat Pack haunt—and current host of The Rat Pack is Back, a fun impersonator's showcase—manages to encompass both old school swank and the popular NASCAR café, themed for the hottest sports franchise in recent years.

Near the NASCAR Cafe is **Cyber Speedway,** a $15-million virtual reality race car–driving experience, where 3-D motion-simulator rides make audience members feel as though they're driving on the Las Vegas Motor Speedway or the Las Vegas Strip.

The Sahara's signature roller coaster, **Speed–The Ride,** uses magnetic technology to propel riders through a tunnel, around a loop, and in and out of the casino at speeds of more than 70 mph. Then you do the entire thing again—backwards. ✉ *2535 Las Vegas Blvd. S, North Strip,* ☎ *702/737–2111 or 800/634–6666, NASCAR Cafe 702/737–2750,* WEB *www.saharahotelandcasino.com.* ✉ *Rides $8.* ☯ *Speed—The Ride weekdays 10–10, weekends 10 AM–midnight; Cyber Speedway weekdays 10–10, weekends 10 AM–11 PM.*

Chaos. ⊠ *2880 Las Vegas Blvd. S, North Strip,* ☎ *702/734–(*
800/634–3450, WEB *www.circuscircus-lasvegas.com.* 🖭 *Adv*
dome free, individual rides $2–$5 or all-day wristbands $16.
Amusement park Mon.–Thurs. 10–6, Fri.–Sat. 10 AM–midnight,
10–8; carnival midway daily 10 AM–midnight.

㉕ Elvis-A-Rama Museum. The quintessential Elvis experience ca
found at this spot on Industrial Road (behind the Fashion Show M
The must-see museum (for Elvis fans, at least) houses four o
King's cars, including his purple Lincoln and his 1955 Fleetwood l
More than 2,000 of Elvis's personal items are on display, including
jewelry, clothing, letters, and records. Every hour an Elvis impers
ator croons to fans on a small stage; various impersonators cover (
ferent decades of his career. Buy Elvis clocks, key chains, pins, boo
and other collectibles in the gift shop. Call the museum to arrange f
a free shuttle pick-up from any major hotel on the Strip. ⊠ *3401 I*
dustrial Rd., North Strip, ☎ *702/309–7200,* WEB *www.elvisarama.con*
🖭 *$9.95.* ☉ *Daily 10 AM–7 PM.*

㉖ Fashion Show Mall. With shops such as Saks Fifth Avenue and Neima
Marcus, among others, you'll be sure to find what you're looking
for—and more. Shoppers will eventually have triple the space to peruse as the mall expands. The first phase is scheduled for completion
in 2003. ⊠ *3200 Las Vegas Blvd. S, North Strip,* ☎ *702/369–8382,*
WEB *www.thefashionshow.com.* ☉ *10–5 daily.*

㉙ Guardian Angel Cathedral. The busiest church in town has standing
room only on Saturday afternoon as visitors pray for luck and drop
casino chips in the collection cups during a special tourist mass. Once
a week a priest takes the chips to Caesars Palace to cash them in (he's
known as the "chip monk"). The 4 PM mass on Saturday is so crowded,
usually with 300 standees, that visitors are asked to attend the 5:15
mass on Saturday or one of five on Sunday instead. ⊠ *336 E. Desert*
Inn Rd., North Strip, ☎ *702/735–5241.* ☉ *Sat. mass 2:30, 4, 5:15; Sun.*
mass 8, 9:30, 11, 12:30, 5.

㉟ Guinness World of Records Museum. One of numerous Guinness museums around the country, the Las Vegas version has colorful displays,
video footage, and computer data banks of various Guinness world
records (the most-married man, the smallest woman, the largest snow-
plow)—the best, biggest, and most bizarre in sports, science, nature,
entertainment, and more. The Las Vegas display alone, which includes
information on celebrities married in Vegas, the Stratosphere, and
Hoover Dam, is worth the price of admission. ⊠ *2780 Las Vegas Blvd.*
S, North Strip, ☎ *702/792–3766,* WEB *www.guinnessmuseum.com.* 🖭
$6. ☉ *Daily 9–5:30.*

㊶ Las Vegas Convention Center. More than 1,000 conventions of varying sizes are held here every year. A handful of them, such as Comdex
and the Consumer Electronics show, are among the largest in the country. Conventions large and small account for about 15% of the city's
visitor volume. One of the most attractive aspects of the convention
center for conventioneers is its proximity to all the hotels and the airport, and there's a visitors center right off the lobby. ⊠ *3150 Paradise*
Rd., North Strip, ☎ *702/892–0711,* WEB *www.lasvegas24hours.com.*

㊵ Las Vegas Hilton. Barbra Streisand opened this hotel with a four-week
gig and was followed by Elvis Presley, who made the Hilton his official Las Vegas venue throughout the 1970s; you can still stay in the
Elvis Suite on the 31st floor, where the king of rock and roll resided
when he played here. Though the Hilton, which is adjacent to the Las
Vegas Convention Center, no longer holds the title of largest hotel in

⑳ Stardust Hotel and Casino. The Stardust has one of the best neon facades on the Strip: pink and blue neon tubes run down the front of the hotel, leading to a 183-ft programmed sign that erupts in bursts of neon stars. On its debut in 1958, the sign was the largest and brightest in Las Vegas, its glow visible for miles. The vision for the Stardust came from mobster Tony Cornero, who in the 1930s ran gambling ships off the southern California coast; he owned a small club out on Boulder Highway and dreamed of building the biggest, classiest casino in town. Cornero didn't live long enough to realize his dream, however; one morning, while shooting craps at the Desert Inn, he had a heart attack, dying with the dice in his hands. Today the Stardust belongs to the Boyd Corporation, the operators of middle-market hotels (Sam's Town, the Fremont, the California, and Main Street Station) that emphasize slots, low table minimums, and good deals on food. The Stardust does have the distinction of hosting Wayne Newton, "Mr. Las Vegas" himself, exclusively in a showroom named for him. ✉ *3000 Las Vegas Blvd. S, North Strip,* ☎ *702/732–6111 or 800/634–6757,* WEB *www.stardustlv.com.*

NEED A BREAK?	Between the Stardust and the Westward Ho is a **McDonald's** (✉ 2880 Las Vegas Blvd. S, North Strip, ☎ 702/731–1575) with the golden arches all decked out in neon and flashing lights. The window seats inside this frantic franchise provide a good view of the automobile, pedestrian, and pigeon traffic on the Strip.

☺ **㊴ Stratosphere Hotel Tower and Casino.** The view from the tower and the thrill rides at the top, as well as good odds and a good slot club, make it worth the extra effort to get to this hotel-casino, which occupies a sort of no-man's land a few blocks north of the northern end of the Strip.

The aforementioned view has no peer— you'll be looking down at Las Vegas from the top of the the tallest **observation tower** in the United States, dominating the Las Vegas skyline at 1,149 ft. Although the view is impressive enough during the day, save a trip to the tower for the evening.

High above the Las Vegas Strip are the Stratosphere's two **thrill rides:** Big Shot and the High Roller. The Big Shot would be a monster ride on the ground, but being high atop the Stratosphere Tower makes it twice as wild. Four riders are strapped into chairs on four sides of the needle, which rises from the Stratosphere's observation pod (the base of the ride is on the 112th floor). With little warning, you're flung 160 ft up the needle, then dropped like a rock. The whole thing is over in less than a minute, but your knees will wobble for the rest of the day. The High Roller is a roller coaster that, although tame by ground standards, is quite thrilling owing to its perch high atop the tower.

For the less daring, Stratosphere also has the revolving Top of the World restaurant and lounge. Set 900 ft above the valley, it makes a complete revolution once every hour or so and offers big views. The shopping plaza between the casino and entrance to the tower houses more than 50 eateries and retail stores. And the Strat-O-Fair, at the base of the tower, has a small Ferris wheel and other rides suitable for children. ✉ *2000 Las Vegas Blvd. S, North Strip,* ☎ *702/380–7777 or 800/380–7732,* WEB *www.stratlv.com.* ✉ *Big Shot $11, High Roller $9; prices include admission to the tower elevator. Both rides and tower admission $15. Strat-O-Fair rides $3.* ☉ *Rides Sun.–Thurs. 10 AM–1 AM, Fri.–Sat. 10 AM–2 AM.*

㉛ Westward Ho. The Westward Ho is a rarity on the Strip: a sprawling low-rise motel. With 1,000 rooms (some of them three-room suites), the Ho claims to be the largest motel in the world. It has seven pools and no elevators. The casino is for gamblers, not gawkers, and has a dizzying array of slot machines and low-minimum table games. The snack bar is a local favorite, serving a huge strawberry shortcake. ⊠ *2900 Las Vegas Blvd. S, North Strip,* ☎ *702/731–2900 or 800/634–6803,* WEB *www.westwardho.com.*

☺ ㊱ **Wet 'n' Wild Water Park.** This 26-acre water park provides family-oriented recreation in a 500,000-gallon wave pool, three water flumes, a water roller coaster, slides, cascading fountains, and lagoons. Showers, changing rooms, and lockers are available, and inner tubes and rafts are for rent. Shops and concession stands sell souvenirs and food. ⊠ *601 Las Vegas Blvd. S, North Strip,* ☎ *702/737–3819,* WEB *www. wetnwildlasvegas.com.* ⊠ *$25.95.* ◷ *May–Oct., opens daily at 10 AM, closing times vary.*

㉗ **Wynn Collection.** Steve Wynn enjoys two things: building bigger and better resort hotels, and collecting art. While he indulges his first passion on the lot next door—LaReve, a 3,000 room luxury hotel under construction—he shares his other joy in a gallery inside one of the former Desert Inn hotel wings. The Wynn Collection is world-class, including works by Matisse, Van Gogh, Modigliani, and, naturally, Picasso's "La Reve." His collection equals the Guggenheim-Hermitage in quality, and is well worth seeing. ⊠ *3145 Las Vegas Blvd. S, North Strip,* ☎ *702/733–4100,* ⊠ *$10.* ◷ *Weekdays 10–9, Sat. 10–7, Sun. noon–6.*

DOWNTOWN

If you've never traveled north of the Stratosphere Tower, you're missing a vital piece of Las Vegas. Downtown Las Vegas is where Sin City was born. Vegas's first telephone was installed here; its first concrete building was built here (The Golden Gate Casino, opened in 1906 and still going strong); its first train station was at the tip of Fremont Street. And the notorious "Block 16," a block of gambling halls, bars and legal brothels, remained in business until 1941. It was the last time prostitution was legal within city limits.

The pioneering spirit of those days lives on Fremont Street. Even though the world-famous "Glitter Gulch" was closed to automobiles and transformed into a pedestrian mall several years ago, the hotels of Fremont still seem like they should have hitching posts in front of them. The lights down here literally turn night to day, and the street's patron saints, the 50-ft-tall neon cowboy Vegas Vic and his gal Vegas Vickie, still welcome visitors with a sincere "howdy."

And Fremont Street has one of Vegas's most spectacular sights—the four-block long Fremont Street Experience light canopy. In essence the largest electronic sign in the world, the Experience employs 2.1 million lights and a 540,000-watt sound system. The shows that run on it hourly, though a bit corny, have to be seen to be believed.

The best way to see Fremont Street is to go with its flow—accept the free slot pulls and roulette spins you're offered, watch the shows on the light canopy, shop the weird souvenir stands, accumulate free souvenirs, and enjoy the inexpensive food and drink. You're on Fremont Street now, and like visitors of long ago, you're seeing the real Las Vegas for the first time.

Numbers in the text correspond to numbers in the margin and on the Las Vegas Downtown map.

EXCURSIONS WITH THE KIDS

OF THE ROUGHLY 35 MILLION VISITORS to Las Vegas each year, 12% are under 21. If you're the parent of one of these too-young-to-gamble tourists, you know that the hotel pool will only occupy them for so long. Fortunately, there's lots for kids to do in Vegas, and any of the following destinations are sure to be a hit. Also, check out the Side Trips chapter for everything from visiting a Wild West town to scrambling around in Red Rock.

Las Vegas Natural History Museum. The museum has displays of mammals from Alaska to Africa, and has rooms full of sharks (including live ones), birds, dinosaur fossils, and hands-on exhibits. The big gift shop is full of games, puzzles, books, clothes, and animals. The Young Scientists area has child-oriented interactive displays such as the Dig-A-Fossil area, Rub-A-Dino, a Paleontologist Lab, and a robotic baby dinosaur youngsters can control. ⊠ 900 Las Vegas Blvd. N, Downtown, ☎ 702/384–3466. ⊡ $5.50 for adults, $3 for children 4–12. ☉ Daily 9–4.

Lied Discovery Children's Museum. One of the largest children's museums in the nation at roughly 25,000 square ft, the Lied (pronounced *leed*) contains more than 100 hands-on exhibits covering the sciences, arts, and humanities. Children can pilot a space shuttle, perform on stage, or stand in a giant bubble. In the Desert Discovery area for children age five and under, youngsters are entertained and educated with a number of hands-on interactive displays, including Boulder Mountain, where children don hard hats and mine soft sculpture boulders in geometric shapes; and Cactus Construction, where children build with, sort, and organize the boulders. Also in Desert Discovery is the Baby Oasis, a safe haven for tots who aren't yet walking that has colorful and stimulating props and toys, including a mirrored pull-up bar and a crawling structure of gently inclined ramps that encourage large-mus-

cle development. ⊠ 833 Las Vegas Blvd. N, Downtown, ☎ 702/382–3445, WEB www.ldcm.org. ⊡ $6 for adults, $5 for children 1–17. ☉ Tues.–Sun. 10–5.

Mountasia Family Fun Center. This amusement park in Green Valley, a fast-growing suburb in southeastern Las Vegas, has two 18-hole miniature-golf courses, a roller-skating rink, go-carts, bumper boats, and an arcade with 75 video games. A fun package includes a round of minigolf or roller skating, two rides (bumper boats or go-carts), and five arcade tokens. ⊠ 2050 Olympic Ave., Henderson, ☎ 702/454–4386. ⊡ $4.50 per ride, fun package $15 (only available on Fri.). ☉ Mon.–Thurs. 3 pm–9 pm, Fri. 3 pm–11, Sat. 11–11, Sun. noon–9.

Scandia Family Fun Center. The center has three 18-hole miniature-golf courses, a video arcade with more than 100 games, 11 batting cages, bumper boats, and the Li'l Indy Raceway for miniature-car racing. You can pay by the ride/activity or purchase a Supersaver package (18 holes of golf, a Li'l Indy ride, a bumper-boat ride, and five game tokens) or a wristband (unlimited rides, golf, and 10 arcade tokens). ⊠ 2900 Sirius Ave., West Side, ☎ 702/364–0070. ⊡ Free admission; individual rides $4.50 each; unlimited pass $16.95. ☉ Sun.–Thurs. 10–10, Fri.–Sat. 10 am–midnight.

Zoological–Botanical Park. Five minutes from downtown, you'll find the last family of Barbary apes in the United States, along with chimpanzees, eagles, ostriches, emus, parrots, wallabies, flamingos, endangered cats (including tigers), and every species of venomous reptile native to southern Nevada. One exhibit features species native to Nevada such as coyotes, golden eagles, and deer; an underwater exhibit stars a 7-ft-long alligator named Elvis. The park has easy-view animal enclosures and a petting zoo with smaller animals. ⊠ 1775 N. Rancho Dr., Rancho, ☎ 702/648–5955. ⊡ $5.95. ☉ Daily 9–5.

A Good Walk

Two miles north of the northern end of the Strip (at Sahara Avenue), Las Vegas Boulevard meets Fremont Street in downtown Las Vegas. Fremont Street runs east from Main Street, which is five blocks west of, and parallel to, Las Vegas Boulevard. At the corner of Main and Fremont is **Jackie Gaughan's Plaza Hotel-Casino** ①, one of the best casinos for low rollers in town.

The heart of downtown Las Vegas, called Glitter Gulch, is the four-block stretch of Fremont Street that begins at the Plaza. It's where you'll find the pedestrian mall and high-tech canopy known as the **Fremont Street Experience** ②. At the mall entrance, on the northeast corner of Fremont and Main streets, is the **Las Vegas Club Hotel and Casino** ③, with a sports theme and a roomy casino. Walk a block northeast to Main and Stewart for **Main Street Station Casino, Brewery & Hotel** ④, one of the most aesthetically pleasing casinos in Las Vegas, with its antiques, stained glass, and exquisite workmanship. Take the overhead pedestrian bridge from Main Street Station to the **California Hotel and Casino** ⑤, where the clientele is almost entirely Hawaiian.

Back on Fremont Street, between 1st and 2nd streets, is the block-long **Binion's Horseshoe Hotel and Casino** ⑥, Las Vegas's quintessential old-time gambling den and the scene of some of the most intense action in town. Across 2nd Street is the **Fremont Hotel and Casino** ⑦, with a photogenic neon sign outside and the superb Second Street Grill inside.

At Ogden Avenue and 3rd Street is the crowded **Lady Luck Casino and Hotel** ⑧, which, with its big picture windows, is the brightest and airiest casino downtown. East two blocks on Ogden Avenue between 6th and 7th streets is the city's oldest standing casino, **Jackie Gaughan's El Cortez Hotel** ⑨, which opened for business in 1941; Bugsy Siegel started his short but memorable Vegas career here.

A two-block stroll south on 7th Street to Bridger Avenue will take you miles from the honky-tonk of downtown and bring you to the everyday life of the **Las Vegas Academy of International Studies, Visual and Performing Arts** ⑩, which, until 1993, was the venerable Las Vegas High School.

Back on Fremont and 7th streets, walk three blocks west to the 34-story, leprechaun-theme **Fitzgeralds Hotel and Casino** ⑪, the tallest building in Nevada until Stratosphere topped it—by a mere 700 ft. Coming out of the Fitz, walk a few feet west to 3rd Street and cross the street to get to the **Four Queens Hotel and Casino** ⑫, serving downtown low rollers since 1965.

The Four Queens occupies an entire block. If you walk all the way through the casino, you exit at the corner of 2nd and Fremont. Cross 2nd Street and visit the upscale **Golden Nugget Hotel and Casino** ⑬ to see the world's largest gold nuggets.

Across 1st Street, atop the Fremont Street Experience logo shop, is **Vegas Vic** ⑭, who's been welcoming people to downtown Las Vegas since 1951. Back at the southeast corner of Fremont and Main is the venerable **Golden Gate Hotel** ⑮. Stripped of a facade that was installed over the original adobe in the mid-1950s, this building has been restored to its original appearance in the early days of Las Vegas. The Victory Hotel, a block south on Main Street, was built in 1910 and retains its original balcony and veranda.

If you have a car or want to hop in a cab (don't walk—you pass through a pretty rough area), you can head over to **Cashman Field** ⑯ and **Old Las Vegas Mormon Fort** ⑰, which are on the same site at the corner of Las Vegas Boulevard North and Washington Street, roughly 2 mi north of downtown. Two miles west of downtown, on Twin Lakes Dr., is the **Nevada State Museum and Historical Society** ⑱.

TIMING

If you're staying within the tight confines of the central casino core of downtown, and not straying outside of Ogden Avenue and Fremont Street between Main and 6th streets, you can do a walking tour any time of the day or night and feel perfectly secure. But downtown is a little rough around the edges, so venturing beyond the security of the lights and crowds of the casino center after dark is not recommended. Extra-cautious travelers might want to walk to the Gold Spike (at Ogden Avenue and 4th Street) or the El Cortez (at Fremont and 6th streets) during daylight hours only. In conjunction with the opening of the Fremont Street Experience pedestrian mall, the city and casinos beefed up police (astride mountain bicycles) and security-guard presence in the downtown core, and it now seems safer than ever. But farther afield is still a no-man's-land when the sun is shining on the other side of the world.

This walk is only 8–10 city blocks long; all the casinos are small in comparison to those of the Strip, and most are right next to each other. To see everything in detail will take only a couple of hours.

Sights to See

⑥ **Binion's Horseshoe Hotel and Casino.** Benny Binion wanted the Horseshoe to be a gambler's haven. So while other casinos are morphing into family attractions, Binion's is still holding true to its founder's vision. With low ceilings and an Old Vegas charm, Binion's Horseshoe is a place to lay your money on the table, as many do for a living: Binion's hosts the World Series of Poker, an event that draws professional poker players from all over the world each spring. If you're keen to participate, all you need is a $10,000 ante and a lot of guts. But don't think of making a grab—Binion's also has one of the few remaining displays of guns in a casino in Nevada (including several of Benny's custom-gilt rifles and pistols). For a glimpse of what Vegas used to be, there's no other place than Binion's. ⊠ *128 E. Fremont St., Downtown,* ☎ *702/382–1600 or 800/237–6537,* WEB *www.binions.com.*

⑤ **California Hotel and Casino.** While it isn't so very different from most other downtown casinos (low ceilings and old school charm), there is one quirk about this place: the California is the chief hangout for Hawaiians in Vegas. Though there's no real island theme, this hotel-casino has built a reputation for serving tourists from America's 50th state with enthusiastic hospitality. Saimin is served at the snack bar, the dealers wear Hawaiian shirts, and the carpeting is patterned with tropical flora. Upstairs is a karaoke bar; the later it gets in the evening (and the more inebriated the performers), the more fun it can be. A pedestrian bridge connects to Main Street Station across the street, with a few shops on either side. ⊠ *12 E. Ogden Ave., Downtown,* ☎ *702/ 385–1222,* WEB *www.thecal.com.*

⑯ **Cashman Field.** For a look at Las Vegas's other convention center, which doubles as a sports venue, drive a mile north from Fremont Street on Las Vegas Boulevard. The attractive facility has a 100,000-square-ft exhibit hall, 17,000 square ft of meeting space, and the 2,000-seat auditorium that was used as the courtroom for the trial of Wayne Newton's libel suit against NBC News. ⊠ *850 Las Vegas Blvd. N, Downtown (2 mi north of its corner with Fremont St. downtown),* ☎ *702/386–000.*

36

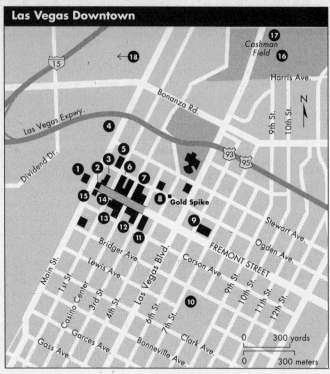

Las Vegas Downtown

⑪ **Fitzgeralds Hotel and Casino.** It's hard to miss this place. With "Mr. O'Lucky"—a 50-ft-tall leprechaun—inviting visitors into Vegas's Irish oasis, Fitzgeralds is easy to spot along Fremont Street's packed pedestrian mall. Inside, the entire casino is decked out in green—money and otherwise. There are six Blarney Stones on display, direct from Ireland's famous Blarney Castle. Lucky's Lookout (off the Sports Bar) has the only second-floor outdoor balcony along Fremont Street. It is one of the best spots from which to watch the Experience light-and-sound shows. Arrive early to grab one of the patio lounge chairs. ⌧ *301 E. Fremont St., Downtown,* ☎ *702/388–2400 or 800/274–5825,* Ⓦ *www.fitzgeralds.com.*

⑫ **Four Queens Hotel and Casino.** In the heart of Fremont Street, the Four Queens' radiating neon rivals the canopy's lightbulb display. Inside, the casino is dark and lushly appointed. A "Big Bertha" slot machine attracts attention at the 2nd Street entrance; at the 3rd Street entrance there's usually a free-pull promotion going on. Otherwise, the Four Queens is typical of the downtown grind joints: the gambling is the thing. ⌧ *202 E. Fremont St., Downtown,* ☎ *702/385–4011 or 800/ 634–6045,* Ⓦ *www.fourqueens.com.*

⑦ **Fremont Hotel and Casino.** A downtown staple since original owner Sam Levinson switched on its fiery neon back in 1956, the Fremont is a Vegas landmark. It was the first high-rise hotel on Fremont Street. Wayne Newton made his Vegas debut here. Even after Boyd Gaming bought the hotel in 1985, the Fremont has remained one of the city's cornerstones. Inside, the old-style casino is reminiscent of many of the other gambling halls downtown, although the neon surrounding the main pit is unique. The poker room walls are graced with interesting

Western murals. ✉ *200 E. Fremont St., Downtown,* ☎ *702/385–3232,* WEB *www.fremontcasino.com.*

❷ **Fremont Street Experience.** In an effort to revive downtown Las Vegas, a partnership consisting of 10 hotels, the city, a privately owned corporation, and the Las Vegas Convention and Visitors Authority created the $70-million Fremont Street Experience, which debuted in 1995. The resulting pedestrian mall is festooned with souvenir stands and cafés, and features live entertainment ranging from mimes to rock bands, but the real attraction is overhead. The sign above this pedestrian mall is the largest electric sign in the world. (The next-largest sign, at the Las Vegas Hilton, is a 50th of its size.) The display is the length of 4½ football fields; the 2 million lightbulbs can produce 65,000 colors; the electricity required to run it could power nearly 2,000 homes; 208 speakers operate independently but combine for 540,000 watts of sound. Six-minute light shows are presented on the hour after dark; it takes 31 computers and 100 gigabytes of memory to run the shows, and it's a don't-miss, only-in-Las Vegas experience. ✉ *Fremont St. from Main to 4th Sts.,* ☎ *702/678–5600,* WEB *www.vegasexperience.com.*

⓯ **Golden Gate Hotel.** Former Las Vegas mayor Jan Laverty Jones declared the Golden Gate the city's "most historic hotel." It stands proudly, though dwarfed by the high-rises that have been built around it during its 95-year history. The tiny hotel-casino opened in 1906 (as the Hotel Nevada) and not much has changed here since then. Many of the original fixtures are still in place. This was the first hotel-casino to introduce the cheap shrimp cocktail to Vegas, and many still regard the Golden Gate's as the best in town. A piano player entertains the crowds eating the crunchy crustacean cocktails in the Deli—some of the only live music (and the only soloist) downtown. Note the San Francisco–inspired decor, especially the large historical photographs. ✉ *1 Fremont St., Downtown,* ☎ *702/385–1906,* WEB *www.goldengatecasino.net.*

⓭ **Golden Nugget Hotel and Casino.** Though no longer owned by Steve Wynn (it's now a part of the MGM Grand conglomerate of casinos), the Golden Nugget is still the classiest joint downtown. The white marble walls, gold-plated slots, and etched-glass windows all stand in stark contrast to the many dark and rustic hotels that surround Fremont Street. The Golden Nugget is also the largest hotel-casino downtown, encompassing 2½ city blocks (including the big parking garage). And it has the biggest and best pool downtown, a concrete courtyard surrounded by the hotel towers, always crowded with sunbathers and swimmers. The most amazing thing about the Golden Nugget, though, is the display of gold nuggets just off the lobby. Here you'll find the world's largest nugget, the 61-pound "Hand of Faith," along with several dozen other stunning specimens of the precious metal. ✉ *129 E. Fremont St., Downtown,* ☎ *702/385–7111 or 800/634–3454,* WEB *www.goldennugget.com.*

❾ **Jackie Gaughan's El Cortez Hotel.** Bugsy Siegel showed up in Las Vegas in 1942 and immediately began to muscle into whatever downtown joints didn't resist him. He started out at the El Cortez, then sold his share and bought into the El Rancho Vegas, then sold that for $1 million, his seed capital to build the Flamingo. Though nothing from that time remains of the other joints, the original El Cortez still stands on the corner of Fremont and 6th streets, including the 60-year-old marquee. Inside, the old wing is delightfully frayed around the edges (contrary to appearances and popular opinion, the carpeting *has* been replaced since it opened) and a great place to people-watch. The coffee shop serves the last round-the-clock $1 bacon-and-eggs breakfast special in town. The "new" wing, built in the early 1980s, houses the race and sports book, hotel lobby, and Roberta's, one of Las Vegas's great "bargain gourmet" restaurants. ⊠ *600 E. Fremont St., Downtown,* ☎ *702/385–5200 or 800/634–6703,* WEB *www.elcortez.net.*

❶ **Jackie Gaughan's Plaza Hotel-Casino.** Jackie Gaughan is a Las Vegas legend. He spent time in Nevada during World War II, first in Las Vegas and later in Tonopah, where he trained gunners for the Air Corps' B-17 bombers. He and his wife Roberta (Bertie) and their two sons, Jackie Jr. and Michael (who became a casino mogul himself), settled here for good in 1951. He bought a 3% interest in the old downtown Boulder Club on Fremont Street, where the Horseshoe now stands. A short time later he bought a 3% interest in the Flamingo Hotel on the Strip. In 1961, he opened the Las Vegas Club and in 1963 he bought the Cortez. He purchased the Union Plaza Hotel & Casino in 1971 and the Gold Spike Hotel & Casino in 1983. Jackie Gaughan's Plaza sits at the end of Fremont Street, looming over the Fremont Street Experience. It's a sleeper, but well worth looking around in for its low table minimums and great nickel machines, live lounge entertainment, excellent snack-bar food at rock-bottom prices, and hall of mirrors lining the south staircase. The Plaza also has the largest showroom downtown (one of only three), a second-floor pool deck, and the Centerstage Restaurant, which sits in a dome looking right down the throat of Glitter Gulch. ⊠ *1 Main St., Downtown,* ☎ *702/386–2110 or 800/634–6575,* WEB *www.plazahotelcasino.com.*

❽ **Lady Luck Casino and Hotel.** The Lady Luck started out as Honest John's newsstand in 1964. It's grown a bit since then. The high-rise casino now includes 40,000 square ft of casino space designed specifically for tourists looking to lay their money down. A large neon arch beckons one and all. The prime-rib specials in the coffee shop are locally famous, as is the funbook handed out free to all comers; one of the coupons is good for a free three-minute long-distance phone call from a 1950s English phone booth. ⊠ *206 N. 3rd St., Downtown,* ☎ *702/477–3000 or 800/634–6580,* WEB *www.ladylucklv.com.*

❿ **Las Vegas Academy of International Studies, Visual and Performing Arts.** This historic structure, the oldest permanent school building in Las Vegas, was built as a high school in 1930 for $350,000. It's a state historical landmark, the only example of 1930s Art Deco architecture in the city. ⊠ *315 S. 7th St., Downtown,* ☎ *702/799–7800.*

❸ **Las Vegas Club Hotel and Casino.** Established in the early 1900s, the Las Vegas Club is a sports-theme casino and hotel. There's not much in the way of entertainment here, but value seekers are sure to appreciate the low-price meals and drinks. It was expanded in 1996 and is now a bit of a maze, covering half a city block. The Las Vegas Club also houses a large private collection of sports memorabilia, some of which is displayed throughout the property. ⊠ *18 E. Fremont St., Downtown,* ☎ *702/385–1664 or 800/634–6532,* WEB *www.playatlvc.com.*

❹ **Main Street Station Casino, Brewery & Hotel.** Downtown's largest and best buffet can be found here, along with the only microbrewery downtown (the Triple 7 Brew Pub, with live entertainment every weekend night). The hotel has a fabulous collection of antiques, artifacts, and collectibles. There are self-guided tours of the collection, which includes Buffalo Bill Cody's private rail car; a fireplace from Scotland's Prestwick Castle; lamps that graced the streets of 18th-century Brussels; and beautiful statues, chandeliers, and woodwork from American mansions of long ago. There's even a piece of the Berlin Wall—in the men's room off the lobby. ⊠ *200 N. Main St., Downtown,* ☎ *702/387–1896 or 800/713–8933,* WEB *www.mainstreetcasino.com.*

(ꆤ **⑱** **Nevada State Museum and Historical Society.** Regional history, from the time of the Spanish exploration to the building of Las Vegas after World War II, is the subject of this museum, which also covers the archaeology and anthropology of southern Nevada. It is by the lake in Lorenzi Park, an open space dotted with ponds and home to plants and animals native to the region. ✉ *700 E. Twin Lakes Dr., Downtown (2 mi west of the corner of Fremont and Main Sts.),* ☎ *702/486–5205.* ▱ *$2.* ☉ *Daily 9–5.*

(ꆤ **⑰** **Old Las Vegas Mormon Fort.** Southern Nevada's oldest historical site was built by the Mormons in 1855 as an agricultural mission to give refuge to travelers along the Salt Lake–Los Angeles trail, many of whom were bound for the California gold fields. Left to the Native Americans after the gold rush, the adobe fort was later revitalized by a miner and his partners. In 1895 it was turned into a resort, and the city's first swimming pool was constructed by damming Las Vegas Creek. Today the restored fort contains more than half the original bricks. Antiques and artifacts help re-create a turn-of-the-20th-century Mormon living room. ✉ *Washington Ave. and Las Vegas Blvd. N, at Cashman Field (enter through parking lot B), Downtown,* ☎ *702/486–3511,* WEB *www.state.nv.us.* ▱ *$2.* ☉ *Daily 8:30–4:30.*

⑭ **Vegas Vic.** The famous Las Vegas icon known as Vegas Vic is about the same age as the average Las Vegas visitor. The original version of this well-known landmark was unveiled in 1947, but was replaced by a newer version in 1951. Now Vegas Vic, a 50-ft-tall neon cowboy, stands outside the Pioneer Club, waving to visitors. Vegas Vic's neon sidekick, Vegas Vickie, went up across the street in 1980.

3 CASINOS

In a town with over one hundred hotel-casinos, all pushing basically the same product, each has to outsell the next. Some joints discount the product more than others. Some use loss leaders to attract customers into the store. Some emphasize service, while others tout exclusivity. Gimmicks, glitz, flesh, and gluttony are all employed in the merchandising. Part of the fun of Las Vegas is to surrender to your temptations. Chances are you'll only remain seduced for a few days, and win or lose, you'll take home very fond memories.

By Deke
Castleman

Updated by
M. Elizabeth
Leong

CONVENTIONAL WISDOM NOTWITHSTANDING, you *can* win in the casinos and many people do. But, as explained in Chapter 10, the odds are riding against you. And that's just for starters. The dazzling lights, the free beer and cocktails, the play money, the absence of windows and clocks, even the oxygen—and, lately, seductive aromas—pumped into the air are all calculated to overwhelm you with a sense of holiday impetuousness that keeps you reaching into your pocket or purse for the green.

Tens of millions of people who *don't* know the odds of, or the strategies for, casino games come to Las Vegas every year, and some of them even win now and then. But let's face it: most people go home with a lighter wallet. Las Vegas casinos make a fortune by taking a big bite out of millions of bankrolls. With table games they keep on average 15% of the cash a player gives for chips; with the slot machines they hold around 25%.

So walk into the casino knowing that the house always has the edge. But who knows, you could beat the odds and walk away a winner. Spend a little time beforehand memorizing the game rules, studying casino etiquette, and taking one of the free gambling lessons offered at most casinos. Then you can join the tables with the all the aplomb of James Bond.

Casino Etiquette

Getting In and Around

Casinos can be confusing places for the first-time visitor. They tend to be large, open rooms full of people who seem to know exactly what they're doing, while you wander around lost. Cameras hung from the ceiling watch your movements, and all the security guards, pit bosses, and dealers seem to be doing the same. Worst of all, there are no signs, announcements, or tour guides to inform newcomers of the rules of behavior. So we'll do that right here.

All players must be at least 21 years of age with no exceptions. A pit boss or security guard is likely to ask to see your ID if you look underage. If you're playing a slot with a child by your side, a security guard will quickly appear (dispatched by casino surveillance) and ask you to leave. But you can walk through the casino with your youngster in tow; as long as you're on the move, you're OK. For families the off-strip casinos frequently provide free child care. *See* Children in Las Vegas *in the* Smart Travel Tips A to Z *section for more information on these and private baby-sitting services.*

Your personal electronic items are also frowned upon in the casino. No electronics, including cell phones, can be used while seated at a casino game. You'll have to step away from the table or machine to talk on the phone. The thick walls of most large casinos block cell phone reception anyhow so you'll have to walk outside to get a dial tone. In the sports book of the casino, pagers and cell phones cannot be used at all.

No photographs may be taken in most of the casinos: Management fears that players may feel uncomfortable if captured on film and will get up and leave. (The exceptions are the Four Queens, Excalibur, and Harrah's casinos, which do allow you to take pictures.)

Smokers on the other hand find casinos a welcome relief. Puff to your heart's content at your favorite slot machine while cigarette girls hustle by with extra smokes. Those who are annoyed by cigarette or cigar smoke will need to find a non-smoking table or slots area. The casinos' smoke permeates clothing quickly so don't count on rewearing too many outfits.

The security of your person and pocketbook shouldn't be forgotten in the bustle of the casino. While the casino tries to protect its patrons with omnipresent security cameras and guards, the crowds and distractions overwhelm their vigilance. You probably won't be mugged inside a casino, but theft or short-changing can easily happen.

Do not leave purses on a table or hanging off the back of a chair. Instead, keep the purse in your lap. Casino chips should not be left on the table under the dealer's protection while you take a quick bathroom break. Recount any chips and cash that casino personnel hand over to you immediately—once you leave the table or cage, you cannot get a mistake corrected. Finally, do not hesitate to request a security guard escort you to the casino parking lot late at night, especially in downtown Las Vegas.

Joining The Games

Always take a few moments to orient yourself when you first walk into the flashing lights and noise of a casino. Allow your senses to become accustomed to the surplus of stimuli. Almost all casinos offer craps, blackjack, slots, video poker, and roulette. The major casinos will, in addition, have live poker, sports betting, baccarat, keno, and an ever-growing list of table games. Stick to video poker, slots, and roulette if you're nervous about the arcane rules and want a relaxing visit.

Table games, especially blackjack and craps, offer the novice the greatest challenges. However, these games remain two of the most popular in Las Vegas. Free daily lessons at most Strip casinos will get the dice rolling for you at blackjack and craps. Call and check with the casino beforehand since the lesson schedule changes frequently. The beginner's course will let you belly up to the tables with confidence. Don't hesitate to ask any question you like at the table. If a dealer doesn't answer, or is rude, walk away to another table—or another casino.

At some of the smaller and less crowded gambling houses, dealers will take time to orient players to new games. If you're a newcomer to the tables, avoid the larger houses, especially at peak hours, because the personnel may be too busy to help you.

Before you sit down at a table, be sure to look at the little placard that announces the betting minimum and maximum. Most casinos offer a range of betting minimums, but the low minimum tables tend to be packed. For example, blackjack tables have minimums of $1 to $500 and maximums up to $10,000. Minimums in casinos on the Strip are generally higher than those of downtown casinos.

Consider also the timing of your casino visit. Las Vegas wakes up around lunchtime, then peaks between 11 PM and midnight. If you like your action rammin' and jammin', you won't mind playing during prime time. If you arrive at a busy hour, tables may be scarce at the minimums you desire. Weekends are also the busiest time of the week for Vegas as half of California drives in for a quick roll.

Comps and Tipping

Within a few minutes of joining any table, you'll be offered your first casino comp, or complimentary gift: "drinks, anyone?" The cocktail waitress will smilingly offer free alcohol and other liquids as long as you keep playing. Comps go way beyond free booze to include free rooms, shows, meals, gifts, limos, and airfares. It all depends on your rating, the casino's estimate of how much you bet and for how long.

The rating determines how much in comps you'll receive. Comps include stuffing your mailbox with outstanding coupons to entice you to return even if you only bet a little. Smaller casinos may even give you coupons just for walking onto their property.

To get on the comps gravy train, get a player's card, either from the pit boss or the player's club. Make sure that all of your gambling is rated, or recorded by the casino. Slot machines have small slots for the player's card, but at table games you'll have to make sure the pit boss receives your card. After about 30 minutes of play you can try to ask politely for a buffet comp, a relatively easy comp to earn. Perhaps he sniffs at your request—but then again you might have a free meal!

Tipping the dealers and cocktail waitresses is also a key element of casino etiquette. Dealers are paid minimum wage at the casinos, and they expect to be tipped when you are winning. It's neither mandatory nor necessary, however, it's only up to your own discretion. Some dealers will "suggest" a tip of 10% of your net win, but this is very generous on your part. Slipping a dealer or change person a chip is like any other tip: a small gratuity for services rendered. This small generosity usually relaxes the dealer, and thus the game, considerably. At most casinos, dealers pool their tips and then split them evenly. So be aware that no matter how much you toke a good dealer, he or she will receive only a percentage. Cocktail waitresses expect $1 for each drink brought to you.

How Not to Go Broke

You should decide before leaving on your vacation how much money you will spend on gambling. This is your gambling bankroll. Gambling newbies will be shocked at how quickly the bankroll disappears at the table. As a rule of thumb, a $1,000 bankroll for a weekend trip of gambling will let you bet $5 to $10 a hand at blackjack or play 25¢ slots. That's it if you hope to get in five hours of gambling. If you bet $25 a hand at blackjack with the $1,000 bankroll you will most likely run out of money within an hour. ATM or credit card cash withdrawals carry hefty surcharges and should be avoided at all times. A cash advance also leads to you gambling with money you don't have and its devastating consequences.

If you want to shrink the casino's edge over you, take the time to read up on the game strategy in Chapter 10. Then, when you have some idea of the basics, attend the free gambling lessons provided at most major casinos. Even if you think you know the rules, these lessons will give you an opportunity to play the game at an actual session and learn the etiquette using practice chips instead of your own cash. Call ahead and get the exact schedule of these free lessons. Most gift shops will also sell you a small plastic card of a rough strategy for the various games. You can have one in hand as you play your game of choice.

THE CASINOS

Our review begins with casinos on the Strip, or Las Vegas Boulevard, then continues to the growing ranks of major off-Strip and "locals" casinos (those frequented by area residents). After that we focus on the downtown casinos on and near Fremont Street, then the casinos on the "Boulder Strip" and the "Rancho Strip." Finally, we cover the farthest-out casinos in the fast-growing suburb of Henderson. The listings in each area are arranged in alphabetical order. These descriptions are intended to help you find the casinos that will most appeal to you. If you'd like to save time by sleeping where you gamble, Chapter 5 has

LAS VEGAS LINGO

BEFORE YOU START GAMBLING, you'll want to learn some key words in the local language.

Bankroll. The amount of cash an individual has to gamble with.

Black chip. $100 casino chip, usually black.

Buy-in. The amount of cash with which a player enters a game.

Cage. The casino cashier station where you can exchange your chips for cash.

Check. Another name for a casino chip.

Comp. A gift from the casino of a complimentary drink, room, dinner, or show; a freebie.

Eye. The overhead video surveillance system and its human monitors in a casino. All videotapes are kept for seven days in Nevada.

Full-pay video poker. A video poker game that, if you know perfect strategy, gives you an edge over the casino. Perfect video poker strategy is very difficult to memorize and the casino's counting on player errors.

Green chip. $25 casino chip, usually green.

Grind joint. A gambling house that promotes low table minimums and slot denominations. You won't find too many high rollers at one.

High roller. A casino customer who plays with a bankroll of $5,000 or more. Some grind joints consider a $1,000 bankroll to be high-roller action; some premium joints require a $10,000 bankroll.

Hold. The house profit from all the wagers; what the casino wins.

Live poker. Traditional poker games such as seven-card stud that are played against other individuals and not the casino.

Low roller. A typical tourist making 25¢ slot-machine bets or $1 and $2 table-game bets.

Marker. A casino IOU. Players sign markers and get chips at the tables; they then pay off the markers with chips or cash.

Pit. A group of tables forming a closed circle on the casino floor. The pit bosses and dealers stand in the middle and serve the customers who sit on the outside. Visitors can't walk into the middle of the pit.

Pit boss. The person who supervises the action on the gaming tables. The pit boss's domain, the pit, is an area surrounded by tables that is off-limits to the general public.

Player's card. A card with a magnetic stripe on it used to track a gambler's activities in a casino. A player's card makes it easy for the casino to rate you and therefore give you comps.

Rating. Tracking a gambler's average bet, length of time played, and net loss. Getting rated helps you get comps.

RFB. The cream of comps—room, food, and beverage, courtesy of the casino. All you have to do is play (depending on the casino) $75–$250 a hand for four hours a day.

Red Chip. $5 casino chip, usually red.

Shill. A person employed by the casino to sit at the tables and play games during the less busy hours—with the casino's money. Shills are only used in live poker games.

Sports Book. The casino area for sports betting. Cell phones and pagers are prohibited in sports book.

Sweating the money. Pit boss nervousness and anger toward a winning player.

Table Games. All games of chance such as blackjack and craps played against the casino with the help of a dealer.

Toke. A tip (short for token, or token of your esteem). This may be the word you'll hear most often; many of the folks you encounter will be expecting a toke.

details on the hotels in which most of these casinos are found. All the casinos have restaurants and most have all-you-can-eat buffets so you can also eat where you sleep and gamble.

The Strip

The Strip casinos, all along Las Vegas Boulevard, are packed in so tight you'll see nothing driving by but one frenetic neon sign on top of another. Strip casinos run the gamut in size and style, from the overwhelming spectacle of the MGM Grand to the small pit at Slots-A-Fun, and from low-roller heaven at Circus Circus to high-roller tension at Bellagio. In general Strip casinos are big and ritzy, with high playing minimums and few comps to give to visitors. Keep in mind, though, that Las Vegas casinos, whether premium or shabby, welcome all comers, no matter what they're wearing. When it comes right down to it, the casinos really care about only one aspect of your attire: that it include a wallet or purse from which you can easily remove your cash.

Aladdin Resort and Casino. With a lavish *Arabian Nights* theme, the Aladdin's huge gaming floor draws a young and hip crowd. From its many balconies the Aladdin wows 'em with the many flashing jewels pulsing in rhythm to the pop music. The casino bars are adorned with figures from Scheherazade's tales: atop the Lamp Bar is a 36-ft-long Aladdin's lamp, and the Roc Bar is guarded by the giant bird from Sinbad the Sailor. The cocktail servers' costumes are straight out of the Sultan's harem. Aladdin's casino includes a high-roller salon operated by London Clubs International, a British luxury casino company. On the second floor, the understated elegance of the London Club attracts older gamblers. Parking at the Aladdin involves a wearying walk through the shopping mall, so use the valets if possible. ⊠ *3667 Las Vegas Blvd. S Center Strip,* ☎ *702/785–5555 or 877/333–9474.*

Bally's Las Vegas. Bally's owns a huge chunk of one of the most popular intersections in the world—it's across the street from the Flamingo, Caesars Palace, and the Bellagio—and it accommodates a perpetually large convention crowd of older players. Yet the casino is so roomy that when the crowds become at all oppressive, you can almost always find a more open part of the floor. Bally's tends to attract high rollers, so its table minimums are rarely less than $5. The comp card for Bally's is good at its flashier sister property Paris. You can earn comps at one property and use them at the other. There's a monorail between Bally's and MGM to get you quickly down the Strip. If you're trying to park at Bally's use the Paris garage for a one-minute walk to the casino. ⊠ *3645 Las Vegas Blvd. S, Center Strip,* ☎ *800/634–3434.*

Barbary Coast Hotel and Casino. The Barbary Coast casino is modeled after late 19th-century San Francisco saloons, with Victorian chandeliers and lamps, tasteful stained-glass signs (including the largest stained-glass mural in the world), and cocktail waitresses who wear garters on their thighs. The Coast is known as a "sweat shop" among blackjack and craps players, meaning the bosses take it personally when you win, but casino table minimums are frequently lower than its larger neighbors. The video poker is playable (the pay schedules are not prohibitive) and the slot club is pretty good, with decent, if not great, cash back and benefits. This joint is usually fairly crowded, though not on the same scale as its neighbors—Bally's, the Flamingo, and Caesars. ⊠ *3595 Las Vegas Blvd. S, Center Strip,* ☎ *888/227–2279.*

★ **Bellagio Las Vegas.** Bellagio is the most opulent and expensive casino ever built anywhere on Earth. It's roomy, luxurious, and filled with a big money international elite surrounded by gawking tourists. Under

46

Las Vegas Strip Casinos

its hushed orange canopies you can easily spot a high-roller betting $5,000 a hand as if it were pennies. Yet 5¢ slots are tucked in the back corners somewhere for low rollers and excellent blackjack games are offered for serious players. The outstanding and large live poker room sees some serious piles of chips in the pot, but you're better off playing video poker almost anywhere else. The race and sports book is super high-tech; each seductive leather seat is equipped with its own TV monitor. With good games and posh surroundings, the Bellagio scoffs at even middle-market comp seekers. Parents take note: those under 18 are unwelcome everywhere within Bellagio, but especially in the casino. There's a free monorail to take the footsore to the Monte Carlo. ⊠ *3600 Las Vegas Blvd. S, Center Strip,* ☎ *702/693–7111.*

Caesars Palace. Caesars is the never-ending casino, two sprawling wings in a gentle horseshoe shape that extends from one end of the huge property to the other. Wear your walking shoes and prepare to get lost in this Roman empire which was not designed for the handicapped with its various staircases. The old wing—low ceiling, high stakes—houses *serious* older gamblers, people who are probably comped in Caesars's exclusive suites and are eligible for unlimited room service, too. The newer Olympic Casino wing, with its high ceiling, soaring marble columns, graceful rooftop arches, and lower limits, embraces the middle market with 5¢ slots. The huge, plush race and sports book with its megadisplay must be seen to be believed. You can even get your picture taken with Caesar, Cleopatra, and the Centurion Guard. However, the Emperor does not generously dole out comps to the small-time gambler. ⊠ *3570 Las Vegas Blvd. S, Center Strip,* ☎ *877/427–7243.*

Circus Circus. Only in Las Vegas would you find a 125-ft neon sign of a clown sucking a lollipop next to a statue of a nude dancer. And only in Las Vegas could you find Circus Circus, the tent-shape pink casino with live circus acts performing over the gamblers' heads. The aging Circus Circus is low-roller and poor service central, with nickel slots galore. The two must-see attractions here are the slot carousel—20 slots sit on a revolving platform, and players ride in circles as they operate the machines—and the merry-go-round bar, which sits atop the carousel on the midway, with actual carousel horses. Those under-21 can whoop it up in a glittering arcade of carnival games and circus acts. As part of the Mandalay Resort Group, your Circus Circus comp card is good at all of its sister properties in Las Vegas. ⊠ *2880 Las Vegas Blvd. S, North Strip,* ☎ *877/224–7287.*

Excalibur Hotel and Casino. This giant medieval-theme casino is in one continuous room, and the ringing of the Merlin slot machines can become overpowering at times. At first glance it's a Camelot for low-rollers with $3 blackjack tables and plenty of 5¢ slot machines, but the lousy rules beef up the house's edge way above its Strip rivals. The aging Excalibur is known for a readily available funbook with some good coupons, and there's usually a free-pull promotion going on. A good perch to watch the action is The King's Pavilion, a beautiful circular bar in the middle of the casino. As part of the Mandalay Resort Group, your Excalibur comp card is good at all of its sister properties in Las Vegas. There's also a free monorail between this casino and Mandalay Bay and Luxor. ⊠ *3850 Las Vegas Blvd. S, South Strip,* ☎ *800/937–7777.*

Flamingo Las Vegas. History lovers: this is where modern Las Vegas began, when Bugsy Siegel imported Miami luxury to the desert. Bugsy, of course, wasn't able to hang around long enough to experience the impact of his vision, but his Fabulous Flamingo has had one hell of a run. Unlike many strip casinos, it's a quick stroll from the sidewalk into the air-conditioned tropical pink and aqua casino. Good black-jack games can be found here with reasonable minimums for the moderate stakes gambler. The Irish-theme casino annex next door—the two-story **O'Sheas Casino**—is the place for low rollers, low-limit poker players, and small-time racing and sports bettors. ⌧ *3555 Las Vegas Blvd. S, Center Strip,* ☏ *800/732–2111.*

Harrah's Las Vegas Casino & Hotel. Carnival music from outside of the Mardi Gras–theme Harrah's will get your heart pumping from far down the sidewalk. The slots are mere feet from the sidewalk so step inside for a quick look while you're strolling by. Dealers tend to be friendly in this festive purple, green, and gold casino. Harrah's Total Gold is the only nationwide player's club in the industry: you can play at any of Harrah's two-dozen casinos around the United States using a single account number. Sign up for their comp program for generous coupons from the chain. ⌧ *3475 Las Vegas Blvd. S, Center Strip,* ☏ *800/634–6765.*

Imperial Palace Hotel and Casino. A blue pagoda-style building with an Asian theme, this house of dragons does a booming business with tour groups. Plan on spending a few minutes finding your way around (the fact that there are few signs adds to the sport). However this aging dowager of the Strip generously doles out the comps, so try for a free buffet, but don't expect gourmet food. Table minimums entice low rollers but the rules generally hurt the player. Auto buffs should not miss the casino's classic car museum. ⌧ *3535 Las Vegas Blvd. S, Center Strip,* ☏ *800/634–6441.*

Luxor Resort & Casino. This magnificent bronze-tint pyramid, owned by Mandalay Resort Group, is arguably the most unusual casino in the world, inside and out. Luxor's casino is not only huge, it's also round, so it will take some time to get your bearings. (Orient yourself by looking for periphery landmarks such as the coffee shop, sports book, and lounge.) Comps are tough to come by but, as a Mandalay Resort Group property, Luxor easily transfers your points to its sister properties. You'll find surprisingly fresh air and a muted noise level as a solid middle class and black-clad chic crowd gawk at this eighth wonder of the world. Cool your heels on the free tram to Mandalay Bay and Excalibur. ⌧ *3900 Las Vegas Blvd. S, South Strip,* ☏ *888/777–0188.*

★ **Mandalay Bay Resort & Casino.** Pagodas and gardens rise out of the vast floors of this Asian-theme newcomer to the ranks of luxury high-roller casinos. Drool at the hordes of fabulous beautiful people and millionaires crowding the tables of this very hip casino. Low rollers will find the table limits of these excellent games to be a bit rich for their blood and the comps even tougher to earn. The comp program links Mandalay Bay with its sister properties around Las Vegas, so play here and then try for freebies at other casinos. While its wide-open spaces could terrify an agoraphobe, Mandalay Bay's pleasant walkways make wheelchair navigation a breeze. For a break from the action, sit amid the virtual vegetation, rock waterfalls, and lily pond of the Coral Reef Lounge, one of the largest lounges in town. A free tram connects the property to Luxor and Excalibur. ⌧ *3950 Las Vegas Blvd. S, South Strip,* ☏ *877/632–7000.*

MGM Grand Hotel and Casino. The two Art Deco lions guarding the front door give away the casino's decorating motif: lions and 1920s movie theaters; there's even a lion habitat on the casino's perimeter. The biggest of the Las Vegas casinos, the MGM has 3,500 slot machines and 165 table games with high minimums and tough comp requirements for its crowd of older high-rollers. The MGM offers some of the best games for players, though, in its many pleasant casinos whose only difference seems to be a change of ceiling color. Plan on spending at least an hour going from one end of the casino to the other and back again. The hike from the parking lot to the casino is similarly strenuous. However, those in a wheelchair will appreciate the spacious isles and well-spaced slot machines. Search the back of the MGM for the free monorail to Bally's. ✉ *3799 Las Vegas Blvd. S, South Strip,* ☎ *800/929–1111.*

★ **Mirage Hotel and Casino.** The ultimate carpet joint, the Mirage has high minimums (such as $500 slots and a plush private pit where the minimum bet is $1,000), ionospheric maximums, intense security, and the most professionally trained staff in the casino business. The decor is rain-forest rustic: pits are distinguished by separate thatch roofs. There's even a wonderfully lush tropical garden in the middle of the casino to clean your lungs with fresh air. And don't miss the display of the white tigers of Siegfried and Roy. Blackjack at the Mirage has some of the best rules of of any Strip casino, while single-zero roulette offers the gambler a strong game. The poker room has a stellar reputation for good action, low and high. If your feet are tired there's a complimentary slow-moving tram to Treasure Island next door. ✉ *3400 Las Vegas Blvd. S, Center Strip,* ☎ *800/627–6667.*

Monte Carlo Resort and Casino. Modeled after the opulent Place du Casino in Monaco, the Las Vegas version of Monte Carlo replicates its sophistication and opulence with a bright and graciously laid-out casino. This is the kind of place where you'll feel under dressed if you're not in a tuxedo or evening gown (don't worry though, nobody else will be either). The casino is unpretentious and quietly serves a mainly middle-aged crowd of players. The single-zero roulette wheels are a nice plus here. As a member of Mandalay Resorts Group your comp points are transferrable between sister properties. A free monorail hidden in the back of the casino can quickly whisk you several blocks to the Bellagio. ✉ *3770 Las Vegas Blvd. S, South Strip,* ☎ *800/311–8999.*

New Frontier Hotel and Gambling Hall. Feel right at home in sweatpants and sneakers at this laid-back, sporty casino. It's a Western-style resort for low-rollers; the $3 and $5 tables are always crowded with a youngish clientele. With 10x craps odds and double-deck blackjack cutting the house advantage way down, a beginning player can easily earn comps from this generous casino. The bingo room, walled off from the casino with glass, is the only one on the Strip. Beginning live poker lessons are given every day but Sunday. ✉ *3120 Las Vegas Blvd. S, North Strip,* ☎ *800/634–6966.*

New York–New York Hotel and Casino. The Big Apple theme runs rampant through this casino both outside and in. The casino, like Manhattan itself, is crowded and cramped. The main casino pit has a vague Broadway feel with its noise, overwhelming neon signs, and confusing layout. The tables and video poker have moderate minimums, but the rules are slightly less inviting than a stick-up on the subway. But try and find the roller coaster ride in the back of the casino for an unforgettable upside-down view of the Strip. ✉ *3790 Las Vegas Blvd. S, South Strip,* ☎ *702/740–6969.*

★ **Paris Las Vegas.** The casino is all decked out in Gallic regalia, including three massive legs of the 50-story Eiffel Tower replica jutting through the roof and resting on the floor. Game rules are poor for the player, minimums high, and comps tough to get, but the main casino floor feels just like Paris in springtime under the breezy twilit sky. The attention to French detail, down to fancy floral wash basins in the Provençal-style bathrooms, adds up to a charming yet classy casino. The Paris player's club is the same as Bally's, so you can earn comps to either property. There's even a cobblestone walkway between the properties with some delicious French pastries and a mime on the loose. And as all the dealers say, bon chance at this French beauty of a casino. ✉ *3655 Las Vegas Blvd. S, Center Strip,* ☎ *800/634–6753.*

Riviera Hotel and Casino. This vaguely French-theme casino has a big race and sports book, two keno parlors, a convenient fast-food court, nearly 90 table games, betting minimums that start at $5, and more than 1,500 slot and video-poker machines. Comps are extremely easy to come by at this fading flower of the strip. Supposedly some full-pay video poker lurks in the far corners of the casino. The latest addition to the Riv's casino inventory is Nickel Town, which has low-roller gaming machines, the cheapest snack-bar food on the Strip, and 50¢ draft beers. ✉ *2901 Las Vegas Blvd. S, North Strip,* ☎ *800/634–6753.*

Sahara Hotel and Casino. This middle-market casino has a clean and unobtrusive Arabian theme. Most minimums are in the middle range, except for the blackjack tables—the Sahara is the only joint left in town with primarily $1 tables. Full-pay video poker and very generous slot payouts make this casino a good destination for the gambler minimizing the house edge. The friendly player's club and frequent gambling promotions enhance its popularity. ✉ *2535 Las Vegas Blvd. S, North Strip,* ☎ *702/737–2111.*

Slots-A-Fun. As you leave Circus Circus, you'll be handed a sheet of coupons for free popcorn, 50¢ hot dogs, 99¢ shrimp cocktails, free pulls of a slot machine, and a free gift (usually a key chain). Redeem them at this noisy, smoky casino next door, with lots of slots and $1 and $2 blackjack tables. ✉ *2880 Las Vegas Blvd. S, North Strip,* ☎ *702/734–0410.*

Stardust Hotel and Casino. The Stardust has one of the best neon facades on the Strip, but the casino, which dates back to the 1950s and has been expanded umpteen times, retains the dim ambience of an old-time sawdust joint. Still, because of its size and sprawling layout, the Stardust never feels overly crowded or claustrophobic. It's a good place to play $2 craps, $5 blackjack, and low-limit poker. The slot club offers excellent perks (especially constant free-room offers). The sports book is nationally famous for the "Stardust line," which is usually the first odds posted for upcoming games; for that reason, radio sports talk shows emanate from the Stardust each day. ✉ *3000 Las Vegas Blvd. S, North Strip,* ☎ *800/634–6757.*

Stratosphere Hotel Tower and Casino. The Stratosphere's off-the-beaten-track location forces the casino managers to offer often noticeably better odds at the games. Full-pay video poker, 100x odds at the crap tables, and a single-zero roulette wheel or two give the gambler a good shot at breaking even. The slot club offers frequent promotions, including comps to meals at the top of the tower with its unparalleled view. Parking at the Stratosphere is easy and unsnarled by heavy traffic. Walking here from other casinos will wear out your feet, however. ✉ *2000 Las Vegas Blvd. S, North Strip,* ☎ *800/998–6937.*

Treasure Island Las Vegas. Pirates and players ahoy, head to Treasure Island for first-class service in a more laid-back atmosphere than its bigger sibling the Mirage. TI goes heavy on the juvenile pirate motif, with treasure chests, bone chandeliers, and skull-and-crossbones door handles festooning the joint. The seven-minute pyrotechnic pirate show in Buccaneer Bay, which fronts the Strip, is one of the best free shows in town. However, the crowds—ferocious any time of the night and day—are especially troublesome when one of the six pirate performances ends. At those times the population of the casino reaches critical mass, and it's best to try and sip on a comped drink until the throngs disperse. The table limits are high but expect to earn comps much faster than at the very similar Mirage and Bellagio. A free tram can take you next door to the Mirage. ✉ *3300 Las Vegas Blvd. S, Center Strip,* ☎ *800/944–7444.*

Tropicana Resort and Casino. The Tropicana's background is one of the lushest in town, having had more than 40 years to fill in. Its luxuriant 5-acre water park has swim-up blackjack: yes, you can actually sit in the pool and play 21. Stuff some cash in your swimsuit pocket and when you reach the table, put it into the Trop's money dryer. If you wind up blowing your soggy bankroll, just return to your breaststroke. Indoors, the casino continues the tropical theme, with palms, parrots, and Polynesiana. An exquisite stained-glass dome extends the length of the main pit but the casino stuffs too many slot machines into its beautiful atrium. However cardsharps may still want to play here since the blackjack rules shrink the house edge greatly. The casino has excellent perks for points accumulated by members of its players club, and the Casino Hall of Fame displays the largest collection of Nevada casino memorabilia in existence. ✉ *3801 Las Vegas Blvd. S, South Strip,* ☎ *800/634–4000.*

Venetian Resort-Hotel-Casino. Walking from the hotel lobby into the casino is one of the great experiences in Las Vegas: overhead, reproductions of famous frescoes, highlighted by 24-karat-gold frames, adorn the ceiling; underfoot, the geometric design of the flat-marble floor provides an M. C. Escher-like optical illusion of climbing stairs. But the pretty pink-and-gold icing of the Venetian is the only plus a gambler will find. Don't look for an Italian hospitality with comps—the Venetian can be very tight. The table-game minimums tend to be high and with very poor rules for the player. The open spaces of this lush casino leave you feeling too exposed to this Venetian duplicate as you scan the thin crowds of hopeful hipsters and high-rollers. At least the player's club employs an ultra-high-tech tracking system that enables you to comp yourself using your slot club points at any machine in the casino. ✉ *3355 Las Vegas Blvd. S, Center Strip,* ☎ *702/733–5000.*

Westward Ho Motel and Casino. The Westward has something few Strip casinos can offer: parking close to the casino. It also has plenty of low-limit blackjack tables, and the progressive video poker machines are among the best on the Strip. Pit bosses practically throw the buffet comps at players. The casino snack bar has good cheap sandwiches and huge servings of strawberry shortcake if you'd rather pay. ✉ *2900 Las Vegas Blvd. S, North Strip,* ☎ *800/634–6803.*

Beyond the Strip

Arizona Charlie's Hotel and Casino West. Like most casinos that cater to area residents, Charlie's tries to attract players by offering the best slot club benefits and the best casino coupons that it can—without giving away the store. The video poker provides the best schedules available, and the slot club is so straightforward that a printed flyer indicates the number of points that anything in the joint costs. Service seems indifferent although the table games have low minimums and average rules. Promotions are continuous; there are three or four good ones almost every day. The buffet is the cheapest in town (and not bad to boot); play on a double-points day for an hour or so, and you'll earn enough points to get it comped. ⊠ *740 S. Decatur Blvd., West Side; take W. Charleston from the corner of Charleston and Las Vegas Blvd. about 2 mi, then go right on Decatur Blvd. for ½ mi; the casino is on the left.* ☎ *800/342–2695.*

Gold Coast Hotel and Casino. Whenever you're at the airport and you see people losing money in the slots, think of the Gold Coast: this casino west of the Strip and west of I–15 was built on airport slot losses. Popular with local gamblers, the Gold Coast shows up regularly in the *Las Vegas Review-Journal*'s reader polls as having some of the loosest slots in town, as well as the best slot club. It also offers a poker room, a bingo parlor, a race and sports book, a 72-lane bowling center, and a movie theater. Like Palace Station, the Gold Coast has low minimums, a friendly atmosphere, and sizable local crowds at times. ⊠ *4000 W. Flamingo Rd., West Side,* ☎ *888/402–6278.*

Hard Rock Hotel and Casino. Owner Peter Morton made his fortune on a trendy international chain of Hard Rock Cafes (and T-shirts advertising the same), with its rock-and-roll memorabilia and cutting-edge concerts. Slots have guitar-neck handles, blackjack layouts are customized with rock-related art, crap tables are adorned with Grateful Dead lyrics, and rock music pervades the place. It's terribly hip with those under 35—actor Ben Affleck and other young Hollywood stars drop their cash at these tables. There's a fun pickup bar in the middle that's designed for eyeballing the miniskirts walking by. But looking is a lot more fun than playing here. The dealers at these very poor games are young, good looking, and with a hyperattitude whose chief concern is carding those under 30. The Hard Rock also has a pool with one of Las Vegas's two swim-up blackjack tables. ⊠ *4455 Paradise Rd., Paradise Road,* ☎ *800/675–3267.*

★ **JW Marriott Las Vegas Casino Resort.** This luxurious, ultra-upscale resort, formerly the Regent Las Vegas, attracts golfers, spa aficionados, and older visitors who want an "alternative" to Las Vegas. The casino is compact but not cluttered. A gorgeous back-lit apricot-color dome decorated with a palm-tree design rises above the pit. Most minimums start at $5 with the plush chairs of outstanding comfort. The roulette wheels are single zero. The sports book is small but elegant, with comfortable couches and picture windows overlooking the lush grounds. The slot club gives you points for anything you buy on the property (including a buffet and a newspaper). This is an excellent place to stop on your way to or from Red Rock Canyon. ⊠ *221 N. Rampart Blvd., Summerlin,* ☎ *877/869–8777.*

Las Vegas Hilton. Under a chandelier the size of an 18-wheeler, the Hilton's main pit runs down the middle of this conservatively attired casino. The sports "super book" is one of Las Vegas's largest and most elegant (with 46 video screens). Because the Hilton is next door to the Las Vegas Convention Center, many delegates stay here, and they pack the casino at all hours along with some older high rollers. Video poker fans can find excellent games with outstanding cash paybacks. However, comps are tough to come by at this casino. Hilton also has a smaller SpaceQuest Casino, which fronts the Star Trek: The Experience attraction; it's the most highly themed and most high-tech casino in town and has a far-out space bar. ⊠ *3000 Paradise Rd., Paradise Road,* ☎ *800/732–7117.*

Orleans Hotel and Casino. Orleans is a big barn of a casino designed for the locals market, with a roomy pit under a high ceiling, scads of full-pay video-poker machines, five comfortable bars (and revealing cocktail-waitress uniforms), and hot lounge entertainment. Lots of locals like to leave their children at the Kid's Tyme child-care center, the 70-lane bowling alley, the 12-theater multiplex, or the big arcade and take advantage of the frequent double- and triple-points slot club promotions, cash drawings, and car giveaways. If you happen to show up here on the night of a particularly lucrative promotion, you might have to park at the far edge of one of the sizable parking lots. ⊠ *4500 W. Tropicana Ave., West Side,* ☎ *800/675–3267.*

★ **Palace Station Hotel and Casino.** Palace Station looks and feels like a railroad station, with Pullman cars for restaurants and a depot for the lobby. For those craving Pai Gow or other Asian games Palace Station has an impressive number of tablesfrom which to pick. The knowledgeable gambler will be interested in 10x odds and good blackjack rules. This is a friendly casino with great food deals whose only fault is that it's so popular with locals that it can become too crowded for comfort. One way around this is to be a member of the Boarding Pass slot club; if you have enough slot-club points, you can get a comp to the restaurants, which lets you march to the head of any waiting list for a table. Boarding Pass members can gamble and redeem their slot-club points at any of the other Station casinos in town. ⊠ *2411 W. Sahara Ave., West Side,* ☎ *800/634–3101.*

The Palms. Striated shadows across the ceiling bring to mind palm fronts in this contempo-California style casino for both locals and hip visitors. While a bit bland in its design, the born-in-2001 Palms is also clean and well-ventilated with slot sections sprinkled comfortably along its length. If you're feeling lucky, get the fortune teller to read your tarot cards and pick a number for you. Palms does take big bets but the game rules are average. A complimentary shuttle bus whisks you to Caesar's Palace on the Strip. ⊠ *4321 W. Flamingo Rd., West Side,* ☎ *866/725–6773.*

★ **Rio All-Suite Hotel and Casino.** Rio Rita symbolizes the Brazilian theme of this popular off-Strip hotel, known for its rainbow neon sign, vibrant Latin character, and 14 restaurants. The Rio now presents " Masquerade Show in the Sky," a free, 12-minute spectacular several times a day; call ahead for the exact schedule. Outrageous Mardi Gras floats crammed with costumed humanity parade above the blackjack and slot players, while dozens of specialty performers sing, dance, mime, and stilt-walk below. You have to see it to believe it. For players Rio tucks away a wide variety of games and slots along its sprawling and confusing length. The player's club at Rio is part of the Harrah's Total Awards Program which enable you to earn Rio comps at Harrah's locations around the country. Remembering where you parked the car may be the biggest challenge of the evening at this lively and friendly casino. ⊠ *3700 W. Flamingo Rd., West Side,* ☎ *800/752–9746.*

Downtown

Fremont Street is the place to come for low table minimums, food bargains, a motley street life, as well as the brightest and most colorful concentration of neon lights in the world. The 100-ft-high awning of the Fremont Street Experience that encloses Glitter Gulch (the core four blocks between Main and 4th streets on Fremont Street) has made a beautiful pedestrian mall of the main street downtown, unifying all the hotels under one roof, so to speak, and providing spectacular entertainment in the form of a noisy 2-million-bulb light show several times an evening. The downtown casinos have enough 25¢ craps, 50¢ roulette, $2–$3 blackjack, and even 1¢ video poker to accommodate Las Vegas's hordes of beginning and low-stakes players, tinhorns, slummers, and, of course, locals. Two signs that downtown will not entirely abandon its Old West motif, which prevailed from Las Vegas's founding in 1905 through the early 1960s, are the pair of neon cowpokes, Vegas Vic and Vegas Vicky, who still preside over Glitter Gulch. Enjoy walking through the street musicians and artists that cram the pedestrian mall, but after dark exercise great care on the sidewalks and parking lots around the downtown area.

★ **Binion's Horseshoe Hotel and Casino.** The Horseshoe is where serious gamblers come to play; the 21 tables are always packed and a single pit holds eight craps tables, all crowded. Behind the hotel, by the parking garage, is a 15-ft statue of Horseshoe founder Benny Binion, wearing a Stetson and sitting on a horse. A former bootlegger, Binion came to Vegas from Texas in the 1940s, set up a respectable shop (though he served time on a tax-evasion charge in the 1950s), and built a joint boasting the highest table limits in the world at that time. No entertainment, no fancy hotel rooms—just good cheap food and gambling. The Horseshoe has seen better days, but its surly dealers still offer one of the best downtown blackjack games: single deck blackjack with good rules. People who have difficulty with tobacco fumes might want to select other casinos, however. This is the home of the annual World Series of Poker in April and May; the final event has a $10,000 buy-in and a $1-million first prize. ⊠ *128 E. Fremont St., Downtown,* ☎ *800/937–6537.*

California Hotel and Casino. Though the name is California, the motif is Hawaiian: all the dealers wear Hawaiian shirts, the carpet has tropical flowers, the snack bars serve Hawaiian dishes, and many of the customers are in fact islanders. Planeloads of Hawaiian tourists on package tours stay at the hotel and enjoy the casual and uncrowded casino, which offers lots of $3 tables and 5¢ slots. The tourists have made a good choice too, since the California serves up good slots, video poker, and blackjack games. ⊠ *12 E. Ogden Ave., Downtown,* ☎ *800/634–6255.*

Fitzgeralds Hotel and Casino. If you don't trust the luck of the Irish, pick up the Fitzgeralds funbook which always includes a good free souvenir and $3–$4 worth of gambling coupons. It also has one of the most high-tech slot clubs anywhere: you can use your club card to pay for rooms and meals and check your point balance on-line. Fitzgeralds makes up for its generosity though with lousy rules on its table games. There's an outdoor balcony right off the second-floor casino, with lounge chairs and tables, a great place for watching the street life below and the Fremont Street Experience above. ⊠ *301 E. Fremont St., Downtown,* ☎ *800/634–6045.*

Four Queens Hotel and Casino. You'll know you've found this casino when you walk along Fremont Street and come upon four painted playing cards in the pavement—four queens, in fact. This is a typical downtown casino, with low minimums, good slot-club benefits, and a cheap coffee shop. Check out the single deck blackjack here to shave the house edge to its lowest level. The Four Queens is also known for frequent free-money promotions: walk in, take a free pull on a slot machine, and get a coupon for two free dollar-slot tokens, or some variation thereof. ⊠ *202 E. Fremont St., Downtown,* ☎ *800/634–6045.*

Fremont Hotel and Casino. In the heart of Glitter Gulch and adding immeasurably to the light show with its block-long neon facade, the Fremont has been a popular landmark since it opened in 1956. The hotel has one of the oldest and most respected race and sports books, which attracts a lot of gamblers, especially during football season. The Fremont also has a keno progressive that often rises into positive territory—rare for keno. Table game rules are OK while the comp program is pretty generous. ✉ *200 E. Fremont St., Downtown,* ☎ *800/ 634–6182.*

Golden Gate Hotel and Casino. The first structure to house Las Vegas's most historic hotel was built in 1906 (it was the first lodging place in Nevada to be built out of concrete). Opened as the Hotel Nevada, it was sold to a group of San Francisco investors in 1955; the famous shrimp cocktail, which started a Vegas tradition, dates from then. The Golden Gate's casino is typical for downtown: cramped, a bit derelict around the edges, and crowded with low rollers playing $3–$5 black-jack at fairly relaxed tables. One unusual feature is the piano player who serenades the deli diners; the sound of tinkling ivories wafts into the pit, making it the only place in town where you can shoot craps to live Scott Joplin or George Gershwin. ✉ *1 Fremont St., Downtown,* ☎ *800/426–1906.*

★ **Golden Nugget Hotel and Casino.** This is the only downtown casino that can truly be called elegant. Don't worry, though, there's still plenty of downtown gaudiness, including gold-plated elevators, pay phones, and slot machines—and the world's largest gold nugget. The games, however, cater to its wealthier and older gamblers : $5 black-jack tables are few and far between, and dollar slots are plentiful. But all is not lost for those with little to lose. Recently, the slot club began recognizing nickel and quarter players, so low rollers can now partake in the good comps here. The relaxed politeness of the entire staff adds to the coziness, although even the President doesn't have this many se-curity guards patrolling his home. One anomaly in the high roller casino is the race and sports book, which is little more than a tiny lounge. ✉ *129 E. Fremont St., Downtown,* ☎ *800/634–3403.*

Jackie Gaughan's El Cortez Hotel. The oldest standing casino in Las Vegas, the Cortez opened for business on Fremont Street in 1941, when cowboys still rode horses up and down the street. The smelly old wing seems little changed from 60 years ago with locals and des-perados cramming the tables. The El Cortez has the best blackjack games in town; where else can you find single-deck blackjack with $3 mini-mums shrinking the house edge to nothing? There is no player's club, however. The food in both the coffee shop (which serves Las Vegas's last 24-hr $1 bacon-and-eggs breakfast) and Roberta's fine-dining room is as inexpensive as the portions are large. However, be careful walking to the generous El Cortez from Fremont Street after dark. ✉ *600 E. Fremont St., Downtown,* ☎ *800/634–6703.*

Jackie Gaughan's Gold Spike Hotel and Casino. This small and odor-ous gambling hall, one block north of Fremont Street, is the sort of place you'd imagine might have lurked in a room behind a cigar or candy store in the old days. The blackjack table limits are unusually low—$1 and $2 mostly, with a $5 here and there. The Spike offers 5¢ video keno and poker machines, live 40¢ keno, and 10¢ roulette. But the casino's unique feature, in terms of both the game and the gamers, is the more than 60 1¢ slot machines, jammed day and night with the hard-core, the desperate, the addicted—in short, the downtown fringe. For a fistful of penny rolls you can join Las Vegas's looniest subcul-ture. ✉ *400 E. Ogden Ave., Downtown,* ☎ *800/634–6703.*

Jackie Gaughan's Plaza Hotel and Casino. Back in the 1920s, when cowboys rode their horses on Fremont Street and miners came to town to buy grub, the corner of Main and Fremont streets was anchored by the railroad depot. It still is, but today that station has a 1,000-room hotel and giant casino around it. The full-hearted Elvis imitation from the nearby stage will keep you chuckling as you play in this smoky low-roller casino. You'll also find low-minimum ($2) table games, some of the best nickel video poker machines in Las Vegas, and a bank of eight 1¢ slots where the jackpots can reach $30,000. ⊠ *1 Main St., Downtown,* ☎ *800/634–6575.*

Lady Luck Casino and Hotel. The Lady Luck, at 3rd and Ogden streets across from the Gold Spike, is a bit off the beaten track, but folks are drawn here by good $1 video-poker machines: 9/6 with a 4,700-coin royal jackpot. Many professional blackjack tournament players come to the Lady's frequent tournaments—with $25 entry fees and $500 first prizes—to hone their skills. The casino is lined with big picture windows, making it the lightest and airiest downtown. Good games, amiable staff, and easy comps make the Lady Luck a low-roller favorite. The casino funbook is famous for its gambling coupons and 75¢ ft-long-frankfurter coupon. ⊠ *206 N. 3rd St., Downtown,* ☎ *800/523–9582.*

Las Vegas Club Hotel and Casino. This casino has been around since day one and has been owned for nearly 50 years by downtown juicemen Jackie Gaughan and Mel Exber. It's a typical Glitter Gulch joint, except for the high ceilings, which give it a roomy and airy feeling, and the pervasive sports theme, with memorabilia all over the walls and dealers in football jerseys. Low limits and easy comps make this a low-roller destination. Las Vegas Club loves introducing new games and rules, so stop by if you're tired of the same old blackjack. You can watch some of the action from a balcony overlooking the casino annex. ⊠ *18 E. Fremont St., Downtown,* ☎ *800/634–6532.*

Main Street Station Casino, Brewery & Hotel. Possibly the classiest casino in Las Vegas, Main Street Station is chock full of antiques, stained glass, bronze bas-reliefs, marble, and wood wood wood. It's a pint-size property, connected to the California by an overhead pedestrian bridge. This place is worth a visit for the aesthetics alone, but as long as you're here, there are plenty of machines (live and electronic) to risk your money on. Games are good with 20x odds on craps and good blackjack rules. ⊠ *200 N. Main St., Downtown,* ☎ *800/465–0711.*

Boulder Strip

The "Boulder Strip" suddenly emerged in 1995 as a destination of its own, competing with downtown and the more famous Strip along Las Vegas Boulevard South. If you're driving to Vegas, the Boulder Strip has some of the nicest facilities at the lowest prices in town, but you'll certainly need a car to get out there.

Boulder Station Hotel and Casino. Boulder Station is an east-side clone of the popular west-side locals casino, Palace Station. The rich wood, stone, even brick floors; the central luxurious pit framed by big stained-glass murals; the plentiful video-poker machines backed by a good slot club that can be used at all Station properties; and the fast-food counters outside the fine restaurants (serving the same food at half the price) all improve on Palace Station's already successful formula. Kids' Quest, a giant indoor play area just off a small satellite pit, makes this the only casino in Las Vegas where parents can play blackjack and watch their children romp at the same time. This is the ultimate indoor playground, 8,000 square ft of fun things to keep youngsters from six weeks to 12 years old happily occupied for hours (there is an hourly fee and a time limit). Boulder Station also has a state-of-the-art 11-plex movie theater. ⊠ *4111 Boulder Hwy., Boulder Strip,* ☎ *800/683–7777.*

Castaways Hotel, Casino, and Bowling Center. The Castaways is the re-named Showboat that was revamped with a Mediterranean seaside

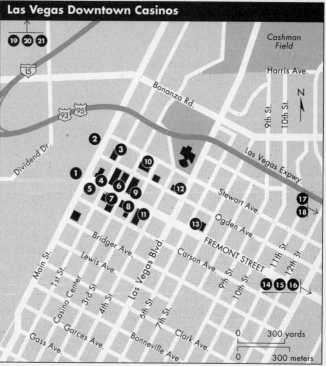

resort theme. Renovating the rundown property with great haste, the new management now aims for a younger and hipper crowd than the current clientele of retirees. Castaways houses the country's largest bowling alley, and the fanciest (and brightest and airiest) bingo hall in town. ✉ 2800 Fremont St., Boulder Strip, ☎ 800/634–3484.

★ **Sam's Town Hotel and Gambling Hall.** About 5 mi from downtown, on the route to Hoover Dam, is Sam's Town, an off-Strip destination for everything imaginable, including an 18-screen movie theater complex, a 1,100-seat event center, and expanded child-care facilities. Sam's motif is touted to be "contemporary western." The casino is built around a 25,000-square-ft indoor park with animatronic howling wolves, saloon fronts, and a waterfall. The two-story casino has row after row of 25¢ video-poker machines, a hardwood floor under the pit, a country band working up a sweat in the lounge, and a dance hall. It also has low-limit table games like 25¢ roulette and $5 blackjack all under large HDTV screens showing every sporting event. For the mid-stakes bettor the great games and OK comps make Sam's Town a recommended watering hole. If you're driving to Hoover Dam (Boulder Highway is much more picturesque than the freeway), you might stop in on your way. ✉ 5111 Boulder Hwy., Boulder Strip, ☎ 800/634–6371.

Rancho Strip

In 1990 the Santa Fe opened in the far northwest part of town, one of the fastest-growing areas of the valley. It "owned" the whole northwest for nearly five years, until the Fiesta opened a couple of miles closer to downtown. The Fiesta was so successful that Texas Station opened directly across the street less than a year later. The competition was particularly intense in the video poker, blackjack, and buffet departments until Station Casinos bought the Fiesta and Santa Fe in 2000. Now Rancho Strip is Station's Strip, but the winners, ultimately, are those of us who patronize the places. A car is mandatory to getting to the Rancho Strip area.

Fiesta Hotel and Casino. Fiesta was a little locals joint with a big, well-deserved reputation, which is probably why Station Casinos bought it. The Fiesta is a popular sports betting venue, thanks to the drive-up betting window complete with pneumatic tubes and teller call buttons. The bingo hall is mind-bogglingly big. Overall, the game rules are poor for the player although comps are doled out to all comers. The Fiesta's Festival Buffet is a perennial favorite, with its gigantic barbecue fire pit, Mongolian grill, and specialty nights. ✉ *2400 N. Rancho, Rancho Strip,* ☎ *800/731–7333.·*

Santa Fe Station Hotel and Casino. Santa Fe offers a 60-lane bowling alley, a 17,000-square-ft ice-skating rink, a 700-seat bingo hall, and a children's nursery. The big casino—2,000 slot and video-poker machines—generally rams and jams and has one of the largest no-smoking sections in Las Vegas. ✉ *4949 N. Rancho, Rancho Strip,* ☎ *702/ 658–4900.*

Texas Station Gambling Hall & Hotel. Texas Station is longhorn territory, with Texas-shape brick sidewalks, Lone Star carpeting design, and a revolving mirrored disco ball that looks like an armadillo. Texas Station's Market Street Buffet is one of the best in Las Vegas, with a Texas chili bar and cooked-to-order fajitas. The casino and race and sports book are huge, with video poker galore and all the usual table games. The player's club is one of the best in town: play at Texas Station and redeem your points at any of the Station casinos. Games overall are only OK for the older clientele. A 16-theater multiplex fills the parking lots nightly, and there's a huge indoor playground called Kids' Quest for children from six weeks to 12 years old. ✉ *2101 Texas Star La., Rancho Strip,* ☎ *800/654–8804.*

Henderson

Henderson was founded in 1940 as a company town for Basic Magnesium, Inc., a giant production plant built to process magnesium mined in huge quantities from a site in central Nevada for the war effort. The site for the factory was selected for its proximity to the unlimited electricity supplied by Hoover Dam; a town to house 10,000 workers was built alongside the magnesium plant. Since then, the magnesium plant has been subdivided into smaller industrial and chemical factories, but Henderson—like its next-door neighbor Las Vegas—has become one of the fastest-growing communities in the country, thanks to the economic boom in southern Nevada over the past decade. Now a vast bedroom community of Vegas, Henderson has overtaken Reno as the second-largest city in Nevada. It has a small downtown, a fine local museum, and several major "locals" casinos.

★ **Green Valley Ranch Resort.** Under the iron scrollwork of this pleasant green and tan Mission-style casino locals are feted in grand style. The Stations company opened Green Valley for its big bettors with high limits, excellent service, and hipper than hip bars and nightclubs. Check out Whisky Sky, a giant bar and garden with acres of vineyards, waterfalls, and fountains. Slots players accustomed to the jingle of coins will be disappointed in the paper payouts of the Green Valley machines. A few full-pay video poker machines lurk in the distant corners here. Comps can be tough to come by but certainly easier than the major strip casinos. As a Station casino the player's card transfers to its other properties. If you're seeking hopping nightlife without the traffic of the Strip, stop by Green Valley. The well-organized parking attendants make finding space stress-free. ✉ *2300 Paseo Verde Pkwy., Henderson,* ☎ *888/319–4661.*

Sunset Station Hotel and Casino. The casino has a Spanish-Mediterranean theme, with ceramic tiles, brick facades, fountains, and wrought-iron balconies. Its size is about standard for a neighborhood joint: 80,000 square ft, with 3,000 slot and video-poker machines, and 50 table games. The video poker is decent, not great, but the slot club is a good one. The middle market Sunset Station is almost always packed with local players, patrons of the excellent buffet and microbrewery, and residents dropping their children at Kids' Quest, the casino's giant indoor play area, on their way to the movies, or going to a show at the rockin' lounge. (Kids' Quest is for children from six weeks to 12 years old; there is an hourly fee and a time limit.) ✉ *1301 Sunset Rd., Henderson,* ☎ *702/547–7777.*

4 DINING

For decades, Vegas dining logic said that bargain buffets, giveaway bacon-and-eggs breakfasts, and cheap steak dinners would attract players whose losses in the casino would more than make up for the hotel's losses in the dining rooms. Change was a long time in coming, but Las Vegas now is finding itself (with some surprise, it seems) increasingly hailed as one of the best restaurant cities in the country—even in the world. You can still save a bundle on prime rib, but in an increasing number of restaurants you might think you're in New York, San Francisco, New Orleans, or Paris.

Updated by
Heidi Knapp
Rinella

L AS VEGAS HAS—HOWEVER IMPROBABLY—BECOME AMERICA'S hottest restaurant market. During the past several years the number of restaurants in the city has nearly doubled to more than 1,000. On average, a new dining establishment opens every week. Each new megaresort brings its own multiple dining options, with celebrity chefs adding clones of famous signature restaurants and newborn establishments to the mix of buffets, coffee shops, and steak houses. Away from the Strip, the unprecedented population growth in the city's newly minted suburbs has brought with it a separate and continuous wave of new restaurants, both familiar chains and independent eateries opened by local entrepreneurs.

Joining a few gourmet pioneers such as Hugo's Cellar and Andre's, and spurred on by Wolfgang Puck who tested the desert waters with a local Spago nearly a decade ago, a flood of newer restaurants has radically changed the experience of eating in Las Vegas. Status-conscious hotel-casinos now compete for star chefs and create lavish, built-to-order spaces for well-known restaurant tenants. These new establishments rival the upscale restaurants of the country's dining capitals in quality, but their prices are often lower than those at their big-city counterparts.

Among the big-name restaurants you'll find in Vegas are six Puck outposts spread among four different hotels (Caesars Palace, Mandalay Bay, The Venetian, and MGM Grand) plus the Bali Hai Golf Club. Other hotels have followed suit. The Bellagio has branches of New York City's famed Le Cirque and Osteria del Circo, along with Jean-Georges Vongerichten's Prime steak house, Julian Serrano's Picasso, and Todd English's Olives, an offshoot of the popular Boston eatery. MGM Grand houses Mark Miller's Coyote Cafe and Emeril's New Orleans Fish House from Emeril Lagasse. The Venetian has Delmonico's, Lagasse's steak house, as well as Star Canyon from Dallas star Stephen Pyles and Valentino from Los Angeles uberchef Piero Selvaggio. In addition to Puck's Trattoria del Lupo, Mandalay Bay offers Charlie Palmer's Aureole (from New York); China Grill (also from New York); Red Square (from Miami Beach); and Border Grill, an L.A. import run by famed TV chefs the Too Hot Tamales (Mary Sue Milliken and Susan Feniger). The Aladdin's Desert Passage shopping area has the first Commander's Palace outside New Orleans, managed by a member of the Brennan family of famed restaurateurs.

The valley's newest hotels—The Palms just off the Strip and Green Valley Ranch in Henderson—have made even more contributions to restaurant quality and diversity in Las Vegas. High atop the 50-plus-story Palms is Alize, the third local restaurant from Andre Rochat of Andre's French Restaurant, where the chef is Michael Demers, who headed Jean-Louis Palladin's Napa. Little Buddha at The Palms is an offshoot of Paris' famed Buddha Bar, and Nine is a branch of the Chicago hotspot.

The restaurant explosion has been partially geared toward satisfying high rollers, who are fed for free as a reward for their often-astronomical bets at the blackjack and baccarat tables, but the city's new reputation as a culinary capital also is drawing attention from those who simply enjoy fine dining. Las Vegas's tendency to do everything to an extreme creates the possibility that too many spectacular restaurants will starve each other, but there's no sign of that yet. While Las Vegas's reputation as being recession-proof may be a bit overstated, the city knows how to continually re-invent itself to ensure that the annual average of 36 million visitors—many of them with fat expense accounts—keep coming.

But even low rollers with thin wallets have plenty of dining options in Las Vegas. Despite the influx of upscale restaurants, you can still find a complete steak dinner for only $4.95 (Ellis Island), a 99¢ shrimp cocktail (Golden Gate), and $2.49 breakfast specials (Arizona Charlie's). And of course, the ever-popular buffet is found in nearly every casino in town.

But crowds at the hotels, long lines at the buffets, and the jangling noise of slot machines prompt some to seek refuge away from the casinos. If you venture into the residential areas, you'll find a steadily increasing variety of restaurants that satisfy every pocketbook. Rosemary's, Andre's, Bonjour Casual French, The Tillerman, and other off-Strip dining rooms satisfy the craving for a civilized meal. And mid-price family eateries (such as Tenaya Creek Restaurant & Brewery, Memphis Championship Barbecue, India Oven, Lindo Michoacán, Dona Maria, and Billy Bob's Steak House) offer reliable quality at reasonable prices.

What to Wear

The dining dress code, like nearly every other social protocol in Las Vegas, is permissive: As long as you wear your wallet, you'll be welcome most anywhere. While the well-heeled new resorts have inspired more people to dress to impress, you'll still see flip-flops and cutoffs in the buffet line and cowboy hats in the steak house. Only the most upscale rooms require that men wear jackets and ties.

Costs

Restaurants, both in and out of hotels, are listed below according to cuisine. A tip of 15%–20% is common practice in Las Vegas restaurants, and in some circumstances you might want to slip the maître d' $5 or $10 for a special table. Some restaurants—particularly the most storied, such as Picasso and Renoir—require reservations, and at any rate, you'd be advised to call ahead to just about any upscale restaurant to inquire about reservation policies, because waits can be long.

CATEGORY	COST*
$$$$	over $30
$$$	$20–$30
$$	$10–$20
$	under $10

*per person for a main course at dinner

American

$$$–$$$$ ✕ **Brown Derby.** The movie-industry elite gathered at the landmark Hollywood original until a wrecking ball demolished it in 1985. The Las Vegas version revives that Golden Era with art deco–style fixtures, lavish floral arrangements, and sketches of popular American stars adorning the walls. The original Cobb salad, Hollywood Shellfish on Ice, Oysters Derbyfeller and broiled lobster and beef Mignonette are on the menu, along with the Brown Derby's signature grapefruit cake. ✉ *MGM Grand Hotel and Casino, 3799 Las Vegas Blvd. S, South Strip,* ☎ *702/891-7318. AE, D, DC, MC, V.*

$$$ ✕ **Lawry's The Prime Rib.** In a city famous for low-price prime rib specials, Lawry's is an upscale, art deco–style palace dedicated to the pursuit of excellence in the guise of slow-roasted, aged prime rib. The dining room, with parquet floors and plush banquettes, is staffed by waitresses in 1930s-style uniforms and white-clad carvers, who roll gleaming domed silver carts up to your table. Atlantic lobster tails and a daily fresh-fish entrée are available for those who don't eat meat. ✉ *4043 Howard Hughes Pkwy., Paradise Road,* ☎ *702/893-2223. AE, MC, V. No lunch.*

$$$ ✕ Nob Hill. Celebrity chef Michael Mina delights Las Vegans (and Las
★ Vegans-for-a-day) with his seafood creations at Aqua at Bellagio, and
now he's doing the same at the MGM Grand. San Franciscan cuisine
is the star here (but you already knew that), with the emphasis on re-
gional favorites such as Gilroy garlic soup, or peppered beef carpac-
cio with Napa Valley tomatoes and chilled pesto linguine, for starters.
Entrées include filet of beef Wellington with lobster cream spinach and
tarragon oil, lobster pot pie, and sautéed Monterey Bay abalone, or
you can get tomato soup with a lobster-and-grilled-cheese sandwich.
The mashed-potato cart is included with dinner, and you can bet the
bread's good. ⊠ *MGM Grand Hotel and Casino, 3799 Las Vegas Blvd.
S, South Strip,* ☎ *702/891–3110. AE, D, DC, MC, V. No lunch.*

$$ ✕ The Broiler. Station Casinos has emerged as one of the front-run-
ning off-Strip casino organizations; its resorts serve as neighborhood
casino outposts of the original Palace Station. Branches of The Broiler,
its good, inexpensive steak and seafood house, are found at both the
Palace and Boulder stations. Both locations have excellent soups,
breads, and a salad bar, which set the stage for medium-price mesquite-
grilled steaks, veal, and chicken. ⊠ *Boulder Station Hotel and Casino,
4111 Boulder Hwy., Boulder Strip,* ☎ *702/432–7777;* ⊠ *Palace Station Hotel and Casino, 2411 W. Sahara Ave., West Side,* ☎ *702/367–
2411. AE, D, MC, V.*

$$ ✕ Tenaya Creek Restaurant & Brewery. Tenaya Creek is a brewpub with
★ a contemporary design, and one that happens to have super customer
service. The menu's contemporary, too—a far cry from the old bar food.
It has such starters as Sedona crab cakes, Singapore Slingers, and house-
made hummus; pizzas, pastas, and sandwiches that include a buffalo
burger; and entrées such as buffalo steak, barbecued honey-beer ribs,
and pork chops marinated in ale. And for dessert, you can even have
beer-a-misu, a tiramisu made with house-brewed ale. ⊠ *3101 N. Tenaya
Way, Northwest Las Vegas,* ☎ *702/362–7335. AE, D, DC, MC, V.*

American/Casual

$$ ✕ Carson Street Cafe. The Golden Nugget is widely considered one of
the gems of Downtown, and the Carson Street Cafe does it proud. The
restaurant has a stylish Southern plantation feel and plays host to
downtown's movers and shakers during weekday breakfast and lunch
hours. Among the breakfast selections are eggs Benedict, a spinach frit-
tata, and the Vegas Experience—banana bread with walnut-cinnamon
cream cheese, bananas, kiwi, and strawberries (and you thought the
Vegas experience was something else!). Standbys on the lunch and dinner menus include rainbow trout, Southern fried chicken, and slabs of
baby-back ribs. Try the prime rib at dinner. ⊠ *Golden Nugget Hotel
and Casino, 129 E. Fremont St., Downtown,* ☎ *702/385–7111. AE,
D, DC, MC, V.*

$$ ✕ Gordon Biersch Brewing Co. This import from Palo Alto, Califor-
nia, is popular with both singles and the power-lunch crowd, thanks
to its trendy warehouse look (there are no old warehouses to retrofit
in such a young city, so Las Vegas builds them from scratch), and lo-
cation in the Hughes Center office park. Glassed-off brewing kettles
are the design centerpiece as well as the main attraction at the square
center bar, which offers specialty brews such as Marzen and Hefeweizen.
The menu has one of the city's most creative selections of appetizers,
including chili- and ginger-glazed chicken wings and crispy artichoke
hearts tossed with Parmesan. Entrées range from pasta and wood-oven
pizza to pan-seared ahi tuna and old-fashioned meat loaf with beer-
mustard gravy. ⊠ *3987 Paradise Rd., Paradise Road,* ☎ *702/312–5247.
AE, D, DC, MC, V.*

64

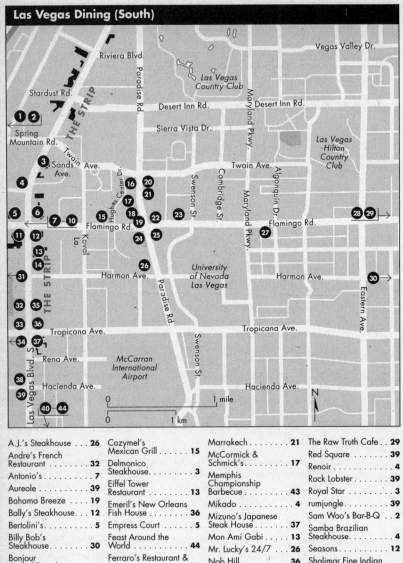

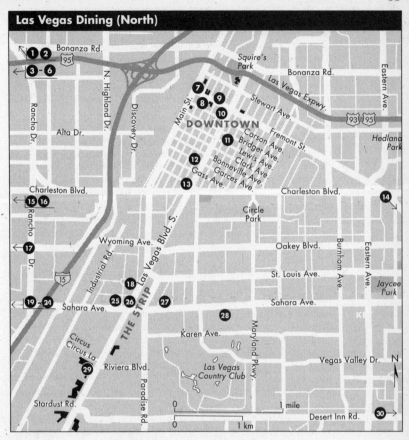

Las Vegas Dining (North)

$$ ✕ **Grand Lux Cafe.** The Venetian's 24-hour operation is no diner/coffee shop. A member of the same family as The Cheesecake Factory, Grand Lux is an attractive, expansive space in contemporary colors. The menu's all over the place, including such items as Asian nachos, oven-roasted mussels, Madeira chicken, and Mongolian steak. And whatever you do, be sure to leave room for dessert. ⊠ *The Venetian Resort-Hotel-Casino, 3355 Las Vegas Blvd. S, Center Strip,* ☎ *702/414–3888. AE, D, DC, MC, V.*

$$ ✕ **Mr. Lucky's 24/7.** The hippest casino coffee shop in Las Vegas is in-
★ side the Hard Rock Hotel, where banks of slot machines bear the likenesses of Jimi Hendrix and Sid Vicious. Clean, modern lines; light-wood floors; and vintage rock-and-roll posters highlight this bubbly, circular café. Menu items range from vegetable omelets and entrée salads to pizza and pasta. More filling options include burgers and fries, steak, grilled salmon, and baby-back ribs. The garlic mashed potatoes are superb. It's open 24 hours, seven days a week—hence the numbers in the name. Beware: the music is loud. ⊠ *Hard Rock Hotel and Casino, 4455 Paradise Rd., Paradise Road,* ☎ *702/693–5000. AE, D, DC, MC, V.*

$ ✕ **5 & Diner.** Meals at this bright and cheerful eatery with multiple locations around town include soup or salad, vegetable, and choice of potato—starting at $5.29. Thick milk shakes, baked homemade meat loaf with rich brown gravy, big hamburgers, spaghetti with garlic bread, chicken-fried steaks, and roast beef are menu mainstays. The quality is surprisingly good, and the atmosphere is friendly. It's open from 6 AM until the wee hours. ⊠ *6840 W. Sahara Ave., West Side,* ☎ *702/368–7903;*⊠ *1825 E. Flamingo Rd., University District,* ☎ *702/892–3510;* ⊠ *1900 N. Buffalo Dr., Northwest Las Vegas,* ☎ *702/804–8044;* ⊠ *8820 S. Eastern Ave., East Las Vegas,* ☎ *702/966–2650;* ⊠ *375 N. Stephanie St., Henderson,* ☎ *702/940–2050. AE, MC, V.*

$ ✕ **Mimi's Cafe.** Mimi's may sound French—a Frenchwoman was the inspiration behind the name of this growing California-based chain—and the decor may look French, but the menu is wide-ranging American. For starters, consider a Thai chicken wrap, Cajun popcorn shrimp, or spinach-and-artichoke dip. Entrée choices include roast pork loin with red cabbage, barbecued meat loaf, capellini with tomatoes and basil, and turkey breast with corn-bread dressing. And don't pass the dessert case without peeking or you might miss the Bananas Foster cheesecake, warm chocolate praline bars, or New Orleans bread pudding. ⊠ *1121 S. Fort Apache Rd., Northwest Las Vegas,* ☎ *702/341–0365. AE, D, MC, V.*

$ ✕ **Roxy's Diner.** Be ready to be entertained at this playful replica of a 1950s-era diner, where you can dig into mammoth hot-fudge sundaes, sizable burgers, fried catfish, old-fashioned thick milk shakes, blue-plate specials that include meat loaf and chicken-fried steak, and other inexpensive American classics. This joint is always jumping. ⊠ *Stratosphere Hotel Tower and Casino, 2000 Las Vegas Blvd. S, North Strip,* ☎ *702/380–7777. AE, D, DC, MC, V.*

Barbecue

$$ ✕ **Memphis Championship Barbecue.** Barbecue the old-fashioned way: that's what fans are looking for, and that's what Memphis Championship Barbecue delivers. The owner/founder hails from Murphysboro, Illinois, which apparently is a well-kept secret as a barbecue stronghold, and cooks Memphis-style; hence the name. If you've got a big appetite—or a big family—try Mama Faye's Down Home Super Dinner for four; you won't go away hungry. Other choices include smoked hot links, barbecued pork shoulder, and catfish. Oh, and on the side, treat your-

self to some fried dill pickles. ⊠ *2250 E. Warm Springs Rd.* ☎ *702/260–6909;* ⊠ *4379 Las Vegas Blvd. N, North I... 702/644–0000. AE, D, MC, V.*

Brazilian

$$$ ✕ **Samba Brazilian Steakhouse.** The Mirag... house presents a lively, colorful, *rodizio* di... style roasted meats, chicken, and fish... table-side, all you can eat. À la carte... crusted halibut to Australian lob... crème brûlée or chocolate mo... adds to the room's exciteme... *Vegas Blvd. S, Center St... No lunch.*

$$$ ✕ **Yolie's.** If you li[k... (a Brazilian "ho... price of $26.9... you-can-ea... steak, al... you c... ad...

chefs, following the example (and success) of California institution Wolfgang Puck, would flock to the desert to bring this city a taste of what they'd been doing in New York, San Francisco, New Orleans, Dallas, and Washington.

The star chefs had nothing to do with the buffets, of course. What they did was raise the bar for Las Vegas' professional kitchens—and the expectations of visitors, who still were looking for great all-you-can-eat deals but were no longer satisfied with the steam-table selections of old.

The first "gourmet buffet" opened with the Bellagio, where it fit in with mogul Steve Wynn's plan for a classier joint. Today, the top three buffets in town are generally considered the Bellagio ($22.95 at dinner, $13.95 at lunch), Paris' Le Village Buffet ($21.95 at dinner, $10.95 at lunch) and the Aladdin's Spice Market Buffet ($19.99 at dinner, $13.99 at lunch).

But nearly every resort of any size presents its own version of the classic buffet. One of the lowest-priced is at Circus Circus ($7.99 at dinner, $5.99 at lunch), where the buffet serves an estimated

Oh, and don't forget the Sunday brunch buffets. Bally's Sterling Brunch ($52.95) is still considered the best in town, and it's pretty much alone in the firmament since MGM Grand's Brown Derby stopped serving its fantastic brunch. Other great brunch bets are Paris ($21.95), especially if you like crepes, and Caesar's Palace ($14.99). There's a Gospel Brunch at House of Blues at Mandalay Bay ($37), jazz brunch at the Aladdin ($25–$35) and margarita brunches at Garduno's at the Fiesta ($11.99) and the Palms ($11.99).

But while much about Las Vegas buffets has changed, some things haven't. There are plenty of long lines at peak times, especially at the best buffets. You'll want to remember to tip; the suggested minimum is $1 per person, depending on service. And here's a tip for you: if you're kind of tricky and very hungry, you can go toward the end of a buffet serving period (the end of the breakfast hour, say) at some buffets and hang around as they start to put out selections for the next meal, saving a few bucks in the process.

— Heidi Knapp Rinella

s Samba Brazilian Steak-
nner—a parade of rotisserie-
cooked on skewers and carved
entrées range from roasted herb-
ter tail. For dessert, try the coconut
usse cake. The sparkling open kitchen
nt. ⊠ *Mirage Hotel and Casino, 3400 Las
rip,* ☎ *702/791–7111. AE, D, DC, MC, V.*

e rodizio served in the fashion of a *churrascaria*
se of meat"), then this is the place for you. The fixed
($14.95 at lunch) gets you bread, soup, sides, and all-
slices of turkey, lamb, brisket, chicken, sausage, and
grilled over a mesquite-fired, glass-enclosed rotisserie that
n see from the dining room. It's a fun place to eat. ⊠ *3900 Par-
se Rd., Paradise Road,* ☎ *702/794–0700. AE, D, DC, MC, V. No
unch weekends.*

$$$ ✕ **The Buffet at Bellagio.** In keeping with the resort, this is one of the most beautifully decorated buffet rooms in town. For cozier dining, it is divided into many alcoves, one of which replicates an outdoor café with umbrellas. But the design isn't the main attraction here; even the most discerning foodie should find something to like with selections that include Kobe beef (yes, Kobe beef), roast sirloin of elk, tandoori game hen, steamed clams and mussels, acorn squash ravioli, white miso soup, and vitello tonnato. The requisite king-crab legs are present as well, and there's quite an array of elaborate pastries—and an in-restaurant bar. ⊠ *Bellagio, 3600 Las Vegas Blvd. S, Center Strip,* ☎ *702/ 693–7111. AE, D, DC, MC, V.*

$$$ ✕ **Le Village Buffet.** Let the other buffets touch on various international foods; Paris Las Vegas owns the world's foremost cuisine and shows it to advantage at Le Village Buffet. The buffet stations are themed to the regions of France; accordingly, you'll find chicken saute chasseur and roasted duck with green peppercorns and peach in Brittany, seafood bouillabaisse in Provence, veal marengo in Burgundy, smoked salmon salad with fresh dill in Normandy, and braised lamb with Riesling and curry in Alsace. Brittany offers dessert crepes, too, and bananas Foster and French bread pudding are served up at the Le Flambe station. ⊠ *Paris Las Vegas, 3655 Las Vegas Blvd. South, Center Strip,* ☎ *702/ 946–7000.. AE, D, DC, MC, V.*

$$$ ✕ **Spice Market Buffet.** This buffet in the traffic-challenged Aladdin Resort & Casino is one of the best in town—and one of the best values. It's probably the only one with a Middle Eastern station (in keeping with the Aladdin's theme), where you'll find such delights as skewered lamb, basmati rice with lentils and raisins, and tandoori chicken. The Italian station offers stromboli, pizza, chicken scallopini, and macaroni with Gorgonzola cream, while the Asian one has super pot stickers, fried rice and spring rolls. ⊠ *Aladdin Resort & Casino, 3667 Las Vegas Blvd. S., Center Strip,* ☎ *702/785–5555. AE, D, DC, MC, V.*

$$$ ✕ **Village Seafood Buffet.** Seafood fans flock to the Rio's nautical-theme buffet, complete with American, Mexican, Italian, and Chinese serv-

ing stations. At the American station you can load up on seafood salads, snow-crab legs, oysters on the half shell, peel-and-eat shrimp, seafood gumbo, grilled salmon, broiled swordfish, oysters Rockefeller, poached roughy, steamed clams, and lobster tails. Then come the ethnic ocean entrées, such as seafood fajitas, cioppino, seafood cannelloni, squid chow fun, and kung pao scallops. To top it all off, the Village Buffet has one of Las Vegas's best selections of high-quality desserts. ⊠ *Rio All-Suite Casino Resort, 3700 W. Flamingo Rd., West Side,* ☎ *702/252–7777. AE, D, DC, MC, V.*

$$ ✕ **Carnival World Buffet.** This was one of the first Las Vegas buffets with separate theme areas; the buffets-within-a-buffet here serve up fresh Mexican, Italian, Chinese, Japanese, American, and other ethnic specialties under one large and colorful roof. The centerpiece is the Mongolian barbecue, where you choose your own meats and veggies to be stir-fried before your eyes on one of two sizzling-hot grills. Hamburgers and french fries, fish and chips, barbecue, sushi, salads, desserts, and more are also available. ⊠ *Rio All-Suite Hotel and Casino, 3700 W. Flamingo Rd., West Side,* ☎ *702/252–7777. AE, D, DC, MC, V.*

$$ ✕ **Feast Around the World.** The buffet at the brand-spankin'-new Green Valley Ranch Station Casino has a similar name as those at some of Station Casinos' other properties, and the options are somewhat similar, but there's no mistaking that the company has improved its offerings with each new casino. A huge display of fresh produce and the use of natural stone and carefully designed lighting lends a decidedly upscale touch to the entrance hall. Specialty stations include a Mongolian grill, Italian, Mexican, and American, plus a good-size salad bar and a belt-busting selection of pastries. ⊠ *Green Valley Ranch, 2300 Paseo Verde Pkwy., Henderson,* ☎ *702/614–5283. AE, D, DC, MC, V.*

Cajun/Creole

$$$$ ✕ **Commander's Palace.** It may not have the gracious Old South atmosphere of the venerable New Orleans institution, but Commander's Palace has managed to replicate every other aspect of the 120-year-old original in its location fronting the Strip at Desert Passage next to the Aladdin. That means classics such as turtle soup, shrimp rémoulade, bananas Foster, bread pudding soufflé, and French Quarter beignets; and updated offerings such as Lyonnaise Gulf shrimp with a potato crust and crispy fennel cabbage slaw, or tasso shrimp Henican with Crystal hot sauce beurre blanc and five-pepper jelly. And don't forget the jazz brunch on Sunday. ⊠ *Desert Passage at the Aladdin, 3663 Las Vegas Blvd. S, Center Strip,* ☎ *702/892–8272. AE, D, DC, MC, V.*

$$$$ ✕ **Emeril's New Orleans Fish House.** A stone courtyard, French doors,
★ and faux willow trees grace the entrance to Chef Emeril Lagasse's first Las Vegas dining spot. The original Emeril's is in New Orleans, and that Cajun feeling prevails here with cayenne-color walls, modern metalwork, and black-and-white photos of Louisiana fishermen. A sampling of Emeril's creative dishes includes Alabama rock-shrimp spring rolls, sweet barbecued salmon, double-cut pork chops with roasted pecan relish, and Creole-seasoned tuna steak with foie gras. Make sure to try his wonderful banana cream pie. ⊠ *MGM Grand Hotel Casino, 3799 Las Vegas Blvd. S, South Strip,* ☎ *702/891–7374. AE, D, DC, MC, V.*

$$–$$$ ✕ **House of Blues.** Mandalay Bay houses a branch of this music-and-restaurant chain that's become a fixture in tourist-friendly cities. Like all of the other Houses, this one is a gaudy, stylized version of a Delta shack with a deliberately ramshackle look (making it easy to find within the tropical-theme hotel), and the HOB compound has a concert hall and the requisite gift shop. Cold beer goes well with just about everything on the menu, from the less expensive smoked pork or mesquite-grilled chicken sandwiches to the center-cut pork chop in bour-

bon sauce, Cajun meat loaf, crawfish and shrimp étouffée, or smoked half-chicken with mashed potatoes and root-beer gravy. ✉ *Mandalay Bay Resort and Casino, 3950 Las Vegas Blvd. S, South Strip,* ☎ *702/632–7777. AE, D, DC, MC, V.*

$$ ✕ **La Louisianne.** This comfortable, New Orleans–style favorite serves seafood and steaks with a Cajun or Creole twist. Among the favorites: New Orleans creole gumbo, catfish, Chilean sea bass, salmon fillet, blackened red snapper, and pork Wellington. For dessert, indulge in such Big Easy specialties as white chocolate–blueberry bread pudding, sweet potato–pecan pie, or Bananas Foster. ✉ *Orleans Hotel and Casino, 4500 W. Tropicana Ave., West Side,* ☎ *702/365–7111. AE, D, DC, MC, V. No lunch.*

$$ ✕ **A Taste of N'Awlins.** It doesn't have to be hot to be good—or authentic—chef/owner Don Gloudé tells us, and he should know; he's New Orleans–born and –bred. Accordingly, his Summerlin restaurant serves dishes that are far more flavorful than they are lip-searing. Try popcorn shrimp with rémoulade sauce for starters, or perhaps some fried oysters, prepared with a cloudlike breading. Entrées include such N'Awlins standards as jambalaya; gumbo and crawfish étouffée, of course; plus less traditional offerings such as barbecued ribs or a rib-eye steak. For dessert, don't miss the bread pudding with vanilla cream sauce. ✉ *9320 Sun City Blvd., Summerlin,* ☎ *702/304–9300. AE, D, DC, MC, V.*

Caribbean

$$$ ✕ **Ortanique.** Chef Cindy Hutson has been celebrating her "cuisine of the sun" at her signature Ortanique in Miami for several years, and in 2001 she shone a little sun on Las Vegas in the walkway between Paris and Bally's. The menu melds flavors from South America, the West Indies and Asia in such appetizers as jerked seared foie gras, and West Indian curried crab cakes with papaya coulis and tropical fruit salsa. Entrées include Rasta Pasta, which is penne pasta topped with sun-dried tomatoes, shiitake mushrooms and tropically seasoned chicken, all in a cream sauce, and island spiced seared ahi tuna with horseradish mashed potatoes. ✉ *Paris Las Vegas, 3655 Las Vegas Blvd. S, Center Strip,* ☎ *702/946–4346. AE, D, DC, MC, V. No lunch.*

$$$ ✕ **rumjungle.** This Mandalay Bay establishment is so hugely popular as a dance club frequented by the see-and-be-seen set that some locals are surprised to learn it even serves food in the evening hours. That's not exactly how it was intended. The intensely themed interior—all waterfalls and fiery displays—was designed with the Brazilian rodizio "fire pit" in mind; a popular choice is the prix-fixe dinner of pork, lamb, chicken, fish, and vegetables served on skewers. Individual entrées include many Caribbean-theme dishes. ✉ *Mandalay Bay Resort and Casino, 3950 Las Vegas Blvd. S, South Strip,* ☎ *702/632–7777. AE, D, DC, MC, V. No lunch.*

$$ ✕ **Bahama Breeze.** No worries, mon; Bahama Breeze is a casual spot with tropical flavors and flair—a bit of Jamaica, a bit of Cuba, a lot of fun. Signature dishes include the satisfying coconut curry chicken, with raisins, cashews, and pineapple; and jerk chicken pasta, with asparagus and mushrooms in an herb cream sauce; as well as such classics as ropa vieja, steak con mojo, conch chowder, and black beans and rice. Starters are tropically flavored, too, such as the tostones con pollo, in which crispy plantains are topped with chicken and cheese, or Jamaican grilled chicken wings. And watch out for those tropical drinks. ✉ *375 Hughes Center Dr., Paradise Road,* ☎ *702/731–3252. AE, D, DC, MC, V. No lunch.*

Chinese

$$$$ ✕ **Empress Court.** This venerable upscale Chinese eatery entered a new era when was it relocated to a spot overlooking Caesars' Garden of the Gods swimming pool and the extensive gardens that surround it. Thai, Malaysian, and Indonesian specialties are part of the program, and seafood plays a starring role. Accordingly, some of the sea creatures can be found swimming in the restaurant's tanks until they're ordered. Offerings include abalone and shark-fin soup, Peking duck, and sautéed scallops with macadamia nuts. ✉ *Caesars Palace, 3570 Las Vegas Blvd. S, Center Strip,* ☎ *702/731–7110. Reservations essential. Jacket and tie. AE, D, DC, MC, V. Closed Tues.–Wed. No lunch.*

$$$$ ✕ **Royal Star.** Seafood-oriented dishes are the center of attention in this simple, emerald-tone dining room with lacquered black furniture. Dim sum is the star at lunchtime, when rolling carts offer a quick but quality feast of pan-fried scallion cakes, barbecue-pork puffed pastries, shrimp-stuffed eggplant, and more. The evening menu ranges from lobster or crab fresh from the tank to regional specials such as spicy garlic scallops and Six Hour Spare Ribs served over a bed of sautéed spinach. And yes, for the less adventurous there are well-executed versions of familiar dishes such as *kung pao* chicken and orange beef. ✉ *Venetian Resort-Hotel-Casino, 3355 Las Vegas Blvd. S, Center Strip,* ☎ *702/ 414–1889. AE, D, DC, MC, V.*

$$$ ✕ **China Grill.** Postmodern architecture and appointments set the stage for Asian dishes with a contemporary accent in this Mandalay Bay restaurant. Start with appetizers such as sake-cured salmon rolls, lobster pancakes, or lamb dumplings. Peking duck and calamari salads join the more pedestrian chicken salad on the salad list. The selection of main dishes leans toward seafood, with options such as barbecued salmon and Shanghai lobster with ginger, curry, and spinach. The menu also mixes offbeat entrées (grilled Australian lamb loin) with more conventional Chinese dishes (Szechuan beef). ✉ *Mandalay Bay Resort and Casino, 3590 Las Vegas Blvd. S, South Strip,* ☎ *702/632–7777. AE, D, DC, MC, V.*

$$$ ✕ **Lillie Langtry's.** This restaurant comes close to turning out the finest
★ Chinese food you'll find this side of Canton, but steaks have a starring role as well. The Cantonese dishes include old familiars such as moo goo gai pan and moo shu pork, plus spicier choices such as Szechuan shrimp. The black-pepper steak is a must for charcoal aficionados, and the lemon chicken is a classic. But if you'd rather, you can always go with a 22-ounce porterhouse or a 28-ounce rib-eye. Don't miss the dragon-eye fruit for dessert. ✉ *Golden Nugget Hotel and Casino, 129 E. Fremont St., Downtown,* ☎ *702/385–7111. AE, D, DC, MC, V. No lunch.*

$$ ✕ **Cathay House.** Cathay House is a bit of a rarity in Las Vegas—a restaurant that has the feel of a mom-and-pop spot, but with a sophisticated atmosphere and a menu that combines the best of both worlds. Among appetizers are the classic soups plus sizzling rice soup, curry puffs, and Hawaiian-style skewered beef and chicken; house entrée specialties include strawberry chicken and sautéed crystal shrimp. The location affords diners fantastic views of the city. ✉ *5300 W. Spring Mountain Rd., West Side,* ☎ *702/876–3838. AE, D, MC, V.*

$$ ✕ **Peking Market.** An 800-gallon tropical aquarium, pastoral murals, and oversize tables accent this Chinese restaurant that serves such dishes as moo goo gai pan; orange-peel beef; and, for dessert, fried banana fritters with whipped cream. The Market's attentive staff speaks Vietnamese, Thai, and several Chinese dialects to serve the specific needs of its Asian customers. Off-the-menu orders are also welcome. ✉

Flamingo Las Vegas, 3555 Las Vegas Blvd. S, Center Strip, ☏ 702/
733–3111. AE, D, DC, MC, V. No lunch.

$$ ✕ **P. F. Chang's China Bistro.** "Americanized" versions of Chinese clas-
sics are served at this high-energy off-Strip eatery. Chinese sculptures
and murals are offset by high-tech lighting fixtures and a modern, earth-
tone color scheme. The 60-item menu ranges from basic sweet-and-
sour pork and barbecued spareribs to more adventurous lemon-pepper
shrimp and Chang's spicy chicken. Vegetarians will find plenty of noo-
dle, rice, and vegetable dishes at this East-meets-West hot spot. ✉ 4165
S. Paradise Rd., Paradise Road, ☏ 702/792–2207; ✉ 1095 S. Ram-
part Blvd., Northwest Las Vegas, ☏ 702/968–8885; ✉ Aladdin Hotel
and Casino, 3667 Las Vegas Blvd. S, Center Strip, ☏ 702/785–5555.
AE, MC, V.

Contemporary

$$$$ ✕ **Aureole.** This is the star of Mandalay Bay's world-class restaurants.
  ★   A four-story wine tower, the first of its kind in the world, holds 12,000
bottles that are reached by "wine fairies" who are hoisted up and down
via a system of electronically activated pulleys. Seasonal specialties on
the fixed-price menu include toasted-corn blini with osetra caviar, saf-
fron scallops with creamed potatoes, and bluefin tuna tartare with a
chile-spiced ponzu sauce. For dessert try the decorated lemon custard,
cool banana mousse, or pineapple-citrus cheesecake. ✉ Mandalay
Bay Resort and Casino, 3950 Las Vegas Blvd. S, South Strip, ☏ 702/
632–7401. AE, D, DC, MC, V. No lunch.

$$$$ ✕ **Hugo's Cellar.** Every woman receives a red rose at this romantic down-
  ★   town favorite. Hugo's has been popular with Las Vegas locals since its
opening in 1976. The staff is attentive and the narrow, brick-lined room
has deep, comfortable booths. For starters, try the hot rock appetizer:
you cook marinated meats right at your table on a granite slab that is
heated to 500°F. All meals include salad (a salad cart is brought right
to your table; you choose the items that will be in your salad), an in-
termezzo of raspberry sorbet served in a miniature ice-cream cone, and
chocolate-dipped fruit with whipped cream for dessert. Entrées vary
from veal T-bone to tasty raspberry chicken with whole berries to In-
donesian-spiced rack of lamb. ✉ Four Queens Hotel and Casino, 202
Fremont St., Downtown, ☏ 702/385–4011. AE, MC, V. No lunch.

$$$$ ✕ **Pinot Brasserie.** James Beard Foundation Award–winning chef
Joachim Splichal and his wife and partner Christine have duplicated
their acclaimed Los Angeles Pinot restaurant—an urban-casual bistro
featuring Franco-Californian cuisine. The storefront facade imported
from France allows passersby to glimpse diners at their tables and cooks
at work. The ocean jewels served here include oysters on the half shell
(imported from wherever they are the freshest), scallop tartare, Pacific
shrimp, Dungeness crab, and lobster. From terra firma come openers
and entrées such as sweetbreads, foie gras, lamb, venison, and poul-
try. The bustle of this spot near the casino floor is softened somewhat
by friendly staff and banquette seating. ✉ Venetian Resort-Hotel-
Casino, 3355 Las Vegas Blvd. S, Center Strip, ☏ 702/735–8888. AE,
D, DC, MC, V.

$$$$ ✕ **Postrio.** Wolfgang Puck's fifth Las Vegas venture is a spin-off of his
  ★   San Francisco seafood house. In many ways, this location in the Vene-
tian's retail mall is the most elegant of his Las Vegas rooms. Like most
Puck places there's an "outdoor" sidewalk café in front of a formal
dining room, which is trimmed in rich burgundy and accented with
jeweled stained-glass pieces, curved to resemble film strips in a slightly
Gaudí-like effect. The lunch and menu includes the familiar Puck piz-
zas, but also something as different as a lobster club sandwich. For din-

ner, the emphasis is on seafood with Mediterranean influences: choose from seafood pastas or such dishes as seared black bass with sautéed winter greens and warm lentil vinaigrette, or roasted turbot with sautéed wild mushrooms and leeks. ⊠ *Venetian Resort-Hotel-Casino, 3355 Las Vegas Blvd. S, Center Strip,* ☎ *702/796–1110. AE, D, DC, MC, V.*

$$$$ ✕ **Seasons.** Booths, intimate alcoves, antiques, and table-side preparation make for glamorous dining here. Among the appetizers are grilled day-boat sea scallops with horseradish vinaigrette and Burgundy escargot with brioche, pancetta, and Roquefort. Entrées include roasted sea bass with basil ratatouille, sautéed medallions of veal with white mushrooms and champagne sauce, and sautéed jumbo prawns in a tarragon and anise broth. Be sure to save room for dessert; offerings include molten Belgian chocolate cake with orange sorbet and Tahitian vanilla crème brûlée. ⊠ *Bally's Casino Resort, 3645 Las Vegas Blvd. S, Center Strip,* ☎ *702/967–4651. AE, D, DC, MC, V. Closed Sun.–Mon. No lunch.*

$$$$ ✕ **Spago Las Vegas.** His fellow chefs stood by in wonder when Wolf-
★ gang Puck opened this branch of his famous Beverly Hills eatery in the culinary wasteland that was Las Vegas in 1992. In 2001, Puck spent $1 million to renovate the place. The café section, which overlooks the busy Forum Shops at Caesars, is great for people-watching; the inside dining room is more intimate. Menu offerings include roasted pumpkin ravioli with spinach, endive, and hazelnuts, as well as sautéed giant prawns with steamed bok choy, ginger, and Chinese black beans. Desserts include spiced apple tart with cinnamon-caramel glaze. It's no wonder Spago is always hopping. ⊠ *Forum Shops at Caesars, 3500 Las Vegas Blvd. S, Center Strip,* ☎ *702/369–6300. AE, MC, V.*

$$$ ✕ **Chinois.** Yet another Wolfgang Puck creation, the high-end Chinois has a Pacific Rim flair. The menu lineup changes daily, but you can bet that whatever's offered is among the most unusual fare in town: sea-scallop salad, sautéed foie gras, roasted venison loin, pan-roasted black cod, barbecued baby pork ribs, Shanghai lobster, and the like. Ask about the prix-fixe tasting menus ($38 or $45), which allow you to sample a variety of dishes. ⊠ *The Forum Shops at Caesars, 3500 Las Vegas Blvd. S, Center Strip,* ☎ *702/737–9700. AE, D, DC, MC, V.*

$$$ ✕ **Mayflower Cuisinier.** You'll find creative Chinese dishes with Californian and Pan-Asian accents and an occasional French flair on the progressive menu at this off-Strip eatery. Try the ginger-chicken ravioli, Asian Portobello mushroom burrito, peppercorn-crusted ahi tuna with wasabi-soy sauce, pistachio-encrusted salmon with ginger-caper sauce, or Mongolian lamb chops with creamy cilantro sauce. The small selection of pastas—such as the Chinese pasta with shrimp, scallops, and salmon—is bolstered by high-quality soups and desserts, such as a delectable trio of crème brûlées flavored with almond, orange, and pineapple-ginger. There's also a patio area. ⊠ *4750 W. Sahara Ave., West Side,* ☎ *702/870–8432. AE, D, DC, MC, V.*

$$$ ✕ **Red Square.** This Soviet-chic restaurant is one of several China Grill–group eateries in Mandalay Bay that manage to tastefully combine theatrical interior design with fine dining. There are 100 varieties of vodka, and a walk-in vodka freezer (in which frequent patrons can rent their own space). For starters, consider the variety of caviars, a crab-stuffed Portobello mushroom, or tuna and smoked salmon tartare. Entrées include potato-crusted snapper, lobster and black-truffle fettuccine, and Roquefort-crusted filet mignon. For dessert try the warm chocolate cake or crème brûlée. ⊠ *Mandalay Bay Resort and Casino, 3950 Las Vegas Blvd. S, South Strip,* ☎ *702/632–7777. AE, D, DC, MC, V. No lunch.*

$$$ ✕ **Rosemary's.** Here's a breath of fresh air: a privately owned restau-
★   rant with the quality and variety of Strip landmarks but without the
traffic, crowds, and stratospheric prices. Husband and wife Michael
and Wendy Jordan, both skilled chefs (he honed his skills under celebrity
chef Emeril Lagasse), preside here, and their restaurant celebrates and
shares their love of food. Among signature dishes are the starter of veal
sweetbreads and wild mushroom–garlic toast and such main courses
as rosemary roasted lamb, brick quail, and Texas barbecued shrimp.
For dessert try the chocolate beignets. ✉ *8125 W. Sahara Ave., West
Side,* ☎ *702/869–2251. AE, D, DC, MC, V. No lunch weekends.*

$$$ ✕ **Roy's.** Don't worry about fusion confusion here; Roy Yamaguchi
★   practically invented the trend. His latest restaurant, which opened in
suburban Las Vegas in 2001, is bedecked with tropical paintings and
features an exhibition kitchen. The menu changes daily to reflect whatever's freshest at the market, but you can expect appetizers such as seared
shrimp on a stick with wasabi cocktail sauce or Hawaiian crispy crab
cakes in sesame beurre blanc. Entrées might include signature Yam-
aguchi dishes such as blackened ahi tuna in a spicy hot soy mustard
sauce, or teriyaki hibachi-grilled salmon with Japanese vegetable salad
and citrus ponzu sauce, hoisin-glazed pork, or charred sea scallops. ✉
8701 W. Charleston Blvd., West Side, ☎ *702/838–3620. AE, D, DC,
MC, V. No lunch.*

$$$ ✕ **Second Street Grille.** Although you'll find steaks, Chinese roast
★   duck, and Mongolian rack of lamb on the menu, seafood is the spe-
cialty here. Daily specials are flown in fresh from Hawaii. For starters,
try the Mongolian seafood pot filled with fish, clams, crab, and scal-
lops; the *ahi* sashimi; panfried crab cakes; or seared sea scallops. For
an entrée opt for the cedar-grilled salmon, sautéed soft-shell crab,
thick swordfish steak, or whole Thai snapper. The room is dark and
intimate; the service is professional but not pretentious; and, best of
all, Second Street Grille is relatively unknown in the Las Vegas fine-
dining firmament, so you can count on same-day reservations, at least
at press time. ✉ *Fremont Hotel and Casino, 200 E. Fremont St.,
Downtown,* ☎ *702/385–3232. AE, D, DC, MC, V. Closed Tues.–Wed.
No lunch.*

$$$ ✕ **WB Stage 16.** Theme restaurants may tend to lean toward the tacky,
★   but that's not the case with Warner Brothers' venture at capitalizing
on its famous movies. Diners enter an "outdoor" scene suggesting the
Burbank studio lot, then have their seating choice of "sets" inspired
by *Batman, Casablanca,* the original *Ocean's Eleven,* and the Busby
Berkeley musical *Gold Diggers of 1933.* The second-floor Jack's Velvet Lounge suggests the studio in its 1940s prime, with plush sofas and
open-balcony views of the Treasure Island pirate show across the
street. The menu includes starters such as barbecued duck spring rolls
with mango-cactus pear jam, pasta dishes such as linguine pronto and
smoked chicken penne, and entrées such as turkey and shiitake mushroom meat loaf and lobster strudel with vanilla Stoli beurre blanc. ✉
*Grand Canal Shoppes at the Venetian, 3355 Las Vegas Blvd. S, Cen-
ter Strip,* ☎ *702/414–1699. AE, MC, V.*

$$ ✕ **Rock Lobster.** The emphasis is heavy on lobster here—everything from
lobster club sandwiches, potpies, bisque, and tacos to $65 lobster din-
ners—but this restaurant owned by the China Grill group also serves
such favorites as New York strip, porterhouse, shrimp-and-scallop
sauté, and even hamburgers. The decor's in keeping with the theme—
the "rock" refers to music as well as lobster—and is slightly reminis-
cent of *Blade Runner* with huge video walls showing music clips and
a conveyor belt running plates of sushi along the central bar. This noisy,
hip place attracts a young L.A.–type crowd at night. ✉ *Mandalay Bay*

Resort and Casino, 3950 Las Vegas Blvd. S, South Strip, ☎ *702/632–7405. AE, D, DC, MC, V. No lunch.*

$$ ✕ **Wolfgang Puck Cafe.** An open-air venue inside the MGM Grand Hotel, this casual eatery is literally two steps off the casino floor. (You may have to speak up to be heard above the sounds of the slot machines and sports book.) It offers a leaner version of the basic Spago patio menu of gourmet pizzas, pasta, salads, and meat loaf. ⊠ *MGM Grand Hotel and Casino, 3799 Las Vegas Blvd. S, South Strip,* ☎ *702/ 891–1111. Reservations not accepted. AE, DC, MC, V.*

Continental

$$$$ ✕ **Picasso.** At this restaurant adorned with the artist's original works, ★ versatile chef Julian Serrano prepares innovative takes on the regional cuisines of France and Spain. Appetizers might include warm quail salad with sautéed artichokes and pine nuts, green asparagus with ragoût of fresh morels, and poached oysters with osetra caviar and vermouth sauce. Some entrée choices are sautéed medallions of fallow deer, slow-roasted short ribs, and roasted Atlantic turbot with carpaccio of potatoes. If that isn't enough, indulge in dessert: gratin of cinnamon with a crust of black walnuts and Port-butter ice cream, caramelized pineapple with coconut-lime sorbet, or warm pumpkin-and-walnut cake with pumpkin seed–brittle ice cream and cranberry syrup. Dinners are prix-fixe, with four- or five-course menus. ⊠ *Bellagio, 3600 Las Vegas Blvd. S, Center Strip,* ☎ *702/693–8105. AE, D, DC, MC, V. Reservations essential. Closed Wed. No lunch.*

$$$$ ✕ **Renoir.** The Mirage's showcase for the contemporary French cui- ★ sine of Chef Alessandro Stratta lives up to its name; genuine Renoir paintings decorate the interior. Stratta's cooking is equally artful, with lobster, scallops, and shellfish dishes among his most popular creations. The á la carte menu offers Santa Barbara prawns; ahi tuna and house-cured salmon Napoleon; roasted breast of pheasant with foie gras, potato, and artichoke confit; pancetta-wrapped veal tenderloin with lentils, arugula, and chanterelles; slow-baked salmon with roasted cauliflower; and braised veal cheeks with Swiss chard, black olives, and creamy polenta. Those who want the full Stratta experience, however, will select the five-course tasting menu. For dessert you might be tempted by crème brûlée or apple and caramel tarte Tatin with ice cream. ⊠ *Mirage Hotel and Casino, 3400 Las Vegas Blvd. S, Center Strip,* ☎ *702/791–7111. Reservations essential. Jacket required. AE, D, DC, MC, V. No lunch.*

$$$$ ✕ **Top of the World.** Dining rooms with a view have historically been hard to come by in Las Vegas, but the 1996 opening of the Stratosphere Hotel Tower and Casino gave the city a striking landmark and a restaurant with stunning views. Rounded, floor-to-ceiling windows at this airy eatery near the top of the 1,149-ft tower give 360-degree views of the Vegas Valley. The entire dining room revolves once each hour. The fare here is standard Continental with a few twists: tequila-lime shrimp, spinach and wild mushroom salad, pastas, steaks, and sandwiches. There's also a (non-rotating) cocktail lounge for casual dining. ⊠ *Stratosphere Hotel Tower and Casino, 2000 Las Vegas Blvd. S, North Strip,* ☎ *702/380–7711. Reservations essential. AE, D, DC, MC, V.*

$$$ ✕ **Pietro's.** Customers here face the difficult choice of which creations to try: pâté en croûte with lingonberry sauce, coquilles St. Jacques, and Nova Scotia smoked salmon are among the appetizers. Breast of capon Kiev with wild rice and roast duckling à l'orange or Montmorency (flamed with Bing cherries) are among the favored entrées. Prepared with flair for two are Châteaubriand and roasted rack of lamb. Among the desserts are Cherries Jubilee, bananas Foster, tiramisu, and baked

Alaska. Pietro's French provincial dining room is intimate (only 40 seats), and tables are adorned with fresh flowers. ⊠ *Tropicana Resort and Casino, 3801 Las Vegas Blvd. S, South Strip,* ☎ *702/739–2341. AE, D, DC, MC, V. Closed Tues.–Wed. No lunch.*

Eclectic

$$$$ ✕ **Caesar's Magical Empire.** The food's not the main attraction here
★ (though it's pretty good); magic and a trip through the almost mystical catacombs beneath Caesars Palace are what make a trip to Caesar's Magic Empire worthwhile. The three-course dinner is a choice of beef, chicken, salmon, or a vegetarian entrée, and wines are included. There's magic (of the non-culinary kind) before and during dinner, and after, when you have the opportunity to wander through the catacombs and take in a number of magic shows. It's an only-in-Vegas, only-at-Caesars experience. ⊠ *Caesars Palace, 3570 Las Vegas Blvd. S, Center Strip,* ☎ *702/731–7333. AE, D, MC, V.*

$ ✕ **J. C. Wooloughan.** What do you get when you build a pub in Ire-
★ land, dismantle it, and ship it across the ocean, to be reconstructed in the desert? An Irish pub in an upscale Las Vegas off-Strip resort that looks like a wee bit o' the Emerald Isle. J. C. Wooloughan offers plenty of Irish beers and beer blends and lots of Irish foods, both familiar and not-so. Cheek-by-jowl with the corned beef and cabbage and fish and chips, you'll find beef and Guinness pie, all-day Irish breakfast, or a Murphy's beef or vegetable curry boxty (a sort of stuffed potato omelet). For dessert, the fantastic Aunt Maura's Sticky Toffee Pudding and Irish mousse cheesecake are among the choices. Soups, sandwiches, salads, and the like also are available at this 24-hour establishment. ⊠ *JW Marriott Casino Resort, 221 N. Rampart Blvd., Summerlin,* ☎ *702/869–7777. AE, D, MC, V.*

French

$$$$ ✕ **Andre's French Restaurant.** Cynics predicted an early demise for Andre
★ Rochat's venture when he opened a classic French restaurant in an ivy-covered 1930s-era home several blocks from the bright lights of downtown's famous Glitter Gulch. That was in 1980, and Las Vegans and visiting conventioneers are still savoring his oven-roasted rack of lamb with mustard and herb sauce, filet mignon in green-peppercorn sauce, and amazing soufflés. You'll also find more updated creations ; the selections change daily depending on the availability of fresh ingredients. A second location at the Monte Carlo serves French food that's just as fine, but in a much more spectacular room, and his latest venture, Alize, is high atop The Palms, more than 50 stores above the Las Vegas Strip. ⊠ *401 S. 6th St., Downtown,* ☎ *702/385–5016;* ⊠ *Monte Carlo Resort and Casino, 3770 Las Vegas Blvd. S, South Strip,* ☎ *702/ 798–7151. Reservations essential. AE, DC, MC, V. No lunch.*

$$$$ ✕ **Eiffel Tower Restaurant.** The signature restaurant of Paris Las Vegas
★ is a room with a view, all right. What's special is not so much the 11-story height as the dramatic perch—about a third of the way up the hotel's half-scale Eiffel Tower replica, with views from all four glassed-in sides. A dedicated elevator whisks patrons straight to the room. The French-accented menu is varied but not overly cluttered. Appetizers include cold smoked salmon, sea scallops, and Russian caviar. Entrées are also weighted toward seafood dishes, including Atlantic salmon in pinot noir sauce and the house specialty, lobster Thermidor. Meat offerings include roasted rack of lamb Provençal, filet mignon in a mushroom sauté, and braised ballantine of quail *en cocotte.* ⊠ *Paris Las Vegas, 3655 Las Vegas Blvd. S, Center Strip,* ☎ *702/948–6937. AE, D, DC, MC, V. Reservations essential. Jacket and tie. Closed Mon. No lunch.*

$$$$ ✗ **Le Cirque.** This sumptuous restaurant, a branch of the New York City landmark, is one of Bellagio's best. The well-heeled diners here seem to know their food and look right at home in the mahogany-lined room, which is all the more opulent for its size: in a city of mega-everything, Le Cirque seats only 80. Even with a view of the hotel's lake and its mesmerizing fountain show, you'll only have eyes for your plate when your server presents to-die-for dishes such as sea scallops layered with black truffles and wrapped in spinach and puff pastry. The wine cellar contains more than 500 premium selections representing every wine-producing region of the world; caviar is available by the ounce. ⊠ *Bellagio, 3600 Las Vegas Blvd. S, Center Strip,* ☎ *702/693-8100. Reservations essential. AE, D, DC, MC, V. Jacket and tie. No lunch.*

$$$$ ✗ **Lutece.** The famed New York eatery has an outpost at the Venetian, with a circular, postmodern dining room. (For those who find the interior too intense, there's also dining on an outdoor patio with views of the Strip.) Among the appetizers are lobster medallions with port wine–roasted grapes, and sautéed foie gras with blood oranges poached in Sauternes. Entrées from the modern French bill of fare include applewood-smoked codfish with arugula and white truffle oil and roasted rack of lamb with an herbed goat cheese crust. Those who want to leave the driving to the chef can go with the seasonal prix-fixe menu, which offers entrées such as crisp black bass with lobster sauce or rack of lamb. ⊠ *Venetian Resort-Hotel-Casino, 3355 Las Vegas Blvd. S, Center Strip,* ☎ *702/414-2220. AE, D, DC, MC, V.*

$$$ ✗ **Mon Ami Gabi.** The Lettuce Entertain You company's French steak house has the highest-profile location inside Paris Las Vegas. It's the rare restaurant with a claim to sidewalk dining on the Strip. For those who prefer a less lively atmosphere, a glassed-in atrium just off the street still conveys an outdoor feel, and there are still-quieter dining rooms inside, adorned with chandeliers dramatically suspended three stories above. Numbered wine racks run from floor to ceiling in the lounge. The specialty of the house is steak frites, offered four different ways: classic, au poivre, Bordelaise, and Roquefort. There are fish and poultry dishes as well, and *plats du jour* such as roast duck and coq au vin on given days of the week. ⊠ *Paris Las Vegas, 3655 Las Vegas Blvd. S, Center Strip,* ☎ *702/946-7000. Reservations essential. AE, D, DC, MC, V.*

$$$ ✗ **Pamplemousse.** This restaurant (the name means grapefruit in
★ French) was named on a whim by late singer—and restaurant regular—Bobby Darrin. The dominant color here is burgundy, orchestral music is played over the stereo system, and the food is classic French. Because the entrées change daily, there is no printed menu; instead, the waiter recites the bill of fare. Specialties of the house include roast duckling with cranberry and Chambord sauce and Norwegian salmon with curry sauce. All dinners include salad, bread, steamed vegetables, and crudités. This room is small and popular with the convention trade, so be sure to make reservations as far in advance as possible. ⊠ *400 E. Sahara Ave., East Side,* ☎ *702/733-2066. Reservations essential. AE, D, DC, MC, V. Closed Mon. No lunch.*

$$ ✗ **Bonjour Casual French.** The *hauteur* that French restaurants are fa-
★ mous for is about all that's lacking at Bonjour, which says it's casual and means it. The food at this charming country-French spot is a blend of the classic and the innovative. Among the appetizer offerings are a warm Roquefort-and-pear Napoleon and onion soup gratinée; entrée choices include crusted salmon with spinach, pine nuts, and tarragon sauce, and vegetable ravioli with wild mushrooms and artichokes. A tarte Tatin is a fine finish. ⊠ *8878 S. Eastern Ave., South Las Vegas,* ☎ *702/270-2102. AE, D, DC, MC, V.*

Indian

$$ ✗ **Gandhi India's Cuisine.** If you're tired of all of the cheap steak and prime-rib specials offered in town, try this alternative. Gandhi offers dishes from major regions of India; large *thali* platters range from milder North Indian tandoori dishes to spicier versions favored in the country's southern regions. A vegetarian thali includes *samosas* (vegetable fritters), *alu Gobi* (cauliflower and baked potatoes), and *mattar panner* (peas with homemade cottage cheese). Colorful Indian fabrics decorate this airy eatery; there's a small loft for more intimate dining. A buffet lunch is served weekdays. ⊠ *4080 Paradise Rd., Paradise Road,* ☎ *702/734–0094. AE, D, DC, MC, V.*

$$ ✗ **India Oven.** There are a number of super Indian restaurants in Las Vegas, but India Oven stands tall among them. The inside is plain, the outside even plainer. But the location—sort of diagonal from the Sahara Hotel and Casino—makes India Oven easy for tourists to find, and its food makes it a favorite among locals—especially Indians, who make up a large part of the clientele. The menu is typically wide-ranging Indian, with tandoori meats and nan bread prepared in the tandoor oven; other specialties include lamb korma with cashews, almonds, and raisins, and chicken vindaloo. Among the creamy, satisfying desserts are a cardamom-flavored rice pudding and kulfi ice cream with pistachios. ⊠ *226 W. Sahara Ave., West Side,* ☎ *702/366–0222. AE, D, MC, V.*

$$ ✗ **Shalimar Fine Indian Cuisine.** Las Vegan Wayne Newton is a frequent visitor to this sedate restaurant just minutes from the Strip. White tablecloths, hanging brass lamps, and taped Indian music provide a comfortable spot for excellent North Indian cuisine. House specialties include eight lamb dishes that can be prepared mild, wild hot, crazy hot, and one-way ticket to the moon, plus marinated seafood and chicken tandoori dishes cooked over a mesquite grill. The weekday luncheon buffet includes 25 different dishes. ⊠ *3900 S. Paradise Rd., Paradise Road,* ☎ *702/796–0302. AE, D, DC, MC, V.*

Italian

$$$$ ✗ **Osteria del Circo.** With a view of the lake, this is one of Bellagio's prime dining spots. The colorful Circo, with its velveteen harlequin-patterned seats and whimsically decorated chandeliers, serves home-style Tuscan food. Among the appetizers are prosciutto with seasonal fruit. The Tuscan fish soup is made with lobster, prawns, calamari, monkfish, clams, and mussels. The homemade pastas include ravioli with spinach and sheep's milk ricotta in a butter-sage or fresh tomato sauce, and spinach-potato dumplings with Romano cheese and thyme. Caviars by the ounce are offered for dinner, and the extensive wine cellar has selections from every wine-producing region of the world. ⊠ *Bellagio, 3600 Las Vegas Blvd. S, Center Strip,* ☎ *702/693–8150. AE, D, DC, MC, V.*

$$$$ ✗ **Terrazza.** This dazzling Italian eatery in Caesars' spectacular Palace Tower has great views of the 4-acre Garden of the Gods pool; you also can dine alfresco on a terrace adjacent to the pool area. The ultraposh Terrazza offers excellent Caesar salads, designer pizzas, mushroom ravioli, lamb, veal chops, and steaks. Imported Italian beers and mineral waters are available. ⊠ *Caesars Palace, 3570 Las Vegas Blvd. S, Center Strip,* ☎ *702/731–7110. AE, D, DC, MC, V. No lunch.*

$$$$ ✗ **Zeffirino.** Everything—from the tile work to many of the employ-★ ees—comes straight from Italy, and all who enter here feel Italian, at least for the day. Located in the Venetian's retail court, the two-story establishment has an impressive facade adorned with dark wood and marble. Seafood dominates the menu, which includes sautéed lobster,

red snapper, and swordfish steak with herbs. Some dishes, such as the seafood symphony, bring the chef from the kitchen to layer assorted seafood and pasta in heated olive oil at the tableside. The pasta with pesto is said to be a favorite of Pope John Paul II. Desserts include *crema caramella*, tiramisu, and *torta al cioccolato Milanese*. ⊠ *Grand Canal Shops at the Venetian Resort-Hotel-Casino, 3355 Las Vegas Blvd. S, Center Strip,* ☎ *702/414–1000. AE, D, MC, V.*

$$$ ✕ **Antonio's.** Inlaid marble floors, a blue-sky dome, and murals depicting Italian scenes decorate this quiet restaurant, which has an open kitchen. The long menu offers well-prepared northern and southern Italian cuisine with old favorites such as cioppino, eggplant Parmesan, osso buco Milanese, and spaghetti con aragosta. If it's available, order the five-onion soup—and you can ask the waiter for the recipe. Desserts include tiramisu. ⊠ *Rio All-Suite Hotel and Casino, 3700 W. Flamingo Rd., West Side,* ☎ *702/252–7737. AE, DC, MC, V. No lunch.*

$$$ ✕ **Market City Caffe.** Recipes passed down through generations are the centerpiece for this lively restaurant owned and operated by a family with successful eateries in southern California. There's a stunning wine list and a spectacular antipasto bar. The menu includes such hearty selections as pizzas (such as pizza gamberetto, with shrimp, goat cheese, fresh tomatoes and pesto), pastas (such as spaghetti *alla puttanesca*, with a tomato-anchovy sauce), salads (such as insalata di calamari, with calamari, diced tomatoes, capers, and mixed greens) and panini (such as panini di melanzane, with warm grilled eggplant, garlic and red chili flakes, spinach, fresh mozzarella, roma tomatoes, and fresh basil). ⊠ *Monte Carlo Resort and Casino, 3770 Las Vegas Blvd. S, South Strip,* ☎ *702/730–7967. AE, D, DC, MC, V.*

$$$ ✕ **North Beach Cafe.** This restaurant reflects the flavor of San Francisco's famous North Beach Italian neighborhood. The menu highlights the northern Italian cuisine of Genoa, a Mediterranean coastal town where seafood is cooked in a light tomato sauce. Empanadas Argentina, tasty meat pies with hard-boiled eggs, raisins, and green olives, are popular appetizers, as are fried calamari and steamed clams and mussels. If you feel like pasta, try the North Beach Special—linguine with grilled chicken breast, eggplant, and zucchini. ⊠ *2605 S. Decatur Blvd., West Side,* ☎ *702/247–9530. AE, D, DC, MC, V. Closed Sun. No lunch Sat.*

$$$ ✕ **Olio.** A gelato wall, where Jetsonesque gelato girls scrape out just enough for each serving, is part of the fun at Olio, a high-styled Italian eatery that has a screening room so fans can watch "The Sopranos." Customers are invited to partake from the 60-ft antipasto table, where the offerings include grilled artichokes stuffed with goat cheese. Other appetizers are a Gorgonzola souffle with Portobello mushrooms and marinated tomatoes, or soft potato ravioli with pan-seared foie gras. Entrées include canelloni of veal, lamb, beef, and ricotta; osso buco Marsala; or South African lobster tail with broccoli rabe and herbed saffron butter. If gelato's not your thing, consider an upside-down polenta cake with sour cream ice cream for dessert. ⊠ *MGM Grand, 3799 Las Vegas Blvd. S, South Strip,* ☎ *702/891–7775. AE, D, DC, MC, V.*

$$$ ✕ **Onda.** Here's another offering from Chef Todd English, best known for his Boston-area restaurant Olives (and its Las Vegas branch in the Bellagio). Enter this superb ristorante through a piano bar opening onto the casino. Beyond this lounge, which has an arched, stained-glass ceiling and a marble floor, the restaurant proper is tucked behind one-way glass. Diners can watch the folks on the casino floor—but not vice versa. The menu offers seafood choices such as garlic-crusted sea bass and lobster Milanese (breaded and pan-fried) as well as traditional pasta dishes such as lasagna, fettuccine Alfredo, and angel-hair pasta with shrimp, garlic, white wine, tomatoes, and bread crumbs. There's

roasted chicken and chicken cacciatore, too. ⊠ *Mirage Hotel and Casino, 3400 Las Vegas Blvd. S, Center Strip,* ☎ *702/791–7111. AE, D, DC, MC, V. No lunch.*

$$$ ✗ **Piero Selvaggio Valentino and P.S. Italian Grill.** The Italian Grill, the busy front room of this eatery on the Venetian's convention-friendly "restaurant row," has a casual, urban vibe. Choose either appetizer or entrée portions of pasta, or heartier fare such as a New York steak in Tuscan barbecue sauce or pork chops marinated in apple cider. The dining-room menu offers four meat and four seafood dishes, among them possibly Maine scallops with a tomato-horseradish sauce and fresh oregano pesto, and roasted chicken breast wrapped in smoked bacon with red-wine sauce, polenta, and spinach. For an all-out experience, go for the prix-fixe tasting menu, which can include main courses such as buffalo steak with Marsala wine. ⊠ *Venetian Resort-Hotel-Casino, 3355 Las Vegas Blvd. S, Center Strip,* ☎ *702/414–3000. AE, D, DC, MC, V.*

$$$ ✗ **Spiedini Ristorante.** Gustav Mauler, who had long been chef and restaurant developer for the former Mirage Resorts company, got the chance to strike out on his own with this stylish Italian restaurant. The menu is a contemporary take on traditional favorites. Starters include a sumptuous antipasto platter and fried, thinly sliced potatoes and zucchini with a creamy Gorgonzola sauce. Entrées include hand-crafted pastas, a veal chop stuffed with fontina and sage, osso buco, and a lobster-and-shrimp fra diavolo. Desserts often are deliciously whimsical, as in the case of the pineapple carpaccio with raspberry sorbet. ⊠ *JW Marriott Las Vegas Casino Resort, 221 N. Rampart Blvd., Summerlin,* ☎ *702/869–8500. AE, D, DC, MC, V. No lunch.*

$$$ ✗ **Stefano's.** Tiles from Salerno, graceful hand-blown chandeliers from Venice, and colorful murals produce an island of serenity, and singing waiters (how can you not like a place where the waiters sing "Volare" and "Pepino the Italian Mouse"?) establish a light-hearted atmosphere in this ristorante named for Las Vegas legend Steve Wynn. The menu includes such standards as prosciutto with melon or mozzarella marinara as well as updated creations such as pappardella carbonara, lobster tail Milanese, and scampi Bella Anna. ⊠ *Golden Nugget Hotel and Casino, 129 E. Fremont St., Downtown,* ☎ *702/ 385–7111. AE, D, DC, MC, V. No lunch.*

$$$ ✗ **Trattoria del Lupo.** Wolfgang Puck and wife Barbara Lazaroff's first
★ Italian eatery is set in a rustic-looking dining room with a bar and wine room, an exhibition pizza and antipasto station, and a 20-ft communal table. The varied and imaginative traditional and contemporary dishes include grilled vegetables with roasted peppers and marinated artichokes, various pizzas, spinach-and-ricotta cannelloni, saffron risotto with sizzling shrimp and garlic, and grilled Sicilian-style swordfish with raisins and pine nuts. For dessert, try the warm polenta cake with strawberries and cream or the tiramisu cappuccino. ⊠ *Mandalay Bay Resort and Casino, 3950 Las Vegas Blvd. S, South Strip,* ☎ *702/ 740–5522. AE, D, DC, MC, V.*

$$$ ✗ **Venetian.** You can't miss this landmark Italian restaurant, which opened in 1955 as the first pizza place in Las Vegas: murals of Venice grace the exterior and interior walls. Culinary traditions here include a jumbo bowl of pork neck bones in a wine marinade served as an appetizer (use the bib!), and Venetian greens on a bed of pasta. You can't go wrong with any dishes that have a "p" in the name: think pasta, parmigiana, eggplant, pizzaiola, scallopini, peppers. The selection of homemade bread is outstanding. ⊠ *3713 W. Sahara Ave., West Side,* ☎ *702/876–4190. AE, D, DC, MC, V. No lunch.*

$$ ✗ **Bertolini's.** Tables at this sidewalk café inside The Forum Shops at Caesars are set up in the piazza surrounding the Fountain of the Gods.

The outside section is noisy; if you want to talk, take a table in the dark, clubby interior, where booths line the black-and-yellow antiqued walls. An open kitchen turns out soups, salads, wood-fired pizzas, and even wood-fired pastas (!), that include roasted chicken canelloni and rigatoni al forno. And if you'd rather avoid the traffic (both vehicular and pedestrian) of the Strip, there's a slightly more sedate outpost of this restaurant from the Morton's group out in the suburbs. ⊠ *The Forum Shops at Caesars, 3500 Las Vegas Blvd. S., Center Strip,* ☎ 702/735–4663. ⊠ *9500 W. Sahara Ave., West Side,* ☎ 702/869–1540 . *Reservations not accepted. AE, DC, MC, V.*

$$ ✗ **Buca di Beppo.** You want to really have fun dining out? Get together a big group of friends and head to one of the Buca di Beppo locations. While a lot of restaurants aren't particularly welcoming to large groups, Buca di Beppo revels in them. Maybe you can sit at the kitchen table, with its stove-side window seat. Or maybe in the Pope's room, with its papally inspired memorabilia and a bust of the pontiff on a turntable in the center of the room. Dishes are served family-style—and how; a small Caesar salad can easily serve four. You can buy a pocket protector at Buca di Beppo, but dessert is better; options include tiramisu and Buca bread pudding caramello. ⊠ *7690 W. Lake Mead Blvd., Northwest Las Vegas,* ☎ 702/363–6524; ⊠ *412 E. Flamingo Rd., Paradise Road,* ☎ 702/866–2867. *AE, D, DC, MC, V. No lunch.*

$$ ✗ **Carrabba's Italian Grill.** "Chain" may seem like a dirty word to anyone who's especially fond of mom-and-pop Italian joints, but Texas-based Carrabba's manages to put a different spin on things; that's immediately evident when you see the trees on the roof. Relax in the brick-bedecked eatery and enjoy such delights as bruschetta Carrabba (which pairs tomato and mushroom varieties of bruschetta), Cozze in Bianco (mussels steamed in a lovely white-wine mixture), tagliarini Picchi Pacchiu (with a crushed-tomato sauce), or chicken Bryan (with caprini cheese and sun-dried tomatoes). At dessert time, the tiramisu is equalled only by the Chocolate Dream. ⊠ *10160 S. Eastern Ave., Henderson,* ☎ 702/990–0650; ⊠ *8771 W. Charleston Blvd., West Side,* ☎ 702/304–2345. *AE, D, MC, V. No lunch.*

$$ ✗ **Chicago Joe's.** Tucked away in a quiet residential area near downtown, this modest brick house with lace curtains and faded framed photographs offers a welcome respite from the glitzy casino hustle. Chicago Joe's (and the Collura family's recipes, which can be traced to Sicily) has been drawing informed tourists and Vegas locals for more than two decades. The marinara sauce, which tops generous portions of pasta, veal, and chicken, has just the right amount of bite. Order "The Works" on any lunchtime sandwich (rib-eye, sausage, or meatball) and savor a mound of sautéed green peppers, mushrooms, and onions. Extra napkins are essential. ⊠ *820 S. 4th St., Downtown,* ☎ 702/382–5637. *AE, D, DC, MC, V.*

$$ ✗ **Ferraro's Restaurant & Lounge.** Gino Ferraro's dependable Italian cuisine has been a favorite of Las Vegans since 1985. The dining room of this casual restaurant is trimmed with black lacquer and pink neon accents. Family recipes are featured, fresh breads and pastas are made on the premises, the wine list is extraordinary, the osso buco is *magnifico,* and Rosalba's tiramisu is *fantastico.* The service is good and prices are moderate, too. ⊠ *5900 W. Flamingo Rd., West Side,* ☎ 702/364–5300; ⊠ *1916 Village Center Circle, Summerlin,* ☎ 702/562–9666. *AE, D, DC, MC, V.*

$$ ✗ **Il Fornaio.** Cross the Central Park footbridge inside the wonderfully quirky New York–New York Hotel and Casino and you'll come to Il Fornaio, a cheery and bright Italian café. You can dine "outdoors" on the patio by the pond and watch the world go by, or opt for a table inside. And now there's a branch at the new Green Valley Ranch Station Casino, where locals enjoy the spacious, contemporary-style dining room with tile floors and wood accents. An exhibition kitchen prepares fresh fish, wood-oven pizzas, fettuccine with sausage, and spinach linguine with shrimp. Very good breads (including ciabatta) are baked twice daily and you can buy loaves to go. ⊠ *New York–New York Hotel and Casino, 3790 Las Vegas Blvd. S, South Strip,* ☎ *702/650–6500;* ⊠ *Green Valley Ranch Station Casino, 2197 Paseo Verde Pkwy., Henderson,* ☎ *702/614–5283. AE, MC, V.*

Japanese

$$$$ ✕ **Mikado.** Only a few steps from the Mirage's casino, this restaurant provides an oasis from the gambling madness; it's relatively soothing if you're seated far from the door, near the placid streams, delicate gardens, and soft murals. The menu offers standard Japanese fare: steak, chicken, and shrimp prepared *teppanyaki* (chopped, diced, and sautéed on a hot grill) or tempura style; *yaki-tori* (grilled beef in a thick-noodle soup); plus sushi and sashimi from a sushi bar in the corner. ⊠ *Mirage Hotel and Casino, 3400 Las Vegas Blvd. S, Center Strip,* ☎ *702/ 791–7111. AE, D, DC, MC, V. No lunch.*

$$$$ ✕ **Nobu.** Chef Nobu Matsuhisa of New York, London, Aspen, and Bev-
★   erly Hills fame has replicated the decor and menu of his Manhattan Nobu (in the trendy TriBeCa neighborhood) in this sparkling restaurant with bamboo pillars, a seaweed wall, and wooden birch trees. Imaginative specialties include spicy sashimi, caramelized sweet miso–marinated black cod, red-bean and green-tea ice cream, mochi (rice) balls, and a bento box with warm chocolate soufflé. ⊠ *Hard Rock Hotel and Casino, 4455 Paradise Rd., Paradise Road,* ☎ *702/693–5000. AE, D, DC, MC, V. No lunch.*

$$$ ✕ **Hamada of Japan.** No matter what type of Japanese food you're in the mood for, you'll find it here. Hamada of Japan has a teppan room, which offers entrées of the sort found in Japanese steak houses; a sushi bar, with a menu of the familiar and the exotic (and which offers a dish called "sushi for beginners"); and a dining room, with a menu that includes teriyaki and tempura dishes, among others. There's a bit of overlap between menus, so if you're seated in the teppan room, you still can order sushi. There are five smaller Hamada branches—mostly on the Strip and also at the JW Marriott in Summerlin—but the original is only minutes from the Strip. ⊠ *598 E. Flamingo Rd., Paradise Road,* ☎ *702/733–3005;* ⊠ *Stratosphere Tower, 2000 Las Vegas Blvd. S, North Strip,* ☎ *702/380–7777;* ⊠ *JW Marriott Las Vegas Casino Resort, 221 N. Rampart Blvd., Summerlin,* ☎ *702/869–7710;* ⊠ *Polo Towers, 3745 Las Vegas Blvd. S, South Strip,* ☎ *702/736–1984;* ⊠ *The Flamingo, 3555 Las Vegas Blvd. S, Center Strip,* ☎ *702/733–3455;* ⊠ *The Luxor, 3900 Las Vegas Blvd. S, South Strip,* ☎ *702/262–4548. AE, D, DC, MC, V. No lunch.*

$$$ ✕ **Mizuno's Japanese Steak House.** Lobster, steak, and chicken entrées are sliced, diced, and grilled at your teppan table by chefs who wield flashy knives and are possessed of witty tongues. Quality teriyaki and seafood dishes are other pluses at this fun Japanese restaurant. ⊠ *Tropicana Resort and Casino, 3801 Las Vegas Blvd. S, South Strip,* ☎ *702/739–2713. AE, DC, MC, V. No lunch.*

Mediterranean

$$$$ ✕ **Olives.** In the Via Bellagio, this Mediterranean ristorante created by

chef/owner Todd English combines the best features of his Boston-area Olives and Figs restaurants. The patio overlooking the Bellagio's spectacular lake is perfect for alfresco dining. Among the fare are appetizers of beef carpaccio on crispy Roquefort polenta and grilled squid and octopus in a vinaigrette of chickpea, tomato, toasted garlic, and parsley. Entrées include whipped ricotta ravioli with hot Italian sausage, and cod cakes with lobster rémoulade and Boston baked beans. The roasted banana tiramisu is tantalizing. English also has a ristorante, Onda, in the Mirage. ✉ *Bellagio, 3600 Las Vegas Blvd. S, Center Strip,* ☎ *702/693–8181. AE, D, DC, MC, V.*

$$ ✕ **Grape Street Cafe, Wine Bar & Grill.** Grape Street's menu is designed
★ to coordinate nicely with the restaurant's interesting—and not stratospherically priced—wine list, and it follows that most of the dishes on it would carry a Mediterranean influence. There are salads, sandwiches, pizzas and the like, plus dinner specials such as filet mignon topped with a crab-stuffed shrimp and served with potato-Gorgonzola ravioli, or baked Alaskan halibut with Brie, crab, and shrimp stuffing. Desserts range from austere Stilton and Port to positively decadent dark-chocolate fondue. Grape Street is brick-lined, candle-lit, and cozy, and there's a patio for pleasant evenings. ✉ *7501 W. Lake Mead Blvd., Northwest Las Vegas,* ☎ *702/228–9463. AE, D, MC, V.*

Mexican

$$ ✕ **Cozymel's Mexican Grill.** This Dallas-based chain spotlights fresh seafood (spicy Yucatan sea bass steamed in banana leaves, or grilled ahi tuna in a citrus marinade) in a festive room decorated with fishing nets and indoor palms for a south-of-the-border fishing resort feel. More familiar Mexican dishes (fajitas, enchiladas, and oversize tacos) are available, along with vegetarian dishes and eight flavored margaritas to get you into the beach-party spirit. ✉ *355 Hughes Center Dr., Paradise Road,* ☎ *702/732–4833. AE, D, DC, MC, V.*

$$ ✕ **Dona Maria.** You might forget you're in Las Vegas after a few minutes in one of these relaxed and unpretentious cantinas—one near downtown and the other west of the Strip. Stop in at the downtown location on a Wednesday night and you just might see a crowd of natives gathered for the futbol game on satellite-provided Mexican TV. All of the combinations and specials are good, but the best play here is to order the enchilada-style tamale (with red or green sauce), for which Dona Maria is justly renowned. You also won't go wrong with the queso fundido con chorizo—Mexican-style sports-bar food. ✉ *910 Las Vegas Blvd. S, Downtown,* ☎ *702/786–6358;* ✉ *3205 N. Tenaya Way, Northwest Las Vegas,* ☎ *702/656–1600. AE, D, DC, MC, V.*

$$ ✕ **La Barca Mexican Seafood Restaurant.** If you want to eat where Mexicans eat and have no patience for Texas or California twists on Mexican food, this is the place for you. This busy spot inside the otherwise faded Commercial Center doesn't put chips and salsa on the table and the emphasis is on seafood, not gloppy things covered with cheese. Fish and shrimp tacos are the most popular orders, along with the Seven Seas Soup—a mixture of seafoods with implied medicinal benefits. The Whaler is a 45-ounce shrimp cocktail that creates an instant party. Mariachi bands enhance the weekend-only atmosphere. ✉ *953 E. Sahara Ave., East Side,* ☎ *702/657–9700. AE, D, DC, MC, V. Closed Mon.–Thurs.*

$$ ✕ **Lindo Michoacán.** *Lindo* means pretty; Michoacán is a state in central Mexico. Gavier Baragas, the congenial owner and host of this colorful cantina named for his native state, presents outstanding specialties that he learned to cook while growing up. Many menu items are named for his relatives, including *flautas Mama Chelo* (corn tortillas filled with chicken). Guacamole is made tableside; you can't get any fresher than that. Michoacán is known for its carnitas, so don't miss them. Or try the *cabrito birria de chivo* (roasted goat with red mole sauce). At dessert time, remember that the flan is a silken wonder. ✉

83

2655 E. Desert Inn Rd., East Side, ☎ *702/735–6828;* ☎ *702/257–6810. AE, D, MC, V.*

$$ ✕ **Pink Taco.** Nothing inside the Hard Rock Hotel is boring, and that goes for this over-the-top take on a Mexican cantina. The food is serviceable but takes a decided backseat to the party atmosphere, which includes a huge four-sided bar, patio doors that open onto the hotel's elaborate pool area, and waitresses in soccer jerseys that are low-cut from every direction. The eyebrow-raising name refers, of course, to the grilled salmon taco, one of six special tacos on the menu. Alternatives include the chicken tostada salad and achiote grilled chicken breast. ✉ *Hard Rock Hotel and Casino, 4455 Paradise Rd., Paradise Road,* ☎ *702/693–5000. AE, D, DC, MC, V.*

$$ ✕ **Viva Mercado's.** The explosion of new chain restaurants in suburban neighborhoods makes it easy to forget the charms of the first Las Vegas restaurant to bring a chef's touch to Mexican food. You can get enchiladas and burritos here if you want, and bountiful plates of them at that. More rewarding are the daily specials and fish dishes, such as orange roughy cooked four different ways (including with the ultra-hot *salsa de arbol*), or *banderilla de camaron* (shrimp grilled in garlic, lemon, and pico de gallo). Stucco, fake plants, and tile awnings over rows of booths vaguely suggest an outdoor Mexican plaza, though in a mom-and-pop way compared to the many "theme" and "designed" restaurants around here. ✉ *6182 W. Flamingo Rd., West Side,* ☎ *702/ 871–8826. AE, MC, V.*

Moroccan

$$$ ✕ **Marrakech.** Sprawl out on soft floor cushions and feel like a pampered pasha as belly dancers shake it up in a cozy Middle Eastern–style "tent" with a fabric-covered ceiling and eye-catching mosaics. The prix-fixe feast is a six-course affair that you eat with your hands: shrimp scampi, vegetable salad, lentil soup, Cornish game hen, lamb shish kebab, and the tasty dessert *pastilla,* which is baked phyllo dough layered with apples, peaches, and pecans. Algerian wines flow freely in this upbeat spot where servers wear Moroccan robes and patrons are invited to join the belly dancers if they feel the urge. ✉ *3900 Paradise Rd., Paradise Road,* ☎ *702/737–5611. AE, D, DC, MC, V.*

Pan-Asian

$$ ✕ **Little Buddha.** It may sound like a mixed metaphor—an Asian
★ restaurant in Paris—but France's Buddha Bar has achieved world fame for its food and its music. And now there's a Buddha Bar branch, Little Buddha, at The Palms in Las Vegas. The decor's a wonderful blend of the elegant and the mysterious, with buddhas of every sort bedecking every surface. The kitchen produces such Pacific Rim wonders as Hawaiian smoked pot stickers, wok-fried salt and pepper calamari and frog's legs, grilled Asian pork ribs, and curry shrimp in banana leaf. Finish things off with a sweet touch of coconut sticky rice with mango and Florentine crisp or liquid-center chocolate cake with vanilla ice cream. ✉ *The Palms, 4321 W. Flamingo Rd., West Side,* ☎ *702/ 942–7777. AE, D, DC, MC, V.*

$$ ✕ **Sam Woo's Bar-B-Q.** Barbecued critters hang in the front window of this authentic and always bustling Chinese eatery, which is one of numerous Asian restaurants in the Chinatown Plaza west of the Strip. Sam Woo's is a good, inexpensive choice, serving everything from Japanese sushi to Beijing duck. The house special chow mein and other Hong Kong–style dishes always shine. Try to ignore the fast service aimed at clearing tables for waiting customers. ✉ *4215 W. Spring Mountain Rd., West Side,* ☎ *702/368–7628. No credit cards.*

Seafood

$$$ ✗ **McCormick & Schmick's.** This Portland-based spot has old-tavern charm (complete with stained glass) and offers a huge menu of appetizers, oysters on the half shell, salads, lunch sandwiches, and imaginatively prepared fresh fish dishes (the selection changes daily). Popular choices are Oregon Dungeness crab cakes with red-pepper aïoli, Louisiana catfish with chipotle pepper sauce, Mexican yellowtail tuna with pepper balsamic vinaigrette, Florida stone crabs, and Alaskan troll king salmon with pinot noir sauce roasted on a cedar plank. Desserts include berry sherry trifle and walnut candied upside-down apple pie à la mode. If the weather's pleasant, you can dine on the patio. ✉ *335 Hughes Center Dr., Paradise Road,* ☎ *702/836–9000. AE, D, DC, MC, V.*

$$$ ✗ **The Tillerman.** Its location on Flamingo Road, almost 3 mi east of the Strip, makes the Tillerman a quiet refuge from the casinos. For smokers, the garden setting—the restaurant is built around a huge ficus tree growing in the center of the room—places you under an open skylight on hot desert nights. Those seeking smoke-free dining are seated in a large room in the back. Specialities include fettuccine with lobster, tomatoes, scallions, and cream; grilled swordfish with vegetable confetti and crispy squid ink pasta; and lightly blackened yellowfin tuna with stone-grain mustard sauce. Up to a dozen fresh-fish selections are offered each night, and the steaks are always done just right, too. ✉ *2245 E. Flamingo Rd., East Side,* ☎ *702/731–4036. AE, D, DC, MC, V. No lunch.*

Southwestern

$$$ ✗ **Border Grill.** The hosts of TV's "Too Hot Tamales," Mary Sue Milliken and Susan Feniger, now have two Las Vegas counterparts to their stylish Santa Monica eatery—the first at Mandalay Bay, and a brand-new space at Green Valley Ranch. Appetizers include green-corn tamales, ceviche, and plantain empanadas; for lunch try the turkey tostada, chipotle chicken, or grilled skirt steak; and for dinner the sautéed rock shrimp. Oaxacan mocha cake and Key lime pie are among the desserts. ✉ *Mandalay Bay Resort and Casino, 3950 Las Vegas Blvd. S, South Strip,* ☎ *702/632–7394;* ✉ *Green Valley Ranch Station Casino, 2197 Paseo Verde Pkwy., Henderson,* ☎ *702/614–5283. AE, D, DC, MC, V.*

$$$ ✗ **Coyote Café and Miller's Grill Room.** Mark Miller has transplanted his self-named "gourmet southwestern" food to Las Vegas from the original Coyote Café in Santa Fe. The café out front offers an excellent alternative to the crowded buffets and coffee shops for breakfast through dinner. (Breakfast is a treat—you walk right in, sit right down, and are offered six choices, including *huevos rancheros,* quiche, and fruit and yogurt.) Miller's Grill Room, adjacent to the café, offers an imaginative dinner menu. Appetizers such as Southwestern Painted Soup and tamales complement entrées such as Howlin' Chile Relleno and the Cowboy Rib Chop. ✉ *MGM Grand Hotel Casino, 3799 Las Vegas Blvd. S, South Strip,* ☎ *702/891–7349. AE, D, DC, MC, V.*

$$$ ✗ **Star Canyon.** Straight from Dallas, chef Stephen Pyles brings his inventive "New Texas" fare to the Las Vegas Strip. In an understated room cleverly accented with Lone Star State miscellany, an open grill tempts diners with the scents of chiles and barbecue. But the menu goes far beyond fajitas and ribs. Pyles combines familiar ingredients in pleasing new ways: Hudson Valley foie gras with mole sauce and corn pudding, or crabmeat-stuffed halibut on a cumin-tinged three-bean melange. A wine list with selections from all over the world includes a number of Texas bottles. ✉ *Venetian Resort-Hotel-Casino, 3355 Las Vegas Blvd. S, Center Strip,* ☎ *702/733–5000. AE, D, DC, MC, V.*

$$ ✕ **Garduño's Chili Packing Co.** "So hot it will make your ice melt" is the friendly warning at these colorfully cluttered Mexican and Southwestern warehouse restaurants. The Garduño family imported these spots from Albuquerque along with ongoing shipments of fresh green chiles from Hatch, New Mexico. The chiles are used in many of the spicier dishes; those with more timid taste buds should sample the milder seafood tacos and fajitas that arrive on sizzling iron skillets. The salsa bar has an impressive array of sauces; the bar has an even more impressive selection of tequilas. Meals come with sopaipillas that can be drenched with honey to cool off the chile burn. On Sunday a margarita brunch is served. ✉ *Fiesta Hotel and Casino, 2400 N. Rancho Dr., Rancho Strip,* ☎ *702/631–7000.* ✉ *Palms, 4321 W. Flamingo Rd., West Side,* ☎ *702/942–7777. AE, D, DC, MC, V.*

$$ ✕ **Z' Tejas Grill.** This Austin, Texas–based chain first conquered Las Vegas with a location on the Paradise Road convention corridor, then added a gorgeous building in the fast-growing Peccole Ranch area in the far west end of town. Both locations offer signature dishes such as Voo Doo Tuna (blackened tuna with spicy soy mustard), Jamaica jerk chicken salad, and pork roast Vera Cruz. Both branches also have a Southwestern-style brunch on weekends. ✉ *3824 Paradise Rd., Paradise Road,* ☎ *702/732–1660;* ✉ *9560 W. Sahara Ave., West Side,* ☎ *702/638–0610. AE, D, DC, MC, V.*

Steak

$$$$ ✕ **A.J.'s Steakhouse.** The Hard Rock Hotel offers a time-machine ride back to Old Las Vegas with this retro-style room serving as a tribute to Hard Rock chairman Peter Morton's father, Arnie, a Chicago restaurateur. Behind the oxblood leather front doors lies a dining room decorated with 1950s-style furniture and photos; there's even a piano bar. Among the appetizers are a Gulf shrimp cocktail and smoked Norwegian salmon. Featured steaks include a 20-ounce New York strip sirloin and a 24-ounce prime porterhouse. Alaskan salmon encrusted in horseradish and Hawaiian tuna steak are among the non-beef options. ✉ *Hard Rock Hotel and Casino, 4455 Paradise Rd., Paradise Road,* ☎ *702/693–8105. AE, D, DC, MC, V. Closed Mon. No lunch.*

$$$$ ✕ **Bally's Steakhouse.** The dining room of this traditional steak house has a mirrored food-and-wine display, large fireplace, and comfortable furnishings. The menu includes homemade sausage-filled mushrooms baked with garlic, spinach, and Fontina cheese; Scottish smoked salmon with bagel chips and horseradish crème fraîche; and jumbo pancetta-wrapped sea scallops with fresh-basil relish. Or try the mesquite-grilled 20-ounce bone-in rib eye with garlic-herb butter. Be sure your dessert pocket is not full—among the magnificently presented sweets are chocolate pâté (a trio of chocolates with Grand Marnier vanilla sauce). ✉ *Bally's Casino Resort, 3645 Las Vegas Blvd. S, Center Strip,* ☎ *702/ 967–4661. AE, D, DC, MC, V. No lunch.*

$$$$ ✕ **Charlie Palmer Steak.** The whole idea of putting a Four Seasons hotel inside Mandalay Bay was to have a quiet enclave "hidden" within a busy hotel-casino complex. Charlie Palmer got the idea right away. While his Aureole at Mandalay Bay is ostentatious, the nearby steak house is clubby and understated. The mahogany-lined room off the Four Seasons lobby serves only Black Angus that's been dry-aged for 21 days. There's tuna steak or caramelized chicken for those who don't eat beef. The lounge welcomes the revival of the cigar and has live entertainment on weekends. ✉ *Four Seasons Hotel, 3960 Las Vegas Blvd. S, South Strip,* ☎ *702/632–5120. AE, D, DC, MC, V. No lunch.*

$$$$ ✕ **Delmonico Steakhouse.** Celebrity chef Emeril Lagasse gives the New Orleans touch to this big-city–style steak house at the Venetian. The subdued, modern dining creates a feeling of calm, and friendly but professional staff members make customers feel welcome. Creole-influenced dishes include baked jumbo Gulf shrimp and various oyster-based creations. Delmonico chicken carved tableside for two, Emeril's double-cut pork chop, and bone-in rib-eye steak are simply satisfying. ⊠ *Venetian Resort-Hotel-Casino, 3355 Las Vegas Blvd. S, Center Strip,* ☎ *702/733–5000. AE, D, DC, MC, V.*

$$$$ ✕ **Luxor Steakhouse.** This attractive restaurant, with its classic cherrywood bar and walls, is divided into several rooms and alcoves to afford intimate dining. Hand-painted Egyptian scenes adorn the walls and Egyptian statues grace the room. Whole stuffed artichokes and hearty Portobello mushrooms filled with seafood, spinach, and Gorgonzola are among the favorite appetizers. Succulent entrée selections include the outstanding, thinly sliced Chicken Breast Giza, filled with couscous and spinach and served with pistachio nuts and sun-dried tomatoes. And the steaks, of course, are super-aged prime beef in the usual cuts, including filet mignon, porterhouse, and rib-eye. ⊠ *Luxor Hotel-Casino, 3900 Las Vegas Blvd. S, South Strip,* ☎ *702/262–4778. AE, D, DC, MC, V. No lunch.*

$$$$ ✕ **Prime.** Even among celebrity chefs, Jean-Georges Vongerichten has
★ established a "can't touch this" reputation. Prime—with its gorgeous view of the fountains—has become a place to see and be seen at the Bellagio. In a velvet-draped, gold and burgundy room, eight cuts of beef are presented with a choice of seven mustards and six sauces, from the classic (béarnaise) to the more adventurous (tamarind). Diners can also get a taste of a few signature Vongerichten dishes, such as garlic soup with frogs' legs. ⊠ *Bellagio, 3600 Las Vegas Blvd. S, Center Strip,* ☎ *702/693–8105. AE, D, DC, MC, V. No lunch.*

$$$$ ✕ **Smith & Wollensky.** The legendary New York restaurant has been replicated in a massive free-standing building. With hardwood floors and no plush surfaces to soak up the ricocheting sound, it's a raucous place—but that's part of the fun. This is one of the few places where you can still get Beef Wellington—and a good one, at that; other specialties include Maryland crab cakes, grilled Atlantic salmon, prime steaks, prime rib, lamb and veal chops, and the famous crackling pork shank with applesauce. Wollensky's Grill, a lively, more casual gathering spot that's open until 3 AM, serves the same menu as the more upscale restaurant, as well as more casual fare such as sandwiches and pizzas. ⊠ *3767 Las Vegas Blvd. S, South Strip,* ☎ *702/862–4100. AE, DC, MC, V. Lunch in grill only.*

$$$ ✕ **Billy Bob's Steak House.** Big food is the name of the game at the Western-theme Billy Bob's Steak House at Sam's Town. The 28-ounce rib eye is Texas-sized, the barbecued brisket could feed a rodeo. And then there's dessert: the chocolate eclairs are a foot long, and the chocolate cake could fill up a good chunk of the Grand Canyon. ⊠ *Sam's Town Hotel and Casino, 5111 Boulder Hwy., Boulder Strip,* ☎ *702/456–7777. AE, D, DC, MC, V. No lunch.*

$$$ ✕ **Golden Steer.** In a town where restaurants come and go almost as quickly as visitors' cash, the longevity of this steak house, opened in 1962, is itself a recommendation. And while it changed hands during 2001, the tradition continues; folks still come to this San Francisco Barbary Coast–theme restaurant with red leather chairs, polished dark wood, and stained-glass windows for the huge slabs of well-prepared meat. Steak, ribs, and game are particularly popular. Although you wouldn't know it from the outside, the Steer is cavernous; however, lots of small, intimate rooms break up the space. ⊠ *308 W. Sahara Ave., West Side,* ☎ *702/384–4470. AE, D, DC, MC, V. No lunch.*

$$$ ✕ **Pullman Grill.** It may be situated hard by the end of downtown Las Vegas' Glitter Gulch, but Main Street Station is a quiet island of Vic-

torian elegance, and that old-world feel is magnified in the Pullman Grill. There's carved wood all over, a pressed-tin ceiling, and—here's some truth in advertising—even a Pullman car right there in the restaurant; you can retreat to it for a cigar and a Port after dinner if you'd like. Dinner leans heavily to steaks, but owing to the Hawaiian clientele of the hotel-casino there are a lot of Asian offerings, too, including a sashimi appetizer of sea-breeze-fresh ahi tuna. Other choices include a seafood medley casserole and succulent lamb chops. ⊠ *Main Street Station, 200 N. Main St., Downtown,* ☎ *702/387–1896. AE, D, DC, MC, V. Closed Mon.–Tues. No lunch.*

$$$ ✕ **Sonoma Cellar.** Sonoma Cellar was one of the first upscale restaurants in a locals casino, and it hasn't lost its verve. It still has an elegant, serene feel as well as a redwood wine cellar and a cigar lounge. The menu includes, in addition to steaks, such classics as oysters Rockefeller, lobster bisque, and clams casino and more updated offerings such as Mediterranean shrimp, crab-stuffed Portobello mushroom, and mesquite-grilled or pan-seared salmon fillet. Alaskan king crab legs and mesquite-grilled or thermidor-style Australian lobster tail are also available. ⊠ *Sunset Station Hotel and Casino, 1301 W. Sunset Rd., Henderson,* ☎ *702/547–7898. AE, D, DC, MC, V. No lunch.*

$$$ ✕ **Steak House.** Believe it or not, many local residents think this steak house set within the craziness of Circus Circus is among the best in town. Totally unlike the rest of Circus Circus, wood paneling and antique brass furnishings adorn a dark, quiet room reminiscent of 1890s San Francisco. A ton of beef—aged 21 days—is displayed in a glassed-in area at the side; the cooking takes place over an open-hearth mesquite grill. Steaks, chops, chicken, and seafood make up the menu, and all entrées are accompanied by soup or salad, fresh bread, and a giant baked potato. ⊠ *Circus Circus, 2880 Las Vegas Blvd. S, North Strip,* ☎ *702/ 734–0410. AE, D, DC, MC, V. No lunch.*

Vegetarian

$ ✕ **The Raw Truth Cafe.** The name of this vegetarian café refers to the fact that nothing is cooked at temperatures higher than the 100-plus degrees it takes to make flat breads and pizza dough. And yet, reasonable facsimiles of pizza (made of dehydrated sprouted bread and fermented almond cheese) and lasagna take their place alongside the expected salad choices. ⊠ *3620 E. Flamingo Rd., East Side,* ☎ *702/450–9007. AE, D, DC, MC, V.*

$ ✕ **Wild Oats Community Market.** Wild Oats has all the stuff you'd expect in the small café of a whole foods market—an extensive salad bar, for example, and smoothies and vegetable juices—but a lot of the unexpected as well; for example, somebody's enlightened enough to separate vegan dishes (biryani, stuffed tofu pockets) from regular vegetarian (kung pao tofu, traditional slaw) in the deli. Selections include a Reuben sandwich that combines smoked tomato slices with sauerkraut, Swiss cheese, and Thousand Island dressing, and a tomato wrapper filled with carrots, cucumbers, tomato, zucchini, and bean sprouts and topped with hummus, grilled tofu, and pepper jack soy cheese. ⊠ *7250 W. Lake Mead Blvd., Northwest Las Vegas,* ☎ *702/942–1500;* ⊠ *517 N. Stephanie St., Henderson,* ☎ *702/458–9427. AE, D, DC, MC, V.*

5   LODGING

Las Vegas has upward of 130,000 hotel rooms, and it probably offers more choices and types of accommodations than anywhere else, from 95-year-old downtown digs to exclusive hotels with 10,000-square-ft penthouse villas. No matter where your head hits the pillow, though, there's sure to be a casino, coffee shop, buffet, lounge, convenience store, and neon sign within shouting distance.

Updated by
Haas Mroue

AS VEGAS IS NOW HOME to 9 of the 10 largest hotels in the United States. If 130,000 hotel and motel rooms seems like a lot, consider that visitor volume in 2003 is projected to near 36 million. That means well over a half-million visitors a week—the equivalent of every man, woman, and child living within Seattle's city limits being suddenly transported to Las Vegas. In short, accommodations fill up fast around here, even when no major conventions or events are in town.

When it's time for a major convention, it's not unusual for Las Vegas to sell out completely. Nearly two dozen conventions a year each attract more than 25,000 participants. Combine those with three-day weekends, holidays, large sporting events, and normally crowded weekends, and you can see why it's wise to make your lodging arrangements as far ahead of your visit as possible. On the other hand, things change quickly in Las Vegas. If you arrive at the last minute without accommodations, you'll almost always be able to find a room somewhere in town—though the price might be double or triple what you would have paid with reservations. And if your original room is not to your liking, you can usually upgrade it around checkout time the next day.

In general, rates for Las Vegas accommodations are far lower than those in most other American resort and vacation cities, but the situation is a wacky one indeed. There are a hundred different variables, depending on who's selling the rooms (reservations, marketing, casino, conventions, wholesalers, packagers); what rooms we're talking about (standard, deluxe, minisuites, standard suites, deluxe suites, high-roller suites, penthouses, bungalows); demand (weekday, weekend, holiday, conventions, or sporting events in town); and management whim (bean-counter profit models, revenue-projection realities, etc.). When business is slow, many hotels reduce rates on rooms in their least desirable sections, sometimes with a buffet breakfast or even a show included. Most "sales" occur from early December to mid-February and July through August, the coldest and hottest times of the year. Members of casino slot clubs often get offers of discounted or even free rooms, and they can almost always reserve a room even when the rest of the hotel is "sold out." The cost structure we're quoting is for a standard room on a regular weekday; expect that room rates might be twice the weekday rate on a regular weekend (no holiday or special event).

One useful guide to bargain rates is the Sunday "Calendar" section of the *Los Angeles Times,* where most Las Vegas hotels advertise. Call a hotel's toll-free number and ask what package deals it has for your vacation dates. Checking the hotel's Web site is always a good idea as many specials are offered on the Internet only. If the hotel reservations clerks continually tell you they're sold out, try the **Las Vegas Convention and Visitors Authority** room reservations center (☎ 800/332–5333), which has access to a good selection of the rooms available for any given day. A good source of available rooms and discounts is the **Las Vegas Reservations Bureau** (☎ 800/831–2754). They may be able to place you in the hotel of your choice.

CATEGORY	COST*
$$$$	over $150
$$$	$100–$150
$$	$70–$100
$	under $70

*All prices are for a standard double room, excluding service charge and 10% tax.

The Strip

$$$$
★ 🏨 **Bellagio Las Vegas.** This luxury hotel, which opened in 1998, has more than a thousand fountains—nozzles that erupt in a choreographed water ballet—surrounding a man-made lake; an art gallery; 12 restaurants, including New York's Le Cirque, Boston's Olives, and San Francisco's Aqua; and one of the most stunning shows on the Strip, Cirque du Soleil's O. A breathtaking lobby, an indoor botanical conservatory, a full-service spa, two wedding chapels, and an upscale shopping arcade complete the extravagant picture. Bellagio also has one of the best buffets in town, where the wait can sometimes exceed two hours. This is the hardest place in Vegas to land good deals, although it wouldn't hurt to check the hotel's Web site for Internet specials. The rooms are standard size, but continue the opulent theme with luxurious fabrics and Italian marble. Parents take note: no one under 18 is allowed on the property unless they are staying at the hotel—and families with children are encouraged to find lodging elsewhere. ✉ *3600 Las Vegas Blvd. S, Center Strip 89109,* ☎ *702/693–7111 or 888/987–6667,* FAX *702/693–8546,* WEB *www.bellagiolasvegas.com. 2,684 rooms, 316 suites. 12 restaurants, in-room data ports, in-room safes, 6 pools, health club, spa, lounge, casino, showroom, shops, laundry service, concierge, business services, meeting room. AE, D, DC, MC, V.*

$$$$
★ 🐨 🏨 **Four Seasons Hotel.** On the top (36th through 39th) floors of the Mandalay Bay complex, with its own private entrance, express elevators, pool, health club, recreation area, parking, restaurants, and meeting area, this is one of the finest and most luxurious hotels in Las Vegas. It's also one of the only places in town with no slot machines or gaming tables and is perfect for families. Children will find a stuffed animal and cookies and milk awaiting their arrival. An added bonus is the complimentary use of the hotel's strollers and playpens. All this said, this luxury hotel is by no means teeming with children; in fact, it's the quietest and most relaxing hotel on the Strip, where a guest's well-being is the number-one priority. Rooms have views of the mountains, desert, pool and gardens, and the Strip. Afternoon tea is served daily in the Verandah lounge. The newly expanded spa (for hotel guests only) is luxuriously intimate and full access to all of Mandalay Bay's facilities is also included. ✉ *3960 Las Vegas Blvd. S, South Strip 89109,* ☎ *702/632–5000,* FAX *702/632–5222,* WEB *www.fourseasons.com. 338 rooms, 86 suites. 2 restaurants, room service, in-room data ports, in-room safes, minibars, in-room VCRs, pool, health club, hot tub, massage, sauna, spa, steam room, bar, laundry service, concierge, business services, meeting room, car rental, no-smoking rooms. AE, D, DC, MC, V.*

$$$$
🏨 **Venetian Resort-Hotel-Casino.** Opened in 1999, this luxurious resort offers some of the largest and plushest rooms on the Strip. The 700-square-ft guest quarters, richly appointed in modified Venetian style, have a sunken living room with dining table and convertible sofa, walk-in closets, separate shower and tub, three telephones (including one in the bathroom), two 27-inch TVs, and a desk with fax machine. Also on the property are the Guggenheim Las Vegas Museum, the largest retail mall in Nevada (complete with a replica Grand Canal plied by gondolas); reproductions of various Venetian landmarks; 11 restaurants; two ultra-hip bars and lounges; the four-level C2K (Carnevale 2000) entertainment complex; Warner Brothers Stage 16, another entertainment complex; and branches of the famous Canyon Ranch SpaClub and Madame Tussaud's Wax Museum. ✉ *3355 Las Vegas Blvd. S, Center Strip 89109,* ☎ *702/733–5000 or 888/283–6423,* FAX *702/414–4805,* WEB *www.venetian.com. 3,036 suites. 11 restaurants, room service, in-room data ports, in-room safes, minibars, 5 pools, health club, hair*

92

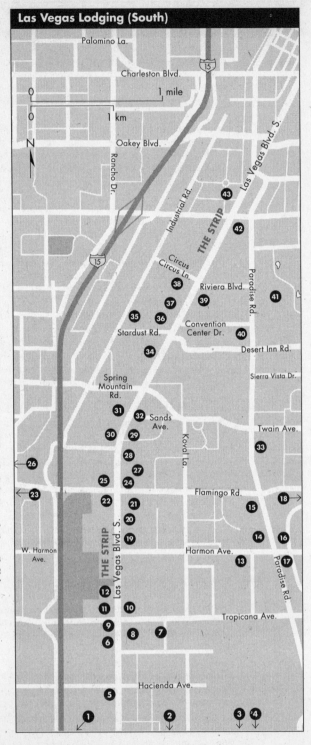

When you pack your MCI Calling Card, it's like packing your loved ones along too.

Your MCI Calling Card is the easy way to stay in touch when you travel. Use it to call to and from over 125 countries. Plus, every time you call, you can earn frequent flier miles. So wherever your travels take you, call home with your MCI Calling Card. It's even easy to get one. Just visit **www.mci.com/worldphone** or **www.mci.com/partners**.

EASY TO CALL WORLDWIDE

1. Just enter the WorldPhone® access number of the country you're calling from.
2. Enter or give the operator your MCI Calling Card number.
3. Enter or give the number you're calling.

Aruba ⁜	800-888-8
Bahamas ⁜	1-800-888-8000

Barbados ⁜	1-800-888-8000
Bermuda ⁜	1-800-888-8000
British Virgin Islands ⁜	1-800-888-8000
Canada	1-800-888-8000
Mexico	01-800-021-8000
Puerto Rico	1-800-888-8000
United States	1-800-888-8000
U.S. Virgin Islands	1-800-888-8000

⁜ Limited availability.

EARN FREQUENT FLIER MILES

Find America *with a Compass*

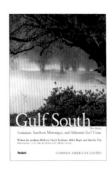

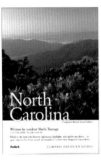

Written by local authors and illustrated throughout
with spectacular color images, Compass American
Guides reveal the character and culture of more than
40 of America's most fascinating destinations. Perfect
for residents who want to explore their own backyards
and for visitors who want an insider's perspective
on the history, heritage, and all there is to see and do.

Fodor's COMPASS AMERICAN GUIDES

At bookstores everywhere.

salon, spa, 4 lounges, casino, showroom, shops, laundry service, concierge, business services, convention center, travel services, no-smoking floor. AE, D, DC, MC, V.

$$$ 🏨 **Aladdin Resort and Casino.** It was the end of an era. After 22 years in operation, on April 27, 1998, 860 charges of dynamite brought down the original Aladdin in a cloud of dust and rubble. Just over two years later, in August 2000, the Aladdin was reborn as one of Las Vegas' modern-day megaresorts. Costing more than $1.3 billion to build, the Aladdin is still themed after the legendary tale from the *Arabian Nights.* The casino has everything from flying horses to a giant version of Aladdin's lamp; the property also includes the Desert Passage mall, a 7,000-seat performing arts center, and a wedding chapel. Rooms are decorated with Arabian flair, but are more geared toward the business world than traveling sheiks. In addition to marble bathrooms and custom furniture, the oversize rooms have high-speed Internet access for those who need to stay connected. ⊠ *3667 Las Vegas Blvd. S, Center Strip 89109,* ☎ *702/736–0111 or 877/333–9474,* ℻ *702/736-7107,* WEB *www.aladdincasino.com. 2,344 rooms, 223 suites. 21 restaurants, in-room data ports, 2 pools, health club, spa, lounge, casino, theater, shops, business services, meeting room. AE, D, DC, MC, V.*

$$$ 🏨 **Bally's Las Vegas.** Opened in 1973 as the original MGM Grand Hotel, this venerable Las Vegas resort had an ultrasplashy beginning with Cary Grant and Dean Martin on hand the day it opened. Now, it's still one of the largest resorts on the Strip; with nearly 3,000 rooms, six restaurants, three showrooms, a wedding chapel, and a 40-store mall, it's clear why this hotel calls itself "a city within a city." The hotel also has a huge casino, separate health spas for men and women, an attractively landscaped outdoor pool, and a terminal for the monorail to MGM Grand. The large rooms are full of bright, overstuffed furniture, and have great views of Vegas's parade of neon. ⊠ *3645 Las Vegas Blvd. S, Center Strip 89109,* ☎ *702/967–4111 or 888/742–9248,* ℻ *702/739–4405,* WEB *www.ballyslv.com. 2,567 rooms, 265 suites. 6 restaurants, in-room data ports, 8 tennis courts, pool, health club, spa, lounge, casino, comedy club, 3 showrooms, shops, concierge. AE, D, DC, MC, V.*

$$$ 🏨 **Caesars Palace.** If the opulent entrance, fountains, Roman statuary, bas-reliefs, roaming centurions, and handmaidens all look vaguely familiar, it's because you may have seen this quintessential Las Vegas hotel in such movies as *Electric Horseman* and *Rain Man.* The Forum Shops at Caesars are among the most extravagant in town and Cleopatra's Barge lounge is one of a kind. The hotel also hosts world-class sporting events and performances by top superstars. Celine Dion will be performing here for many years to come. While the Palace Tower's spacious rooms offer everything from vaulted ceilings to whirlpool baths to four phone lines, the smaller rooms at the front of the recently renovated Forum Tower have a spectacular view of the Strip, including the Flamingo's fabulous swath of neon. ⊠ *3570 Las Vegas Blvd. S, Center Strip 89109,* ☎ *702/731–7110 or 800/223–7277,* ℻ *702/731–6636,* WEB *www.caesars.com. 2,364 rooms and 100 suites. 7 restaurants, in-room data ports, 4 tennis courts, 3 pools, health club, spa, squash, lounge, casino, showroom, theater, shops, concierge, business services, meeting room. AE, D, DC, MC, V.*

$$$ 🏨 **Luxor Resort & Casino.** This 36-story, pyramid-shape hotel-casino is pure Egyptian, Vegas-style. Four "inclinators" travel the 39-degree incline of the pyramid to the guest rooms; "hallways" to the rooms overlook the world's largest atrium. Two "step towers," each with almost 1,000 rooms, were added in 1996, making Luxor the second-largest hotel in Las Vegas. Rooms are large and continue the Egyptian motif. Palm trees grow right up out of the pool. There is a video arcade on

two levels, with interactive race cars, small motion simulators, state-of-the-art video machines, and a roomful of air-hockey games. A tram connects Luxor with its sister casinos, Mandalay Bay and Excalibur. ⊠ *3900 Las Vegas Blvd. S, South Strip 89119,* ☎ *702/262–4000 or 800/288–1000,* FAX *702/262–4452,* WEB *www.luxor.com. 4,476 rooms. 6 restaurants, in-room data ports, 5 pools, health club, spa, lounge, casino, 3 theaters, showroom, shops, meeting room, airport shuttle. AE, D, MC, V.*

$$$ ⊡ **Mandalay Bay Resort & Casino.** When it opened in 1999, Mandalay
★ Bay quickly became one of the city's most popular megaresorts. It's easy to see why. It's a hip, fun, imaginative joint, with some unique elements: a small museum displaying rare coins and currency, a wave pool with 5-ft swells, a million-gallon walk-through aquarium, and a 12,000-seat arena complex that hosts major sporting contests and superstar concerts. The House of Blues operates not only a restaurant and a 1,800-seat concert hall, but the entire 34th floor, and the fabulous rumjungle restaurant turns into the city's hippest nightclub after 11 PM. The rooms on 34 are decorated in either the folk art that adorns the restaurant or in the East Indian crafts that layer the Foundation Room, H.O.B.'s exclusive club on the top floor. While the rest of the guest rooms don't have as much flair, they are spacious, with extra large beds and separate tubs and showers. Those in the back have a great view of Mandalay Bay's beach and wave pool. ⊠ *3950 Las Vegas Blvd. S, South Strip 89109,* ☎ *702/632–7777 or 877/632–7400,* FAX *702/791–7446,* WEB *www.mandalaybay.com. 3,700 rooms. 11 restaurants, in-room data ports, minibars, refrigerators, pool, health club, spa, lounge, casino, concert hall, nightclub, showroom, shops, meeting room. AE, D, DC, MC, V.*

$$$ ⊡ **MGM Grand Hotel and Casino.** The largest hotel in the world was
☾ built in the early 1990s at the cost of $1 billion. The four emerald-green towers, three of them 30 stories high, are set on 112 acres and house over 5,000 guest rooms, including 733 Hollywood-inspired suites. Also here are the world's largest casino, nine restaurants (not including the fast-food court), two showrooms, a special-events arena, a nightclub, a lush and extensive pool area, a complete day-care facility, a wedding chapel, and a lion habitat. Rooms are of average size, with Hollywood decor and picture windows. The newly renovated bungalow suites in the Grand Tower have plush fabrics, polished wood, and black and white Italian marble bathrooms. You can now check-in at the airport (by the baggage carousel) and avoid the long lines at the hotel. ⊠ *3799 Las Vegas Blvd. S, South Strip 89109,* ☎ *702/891–7777 or 800/929–1111,* FAX *702/891–1030,* WEB *www.mgmgrand.com. 5,005 rooms. 10 restaurants, in-room data ports, 4 tennis courts, 5 pools, health club, spa, 2 lounges, casino, nightclub, 2 showrooms, shops, business services, meeting room. AE, D, DC, MC, V.*

$$$ ⊡ **Mirage Hotel and Casino.** The $630-million South Seas–theme re-
★ sort is appropriately named. This property—including a rain forest with 3,000 tropical plants, palm and banana trees, and lagoons; a habitat for tigers; a 53-ft-long aquarium filled with tropical fish, including baby sharks; seven dolphins frolicking in the largest saltwater pool in the world; and a 50-ft waterfall that becomes an exploding volcano after dark—seems at times to have been created by resident master illusionists Siegfried and Roy. The rooms, all immaculate and featuring botanical colors and pleasant furniture were renovated in early 2002. Bathrooms, however, tend to be rather small. Request a room with a view (at check-in, for no extra charge) and you may have an eye-popping view of the Strip and the volcano. Chef Alessandro Stratta captures the flavors of the French Riviera at the outstanding Renoir restaurant. ⊠ *3400 Las Vegas Blvd. S, Center Strip 89109,* ☎ *702/791–7111 or*

800/627–6667, FAX 702/791–7446, WEB *www.themirage.com. 2,825 rooms, 224 suites. 11 restaurants, café, 2 pools, spa, lounge, casino, showroom, shops, business services, convention center, meeting room. AE, D, DC, MC, V.*

$$$ **Monte Carlo Resort and Casino.** This gigantic $350-million, 3,002-room megaresort opened in 1996. Modeled after the opulent Place du Casino in Monaco, the Las Vegas version of Monte Carlo replicates its fanciful arches, chandeliered domes, ornate fountains, marble floors, gas-lit promenades, and Gothic glass registration area overlooking the lush pool area. However, don't expect high glamour here. Underneath the pseudo-Euro ambience, there are a lot of family-friendly features: a fast-food court; a cheap and good buffet; a high-tech video arcade with some mind-numbing games; and a water park consisting of adults' and children's pools, a hot tub, and a wave pool and "lazy river" combo. The standard-size rooms are packed with cherrywood furniture and Italian marble. Best of all, with all those rooms to fill, surprisingly good lodging deals are often found here. ⊠ *3770 Las Vegas Blvd. S, South Strip 89119,* ☎ *702/730–7777 or 888/529–4828,* FAX *702/730–7200,* WEB *www.monte-carlo.com. 2,746 rooms, 259 suites. 7 restaurants, in-room data ports, 3 tennis courts, pool, health club, hot tub, spa, lounge, casino, showroom, shops, meeting room. AE, D, DC, MC, V.*

$$$ **New York–New York Hotel and Casino.** Outside, the mini New York skyline includes half-size re-creations of the Statue of Liberty and the Empire State Building; the New York Public Library and other land-mark buildings; Grand Central Terminal; and the Brooklyn Bridge. Inside, it's no less thematically realized: everywhere you look is another clever reproduction of a Big Apple icon. The only detail missing is the NYC attitude: everyone is more than willing to lend you a hand. That said, this $460-million, 2,024-room megaresort does have its downside: the public areas are cramped and crowded, just like Manhattan; it's a long trek from the front desk to some of the towers; and the rooms can be noisy, thanks to the roller coaster. But the accommodations are fairly large, with elegant cherry furniture, and some have separate sitting areas with sofas. Sports fans will delight in the ESPN Zone, a mega-sports grill and a huge screening room to view the big games. ⊠ *3790 Las Vegas Blvd. S, 89109,* ☎ *702/740–6969 or 800/693–6763,* FAX *702/740–6700,* WEB *www.nynyhotelcasino.com. 2,024 rooms. 10 restaurants, in-room safes, pool, health club, spa, lounge, casino, showroom, shops, business services, meeting room. AE, D, DC, MC, V.*

$$$ **Paris Las Vegas.** In addition to reproductions of the Arc de Triomphe and the Eiffel Tower, the 2,900-room, $785-million Paris, which opened in 1999, includes 13 restaurants, a 200-ft-tall sign resembling a hot-air balloon, an in-house parfumerie, a patisserie, a wedding chapel, and a tunnel to Bally's (also owned by Park Place). Fountains and statues are everywhere. Each spacious room has custom-designed furniture, rich French fabrics, and separate marble bath tubs and showers. Request a Strip view and you'll get to see the Bellagio fountains dancing right from your room. Otherwise your room may overlook the pleasant pool area. The fabulous buffet features dishes from five different French regions. ⊠ *3655 Las Vegas Blvd. S, Center Strip 89109,* ☎ *702/739–4111 or 888/226–5687,* FAX *702/946–4405,* WEB *www.paris-lv.com. 2,621 rooms, 295 suites. 13 restaurants, in-room data ports, in-room safes, pool, health club, spa, 5 lounges, casino, show-room, shops, business services, meeting room. AE, D, DC, MC, V.*

$$$ **Treasure Island Las Vegas.** Think of it as the Vegas version of Dis★ ney's "Pirate of the Caribbean Ride." Based on the stories of Robert Louis Stevenson, Treasure Island is full of swords, eye patches, hidden treasure, and more. The casino facade wraps around Buccaneer Bay, a marvelously detailed replica of a South Seas pirate village, where six

GETTING THE SPA TREATMENT IN LAS VEGAS

ONE OF THE NEWEST TRENDS in Las Vegas is the luxury spa. You'll now find a spa in most every large Strip hotel. However, you'll pay for the privilege of being pampered, anywhere from $15 to $30 just for a day's admission to use the health club facilities. Skin and hair treatments, massages, and personal training sessions are an additional cost, though many spas waive the daily facility fee on the day that you purchase a treatment. Most spas are open to the public, but some are available only to guests of the hotels in which they are located. The hotels listed below have some of the better spas, but these are by no means the only spas in town. There are over 30 in Las Vegas and the surrounding area.

Bellagio. Spa Bellagio has a beautiful, marble-clad area with hot and cold soaking pools and a relaxation lounge. A wide variety of treatments is offered, and there is a busy exercise room. Open to hotel guests only.

Caesars Palace. While the 6,500-square-ft fitness facility has a rock-climbing wall and a large selection of weight machines, the spa offers a range of luxurious, sometimes exotic, treatments. Open to the public weekdays and Sunday, hotel guests only Friday–Saturday.

Four Seasons. In addition to a relatively small fitness facility, the full-service spa offers skin treatments and salon services. You may also use the larger Mandalay Bay facility. Open to hotel guests only.

Hard Rock Hotel. Though somewhat smaller than its Strip counterparts, the Rockspa offers the same range of salon and body treatments, along with spacious health club facilities, including a climbing wall. Open to the public.

Hyatt Regency Lake Las Vegas Resort. Far removed from the Strip, this resort's spa has unusual treatment offerings, including a tandem massage with two masseurs. There is a fitness center and sauna. Open to the public.

JW Marriott. The 40,000-ft Aquae Sulis spa offers treatments from the usual to the unusual, plus a large fitness facility with daily exercise classes. Open to the public.

Luxor. The Oasis Spa is one of the few 24-hour facilities in Las Vegas. It offers a range of treatments and has a good fitness center. Open to the public.

Mandalay Bay. The 30,000-square-ft Spa Mandalay is decked out like an Eastern European Turkish-style bath and has a good fitness facility. Open to the public.

MGM Grand. The MGM Grand Spa is one of the best in Las Vegas, and the health club facilities are also good. Open to the public Sunday–Thursday, to hotel guests only Friday–Saturday.

The Venetian. The Canyon Ranch SpaClub here is operated by the famed Canyon Ranch in Tucson and is one of the best day spas in the country; the health club has a large, 40-ft climbing wall. The adjoining café serves healthy cuisine. Open to the public.

times a night you can watch pirates and sailors duke it out aboard the *Hispaniola* and HMS *Britannia*. If you want something even more jaw-dropping, see the Cirque du Soleil production *Mystère*, which has a permanent home here. After a complete renovation at a cost of $65 million, Treasure Island has undergone a dramatic change and is geared to the upscale traveler without children. The opulent lobby overlooks the tropical pool and the newly redecorated rooms are modern and inviting with soft hues, plants in ceramic pots, and marble bathrooms. The pool area is very pleasant, and at night you can have drinks outdoors at the "Kahunaville" tropical nightclub. ⊠ *3300 Las Vegas Blvd. S, Center Strip 89109,* ☎ *702/894–7111 or 800/944–7444,* FAX *702/894–7414,* WEB *www.treasureislandlasvegas.com. 2,885 rooms. 7 restaurants, in-room data ports, in-room safes, pool, health club, spa, lounge, casino, nightclub, showroom, meeting room. AE, D, DC, MC, V.*

$$ ⊞ **Barbary Coast Hotel and Casino.** The Barbary Coast has one of the most central locations in Las Vegas, across from Caesars and next-door to the Flamingo. It's a fun place with a San Francisco Gold Rush theme. Victorian-style rooms have brass four-poster beds with canopies, old-fashioned lamps, lacy curtains, etched mirrors, separate eating areas, and good rates. The views are of the Strip or the Flamingo. Because there are only 208 rooms and suites here, it's not always easy to get one. The hotel's upscale restaurant, Michael's, is similarly in demand. ⊠ *3595 Las Vegas Blvd. S, Center Strip 89109,* ☎ *702/737–7111 or 888/227–2279,* FAX *702/737–6304,* WEB *www.barbarycoastcasino.com. 196 rooms, 12 suites. 3 restaurants, in-room data ports, lounge, casino. AE, D, DC, MC, V.*

$$ ⊞ **Excalibur Hotel and Casino.** Some folks have dubbed this 4,008-room megaresort "Castle Castle." The property's restaurants and 20-plus-shop Renaissance Village have an Arthurian theme, complete with strolling performers. At the wedding chapel you can tie the knot with all the trappings of King Arthur and Lady Guinevere. The Excalibur is also notable for its good-value accommodations. You get what you pay for: the standard-size rooms, decorated in bright colors, aren't spectacular, but the occupancy rate is almost always 100%. So don't be surprised at long lines to check-in and crowded public areas. The hotel's own Web site posts discounted nights months in advance, so if you're looking for a bargain for a specific date you may be in luck here. Try to get a room that overlooks the Strip (rather than the hotel's back parking lot). ⊠ *3850 Las Vegas Blvd. S, South Strip 89119,* ☎ *702/597–7777 or 877/750–5464,* FAX *702/597–7040,* WEB *www.excaliburcasino.com. 4,008 rooms. 6 restaurants, 2 pools, casino, showroom, shops, meeting rooms. AE, D, DC, MC, V.*

$$ ⊞ **Flamingo Las Vegas.** The Fabulous Flamingo that opened in 1946 with everyone—from Bugsy down to the janitors—dressed in tuxedos was a 98-room oasis with palm trees imported from California. The Flamingo has changed a lot since then: today its six high-rise towers overlook a 15-acre pool area where the original low-rise bungalows once stood. The Flamingo is pervasively pink, from the outside neon sign to the lobby carpeting to the in-room vases and pens. The spacious rooms in the towers offer expansive views of the Strip. The swimming-pool area is one of the largest and prettiest in town, and—an unusual feature—the registration area is on the side of the hotel near the elevators, so you won't have to carry your luggage through the casino. ⊠ *3555 Las Vegas Blvd. S, Center Strip 89109,* ☎ *702/733–3111 or 800/732–2111,* FAX *702/733–3353,* WEB *www.flamingolasvegas.com. 3,466 rooms, 176 suites. 8 restaurants, 4 tennis courts, 3 pools, health club, spa, lounge, casino, showroom, shops, business services, meeting room. AE, D, DC, MC, V.*

$$ ⊞ **Harrah's Las Vegas Casino & Hotel.** A Holiday Inn when it opened in 1973, the flagship of the large Harrah's casino fleet has sailed under the same banner since 1992. In 1997 Harrah's completed what could turn out to be its final expansion and renovation, adding a 35-story, 1,000-room tower and retail and restaurant space; expanding the casino; and replacing the facade, all to the tune of $250 million. The rooms are modest and have lavender doors, gray walls, blue bedspreads and matching curtains, and dark-wood furniture. ⊠ *3475 Las Vegas Blvd. S, Center Strip 89109,* ☎ *702/369–5000 or 800/427–7247,* FAX *702/369–5008,* WEB *www.harrahs.com. 2,651 rooms, 49 suites. 7 restaurants, in-room data ports, pool, health club, hair salon, spa, lounge, casino, showroom, business services, meeting rooms. AE, D, DC, MC, V.*

$$ ⊞ **Imperial Palace Hotel and Casino.** The Imperial Palace was the first hotel built in Las Vegas around an Asian theme, featuring crystal, jade, and carved wood. In the heart of the Strip, it houses one of Las Vegas's most popular long-running shows, *Legends in Concert,* and one of Las Vegas's most popular tourist attractions, the Automobile Museum. The hotel offers eight restaurants and two buffets, the only multi-tier sports book in Las Vegas, and its own wedding chapel. Rooms are of standard size and look out at Caesars Palace and the Mirage. ⊠ *3535 Las Vegas Blvd. S, Center Strip 89109,* ☎ *702/731–3311 or 800/634–6441,* FAX *702/735–8578,* WEB *www.imperialpalace.com. 2,412 rooms, 225 suites. 8 restaurants, pool, health club, massage, lounge, casino, showroom, shops. AE, DC, MC, V.*

$$ ⊞ **New Frontier Hotel and Gambling Hall.** While the Frontier of today stands on the same property as the original 1942 hotel, it bears no resemblance to the old place. An Old West motif prevails, but the rooms have been upgraded, and you won't find cacti or branding irons on the walls as in the original. The Atrium Tower has minisuites decorated in earth tones, with separate dining areas and views of the Strip or the Frontier garden area; the center of the 14-story tower is open to the sky. These rooms are some of the best lodging deals in town. ⊠ *3120 Las Vegas Blvd. S, North Strip 89109,* ☎ *702/794–8200 or 800/421–7806,* FAX *702/794–8326,* WEB *www.frontierlv.com. 986 rooms, 396 suites. 3 restaurants, 2 tennis courts, pool, lounge, casino, showroom, business services, meeting rooms. AE, D, DC, MC, V.*

$$ ⊞ **Riviera Hotel and Casino.** Once upon a time, there was a nice nine-story hotel-casino on the Strip that styled itself after the Miami resorts of the 1950s and tried to capture the feeling of the French Riviera. As time went on, an owner decided to expand by adding a tower. Then a new owner added another tower and enlarged the casino. Still another owner tacked on two more towers and moved the casino walls yet farther apart. It could be argued that one of them should have torn it all down and started from scratch, but what's done is done. Though the casino itself has become less of a maze since the completion of the last expansion in 1991 (it's now basically one huge room), it's still a ramble to locate the proper elevator to the correct tower to your room. Most of the accommodations are large, fairly modern affairs with maroon bedspreads and carpeting, teak furniture, and dining areas. ⊠ *2901 Las Vegas Blvd. S, North Strip 89109,* ☎ *702/734–5110 or 800/634–6753,* FAX *702/794–9451,* WEB *www.theriviera.com. 1,942 rooms, 158 suites. 5 restaurants, 2 tennis courts, pool, health club, hair salon, spa, lounge, casino, 4 showrooms, business services, meeting rooms, car rental. AE, DC, MC, V.*

$$ ⊞ **Stardust Hotel and Casino.** Emblazoned with an amazing amount of neon, the 2,500-room Stardust is owned by the Boyd Corporation, the operators of middle-market hotels that emphasize slots, low table minimums, and good deals on food. The tower rooms offer a great view of the Strip or the hotel garden and pool area and are among the largest in town. ⊠ *3000 Las Vegas Blvd. S, North Strip 89109,* ☎ *702/732–6111 or 800/634–6757,* FAX *702/732–6257,* WEB *www.stardustlv.com. 2,500 rooms. 6 restaurants, in-room data ports, in-room safes, 2 tennis courts, 2 pools, health club, lounge, casino, showroom, meeting room, car rental, laundry service, no-smoking rooms. AE, DC, MC, V.*

$$ ⊡ **Stratosphere Hotel Tower and Casino.** In 1996, Stratosphere opened on the site of the old Bob Stupak's Vegas World. In addition to the 1,444 hotel rooms, this complex includes the tallest observation tower in the United States (1,149 ft), the world's two highest thrill rides, a shopping mall, a showroom and lounge, six restaurants, several fast-food outlets, and a 97,000-square-ft casino. A 24-story tower opened in June 2001 and added another 1,002 rooms as well as a huge outdoor pool and recreation area where concerts and high-roller parties are held. The accommodations are standard, but the newer tower's rooms are more modern than the older building and due to Stratosphere's out-of-the-way location, room deals abound. But beware: it does get crowded. The expensive Top of The World restaurant offers sweeping 360° views as it slowly circles above the city. ⊠ *2000 Las Vegas Blvd. S, North Strip 89109,* ☎ *702/380–7777 or 800/998–6937,* FAX *702/739–2448,* WEB *www.stratlv.com. 2,346 rooms, 100 suites. 6 restaurants, in-room safes, pool, health club, spa, lounge, casino, showroom, shops, no-smoking floors. AE, D, DC, MC, V.*

$$ ⊡ **Tropicana Resort and Casino.** While the Tropicana positions itself
☾ as an adult-oriented hotel, it's a great place for families. The Trop is a beautifully landscaped hotel-casino, with an especially lush 5-acre pool area, including a meandering swimming pool, swim-up bars, and a child-pleasing 110-ft-long water slide. The theme is, as you would expect, tropical, with neon palms and colorful birds on the "Wildlife Walk" between towers. Rooms vary in size, depending on whether you're staying in the newly renovated Paradise Tower (standard size), one of the Garden rooms by the pool (somewhat larger), or in the rear Island Tower (spacious). All have rattan furnishings and some even have a terrace (again, a plus for families). ⊠ *3801 Las Vegas Blvd. S, South Strip 89109,* ☎ *702/739–2222 or 888/826–8767,* FAX *702/739–2448,* WEB *www.tropicanalv.com. 1,708 rooms, 200 suites. 5 restaurants, 4 tennis courts, 3 pools, health club, massage, spa, racquetball, lounge, casino, showroom, business services, meeting room. AE, D, DC, MC, V.*

$ ⊡ **Circus Circus.** Beware of Circus Circus—this place is both a madhouse
☾ and a maze. Upstairs in the old towers you'll find painted circus tents in the hallway and some of the most garishly appointed guest rooms in Las Vegas: bright red carpets; matching red chairs; pink walls; and, on one wall, red-, pink-, and blue-stripe wallpaper. The newer tower's rooms are more subdued. The casino attracts so many visitors that drivers will find it a major achievement just getting into the parking lot. On a Saturday night the stretch of Las Vegas Boulevard leading up to Circus Circus is often gridlocked; the valet parking sign reads FULL and the nearest parking space is halfway to Arizona. (If you spend a few minutes learning the back way in, from Industrial Road, you'll save yourself a lot of grief.) Circus Circus is a favorite of families: parents can drop the children off at the midway to play games or watch the circus acts while the adults hit the slots; five-minute circus acts are performed every 20 minutes from 11 AM to midnight. The Adventuredome, a 5-acre theme park with a flume ride, a roller coaster, bumper cars, laser tag, and kiddie rides, is directly behind the hotel. ⊠ *2880 Las Vegas Blvd. S, North Strip 89109,* ☎ *702/734–0410 or 877/224–7287,* FAX *702/734–2268,* WEB *www.circuscircus.com. 3,774 rooms. 8 restaurants, 3 pools, casino, meeting room. AE, D, DC, MC, V.*

$ ⊞ **Sahara Hotel and Casino.** The oasis theme, established in 1952 when the Sahara opened for business, still remains 50 years later—an eternity in Las Vegas. Like many of its neighbors, the Sahara began as a small motor hotel and grew by adding towers, towers, and more towers. In 1997 the Sahara completed its largest expansion in nearly 20 years, doubling the size of the casino, replacing the facade and sign, and adding a parking garage. Another $100-million makeover added the NASCAR Cafe; a roller coaster; and Speedworld, offering virtual-reality race-car-driving experiences. The original bungalow rooms have all been torn down; the tower rooms are large, with king-size beds and views of either the Strip or Paradise Road. Of the many value properties in Las Vegas, the Sahara offers the nicest rooms. ⊠ *2535 Las Vegas Blvd. S, North Strip 89101,* ☏ *702/737–2111 or 888/696–2121,* FAX *702/791–2027,* WEB *www.saharalv.com. 1,961 rooms, 75 suites. 5 restaurants, room service, 2 pools, health club, 2 lounges, casino, showroom, business services, car rental. AE, D, DC, MC, V.*

$ ⊞ **Westward Ho Motel and Casino.** The largest motel in the world, with 1,000 rooms, seven swimming pools, and a casino, the Ho is strategically located between the Stardust and Circus Circus. The location is also a drawback, however: on Saturday night, this part of town is gridlocked, and returning to your room by car will take considerable time—unless you learn the shortcut from Industrial Road through the Stardust parking lot. Because of its size, location, and deals, it's often crowded with conventioneers, slot-club members, and tournament players. ⊠ *2900 Las Vegas Blvd. S, North Strip 89109,* ☏ *702/731–2900 or 800/634–6803,* FAX *702/731–6154,* WEB *www.westwardho.com. 1,000 rooms. Restaurant, café, 7 pools, casino. AE, D, DC, MC, V.*

Beyond the Strip

$$$$ ⊞ **Green Valley Ranch Resort.** Opened in December 2001, a 10-minute drive from the Strip, this is Station Casino's first luxury property. The lobby, built to resemble an intimate country club, opens up onto 2 acres of vineyards, a strikingly modern pool with a small soft-sand beach and an outdoor patio area. Rooms come with every amenity including plush cotton sheets and down comforters. The hotel has several excellent restaurants and lounges including Whiskey Sky—a hot-spot for the young and the fabulous with king-size mattresses strewn about the outdoor patio overlooking the pool. There's also a European day spa with cascading waterfalls, a cinema, and a casino. ⊠ *2300 Paseo Verde, Henderson 89052,* ☏ *702/617–7777 or 866/617–1777,* FAX *702/617–7778,* WEB *www.greenvalleyranchresort.com. 201 rooms. 7 restaurants, in-room data ports, in-room safes, minibars, pool, health club, spa, 2 lounges, casino. AE, D, DC, MC, V.*

$$$$ ⊞ **Hyatt Regency Lake Las Vegas Resort.** Just 15 mi from the city but
★ ☾   a world away on the shores of Lake Las Vegas, this is a luxurious oasis in the middle of the desert. Opened in January 2000 and designed to mirror a Moroccan castle, this lovely hideaway is your perfect choice for seclusion, yet it's a relatively short drive to the Strip. Set against the backdrop of hills, a championship golf course, and a sparkling 320-acre lake, this is a world unto itself, and a tranquil one indeed. Plush rooms continue the Moorish theme with rich earth tones complementing the sweeping views of the lake and desert. Children will delight in the water slide at the activities pool (separate from the adult pool so you don't have to worry about screaming kids). There's even a small beach where 8 tons of soft, white sand is trucked in every summer. Free shuttle service to the Strip is provided. ⊠ *101 MonteLago Blvd., Henderson 89011,* ☏ *702/567–1234,* FAX *702/567–6067,* WEB *www.lakelasvegas.hyatt.com. 449 rooms, 47 suites. 2 restaurants, deli,*

room service, in-room data ports, in-room safes, refrigerators, 18-hole golf course, 2 pools, lake, health club, spa, boating, lounge, casino, children's programs, concierge floor, car rental, meeting rooms. AE, D, DC, MC, V.

$$$$ 🏨 **JW Marriott Las Vegas Casino Resort.** Sometimes all that neon can
★ just be too much, so you just have to get away. Overlooking two of the city's most popular golf courses and within a few miles of Red Rock Canyon, the JW, which used to be the Regent Las Vegas, is still the perfect luxurious escape from the hectic Strip. Combining elegance with an urge to soothe, the ultra-upscale resort is designed to help you unwind. The Aquae Sulis Spa will work all the knots out, and the plush and spacious rooms—featuring everything from a marble bathroom with a separate whirlpool and shower to cordless Internet connections—are designed for comfort. The nine restaurants offer some of the best dining in the city, and on weekends J. C. Wooloughan's, an Irish pub, is always a good time. ⊠ 221 N. Rampart Blvd., Summerlin 89128, ☎ 702/869–7777 or 877/869–8777, FAX 702/869–7325, WEB www.jwmarriottlv.com. 541 suites. 9 restaurants, in-room data ports, in-room safes, minibars, refrigerators, pool, health club, spa, 3 lounges, casino, business services, meeting rooms. AE, D, DC, MC, V.

$$$$ 🏨 **The Palms.** Opened in November 2001, this is the city's first true luxury boutique hotel. Just minutes off the Strip, the $265 million Palms was designed with glamour and high fashion in mind. Its lounges, clubs, and restaurants attract a young wealthy crowd who keep the public places hopping every weekend night. Rooms are large, opulent, and modern, with some unusual amenities for Las Vegas—such as ultra-special beds with firm mattresses, duvets, coffeemakers, and Neutrogena products. Most rooms provide a good view of the city and you don't have to venture far to enjoy the hopping nightlife at the hotel's popular "Rain" nightclub. ⊠ 4321 W. Flamingo Rd., West Side 89103, ☎ 702/942–777 or 866/942–7777, FAX 702/942–7001, WEB www.palms. com. 447 rooms. 7 restaurants, in-room data ports, in-room safes, minibars, pool, health club, hair salon, spa, 4 lounges, casino, cinema. AE, D, DC, MC, V.

$$$ 🏨 **Crowne Plaza.** This all-suites hotel close to the convention center caters to business travelers and is quiet and intimate. The lobby is expansive with its glass atrium leading to modern and comfortable rooms with separate sleeping areas and small kitchenettes with coffeemakers. You'll find two TVs in every suite as well as a sleeper sofa in the living room. There's a small pool and hot tub; complimentary airport shuttle is available 24 hours a day. ⊠ 4255 S. Paradise Rd., Paradise Road 89109, ☎ 702/369–4400, FAX 702/369–3770, WEB www.crowneplaza. com. 201 suites. Restaurant, in-room data ports, refrigerators, pool, gym, outdoor hot tub, bar, airport shuttle. AE, DC, MC, V.

$$$ 🏨 **Hard Rock Hotel and Casino.** It's impossible to forget you're in the Hard Rock, no matter where you go in this rock-fixated joint: even the hall carpeting is decorated with musical notes. The DO NOT DISTURB signs read I HEAR YA' KNOCKIN', BUT YA' CAN'T COME IN. The art-deco rooms are large and sparsely furnished; beds have leather headboards, bathrooms have stainless-steel sinks, soaking tubs, and low-flow toilets, and there are double French doors that actually open. The Lagoon pool has a sandy bottom, a water slide, floating craps tables, a "swirling Coriolis" (circular current), and, of course, rock music piped underwater. The hotel runs a free shuttle to the Strip. The hippest hang-out in Las Vegas for twentysomethings is the fun "Pink Taco" restaurant and bar, packed to the gills on weekend nights and serving the best tacos in town. If you do stay here be prepared for very crowded (but fun) public areas. ⊠ 4455 Paradise Rd., Paradise Road 89109, ☎ 702/693–5000 or 800/693–7625, FAX 702/693–5010, WEB www.hardrockhotel.

com. 668 rooms. 7 restaurants, in-room data ports, pool, health club, spa, lounge, casino, showroom. AE, D, DC, MC, V.

$$$ 🏨 **Las Vegas Hilton.** Though the Hilton, which is adjacent to the Las Vegas Convention Center, no longer holds the title of largest hotel in town, it's still a sight to see—best of all by standing at its foot and staring up at the 29-story three-wing tower. The rooms are spacious, with soft colors, large beds, and telephones in the lavatories; those on the higher floors have great views of the city. The two-story lounge seats 900, there's a wedding chapel, and the buffet features all the cold king crab you can eat. There's a fabulous pool area next to a spacious recreation deck with lighted tennis courts for night games. ⊠ *3000 Paradise Rd., Paradise Road 89109,* ☎ *702/732–5111 or 800/732–7117,* FAX *702/732–5834,* WEB *www.lv-hilton.com. 2,617 rooms, 124 suites. 12 restaurants, in-room data ports, 18-hole golf course, putting green, 6 tennis courts, pool, health club, spa, lounge, casino, showroom, children's programs, business services, meeting room. AE, D, DC, MC, V.*

$$$ 🏨 **Residence Inn by Marriott.** This town house–style all-suite hotel on nicely landscaped grounds is across the street from the convention center and a short cab ride (1¼ mi) from the Strip. Complimentary breakfast and a complimentary weekday dinner buffet are included in the room rate. The studios and two-bedroom suites all have kitchens. Curbside parking is a plus. ⊠ *3225 Paradise Rd., Paradise Road 89109,* ☎ *702/796–9300 or 800/331-3131,* FAX *702/796–9562,* WEB *www.residenceinn.com. 144 studios, 48 2-bedroom suites. Tennis court, pool. AE, D, DC, MC, V. BP.*

$$$ 🏨 **Rio All-Suite Hotel and Casino.** The Rio was the first all-suite hotel with a casino in Las Vegas. The striking blue-and-red, four-tower hotel is off the Strip (west of I–15)—a good location if you prefer quieter surroundings—and has a Brazilian theme, including the sandy beach beside the pool. While suites here don't have separate bedrooms, they're spacious with extra-large sofas, sitting areas, minifridges, dining tables, big bathrooms, and floor-to-ceiling windows. The roominess makes them nice for those traveling with children. The Rio's 41-story room tower, one of the tallest in the country, has a large casino, four restaurants, and an excellent seafood buffet. Every two hours there's a free spectacle, *Masquerade Show in the Sky,* where dancers and singers circle the casino in floats suspended from the ceiling, tossing Mardi Gras–style beads and free-drink coupons. Casino guests may take part in the parade, wearing costumes and riding on one of the floats (for $9.95 per person). ⊠ *3700 W. Flamingo Rd., West Side 89109,* ☎ *702/252–7777 or 800/888–1808,* FAX *702/253–6090,* WEB *www.playrio.com. 2,554 suites. 14 restaurants, pool, health club, spa, lounge, casino, showroom, business services, meeting room. AE, D, DC, MC, V.*

$$ 🏨 **Alexis Park Resort Hotel.** Will businesspeople come to a hotel in Las Vegas that has no neon, no gaming tables, and no slots? The Alexis Park opened in 1984 and discovered that the answer is yes. Halfway between the convention center and the airport, this is a favorite spot for conventioneers who want as "normal" a living experience as possible during their business trip. The individual buildings of the all-suite desert hotel are two-story, white-stucco blocks with red-tile roofs, all set in a water garden. Views are of either a rock pool or a lawn, but neither is anything too special. Rooms are clean and adequate and all come with wet-bars; some have fireplaces or Jacuzzis. ⊠ *375 E. Harmon Ave., Paradise Road 89109,* ☎ *702/796–3300 or 800/582–2228,* FAX *702/796–0766,* WEB *www.alexispark.com. 500 suites. Restaurant, in-room data ports, 9-hole putting green, 2 tennis courts, 3 pools, spa, lounge. AE, D, DC, MC, V.*

$$ ⛨ **DoubleTree Club Hotel.** Close to the airport and popular with pilots and airline personnel, this immaculately maintained hotel is located just off the Airport Connector and I–215 and a few minutes' drive from the Strip. Geared toward the business traveler with easy, ample outdoor parking just outside the hotel's entrance, this is a good place to avoid crowded check-in lines and lengthy walks from parking lots. The rooms are modern and colorfully elegant, and all come with an oversize work desk, two dual-line speaker phones with voice-mail, and coffeemakers. There's also a free shuttle to the strip and to the airport. ⊠ *7250 Pollock Dr., 89119,* ☎ *702/948–4000 or 800/222–8733,* FAX *702/948–4100,* WEB *www.doubletree.com. 190 rooms. Café, deli, in-room data ports, pool, gym, business services, meeting room, airport shuttle. AE, D, DC, MC, V.*

$$ ⛨ **Embassy Suites.** A block away from the Hard Rock Hotel, this at-
🐾 tractive property opened in 1999 and has the signature airy and expansive atrium unique to Embassy Suites, where a complimentary cooked-to-order breakfast is served every morning. Every suite has a separate living area and all are attractively furnished and geared towards the business traveler with a desk and four telephones with voice-mail and Internet connection. There are two TVs in each unit, a microwave, refrigerator, and coffeemaker, and a complimentary newspaper is delivered to your door each morning. The Neutrogena bath products are a nice touch in the bathrooms. Children will enjoy the large pool area and the two resident swans: Elvis and Priscilla. The hotel provides a free shuttle to the Strip. ⊠ *4315 Swenson St., Paradise Road 89119,* ☎ *702/795–2800,* FAX *702/795–1520,* WEB *www.embassylasvegas.com. 220 suites. Restaurant, in-room data ports, refrigerators, pool, gym, lounge, shop, meeting room, airport shuttle. AE, D, DC, MC, V. BP.*

$$ ⛨ **Embassy Suites Convention Center.** This very attractive newer Embassy suites caters to business and leisure travelers who crave space. Each suite is modern and spacious and comes with separate bedroom and living room with sofa sleeper. Every suite has its own kitchen equipped with microwave, coffeemaker, and refrigerator. Web TV is available as well as a complimentary newspaper each morning. Full breakfast is included and complimentary shuttle service to the Strip and the airport is provided. ⊠ *3600 Paradise Rd., Paradise Road 89109,* ☎ *702/893–8000,* FAX *702/893–0378,* WEB *www.eslvcc.com. 286 suites. Restaurant, in-room data ports, refrigerators, bar, airport shuttle. AE, D, DC, MC, V. BP.*

$ ⛨ **AmeriSuites.** This all-suite hotel close to the Hard Rock is an excellent value if you're looking for a non-gaming property. It's quiet and fairly modern with bright rooms with separate living rooms and kitchenettes with microwaves and coffeemakers. There's a small exercise room, a pool and free breakfast buffet. ⊠ *4520 Paradise Rd., Paradise Road, 89109,* ☎ *702/369–3366,* FAX *702/369–0009,* WEB *www. amerisuites.com. 202 suites. Refrigerators, in-room data ports, pool, gym. AE, MC, V. BP.*

$ ⛨ **Budget Suites of America.** A nearby alternative to the Westward Ho is this sprawling complex on the corner of Industrial and Stardust roads. Every room here is a minisuite with a living-dining room, a small separate bedroom, and a full kitchenette; the TV is mounted on a swivel between the living room and bedroom. Weekly rates offer a good discount; rooms on the second and third floors are the least expensive and are even cheaper if you bring your own sheets and towels. ⊠ *1500 Stardust Rd., West Side 89109,* ☎ *702/732–1500 or 800/752–1501,* FAX *702/732–2656,* WEB *www.budgetsuites.com. 639 suites. Pool, spa. AE, MC, V.*

$ ⛨ **Motel 6.** Welcome to the largest Motel 6 in the United States, with 877 rooms, a pool, and a big neon sign. Rooms here look like those of any other Motel 6, but when travelers think in terms of cheap accommodations, they think of this chain, so it tends to get booked up fast. ⊠ *195 E. Tropicana Ave., 89109,* ☎ *702/798–0728,* FAX *702/798–5657,* WEB *www.motel6.com. 887 rooms. Pool. AE, D, DC, MC, V.*

$ 🖵 **Sam's Town Hotel and Gambling Hall.** Sam's Town is named for Sam Boyd, the pioneer gambler and owner who built a small grubstake into one of the largest casino companies in Nevada. This simple yet busy hotel is far from the center of activity and close to the desert—it's on the Boulder Strip, 6 mi from downtown. The location gives Sam's Town's Old West decor some authenticity. Indeed, Sam's excels at perpetuating the Western theme: everyone wears garters or string ties; the food is good, plentiful, and inexpensive; and there's a big Western-wear store on the property. The rooms, built around a nine-story glass-roof atrium filled with tall live trees, cobblestone paths, a rock waterfall, and babbling brooks crossed by wooden bridges, are fairly standard, with queen-size beds, large TVs, and soothing colors. ⊠ *5111 Boulder Hwy., Boulder Strip 89122,* ☎ *702/456–7777 or 800/634–6371,* FAX *702/454–8014,* WEB *www.samstownlv.com. 650 rooms. 8 restaurants, pool, bowling, lounge, casino, meeting rooms. AE, D, DC, MC, V.*

$ 🖵 **Texas Station Gambling Hall and Hotel.** This place and its three sis-
🐣 ters—Palace Station, Boulder Station, and Sunset Station—are primarily casinos/entertainment complexes designed for locals, with friendly odds, fast-food joints, expansive buffets, arcades, and large movie theaters. On the northwest side of Vegas, the Lone Star state–theme hotel-casino has all the action and amenities of many Strip properties. Though not lavishly appointed, rooms are large and comfortable, with a separate sitting area and dining tables. The key perk for families is that each Station casino contains a Kids' Quest, a 8,000-square-ft multi-level indoor playground and activity center where children ages 6 weeks to 12 years will be entertained for hours while the grown-ups work the tables. A free shuttle provides transportation to the Strip. ⊠ *2101 Texas Star La., Rancho Strip 89036,* ☎ *702/631–1000 or 800/654–8888,* FAX *702/631–8120,* WEB *www.texasstation.com. 200 rooms. 5 restaurants, food court, lounge, in-room data ports, pool, casino, theater, airport shuttle. AE, D, DC, MC, V.*

Downtown

$$ 🖵 **Golden Nugget Hotel and Casino.** The best hotel downtown, the
★ Nugget was a gambling hall with sawdust on the floors and no hotel rooms when Steve Wynn took it over in the 1970s and decided to go after high rollers. Now red rugs flow over white marble, leading you to the lobby and a large public area with columns, etched-glass windows, and fresh flowers in gold-plated vases. Almost everything here is gold (or, more accurately, brass-plated)—the telephones, the slots, the elevators. Then again, what else would you expect of the home of the world's largest single gold nugget? The well-kept rooms are modern and comfortable, though the bathrooms are considerably smaller than at the newer hotels on the Strip. In addition to the standard double rooms, the Nugget has 27 opulent duplex suites, some with a personal room-service waiter. The pool is the biggest and best downtown. A strong and loyal repeat clientele keep it busy most weekends of the year. ⊠ *129 E. Fremont St., Downtown 89101,* ☎ *702/385–7111 or 800/634–3454,* FAX *702/386–8362,* WEB *www.goldennugget.com. 1,805 rooms, 106 suites. 7 restaurants, in-room safes, pool, health club, spa, lounge, casino, showroom, meeting room. AE, D, DC, MC, V.*

$ 🖵 **Binion's Horseshoe Hotel and Casino.** For more than 35 years, Binion's Horseshoe had 80 rooms; in order to get one of these downtown domiciles, you had to know patriarch Benny Binion. But in 1988, Bin-

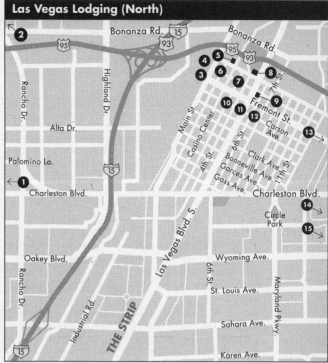

Las Vegas Lodging (North)

ion's bought the 26-floor, 300-room Mint next door. Now known as the West Horseshoe, it has modern, medium-size rooms that are decorated in light colors. The east-side rooms reflect the Western style of the original Horseshoe: they have Victorian-style wallpaper and brass beds with quilted spreads. The pool is on the roof. The snack bars have down-to-earth food and prices; the deli (by the sports book) and steak house (on the 24th floor, reached by a glass elevator) are enormously popular. ⊠ *128 E. Fremont St., Downtown 89101,* ☎ *702/382–1600 or 800/237–6537,* FAX *702/384–1574,* WEB *www.binions.com. 360 rooms. 4 restaurants, pool, casino. AE, D, DC, MC, V.*

$ Fitzgeralds Hotel and Casino. This 34-story hotel was the tallest building in Nevada for 15 years, until it was eclipsed by the Stratosphere Tower. When you reach your room, you'll find it to be clean and comfortable with bright bedspreads. The views are of Fremont Street or the neighboring Four Queens. ⊠ *301 E. Fremont St., Downtown 89109,* ☎ *702/388–2400 or 800/274–5825,* FAX *702/388–2181,* WEB *www.fitzgeralds.com. 624 rooms, 14 suites. 3 restaurants, in-room data ports, shop, lounge, casino, meeting room, business services, car rental. AE, D, DC, MC, V.*

$ Four Queens Hotel and Casino. This prominent downtown hotel has rooms furnished in New Orleans style, with turn-of-the-20th-century wallpaper, vintage lamps, four-poster beds, and views of Fremont Street, Fitzgeralds, or the Golden Nugget. Its coffee shop is one of the least expensive downtown, and people consider Hugo's Cellar one of the better restaurants in this area. ⊠ *202 E. Fremont St., Downtown 89109.* ☎ *702/385–4011 or 800/634–6045,* FAX *702/383–0631,* WEB *www. fourqueens.com. 690 rooms. 2 restaurants, in-room data ports, in-room safes, lounge, casino, no-smoking rooms. AE, D, DC, MC, V.*

$ 🏨 **Jackie Gaughan's El Cortez Hotel.** This is a good deal: a room for two in the downtown area for $22 (including tax) a night—available on a walk-in basis only, and not on Saturday. There are two floors of tiny rooms, each of which has twin beds, a small TV, and a narrow window with a view of Fremont Street. Rooms in the tower are newer, larger, and only a little more expensive—up to $40. ⊠ *600 E. Fremont St., Downtown 89109,* ☎ *702/385–5200 or 800/634–6703,* 𝖥𝖠𝖷 *702/ 385–1554,* 𝖶𝖤𝖡 *www.elcortez.net. 299 rooms. 2 restaurants, lounge, casino, meeting room. AE, D, DC, MC, V.*

$ 🏨 **Jackie Gaughan's Gold Spike Hotel and Casino.** The hotel is billed as "Las Vegas as it used to be," with penny slots and video poker, 40¢ live keno, and $1 blackjack tables. The Spike charges only $22 a night, every night, for a small, plain double room with twin beds, a night-stand, a TV, and a view of East Ogden Avenue. A suite for $33 a night adds a four-poster bed, couch, and balcony. All rates include break-fast. ⊠ *400 E. Ogden Ave., Downtown 89109,* ☎ *702/384–8444 or 800/634–6703,* 𝖥𝖠𝖷 *702/384–8768,* 𝖶𝖤𝖡 *www.goldspikehotelcasino.com. 103 rooms, 7 suites. Coffee shop, casino. AE, D, DC, MC, V. BP.*

$ 🏨 **Jackie Gaughan's Plaza Hotel and Casino.** Opened in 1971, the Plaza anchors Fremont Street and can be seen in the center of nearly every photo of it. The Plaza almost always has a room, even during big conventions. Green-blue decor, bright bedspreads, and mirrors above some of the beds characterize the medium-size rooms. Be sure to ask for one overlooking Fremont Street; otherwise you'll have a view of the railroad tracks. There's a pool, a showroom (the largest down-town), and a wedding chapel on the premises. ⊠ *1 Main St., Down-town 89109,* ☎ *702/386–2110 or 800/634–6575,* 𝖥𝖠𝖷 *702/382–8281,* 𝖶𝖤𝖡 *www.plazahotelcasino.com. 1,037 rooms. 3 restaurants, 4 tennis courts, pool, gym, hair salon, lounge, casino, showroom, meeting rooms. AE, D, DC, MC, V.*

$ 🏨 **Lady Luck Casino and Hotel.** The newer 400-room tower is across the street from the 17-story tower: you travel from the old Lady to the new via a glass-enclosed pedestrian bridge on the third-floor level. Lady Luck has small, bright rooms with white walls and half-windows that look out on Ogden Street. The coffeemaker in each room is an added bonus. There are also 115 junior suites and 385 "senior" suites for the Lady's many high rollers. Why are there so many high rollers at the Lady Luck? Because the casino has some of the least demanding comp criteria in town. ⊠ *206 N. 3rd St., Downtown 89109,* ☎ *702/477–3000 or 800/634–6580,* 𝖥𝖠𝖷 *702/477–3002,* 𝖶𝖤𝖡 *www.ladylucklv.com. 292 rooms, 500 suites. 4 restaurants, refrigerators, pool, casino, show-room, shop. AE, D, DC, MC, V.*

$ 🏨 **Las Vegas Club Hotel and Casino.** Here, a sports theme prevails every-where but in the guest rooms. The walls in the Upper Deck coffee shop are covered with baseball and basketball photos and memorabilia. The small rooms have a light-brown finish, the beds have small awnings, and the tiny half windows overlook Fremont and Main streets. A tower completed in 1996 houses 186 rooms, two restaurants, and a casino annex. ⊠ *18 E. Fremont St., 89109,* ☎ *702/385–1664 or 800/ 634–6532,* 𝖥𝖠𝖷 *702/387–6071,* 𝖶𝖤𝖡 *www.playatlvc.com. 410 rooms. 3 restaurants, in-room data ports, lounge, casino, meeting room, dry clean-ing, laundry service, business services. AE, DC, MC, V.*

$ 🏨 **Main Street Station Casino, Brewery & Hotel.** It's like walking into an antiques dealer's store. Filled with gobs of antiques, collectibles, and memorabilia, Main Street Station is brimming with things to look at, including Theodore Roosevelt's Pullman railroad car, dropped-dome chan-deliers from the El Presidente Hotel in Buenos Aires, and a section of the Berlin Wall. Guest rooms, accented in dark wood, antiques, and gold-framed mirrors, continue the theme. Make sure to get one on the south side of the building, facing Main Street—it's hard to get away from the noise of I–15 on the north side. There's a free shuttle service to the Strip. ✉ *200 N. Main St., Downtown 89101,* ☎ *702/387–1896 or 800/713–8933,* FAX *702/386–4421,* WEB *www.mainstreetcasino.com. 406 rooms. 4 restaurants, in-room data ports, in-room safes, lounge, casino, meeting rooms. AE, DC, MC, V.*

RV Parks and Campgrounds

Las Vegas is an RVer's oasis. The city offers thousands of hook-ups, some next to casinos, some tucked away in private resorts. Nearby options are more limited if you plan to camp, however. Only a small number of places allow tent camping, but with numerous state and national parks within an hour of the city, it's possible to find a place to pitch the pup tent.

$ ⚲ **Boulder Lakes.** Located near Sam Boyd Stadium, Boulder Lakes is a good hike from the Strip. But this 417-site RV park is more for people looking to spend some serious time in Vegas than those who want to just hang out for a weekend. With monthly rates and numerous perks—including a playground, a clubhouse, four pools, three spas, and a ballroom—Boulder Lakes is designed for extended stays. Other on-site facilities include hook-ups, drinking water, showers, toilets, telephones, laundry, cable TV, and a grocery store. Pets are allowed. ✉ *6201 Boulder Hwy., East Side 89122,* ☎ *702/435–1157,* FAX *702/435–1125.* 🖮 *$22. MC, V.*

$ ⚲ **Circusland RV Park.** The only RV park right on the Strip, Circusland makes for easy access to Las Vegas's main drag. The only problem: like Circus Circus, the casino it is attached to, Circusland tends to fill up quickly, often running at capacity on weekends and holidays. It has 399 sites, hook-ups, a dump station, drinking water, showers, toilets, telephones, laundry, a grocery store, and a pool. Pets are allowed. ✉ *500 Circus Circus Dr., North Strip 89109,* ☎ *702/794–3757 or 800/444–2472,* FAX *702/792–2280.* 🖮 *$19–$35. AE, D, DC, MC, V.*

$ ⚲ **KOA Las Vegas.** On Boulder Highway, KOA Las Vegas is a good click from the Strip—at least 15 minutes by the surface streets or the expressway. But the trade-off is familiarity and consistency. Like most KOAs across the country, KOA Las Vegas has good, clean facilities that are hard to beat. It's also one of the few places in Vegas that allows tent camping. It has 40 RV sites, hook-ups, a dump station, drinking water, showers, toilets, telephones, laundry, a grocery store, and a pool. Pets are allowed. There's also a free shuttle to the Strip. ✉ *4315 Boulder Hwy., Boulder Strip 89121,* ☎ *702/451–5527 or 800/562–7782,* FAX *702/434–8729,* WEB *www.koa.com.* 🖮 *$25–$33. AE, D, MC, V.*

$ ⚲ **Oasis Las Vegas RV Resort.** As much a resort as a place to park the mobile kingdom, Oasis Las Vegas is a plush, well-landscaped RV park with 701 sites and lots of amenities—including a pool and its own clubhouse. Just minutes from the Strip—there's even a shuttle that runs from Oasis to the heart of casino row—as well as within walking distance of the Belz outlet mall, Oasis is perfectly situated to enjoy the neon without feeling overpowered. Just make sure to make your reservations early. Though Oasis Las Vegas is the area's largest RV park, it tends to fill up during holiday weekends and winter months. Facilities include hook-ups, a dump station, drinking water, showers, toilets, telephones, laundry, cable TV, and a grocery store. Pets are allowed. ✉ *2711 W. Windmill Rd., South Las Vegas 89123,* ☎ *702/260–2000 or 800/566–4707,* FAX *702/263–5160.* 🖮 *$20–$50. AE, D, MC, V.*

$ ⚠ **Sam's Town RV Park.** There are two separate RV locations, one on Boulder Highway, just to the east of the casino, and one just north on Nellis Boulevard, with 499 sites in all. Both offer the standard amenities—hook-ups, drinking water, showers, toilets, telephones, laundry—as well as child care and shuttle service to the Strip. The only difference is that the Nellis park allows pets. Given Sam's Town's guaranteed price of $18, these are the cheapest places to park the mobile kingdom in town. ⊠ *5225 W. Boulder Hwy., Boulder Strip 89122,* ☎ *702/456–7777 or 800/634–6371,* FAX *702/456–5665.* ▤ *$18. AE, D, DC, MC, V.*

$ ⚠ **Silverton RV Park.** Like the casino it's named for, the Silverton RV Park is all about down-home charm. Located just to the southwest of the Strip, the Silverton RV Park has been rated No. 1 in the West by the Good Sam Club, with 460 sites and telephone and cable hook-ups for every stall. There's also a pool, a recreation room, and an on-site convenience store for all your needs. And when the urge hits, there's a shuttle to the Strip. Other facilities include a dump station, drinking water, showers, toilets, and a laundry. Pets are allowed. ⊠ *3333 Blue Diamond Rd., 89139,* ☎ *702/263–7777 or 800/588–7711,* FAX *702/897–4208,* WEB *www.silvertoncasino.com.* ▤ *$20. AE, D, DC, MC, V.*

6 NIGHTLIFE AND THE ARTS

With Las Vegas–style revues old and new, traditional headliner rooms and concert halls, umpteen lounges, hi-tech discos, low-tech honky-tonks, comedy clubs, free light-and-water shows, amusement parks, magicians, showgirls, and of course people-watching, the only way to arrive in Las Vegas and not be entertained is in a coffin.

T HE VERY NAME "LAS VEGAS" HAS BEEN synonymous with a certain style of showbiz entertainment ever since Jimmy Durante first headlined at Bugsy Siegel's Fabulous Flamingo Hotel in 1946 and *Minsky Goes to Paris* introduced topless showgirls at the Dunes in 1957. In those days the lounges gave up-and-coming performers a chance to polish their acts on their way to the showrooms; the camaraderie and informality lent an anything-can-happen-here-tonight air to the entertainment. Through the years the Entertainment Capital of the World has weathered a number of changes in its stage presentations, policies, and prices, but one thing has remained consistent for the past 50 years—doing things big with as much attention called to the doing as possible.

Updated by
Mike
Weatherford

Headliners such as Tom Jones, David Copperfield, Wayne Newton, and George Carlin still pack the traditional showrooms. Extravagant revues such as *EFX Alive, Folies Bergère,* and *Jubilee!* still stage 12 shows a week, with outrageous sets, costumes, variety acts, and song and dance. But young and exuberant shows such as Cirque du Soleil's *O* and *Mystère* and *Blue Man Group* have modernized the spectacle; while illusionists such as Siegfried and Roy and Lance Burton, who started out as brief breaks for the major action, have gone on to become stars in their own right. Female and superstar impersonators, "dirty" dancers, comedians—all perpetuate the original style of razzle-dazzle entertainment that Las Vegas has popularized for the world.

Some traditions have changed, however. Certain hotels have eliminated nudity and foul language in the name of family entertainment. Some even encourage parents to bring their children along by offering special prices for youngsters (usually in the summer months). And the dinner show has gone the way of the mink stole, unless you count the utensil-free "medieval style" dining at Excalibur's "Tournament of Kings."

In the not-so-old days, the shows were loss leaders, much as the buffets are today: they were intended to draw patrons who would eventually wind up in the casino. Admission prices to shows were dirt cheap, and the programs were fairly short. Nowadays, it will cost you $50 to see Newton or Paul Anka, and a ticket to the biggest production, *O,* will set you back $93–$121. Yet many of the smaller shows have much lower prices. Bargain-hunters have learned to look to afternoon shows, such as Tropicana magician Rick Thomas or the Flamingo's campy burlesque revue "Bottom's Up," as places to hold ticket prices under the $20 line.

There are several kinds of shows in Las Vegas. What used to be known as the "big room headliners" are a vanishing breed, and so are the old table-and-booth showrooms where they used to perform. But you can still find a few of the old names, along with a more recent generation of "resident headliners"—singer Clint Holmes and impressionist Danny Gans—who keep the tradition alive. The big-production spectaculars also remain a Las Vegas trademark, presenting little or no language barrier to the city's large numbers of international tourists. But the classic "feather show"—90 minutes of song, dance, topless showgirls, specialty acts, and special effects—has taken a backseat to the stylized eye candy of Cirque du Soleil, or the avant-garde stunts of the Blue Man Group. Foreign visitors also seem to love magic shows; Siegfried and Roy are to Las Vegas what the Empire State Building is to New York, and you don't have to understand English to enjoy them. The same is true for a number of burlesque-derived revues that still rely on the topless showgirl or dancer, whose blatant charms can be appreciated in any language.

The 1990s also broke down the walls that used to exist between old-school Las Vegas headliners and contemporary concert attractions. It used to be that rockers such as Elton John, the Rolling Stones, Eric Clapton, and Bob Dylan eschewed appearances in Las Vegas, which they felt jeopardized their musical credibility. And the showrooms were simply too small to accommodate the arena-level concert acts. But those days are over. Las Vegas is a hotbed of up-to-the-minute entertainment, thanks to a local population that now exceeds a million, baby boomers finally discovering the joys of a Las Vegas vacation, and the opening of both arenas and rock clubs such as the House of Blues at Mandalay Bay. Las Vegas has become a mandatory tour stop for top-name stars of all ages and musical genres.

Getting into certain shows has become easier than it used to be. Most hotels have switched over to reserved-seat ticketing through corporate networks such as Ticketmaster, much like concerts or events anywhere else. Many Internet-savvy travelers now pick their seats and purchase tickets for some attractions on-line well before their visits. In fact, it's advisable to do so for the hotter shows, such as Gans and the Cirque du Soleil productions.

Other shows have reserved seats but "closed" or "in-house" ticketing networks operating more on a first-come, first-served basis or which restrict advance purchases. On weekends it can be tough getting in to see the top names and production revues. Crowds are large, lines are long, and the prime spots are reserved for comped players. Your chances of getting a seat are usually better when you're staying—and gambling—at the hotel. If you plan on spending a fair amount of time at the tables or slots, call VIP Services or a slot host and find out what their requirements are for getting a comp, tickets that have been withheld, or a line pass (that allows you to go straight to the VIP entrance without having to wait in line with the hoi polloi). Then be sure to have your play "rated" by the pit boss when you gamble, in order to qualify for the privileges.

Computerized ticketing and customer preference for reserved seats have all but eliminated the once-frightening realm of maître d's (who assigned the seats at the door) and captains (who show you to your seats). The Imperial Palace's "Legends in Concert" remains the only show in a mid- to large-size room that still operates on the fabled system of tipping the maître d' for improved seating. To ensure a good seat, arrive early and discreetly toke the maître d' (with bills or chips the denomination of which he can readily see); $5 is usually sufficient.

Finding Out What's Going On

Information on shows, including their reservation and seating policies, prices, suitability for children (or age restrictions), and smoking restrictions, is available by calling or visiting the box offices. It's also listed in several local publications. The **Las Vegas Advisor** is available at its office (✉ 3687 S. Procyon Ave., Las Vegas 89103, ☎ 800/244–2224) for $5 per issue or $50 per year; this monthly newsletter is invaluable for its up-to-the-minute information on Las Vegas dining, entertainment, gambling promotions, comps, and news. You can also pick up free copies of *Today in Las Vegas* and *What's On in Las Vegas* at hotels and gift shops. The *Las Vegas Review-Journal,* the city's morning daily newspaper, publishes a tabloid pullout section each Friday called "Neon." It provides entertainment features and reviews, and showroom and lounge listings with complete time and price information. The

"Neon" section is sold separately for a quarter in some news boxes along the resort corridor. The *Review-Journal* also maintains a comprehensive city Web site, www.lasvegas.com, where show listings are updated each week. The *Las Vegas Sun*—a separately staffed afternoon newspaper published in a joint operation with the *Review-Journal*—maintains a rival Web site, www.vegas.com.

Getting Tickets

Most of the showrooms and concert venues in town are part of the **Ticketmaster** network (☏ 702/474–4000, WEB www.ticketmaster.com), making it possible for you to buy tickets for many Las Vegas shows at your hometown Ticketmaster outlet or through the company's Web site. Local walk-up outlets include Wherehouse and Tower Records stores, Smith's Food and Drug Centers, and Robinsons-May stores, along with each casino's box office. Las Vegas's **Tower Records** store (⊠ 4580 W. Sahara Ave., West Side) is conveniently located for ticket buyers.

The notable holdout from Ticketmaster is the Thomas and Mack Center on the University of Nevada–Las Vegas (UNLV) campus. **Tickets.com** (WEB www.tickets.com) has an exclusive agreement to sell tickets for the Thomas and Mack Center, which hosts Runnin' Rebels basketball, concerts, and special events such as *Disney on Ice*. Tickets can be purchased on-line, by phone (☏ 888/464–2468), or at the arena itself. They can also be purchased at the Galleria at Sunset mall and Mail Boxes, Etc. stores.

Allstate Ticketing and Tours (☏ 800/634–6787, WEB www.showtickets.com) operates box offices all over town, most prominently in casinos without a show of their own. It sells tickets for almost every casino show except the two Cirque du Soleil productions. You'll find offices at Fitzgeralds, the Forum Shops at Caesars, Harrah's, Holiday Inn Boardwalk, Lady Luck, McCarren International Airport, New Frontier, Sahara, and Stratosphere. It's important to know that Allstate works on a system in which producers pay commissions for each ticket sold, which may prejudice a ticket broker's enthusiasm about a particular show. The lesser shows sometimes offer the highest commissions.

Venues

In addition to the hotel showrooms and theaters, Las Vegas has four large entertainment arenas and four smaller performance venues.

Aladdin Theatre for the Performing Arts. The old Aladdin was destroyed and rebuilt around this 7,000-seat concert hall that was spared the wrecking ball and reopened in September 2000 with new seats and sound equipment. Since Las Vegas does not have its own municipal theater, the Aladdin often hosts touring companies for Broadway musicals such as *Les Misèrables*. ⊠ *Aladdin Hotel and Casino, 3667 Las Vegas Blvd. S, Center Strip,* ☏ *702/785–5555.*

Mandalay Bay Events Center. With a capacity of 8,000 to 11,000, this theater is slightly smaller than the city's other two large arenas, the MGM Grand Garden and the Thomas and Mack Center. ⊠ *Mandalay Bay Resort and Casino, 3950 Las Vegas Blvd. S, South Strip,* ☏ *702/632–7777.*

MGM Grand Garden. This arena tends to get the biggest concert names, from Bruce Springsteen to Britney Spears. But to secure the acts with adult appeal, such as Cher and Jimmy Buffett, the MGM has a reputation for outbidding the rival arenas, then passing the costs along to fans in the form of triple-digit ticket prices. It holds from 12,000 to 15,200 people. ⊠ *MGM Grand Hotel Casino, 3799 Las Vegas Blvd. S, South Strip,* ☏ *702/891–7777.*

Sam Boyd Stadium. An outdoor venue, it still hosts the occasional concert that has the ability to pull in 30,000 or more people. But the UNLV-operated stadium has been busier lately with motorcycle and "Bigfoot truck" exhibitions. ✉ *Off Boulder Hwy. on Russell Rd.,* ☎ *702/895–3900.*

Thomas and Mack Center. On campus at UNLV, the center has come to rely on more sporting events such as the National Finals Rodeo since the MGM Grand and Mandalay Bay both built their own concert and sporting arenas. It holds anywhere from 7,000 to 18,000 people. ✉ *Tropicana Ave. at Swenson St., University District,* ☎ *702/895–3900.*

UNLV Performing Arts Center. Like the Thomas and Mack Center, this complex is also on the UNLV campus but tends to stage more genteel events. It is divided into the the 600-seat **Judy Bayley Theatre,** which hosts ballet and plays, and the 1,800-seat **Artemus Ham Concert Hall.** ✉ *4505 S. Maryland Pkwy., University District,* ☎ *702/895–2787.*

Two nightclub/concert hall hybrids divide up most of the market for one-night concert attractions that aren't big enough for an arena, or ones who accepted a lofty paycheck to play a cozier room for their well-heeled fans. Each holds about 1,800. **The Joint** (✉ 4455 Paradise Rd., Paradise Road, ☎ 702/693–5000) is inside the Hard Rock Hotel and Casino. The **House of Blues** (✉ 3950 Las Vegas Blvd. S, South Strip, ☎ 702/632–7600), at Mandalay Bay, is the seventh entry in this chain of successful music clubs.

For those who venture off the Strip, the Station Casinos family caters more to locals, with mid-level concert acts at reasonable prices. **The Railhead** (✉ 4111 Boulder Hwy., Boulder Strip, ☎ 702/432–7777) is in Boulder Station. **Club Madrid** (✉ 1301 E. Sunset Rd., Henderson, ☎ 702/547–7777) is in Sunset Station. These small showrooms have hosted everyone from Toby Keith to Keith Sweat, and from Merle Haggard to Jerry Vale. The Railhead got some competition with the arrival of **Sam's Town Live!** at Sam's Town (✉ 5111 Boulder Hwy., Boulder Strip, ☎ 888/464–2468), a smartly designed concert and convention hall with retractable seating.

NIGHTLIFE

Bars and Lounges

The lounges of the Las Vegas casino-hotels were once places where such headliners as Frank, Dean, and the gang would go after their shows, taking a seat in the audience to laugh at the comedy antics of Shecky Greene or Don Rickles or to enjoy the music of Louis Prima and Keely Smith. Now the lounges have been mostly reduced to small bars within the casino, where bands play Top 40 hits in front of small crowds of people pie-eyed from the slots. Virtually every casino has such a spot; all you need to do is buy a drink or two and you can listen to the music all night long. A few—the Las Vegas Hilton and Treasure Island among them—have computerized lighting and larger dance floors, making them as much a small dance club as a lounge. A few of the nicest lounges are at Paris Las Vegas, the Tropicana, the Stratosphere, Mandalay Bay, and the Orleans.

A couple are worthy of special mention. The **Fontana Lounge** inside the Bellagio (✉ 3600 Las Vegas Blvd. S, Center Strip, ☎ 702/693–7111) is styled like a 1940s-era supper club and offers a spectacular view of the dancing water shows outside. **The Carnaval Court** at Harrah's Las Vegas (✉ 3475 Las Vegas Blvd. S, Center Strip, ☎ 702/369–5000) is the rare outdoor lounge to take advantage of the Strip's parade of street life. Misters cool the scene in the summertime, and performing "flair bartenders" juggle bottles to the awe of customers.

The turn of the 21st century brought an explosion of hybrid nightspots aiming for the middle ground between dance club and conversational lounge. **V Bar** inside the Venetian (✉ 3355 Las Vegas Blvd. S, Center Strip, ☎ 702/733–5000) was launched by the founders of New York's Lotus and Los Angeles' Sunset Room. In the Venetian's retail mall, **Jack's Velvet Lounge** (☎ 702/414–1699) occupies the second floor of the WB Stage 16 restaurant and cranks up ambient and house music on weekend nights. Next door to Jack's in the Venetian's mall is the **Venus Lounge and Tiki Bar** (☎ 702/414–4870), a retro-theme appeal to "Cocktail Nation" nostalgists. Caesars Palace converted one of its traditional lounges into **Shadow** (✉ 3570 Las Vegas Blvd. S, Center Strip, ☎ 702/731–7990), thus named because of the seemingly naked women dancing behind scrims in silhouette. **Ghostbar** on the penthouse level of The Palms (✉ 4321 W. Flamingo Rd., West Side, ☎ 702/942–7777) has a glassed-in view of the city and an outdoor deck cantilevered over the side of the building, with a plexiglass platform that allows revelers to look down 450 ft below. Closer still to a full-bore dance club is the wild scene inside **Drai's** at the Barbary Coast (✉ 3595 Las Vegas Blvd. S, Center Strip, ☎ 702/737–0555), once the tony restaurant's tables are cleared away after evening dining hours. John J. Tunney's **Olio!** inside the MGM Grand Hotel (✉ 3799 Las Vegas Blvd. S, South Strip, ☎ 702/891–7775) looks like an adult playground, with its bold colors and staunch resistance to any right angles, and it aims to be versatile: in addition to the full menu offered until 2 AM, there's a dance floor and a multi-media center.

Away from the Strip, the Las Vegas bar scene is dominated by so-called "video poker taverns," named for the 15 video poker machines they are legally allowed to have. Most are generic, but there are exceptions. **Gordon Biersch Brewing Company** (✉ 3987 Paradise Rd., Paradise Road, ☎ 702/312–5247), also a full-scale restaurant, caters to Las Vegas's new breed of white-collar workers. For the boho crowd, there's the deliberately downscale **Double Down Saloon** (✉ 4640 Paradise Rd., Paradise Road, ☎ 702/791–5775), with a jukebox blasting everything from Patsy Cline to classic punk. Fans of the place include filmmaker Tim Burton. (Don't bother checking it out before midnight, though.) Locals immediately embraced the **J. C. Wooloughan Irish Pub,** at the JW Marriott (✉ 221 N. Rampart Blvd., Summerlin, ☎ 702/869–7777). In order to create the proper environment for serving Guinness, Bass, and Harp, the entire exterior of the 24-hour pub was constructed in Dublin, then shipped to Las Vegas. The crowd is yuppie-leaning after work, then gets more casual and more diverse as the evening wears on. There is live music (usually Celtic rock bands) Wednesday through Sunday nights, but the bands are treated more as incidental additions than as the main attraction.

Comedy Clubs

Even when Las Vegas wasn't the hippest place to catch a musical act, it was always up-to-the-minute in the comedy department. From Shecky Greene to Chris Rock, virtually every famous comedian has worked a Las Vegas showroom or lounge. While the franchised comedy club boom of the 1980s went bust in most cities, the Strip still has five comedy clubs, all with multiple-act formats featuring the best names on the circuit. Cover charges are in the $18 range, but two-for-one coupons are easy to come by in freebie magazines and various coupon packages.

Catch A Rising Star. A former restaurant on the second-floor Attractions level of the Excalibur now houses a spacious 450-seat, budget-minded comedy club with two performers each night. ⊠ *Excalibur, 3850 Las Vegas Blvd. S, South Strip,* ☏ *702/597–7600.* ☉ *Nightly 7:30 and 10.*

Comedy Stop. There are two shows each night at this 400-seat club. Three comedians perform during each show. The price of admission includes two drinks. ⊠ *Tropicana Resort and Casino, 3801 Las Vegas Blvd. S, South Strip,* ☏ *702/739–2714.* ☉ *Nightly 8 and 10:30.*

An Evening at the Improv. This 300-seat showroom is in the old bingo hall on the second floor of Harrah's. The Improv is dark on Monday night, and drinks are not included in the admission price. ⊠ *Harrah's Las Vegas, 3475 Las Vegas Blvd. S, Center Strip,* ☏ *702/369–5111.* ☉ *Tues.–Sun. night 8:30 and 10:30.*

Laugh Trax. This 300-seat club at the locals-friendly Palace Station undercuts the price of its Strip competitors but only books two comedians for each program. Weekends, however, often include a singer-guitarist as a change-of-pace host. ⊠ *Palace Station, 2411 W. Sahara Ave., West Side,* ☏ *888/464–2468.* ☉ *Tues.–Sat. night 7:30 and 10.*

Riviera Comedy Club. There are two shows each night of the week at this cozy 375-seat club. ⊠ *Riviera Hotel and Casino, 2901 Las Vegas Blvd. S, North Strip,* ☏ *702/794–9433.* ☉ *Nightly 8 and 10.*

Dance Clubs

Dance clubs have been the Strip's biggest entertainment innovation of the past few years. Hotels got tired of watching their guests hop a cab to off-Strip nightspots, and built fantasy-theme dance palaces that only establishments with unrestricted budgets could create. Cover charges have correspondingly crept into the $10 to $20 range—and don't be surprised to find that, even in these "enlightened times," men will pay more than women to get in. While that level of capital investment gives these clubs a longevity their New York counterparts don't enjoy, dance clubs are still a fickle, fleeting enterprise by nature.

Each club sets its own dress code standard, but all clubs enforce a fairly rigorous one: no T-shirts, ball caps, or tennis shoes, and no logos that could be affiliated with gangs. Prepare for frustration, depending on the whim of the doorman, if you try to argue for the validity of designer tennis shoes or pullovers without a collar. How much you paid for them doesn't seem to matter.

Baby's. The concept of an "underground" club is literal at the Hard Rock Hotel, which added this mostly buried dance club as part of a 1999 hotel expansion project. An antechamber with a low ceiling, stone walls, and a tiny dance floor gives way to the main room, where a sloping seating area gradually rises to curve around the dance floor at second-story level. Video walls and servers dressed in black leather to match the black-upholstered booths from the 1950s create a futuristic *noir.* Guest big-city DJs play house, trip-hop, and drum and bass dance music. Thursday's "Can You Feel It?" is the signature night for locals and informed clubbers. The club is open Thursday through Saturday from 10:30 PM. ⊠ *Hard Rock Hotel and Casino, 4455 Las Vegas Blvd. S, Paradise Road,* ☏ *702/693–5000.*

The Beach. Life is one nonstop fraternity bash at this two-story club designed to look like a South-of-the-Border party barn. A less-restrictive dress code than that imposed by the hotels and aggressive "ladies' night" promotions make this off-Strip club a hot spot with the college crowd. It's open nightly, but hours vary, especially on weeknights. ⊠ *365 Convention Center Dr., Paradise Road,* ☎ *702/731–1925.* WEB *www.beachlv.com.*

C2K. The Venetian's "megaclub" is a leased-out, separately run operation with an opera-house design. Decorated in black and chrome accented with purple, the club spans three levels and is capable of holding nearly 3,000 people. The upper two levels allow people to look down on the dance floor below, but also offer several nooks and crannies for those seeking a quieter spot. It's open Wednesday through Sunday from 10:30 PM. ⊠ *Venetian Resort-Hotel-Casino, 3355 Las Vegas Blvd. S, Center Strip,* ☎ *702/933–4255.*

Club Rio. This pioneering dance club inside a casino offers all the essentials: wraparound video screens, a big stage, and a large dance floor. To combat the loss of novelty as newer clubs open in other casino-hotels, Club Rio has embraced Latin pop and house music to make Thursday's Latin La-Beat-Oh its signature night. If the dance floor gets too hot, overhead misters cool everyone down. It's open Wednesday through Sunday from 10:30 PM. ⊠ *Rio All-Suite Hotel and Casino, 3700 W. Flamingo Ave., West Side,* ☎ *702/252–7727.*

Light. Nightclub entrepreneurs Keith and Chris Barish, along with operating partner Andrew Sasson, threw their hat into the Vegas club circle in early 2002. This 600-capacity room at the Bellagio emphasized the exclusivity of its 40 reserved tables and expensive "bottle service" in the early going, but it is also open to those of average means. It's open nightly from 9:30 PM. ⊠ *The Bellagio, 3600 Las Vegas Blvd. S, Center Strip,* ☎ *702/693–8300,* WEB *www.lightlv.com.*

Ra. Luxor opened this $20-million hot spot in 1997. It's still the most fancifully designed of the clubs, with a theme park–style interior inspired by the "Egyptian-deco" futurism of the sci-fi movie *Stargate.* Live bands sometimes take to the center stage; dancers gyrate in cages. The club spotlights visiting DJs from other cities and its signature night is Wednesday's "Pleasuredome." Collared shirts *and* sports jackets for men are required. It's open Wednesday through Saturday from 10:30 PM. ⊠ *Luxor Hotel-Casino, 3900 Las Vegas Blvd. S, South Strip,* ☎ *702/262–4949.*

Rain in the Desert. Michael Morton and Scott DeGraff, the Chicago partners who ran the popular stand-alone Drink club during the '90s, were lured into a casino environment at The Palms after the Drink ran its course. The round, 1,500-capacity nightclub and concert house is equipped with dancing waters, video projections on a 40-ft water curtain and occasional blasts of fire. Perhaps because The Palms shares ownership with the Sacramento Kings, the club even includes "skyboxes" for rent. Thursday is the signature night, "Drenched." ⊠ *The Palms, 4321 W. Flamingo Rd., West Side,* ☎ *702/938–9999,* WEB *www.rainatthepalms.com.*

rumjungle. This Mandalay Bay version of a Brazilian paradise drew Disney-style lines from the day it opened. The "fire wall" out front beckons clubgoers into a wild 20,000-square-ft room with waterfalls, dancing girls on platforms above the 85-ft-long bar, giant conga drums, and even aerialists attached to trapezelike harnesses. The house, hip-hop, and Latin music keep the dance floor hoppin'. It's open Thursday through Saturday from 11 PM. ⊠ *Mandalay Bay Resort and Casino, 3950 Las Vegas Blvd. S, South Strip,* ☎ *702/632–7408.*

Studio 54. This tri-level, 22,000-square-ft dance club inside the MGM Grand Hotel and Casino took over the area where a cheesy lion's mouth

Country and Western

Dylan's Dance Hall & Saloon. Once known as R…
der Highway honky-tonk is the spiritual hea…
music. It's open Thursday through Saturd…
Boulder Hwy., Boulder Strip, ☎ *702/45…*

Gilley's Dancehall Saloon & Barbecu…
moved from Texas to Las Vegas, …
dancing, but it's country's hom…
day through Saturday from 6…
nightly for dinner. ⊠ *Ne…*
Las Vegas Blvd. S, So…

Jazz

Jazz is played ar…
ing as part of…
(⊠ 3667 I…
and con…
premi…
sta…

---

scene in its infant days was smaller and so inclusive of gay patrons there was no need to draw distinctions. Now there are quite a few bars and nightclubs catering to different segments of the community. For a more complete list, pick up a copy of the *Las Vegas Bugle* gay monthly or check the listings in *Fodor's Gay Guide to the USA*. Several of the more popular gay and lesbian bars are concentrated around the intersection of Naples Drive and Paradise Road, just north of the airport. Expect cover charges to be around $10 for dance clubs on weekends.

Freezone. A bar that also claims to be the largest gay restaurant in Las Vegas serves a mix of women and men and has different themes each night with drink promotions. ⊠ *610 E. Naples Dr., Paradise Road,* ☎ *702/794–2300.*

Flex. A smaller, more neighborhood-oriented bar/club for men, this place sometimes has live floor shows, contests, and entertainment. ⊠ *4371 W. Charleston Ave., West Side,* ☎ *702/385–3539.*

Gipsy. The oldest, largest and most famous alternative dance club in Las Vegas is within walking distance of the Hard Rock Hotel. Predominantly a male club, it has always welcomed the open-minded regardless of sexual preference. However, competition from new mainstream nightclubs (including Baby's across the street at the Hard Rock) has taken a little of the edge off its crossover appeal outside the gay community. ⊠ *4605 Paradise Rd., Paradise Road,* ☎ *702/733–9677.*

Keys. This piano bar has an older male clientele. ⊠ *1000 E. Sahara Ave., East Side,* ☎ *702/731–2200.*

The Spotlight Lounge. At the entrance to the fading Commercial Center, one of the city's oldest shopping centers, this bar offers everything from video poker and Western barbecue on Sunday evening to male strippers on Friday night. ⊠ *957 E. Sahara Ave., East Side,* ☎ *702/ 696–0202.*

ockabilly's, this Boul-
rt of Las Vegas country
ay from 7:30 PM. ⊠ 4660
1–4006.

e. This institution, which Mickey
as less live music than dee-jayed line
e on the Strip. The club is open Thurs-
PM for dancing, but the restaurant is open
Frontier Hotel and Gambling Hall, 3120
th Strip, ☎ *702/794–8434.*

ound town at various venues and various times. Open-
the resurrected Aladdin, New York's famous **Blue Note**
as Vegas Blvd. S, Center Strip, ☎ 702/862–8307) scaled back
solidated into one room after its original restaurant-showroom
se proved too ambitious. The intimate club still offers jazz main-
ys such as Phil Upchurch and Bill Watrous. Away from the Strip,
the best bet is the **Jazzed Cafe and Vinoteca** (⊠ 8615 W. Sahara Ave.,
West Las Vegas, ☎ 702/233–2859). For information on concerts in
parks and municipal library theaters, call the **Las Vegas Jazz Society**
(☎ 702/455–7340).

Rock

Boston Grill & Bar. This is the no-frills, low-cover place to hear Las Vegas's
own original rock bands. It's open nightly from 8 PM. ⊠ *3417 S. Jones
Blvd., West Side,* ☎ *702/368–0750.*

Junkyard Live. A fashionably downscale spot hosts local bands in all
genres, with jam sessions on Monday, Wednesday, and Thursday. ⊠
2327 S. Eastern Ave., East Las Vegas, ☎ *702/440–8812,* WEB *www.
junkyardlive.com.*

Afternoon Shows

Las Vegas has become a wider reaching and more family-friendly destination. But at the same time, evening show prices have broken into
the triple-digits. These factors are sometimes at odds with one another
and help explain a host of afternoon shows that hold their ticket prices
under the $20 mark. The following are the most proven and popular.

Bottom's Up. Comedian Breck Wall has been a fixture on the Strip since
1964, when his Dallas-based comedy troupe first offered Las Vegas a
campy hour of blackout sketches and burlesque humor that may have
inspired TV's "Laugh-In." (Wall says Rowan & Martin used to catch
the show when they were working in town.) No joke is too old or raunchy
for the only daytime topless show. ⊠ *Flamingo Las Vegas, 3555 Las
Vegas Blvd. S, Center Strip,* ☎ *702/733–3333.* ⊟ *$12.95.* ☉ *Mon.–
Sat. 2 PM and 4 PM.*

☺ **Mac King.** This comic magician keeps the payroll small; the only "exotic animal" is a goldfish that pops out of his mouth at an unexpected
moment. King stands apart from the other magic shows on the Strip
by offering a one-man hour of low-key, self-deprecating humor and
the kind of "close-up" magic that often requires more skill than the
the "cabinet tricks" of the larger shows. ⊠ *Harrah's Las Vegas Casino
& Hotel, 3475 Las Vegas Blvd. S, Center Strip,* ☎ *702/369–5111.* ⊟
$14.95. ☉ *Tues.–Sat. 1 PM and 3 PM.*

↻ **The Illusionary Magic of Rick Thomas.** If you want your children to see a Las Vegas-style magic show without paying Siegfried & Roy-level prices, Rick Thomas's well-paced revue offers an overview of the basic stage illusions and even throws in a white tiger. ⊠ *Tropicana Resort and Casino, 3801 Las Vegas Blvd. S, South Strip,* ☎ *702/739–2222.* 🎫 *$16.95–$21.95.* ☉ *Sat.–Thurs. 2 PM and 4 PM.*

Evening Revues

↻ **American Superstars.** This upstart impersonator show made "Legends in Concert" pick up its energy level by challenging it with rollicking tributes to pop stars such as Ricky Martin and Christina Aguilera. Both shows are better for the competition. ⊠ *Stratosphere Hotel and Casino, 2000 Las Vegas Blvd. S, North Strip,* ☎ *702/380–7711.* 🎫 *$30.* ☉ *Sun.–Tues. 7 PM. Wed. and Fri.–Sat. 7 PM and 10 PM.*

Blue Man Group: Live at Luxor. A perhaps unlikely success story on the Strip is a striking example of how far Las Vegas has come in shedding its old image. The New York–based troupe launched its fourth and largest production at the Luxor just before it became ready for prime-time in a series of high-profile computer processor commercials. Three men in utilitarian uniforms, their heads bald and gleaming from cobalt blue greasepaint, prowl the stage committing twisted "science projects" that are alternately highbrow and juvenile. A civil-engineering lesson might be followed by marshmallow spitting. A seven-piece band plays angular spaghetti Western music to complement the Blue Men's signature percussion instruments made from PVC pipe. ⊠ *Luxor Hotel-Casino, 3900 Las Vegas Blvd. S, South Strip,* ☎ *702/262–4400,* 🌐 *www.blueman.com.* 🎫 *$65–$100.* ☉ *Nightly 7 and 10.*

Crazy Girls. An Americanized, low-rent version of the Crazy Horse Cabaret in Paris offers a topless club experience within the safe confines of the hotel. The basic formula is still a chorus line of topless women who lip-sync songs and gyrate to taped music. ⊠ *Riviera Hotel and Casino, 2901 Las Vegas Blvd. S, North Strip,* ☎ *702/794–9433.* 🎫 *$25–$35.* ☉ *Wed.–Mon. 9 PM.*

↻ **EFX Alive.** Australian pop star Rick Springfield is the fourth star (following Michael Crawford, David Cassidy, and Tommy Tune) to headline an over-the-top production show full of movie-quality special effects (hence the name). Each star has brought his own strengths to the table and modified the show to his talents; Springfield's version aims to be more "rocking" with self-referential humor. But every headliner has worked within the framework of four basic segments: battling dragons in King Arthur's Camelot, helming an intergalactic circus as an ageless P. T. Barnum, defying death and the afterlife as Houdini, and rescuing a fair maiden from the primitive future of H. G. Wells' *Time Machine.* Though the Broadway theatrics are diverting, the emphasis here is on the effects: 2,500 fixed and 300 moving lights, 48-channel digital surround sound, a 3-D segment, and gargantuan sets that fill the 100-ft stage. ⊠ *MGM Grand Hotel Casino, 3799 Las Vegas Blvd. S, South Strip,* ☎ *702/891–7777.* 🎫 *$55–$75.* ☉ *Wed. and Thurs. 7:30 PM; Tues., Fri., and Sat. 7:30 PM and 10:30 PM.*

An Evening at La Cage. This durable female impersonator show has been guided for more than a decade by Frank Marino, whose dead-on take on Joan Rivers provides the live voice to introduce lip-synced musical tributes. ⊠ *Riviera Hotel and Casino, 2901 Las Vegas Blvd. S, North Strip,* ☎ *702/794–9433.* 🎫 *$29.95.* ☉ *Wed.–Mon. 7:30 PM and 9:30 PM.*

Folies Bergère. This classic French topless revue celebrated its 40th year at the Tropicana in 1999; a new finale was added to spruce up the "greatest hits" format in late 2001. The painted flats and dance segments such as the "Can-Can" still show their age compared to newer, hi-tech competition. But now that the Strip has only two classic revues complete with singers, dancers, a comedian or juggler, and, of course, showgirls parading around in feathers, it's easier to appreciate the Folies and to see it more as a nostalgic throwback than as the dinosaur it seemed to be a few years ago. Only the late show is topless. ⊠ *Tropicana Resort and Casino, 3801 Las Vegas Blvd. S, South Strip,* ☎ *702/739–2411.* 🖃 *$45–$55.* ☉ *Fri.–Wed. 7:30 PM and 10 PM.*

Jubilee! Donn Arden, who produced shows in Las Vegas from 1952 until his death in 1994, put together this spectacular stage tribute to Hollywood in 1981 for the old MGM Grand Hotel, now Bally's. *Jubilee!* has been updated in places since then, but it remains your last chance to experience the scope of Arden's over-the-top vision and to sample the "class" (or kitsch) Vegas of old. A cast of 80 or more performs in a theater with 1,100 seats, but the gargantuan sets and props steal the show: The sinking of the *Titanic* is re-created, and when Samson destroys the temple the wreckage goes up in flames. Showgirls parade about in the largest spectacle of feathers and bare breasts you've ever seen. ⊠ *Bally's Casino Resort, 3645 Las Vegas Blvd. S, Center Strip,* ☎ *702/739–4567.* 🖃 *$50–$66.* ☉ *Sat.–Thurs. 7:30 PM and 10 PM.*

La Femme. The MGM Grand Hotel wooed Paris' Crazy Horse Cabaret to Las Vegas by offering to remodel a lounge into a near-spitting image of the French institution. After years of hosting knockoffs such as "Crazy Girls," Las Vegas finally has the original girlie show, a classy affair in which symmetrically matched, naturally endowed women are expertly choreographed and "painted in light" for a succession of humorous or erotically mimed vignettes. ⊠ *MGM Grand Hotel, 3799 Las Vegas Blvd. S, South Strip,* ☎ *702/891–7777.* 🖃 *$49.* ☉ *Wed.–Mon. 8:30 PM and 10:30 PM.*

☺ **Lance Burton: Master Magician.** The eponymous Lance Burton Theater is an opulent 1,200-seat opera house that makes a splendid long-term home for a nice guy from Kentucky who worked his way up the ranks from specialty act to star. He's a charmer with the ladies, and works youngsters into the show like no other act on the Strip. Unfortunately, the small magic—the sleight of hand and close-up tricks that earned him the prestigious Gold Medal from the International Brotherhood of Magicians—is lost from way up in the balcony. Still, the major illusions, such as making cars disappear, are downright stunning. ⊠ *Monte Carlo Resort and Casino, 3770 Las Vegas Blvd. S, South Strip,* ☎ *702/730–7777.* 🖃 *$55–$60.* ☉ *Tues.–Sat. 7 PM and 10 PM, Sun. 7 PM.*

☺ **Legends in Concert.** The durable *Legends* rotates impersonations of Madonna, Liberace, Tom Jones, and others, with the Elvis Presley finale the only non-variable rule. There's no lip-syncing and always a live band. ⊠ *Imperial Palace Hotel and Casino, 3535 Las Vegas Blvd. S, Center Strip,* ☎ *702/794–3261.* 🖃 *$35.* ☉ *Mon.–Sat. 7:30 PM and 10:30 PM.*

☺ **Melinda—First Lady of Magic.** Melinda is a former showgirl and home-grown Las Vegan, and longtime residents have watched her show evolve from the amateurish level of a school play into a fun, fast-moving affair with the feel of a pop video. It's still not the place to see magic that will challenge you, but audiences are forgiving of the likeable star,

The Second City. Shoehorning itself onto a Strip filled w
comedy clubs, Chicago's ensemble comedy institutio
fresh air. It has the class and polish of a theatrical re
to go for the cheap or lowbrow when there's a
Five performers present favorite sketches fro
archives and also pull audience members i
in Bugsy's Celebrity Theatre. ⊠ *Flamin*
Blvd. S, Center Strip, ☎ *702/733–*
Thurs.–Sun. 8 PM and 10:30 PM, W

Siegfried and Roy at the Mira
Las Vegas, having performe
signed them to a $55.5-m
they opened with a gr
under a "lifetime c
tire. Siegfried an
pear and have
white tigers
a robotic
Mich
rag

before the show begins. The music is rousing
batics chilling, and the dance numbers inspiring. The usual circus-type
distractions are kept to a minimum, and there are no animals. The opening of Cirque du Soleil's newer show, *O*, threatened to make this one
seem less special, but so far that hasn't been the case. *Mystère* keeps
the audience closer to the action and the human achievements more
in the spotlight. ⊠ *Treasure Island Hotel and Casino, 3300 Las Vegas
Blvd. S, Center Strip,* ☎ *702/894–7722.* 🎫 *$88.* ☉ *Wed.–Sun. 7:30
PM and 10:30 PM.*

O. Cirque du Soleil's *O* is the most expensive show in history—in Las
Vegas or anywhere else. More than $70 million was spent on the the-
ater at Bellagio, and on the liquid stage that takes over as the real star
of the show. *O* is the pronunciation of *eau*, French for water, and water
is everywhere—1.5 million gallons of it, 12 million pounds of it, con-
tained by a "stage" that, thanks to hydraulic lifts, can change shape.
The intense and nonstop action by the show's acrobats, aerial gym-
nasts and trapeze artists, synchronized swimmers, divers, and contor-
tionists takes place above, within, and even on the surface of the water.
True to Cirque tradition, the costumes, music, sets, and timing greatly
enhance the overwhelming spectacle. So much is going on, in fact, that
at the end of the show you're exhausted from trying to see everything.
⊠ *Bellagio, 3600 Las Vegas Blvd. S, Center Strip,* ☎ *702/693–7111.*
🎫 *$93–$121.* ☉ *Fri.–Tues. 7:30 PM and 10:30 PM.*

The Rat Pack is Back. Purporting to be a night at the Sands in the swingin'
days of 1961, this snappy, well-written show has been embraced for
its sincere attempt to rekindle the glory days of Frank, Sammy, Dino
and Joey (no last names are used, thanks to opposition from the Sinatra estate). ⊠ *Sahara Hotel and Casino, 2535 Las Vegas Blvd. S,
North Strip,* ☎ *702/737–2111.* 🎫 *$40–$50.* ☉ *Tues. and Thurs.–Fri.
8 PM, Mon. and Wed. 6:30 PM and 9 PM.* ⋅

with stand-up
n is a breath of
vue but isn't afraid
good laugh to be had.
Second City's 40-year
nto improvisational games
o Las Vegas, 3555 Las Vegas
333. ✆ $27.95. ⊘ Tues. and
ed. and Fri. 8 PM.

ge. The magic duo is synonymous with
d on the Strip since the 1960s. Steve Wynn
illion contract to star at The Mirage, where
undbreaking production in 1990 and continue
ntract" until their weary bones demand they re-
d Roy have made elephants and motorcycles disap-
levitated each other as well as the lions and signature
, who are their roommates in Las Vegas. The show includes
fire-breathing dragon, lasers, music written and recorded by
el Jackson, plus a home video of the stars' pet tiger cubs. ⊠ Mi-
e Hotel and Casino, 3400 Las Vegas Blvd. S, Center Strip, ✆ 702/
92-7777. ✆ $100.50. ⊘ Sun.–Tues. 7:30 PM, Fri.–Sat. 7:30 PM and
11 PM.

Skintight. This "equal opportunity" topless show includes a dynamic male frontman, Darryl Ross, and male dancers along with women in the chorus. ⊠ Harrah's Las Vegas, 3475 Las Vegas Blvd. S, Center Strip, ✆ 702/369–5111. ✆ $39.95. ⊘ Mon.–Wed. 10:30 PM, Fri. 10 PM and midnight, Sat. 10:30 PM, Sun. 7:30 PM and 10:30 PM.

Splash. The original incarnation of Splash was known for its high-energy staging, loud rock and roll, and nonstop specialty acts. But the show was eclipsed by such spectaculars as EFX and Mystère and has struggled to bring back the excitement. The name is a bit of a misnomer now, since the water is frozen; the trademark tank was removed in 1999 to shift the focus to ice-skating. Some of the skating adagios are impressive, but the classical music is jarring when interspersed with Michael Jackson and Madonna tributes held over from previous versions. Splash used to be live MTV. Now it's just for channel surfers. ⊠ Riviera Hotel and Casino, 2901 Las Vegas Blvd. S, North Strip, ✆ 702/794–9301. ✆ $51.50–$65. ⊘ Sat.–Thurs. 7:30 PM and 10:30 PM.

☙ **Steve Wyrick.** This Texas magician designed a show to match the Sahara's middle-market focus; a production-heavy spectacle in the middle-price range with the feel of a theme park stunt show. The giant sets and props help make up for the star's underwhelming, albeit amiable, stage personality. Youngsters under 12 are always free with a parent. ⊠ Sahara Hotel and Casino, 2535 Las Vegas Blvd. S, North Strip, ✆ 702/737–2111. ✆ $45.95–49.95. ⊘ Wed.–Sat. 7 PM and 10 PM, Sun.–Mon. 7 PM.

Storm. The Strip's latest homegrown extravaganza opened in March 2001, attempting to fuse current Latin pop music with the special effects, aerialists, and environmental theater of other successful shows on the Strip. The Mandalay Bay Theatre was refitted to sport vines hanging from the side walls and rusted-out car bodies in the middle of the audience. But director Jamie King, who directed concert tours for Martin and Madonna, has trouble sustaining his over-the-top, pop video approach without a star as the focal point. The result is a lot of busy, colorful claptrap that doesn't add up to a cohesive whole. ⊠ Man-

dalay Bay Resort and Casino, 3950 Las Vegas Blvd. S, South Strip, ☎
702/632–7777. 🎫 *$55–$65.* 🕐 *Wed.–Mon. 7:30 PM, Sat. 10:30 PM.*

☝ **Tournament of Kings.** One of Las Vegas's most unusual big shows takes
place in a dirt-floor arena, with the audience eating a basic dinner (warning: no utensils) and cheering fast horses, jousting, and swordplay. It's
a wonderful family show—especially for families with pre-adolescents,
who get to make a lot of noise. ✉ *Excalibur Hotel and Casino, 3850
Las Vegas Blvd. S, South Strip,* ☎ *702/597–7600.* 🎫 *$39.95.* 🕐
Nightly 6 and 8:30.

Showrooms

Resident Headliners

The turn of the new century took Las Vegas back to one of the traditions from its past. The success of impressionist Danny Gans opened
the doors to a wave of "resident headliners" who live in Las Vegas and
perform on a year-round schedule comparable to the revues (as opposed
to visiting headliners such as the Moody Blues, Huey Lewis, or Tom
Jones, who stay anywhere from three nights to two weeks).

Clint Holmes, Rita Rudner, and even a certain fellow named Wayne
Newton, all bet that showgoers were tired of special effects and ready
to re-embrace the "down front" performing tradition that put Las Vegas
on the map.

Clint Holmes (Harrah's). Harrah's wagered that Danny Gans lightning
would strike twice when it backed a relative unknown, but strong word-
of-mouth brought Clint Holmes deserved acceptance. The singer has
only one distant hit single to his name: the noncharacteristic "Playground
in My Mind" in 1973. But his endearing persona and his jazzy way
with a baby-boomer pop standard (he prefers 1970s-era material to
the Sinatra classics) allow him to pull off the seemingly impossible task
of becoming a new-generation crooner who isn't a retro throwback to
the swing era. ✉ *Harrah's Las Vegas, 3475 Las Vegas Blvd. S, Center Strip,* ☎ *702/369–5111.* 🎫 *$60.* 🕐 *Mon.–Sat.*

Danny Gans: Man of Many Voices (The Mirage). The impressionist (and
former baseball player) pulled off a near miracle in Las Vegas, coming in from the trade show and convention circuit as a "no name" and
becoming one of the hottest tickets in town. This talented impressionist
leaves 'em standing and cheering every night, after performing upwards
of 60 characters—everyone from Gerald Ford and Kermit the Frog to
Dean Martin and Homer Simpson. Gans is also a singer, dancer, mu-
sician, and comedian, and fronts a live band that provides musical
mimicry. With a show that plays more like a one-man theatrical revue
than a nightclub act, Gans lacks spontaneity but pushes emotional buttons. ✉ *Mirage Hotel and Casino, 3400 Las Vegas Blvd. S, Center Strip,*
☎ *702/791–7111.* 🎫 *$80–$100.* 🕐 *Tues.–Thurs. and Sat.–Sun. 8 PM.*

Rita Rudner (New York–New York). It's rare to be a female comedian
in Las Vegas and rarer still to offer a "clean" act that's still insightful
in its look at domestic life and female obsessions. The folding chairs
in the so-called Cabaret Theatre are nothing to write home about, but
Rita gets the job done for an intimate evening of soft-spoken wit. ✉
New York–New York, 3790 Las Vegas Blvd. S, South Strip, ☎ *702/
740–6815.* 🎫 *$46.* 🕐 *Mon. and Wed.–Thurs. 8 PM, Fri. 9 PM, Sat. 7
PM and 9 PM.*

The Scintas (Rio). After a year in a smaller room at the Las Vegas
Hilton, this Buffalo, NY, quartet of three siblings and a drummer
moved into the Rio in April 2001. The Scintas hearken back to the era

of the "show band," where every member sported double-threat comic and musical duties. The Scintas lay on the schtick pretty thick, but have a loyal, mostly older fan base for an act that can perhaps be described as Wayne Newton meets the Smothers Brothers. ⊠ *Rio All-Suite Hotel and Casino, 3700 W. Flamingo Rd., West Side,* ☎ *702/252–7776.* ▨ *$45.* ☉ *Mon. and Fri.–Sun. 8 PM, Tues. 8 PMand 10:30 PM.*

Wayne Newton (Stardust). Mr. Las Vegas, the Midnight Idol, the King of the Strip: Wayne Newton is in many ways the epitome of the Las Vegas headliner. A homegrown phenomenon, he has been performing here since his teens. On stage Newton gives it the Al Jolson treatment, working and sweating his way through a leisurely two hours—singing, telling jokes, and playing the guitar, violin, and trumpet. Whatever one thinks of his diminished voice or the cornpone, no one would dispute the fact that he knows how to entertain his audience. Seeing him in this appropriately aged showroom (which once housed the *Lido de Paris*) is as much a part of the experience of visiting Las Vegas as gambling and a trip to Hoover Dam. ⊠ *Stardust Hotel and Casino, 3000 Las Vegas Blvd. S, North Strip,* ☎ *702/732–6325.* ▨ *$55.* ☉ *Sat.–Thurs. 9 PM.*

Headliners Showrooms

Who would have thought the day would come when the traditional headliner room was an endangered species on the Strip? Part of it's due to the previously mentioned effect of the concert industry shifting the action to venues such as the House of Blues. A few rooms do still host a rotating roster of names, but much of the action has shifted to the locals scene away from the Strip proper.

Hilton Theater. Once famous as the home base for Elvis Presley, this large showroom with a balcony has since been converted to theater seating. Three acts were signed as "anchor" tenants in 2002 to make sure there would always be a headliner in the room: The Commodores, Righteous Brothers, and Smothers Brothers. ⊠ *Las Vegas Hilton, 3000 Paradise Rd, Paradise Road,* ☎ *702/732–5755.*

Hollywood Theatre. Tom Jones makes regular visits to this contemporary update of the classic showroom at the MGM Grand, which eliminates the long tables to improve sightlines but keeps the booths. The sound system in the 650-seat venue is among the best in town for a roster that also includes comedians George Carlin and Carrot Top. ⊠ *MGM Grand Hotel Casino, 3799 Las Vegas Blvd. S, South Strip,* ☎ *702/891–7777.*

Les Théâtre des Arts. The stage musical "Notre Dame de Paris" failed at Paris Las Vegas in 2000, about the time corporate owner Park Place Entertainment decided to close the Circus Maximus at sister property Caesars. Instead of looking for a new long-running attraction, the company moved such longtime Caesars headliners as the Moody Blues and Natalie Cole into this 1,200-seat auditorium. The hotel planned to continue the policy, adding names such as Vanessa Williams and Jay Mohr to the mix. ⊠ *Paris Las Vegas, 3655 Las Vegas Blvd. S, Center Strip,* ☎ *702/946–4567.*

Orleans Showroom. Theater seating and a super-wide stage (designed to lure TV production) highlight this room slightly west of the Strip at the Orleans, which has proven popular with both locals and tourists. Frequent headliners include Neil Sedaka and Debbie Reynolds. ⊠ *Orleans Hotel and Casino, 4500 W. Tropicana Ave., West Side,* ☎ *702/365–7075.*

Samba Theatre. The Rio didn't really seem to have a plan of action when it built a gorgeous 1,500-seat auditorium, which rivals the municipal auditoriums of any major city with its opulent chandeliers and original artwork in the lobby. Lately the hotel has been using it for headliners such as comic magicians Penn & Teller, and for two-night visits by a variety of acts, from David Spade to Peter Frampton. They also added a late-night adult revue called "Showgirls" as an anchor tenant. ⊠ *Rio All Suite Hotel and Casino, 3700 W. Flamingo Rd., West Side,* ☎ *702/252–7776.*

Suncoast Showroom. The Suncoast is a locals-oriented casino from the Gaughan family that built the Gold Coast and Orleans. While the latter are only a couple of miles away from the Strip, the Suncoast is a determined drive 15 mi or so west of the tourist corridor in Summerlin. A handsome 400-seat showroom with a classic old-Vegas feel was, therefore, something of a risk. But in its early going, acts ranging from Tower of Power to Bobby Rydell were drawing a 60-40 split of locals to tourists. ⊠ *Suncoast, 9090 Alta Dr., Northwest Las Vegas,* ☎ *702/ 365–7075.*

Theatre Ballroom. The Golden Nugget had closed its upstairs cabaret once, leaving downtown short on entertainment. But the cozy 350-seat room reopened in late 2000 with successful numbers for comic magician The Amazing Johnathon and for Las Vegas fixture Tony Orlando. ⊠ *Golden Nugget Hotel and Casino, 129 Fremont St., Downtown,* ☎ *702/796–9999.*

Strip Clubs

Strip clubs have become a cottage industry in Las Vegas, their rise paralleling the growth of the convention industry in Las Vegas as well as their general boom nationwide. Zoning still restricts most clubs to industrial areas off the Strip, but the "upscale" trend within has caused most of them to institute cover charges of $5 to $10. The real money is made on the "table dances" continuously solicited inside. Most of them cost $20 per song.

Newer clubs seem to succeed by sacrificing their liquor license in exchange for full nudity. Let your own preferences be your guide, but remember that the Palomino Club in North Las Vegas is the only place where you can have both. Otherwise, the choice is between booze and g-strings or soft drinks and full nudity.

Club Paradise. Its location—directly across the street from the Hard Rock Hotel—has been a plus for this place. It was also one of the first local clubs to embrace the "gentleman's club" boom of the 1990s. Once a run-down place called the Pussycat Lounge, it renovated, changed its name, suited its bouncers in tuxedos, and put computerized lighting over the stage. ⊠ *4416 Paradise Rd., Paradise Road,* ☎ *702/734–7990.*

Olympic Gardens. Right on the northern edge of the Strip, this is one of the busiest, most easily located jiggle joints in town. It was the first to install several "pod" stages to take the place of the single stage found in older clubs. ⊠ *1531 Las Vegas Blvd. S, Downtown,* ☎ *702/ 385–8987.*

Palomino Club. One of the oldest strip clubs in the area, it is grandfathered into North Las Vegas zoning codes, which means it's allowed to have both a full bar and full nudity. The Palomino combines the generations by keeping its old "burlesque" stage downstairs, while upstairs the dancers perform on mini-platforms and solicit private dances. ⊠ *1848 Las Vegas Blvd. N, North Las Vegas,* ☎ *702/642–2984.*

THE ARTS

While known more for theatrical spectacles than serious theater, Las Vegas does have a lively cultural scene. The groups listed below offer full seasons of productions each year. The **Allied Arts Council** (✉ 3750 S. Maryland Pkwy., East Side, ☎ 702/731–5419) can provide a detailed schedule of local theater, dance, music, and fine-arts exhibits.

Ballet

Nevada Ballet Theatre is the city's longest-running fine-arts organization (this being Las Vegas, it only dates from 1973). Bruce Steivel is artistic director for the troupe, which stages three to five productions each year, anchored by an annual December presentation of *The Nutcracker*. Most performances are held in UNLV's Judy Bayley Theatre. ✉ *4505 S. Maryland Pkwy., University District,* ☎ *702/243–2623 for schedule information; 702/895–2787 for tickets.*

Classical Music

The **Las Vegas Philharmonic** was formed in 1998 when the older Nevada Symphony Orchestra was headed for insolvency. It includes most of the players from the now-defunct orchestra and is conducted by Hal Weller, formerly of the Flagstaff Symphony Orchestra. The Philharmonic performs at Artemus Ham Hall on the UNLV campus. ✉ *4505 S. Maryland Pkwy., University District,* ☎ *702/258–9895 for schedule information; 702/895–2787 for tickets.*

Film

The second half of the 1990s saw an explosion of new multiplex construction in Las Vegas—there are 20 theaters and more than 150 screens in town, a surprising number of them attached to casinos. For the first time ever, there's even an eight-theater multiplex on the Strip. Several theaters are conveniently located. The **Showcase 8** (✉ 3785 Las Vegas. Blvd. S, South Strip, ☎ 702/225–4828) is the only movie theater on the Strip; it's in the Showcase Mall, next to the MGM Grand. The **Century 12** (✉ 4500 W. Tropicana Ave., East Side, ☎ 702/365–7111) is a 12-plex at the Orleans Hotel-Casino. The **Brenden Theatres at the Palms** (✉ 4321 W. Flamingo Rd., West Side, ☎ 702/507–4849) adds 12 more screens to a casino setting in the same area. On the other side of town, the "Boulder strip" in east Las Vegas offers two high-tech multiplexes. The 11-screen **Boulder Cinemas** (✉ 4111 Boulder Hwy., Boulder Strip, ☎ 702/221–2283) is at the Boulder Station. **Century 18 Sam's Town** (✉ 5111 Boulder Hwy. Boulder Strip, ☎ 702/547–7469) is just down the road from the Boulder Station.

♻ The **Luxor IMAX Theatre** (✉ Luxor Resort and Casino, 3900 Las Vegas Blvd. S, South Strip, ☎ 702/262–4000) has multiple daily screenings of movies created for the giant screens of the 70mm IMAX process. Films available in this format usually have appealing scientific or natural-history subjects, such as travel on a space shuttle or explorations of the Grand Canyon, but lately have expanded into more purely entertaining attractions such as the Disney films *Fantasia 2000* and *Beauty and the Beast*.

Theater

Away from the Strip, a booming community theater scene caters to the area's many new residents, retirees in particular, who are looking for a low-cost alternative to the pricey shows. Only **Actors Repertory The-**

atre is considered a professional company in Las Vegas, in that its players are members of the Actors Equity union. Most of its productions are held at the Summerlin Library and Performing Arts Center. ✉ *1771 Inner Circle Dr., Summerlin,* ☎ *702/647–7469 for schedule information; 702/256–5111 for tickets.*

The **University of Nevada–Las Vegas Theater Department** brings in outside professionals and holds community-wide auditions for a full season of productions each academic year. Most performances are held in the Judy Bayley Theatre on campus. ✉ *4505 S. Maryland Pkwy., University District,* ☎ *702/647–7469 for schedule information; 702/ 895–2787 for tickets.*

Las Vegas has two community theater groups. Both have their own performance spaces and concentrate on intimate, easily staged productions. **Las Vegas Little Theatre** (✉ 3850 Schiff Dr., West Side, ☎ 702/362–7996) tends to focus on familiar titles such as Neil Simon comedies or light musicals such as *Nunsense.* **Off Broadway Theater** (✉ 900 E. Karen Ave., East Side, ☎ 702/737–0611) searches for crowd-pleaser productions that can be staged on single sets with small casts. Some of their titles (*Light Sensitive,* for example) aren't very familiar, but depend on word of mouth and a consistent product for supporters. **Nevada Theater Company** (✉ 2928 Lake East Dr., The Lakes, ☎ 702/ 873–0191) has come on strong in recent years, moving into a former video store with more adventurous efforts such as *Psycho Beach Party.*

7 OUTDOOR ACTIVITIES AND SPORTS

What makes Las Vegas a hot spot for outdoor recreation and fitness activities? More than 300 sunny days a year; a flat valley for jogging, walking, and biking surrounded by mountains for hiking, bouldering, and climbing; a fantastic collection of world-class golf courses and tennis courts; swimming in hotel pools; boating and fishing in one of the world's great lakes; and downhill skiing within an hour of the sizzling city. When casino hopping gets old, just step outside. A big world awaits.

Updated by
Mike
Weatherford

T HE PLAYFUL SPIRIT OF LAS VEGAS, epitomized in its casinos, is also very much alive in its sports. With more than 50 golf courses (roughly half public or semiprivate), Las Vegas hosts several prestigious tournaments that include a $1-million stop on the PGA tour. Many boxing superstars—Muhammad Ali, Sugar Ray Leonard, Thomas Hearns, George Foreman, Mike Tyson, and Evander Holyfield—have faced each other in a Las Vegas ring. Las Vegas also hosts the 51s triple-A minor-league baseball team and the Runnin' Rebels college basketball team. The Las Vegas Motor Speedway is one of the largest Indy-style racetracks in the country; every March, the Las Vegas 400, a NASCAR Winston Cup race, attracts more than 120,000 spectators, the largest sporting event held in Nevada. Most locals-oriented casinos now have world-class bowling alleys. There's downhill skiing at Mt. Charleston, a mere hour from the sizzling Strip. Scuba diving and fishing in Lake Mead, hiking and rock climbing at Red Rock Canyon, and biking and horseback riding in the desert round out the outdoor recreation and sports.

Participant Sports and Fitness

Ballooning

Several hot-air balloon companies can take you up, up, and away in their beautiful balloons. The balloon season runs from October through April, depending on the local thermals, though some companies fly year-round. The flights start just before sunrise or sunset, when the air is stillest (you have to get up very early in the morning in the summer so as not to land too long after the sun rises). Most balloon businesses ask for reservations (held by a credit card number) a week in advance. The Las Vegas Balloon Classic, which takes place in October, attracts more than 100 balloons from all across the West.

The Little White Chapel in the Sky. This outfit does hot-air-balloon weddings in a 12-passenger basket (the largest basket in town). You have to plan on a three-day window for getting married, since wind conditions are so variable. A wedding package starts at $650 for the couple, with the cost rising (so to speak) from there: $150 per additional guest; $250 for photography or videotaping; and more for flowers, cake, and music. ⊠ *1301 Las Vegas Blvd. S, Downtown,* ☎ *702/382–5943.*

Nevada High. Champagne is included in the cost ($125 per person) of your one-hour flight. They also offer instruction in flying hot-air balloons in their balloons—or yours. ☎ *702/873–8393.*

Biking

Because the summer heat is intense, the best times to bike in this area are fall and spring. The winter is often warm enough to brave the outdoors on two wheels, but during the summer, unless you get up at first light, it's too bloody hot. Wherever you ride, whatever the season, carry lots of water.

Las Vegas Valley has a handful of good, long rides. One popular trip is the jaunt out to Red Rock Canyon on West Charleston Boulevard; it's 11 mi from the Rainbow Boulevard intersection to the Red Rock Visitors Center. The road has a good shoulder, or dedicated bike paths, the whole way. Once there, you can continue around Red Rock Canyon's moderately difficult 13-mi scenic loop (the road is one-way).

Another good ride is between the entrance to Red Rock Canyon and the city park in the small settlement of Blue Diamond, just under 8 mi south on Highway 159. The road has good shoulders and long gentle grades with flat recuperation stretches.

A third possibility is a ride out Boulder Highway through Henderson. It's best to start east of Tropicana Avenue; there's a shoulder the whole way. If you turn around before climbing up and over Railroad Pass, the round trip is a little less than 40 mi.

Mountain biking is limited primarily to Mt. Charleston and the Bristlecone Trail, accessible at the top of the Lee Canyon ski area parking lot. It's a 6-mi loop and climbs 1,400 ft. Another popular mountain-biking locale is Cottonwood Valley. To get there, take the Blue Diamond exit off I–15 south of Las Vegas, head west for 6 mi, and turn off at the sign. You drive another ½ mi to the PACK-IN PACK-OUT sign, then ride on a 14-mi loop. Any bike store in town can give you a map to the place.

Escape the City Streets (⊠ 8221 W. Charleston Blvd., West Side, ☎ 702/838–6966) is a conveniently located store that rents bikes; it's on West Charleston Boulevard almost halfway between downtown and Red Rock Canyon. Most folks drive to Escape, park there, rent their bikes, and pedal out the rest of the way to Red Rock and back (30 mi round-trip). Bike rentals range from $25 to $50, with both hybrid bikes (fat slick tires) and mountain bikes available. For a fee, Escape will also deliver bikes to your hotel or motel and pick them up again ($12 each way).

If you don't want to pedal, you can rent a scooter. **Las Vegas Scooters** (⊠ 3735 Las Vegas Blvd. S, South Strip, ☎ 702/736–8633) rents by the hour, half-day, or full day.

Boating

All water sports in the Las Vegas area are centered on Lake Mead. You can rent personal watercraft such as small motorboats (complete with waterskiing equipment), Jet Skis, and inner tubes at **Get It Wet** (⊠ 661 W. Lake Mead Dr., Henderson, ☎ 702/558–7547). At the **Lake Mead Resort and Marina** (⊠ 322 Lakeshore Rd., Boulder City, ☎ 702/293–3484) you can choose from a variety of motorboats (and water-ski equipment) for rent by the hour or day.

Bowling

Bowling (and movie theaters) have gone from a novelty to something that locals almost expect at an off-Strip casino. Several casinos have bowling facilities that are open 24 hours a day. And as most facilities were built since the mid-'90s, they include the most up-to-date equipment (automatic scoring, video score screens, and the like), shoe rental, a pro shop, a snack shop, a bar and lounge, and cocktail service. At most places the prices are the same all the time, though at one or two the prices rise a nickel or dime a game on weekends. It's a good idea to call for public bowling hours before you go, since bowling leagues are a major rage in Las Vegas, and the alleys can be closed to the public for hours at a time, especially on weekday evenings.

Santa Fe Station. The 60-lane bowling facility has Bowlervision, which tracks the speed and path of the ball from the time it leaves your hand until it strikes the first pin. It is also equipped with the Frameworx scoring system, which has an instant-replay function. You can leave your children in the nursery while you bowl. ⊠ 4949 N. Rancho Dr., Rancho Strip, ☎ 702/658–4995.

The Castaways Hotel & Bowling Center. With 106 lanes, this is the world's largest bowling alley. (Although given its size, it is surprisingly quiet.)

It hosts the oldest stop on the PBA professional tour, held every January. ⊠ *2800 E. Fremont St., Boulder Strip,* ☎ *702/385–9153.*

Sam's Town (⊠ 5111 Boulder Hwy., Boulder Strip, ☎ 702/454–8022) has a popular 56-lane bowling alley. A good bowling alley open 24 hours is the 72-lane **Gold Coast** (⊠ 4000 W. Flamingo Rd., West Side, ☎ 702/367–4700). **The Suncoast** (⊠ 9090 Alta Dr., Northwest Las Vegas, ☎ 702/636–7400), a sister property to the Gold Coast, opened with 64 lanes. Not too far off the Strip you'll find the 70-lane **Orleans** (⊠ 4500 W. Tropicana Rd., West Side, ☎ 702/365–7111). **Texas Station** (⊠ 2101 Texas Star La., Rancho Strip, ☎ 702/631–1000) has 60 lanes and was the first to declare itself a nightclub hybrid, adding fancy lights and a booming sound system for a "cosmic bowling" concept that's since been initiated at the Gold Coast and Suncoast as well.

Fishing

Lake Mead is the place to fish for largemouth and striped bass, channel catfish, crappie, bluegill, and various types of trout. The lake is stocked with a half-million rainbow trout regularly, and at least a million fish are harvested every year. You can fish here 24 hours a day, year-round (except for posted closings). Limits are 5 trout, 6 largemouth bass, 15 crappie, 20 striped bass, and 25 catfish. Nonresident licenses are $12 a day or $51 for the year.

A good spot to cast your line in Las Vegas itself is the pond at **Lorenzi Park** (⊠ 3333 Washington Ave., West Side, ☎ 702/229–6297), which is stocked with rainbow trout in the winter and channel catfish during the spring and summer; the park is open 7 AM–11 PM. Tule Lake at **Floyd Lamb State Park** (⊠ 9200 Tule Springs Rd., North Las Vegas, ☎ 702/486–5413) is a good place to catch rainbow trout (summer) and catfish (winter). The park is open 8 AM–7 PM in summer, until 5 in winter.

Fishing supplies are available from **Blue Lake Bait and Tackle** (⊠ 5485 E. Lake Mead Blvd., Henderson, ☎ 702/452–8299). A mile outside Henderson, you can stop for supplies at the **Sandy Cove Bait Store** (⊠ 5225 E. Lake Mead Blvd., East Side, ☎ 702/459–2080). For more information on fishing in the Las Vegas area, contact the **Las Vegas Fly Fishing Club** (⊠ Box 13322, Las Vegas, NV 89112, ☎ 702/898–1168).

Golf

With an average of 315 days of sunshine a year and year-round access, Las Vegas's top sports recreation is golf. It's no accident that there are over 50 golf courses in the Las Vegas area and more opening every year. The peak season is from October through May. In May through October only mad dogs and Englishmen are out in the noonday sun, and early-morning starting times are most heavily in demand.

Reservations for tee times can be made up to a week in advance (one or two days are sufficient at some courses, and a select few allow reservations up to three months in advance). Starting times for same-day play are possible, but you're given the first available time. All courses have pros, pro shops, practice facilities, club rentals, and clubhouses. Watch out for the hustlers who hang around the resort courses looking for an easy mark.

Plans called for the Desert Inn Golf Course, the last of three 18-hole courses on the Strip itself, to close for a redesign by Tom Fazio as part of Steve Wynn's Le Reve project. But don't fear. The Bali Hai Golf Club, opened in early 2001 just south of the Mandalay Bay now carries the bragging rights as the only golf course right on the Strip. Otherwise, there are many courses on the outskirts of the city, and a few scattered around Summerlin, Henderson, Primm Valley, and Lake Las Vegas—where Fazio also is designing Rainbow Canyon at the Lake Las Vegas Resort—as well as several other courses dotted around the landscape. Most hotel concierges will help you reserve tee times.

Angel Park (⊠ 100 S. Rampart Blvd., West Side, ☎ 702/254–4653), a municipal course, is an intensely popular 36-hole Arnold Palmer–designed layout. There are three courses here: Palm, Mountain, and Cloud Nine. The 12-hole Cloud Nine replicates a dozen of the world's most famous par-3 holes; nine holes are lighted for night play (hence the name). Call two months prior to set up your tee times as this place fills up fast. Fees range from $135 to $160.

Inspired by the South Pacific, the 18-hole **Bali Hai Golf Club** (⊠ 5160 Las Vegas Blvd. S, South Strip, ☎ 702/450–8000), with its 2,500 palm trees and 7 acres of water is reminiscent of a tropical island. The entrance is a mere 10-minute walk from the Mandalay Bay–making it the only course within easy walking distance of the Strip. The Club house comes complete with a pro shop, Wolfgang Puck–inspired restaurant, and a bevy of tropical plants to round out the tropical paradise theme. Hefty greens fees begin at $250 mid-week, going up to $295 on weekends; ask about twilight specials that start at $150.

Craig Ranch (⊠ 628 W. Craig Rd., North Las Vegas, ☎ 702/642–9700) is a 50-year-old public course. It's short (6,000 yards, par 70) and narrow, with 11,000 trees. It's also the most inexpensive course in Las Vegas, a mere $18 to walk 18 holes ($26 to ride).

The **Desert Rose Golf Course** (⊠ 5483 Clubhouse Dr., East Side, ☎ 702/431–4653), a municipal course, is a 40-year-old course that was recently redesigned by PGA star Jim Colbert. As usual, it has a driving range, three putting/chipping greens, a restaurant, and snack bar. Non-Nevada residents pay $69; or you could take advantage of the twilight rate of $49 offered four hours before sunset.

Las Vegas Golf Club (⊠ 4349 Vegas Dr., West Side, ☎ 702/646–3003), established in 1949, is the oldest golf course in Las Vegas. It's a mature course with lots of trees (though little water). Many local tournaments are sponsored by this popular club, one of three Las Vegas municipal courses. The championship layout is 6,630 yards, par 72. There's a lighted driving range, putting green, restaurant, and snack bar. Non-residents pay upwards of $69 for 18 holes.

Fifteen miles from the Strip, the Jack Nicklaus–designed **Reflection Bay Golf Club** (⊠ 75 MonteLago Blvd., Henderson, ☎ 702/740–4653) is set in a beautiful location fronting Lake Las Vegas, minutes from the Hyatt resort. The course, which has 1½ mi of lakefront beach, hosts the Wendy's Three Tour Challenge. La Chandele Restaurant in the elegant clubhouse has a large patio overlooking the lake. If you're staying at the Hyatt Lake Las Vegas Resort you may reserve your tee times up to three months in advance. Fees to play are $250.

The $52-million **Shadow Creek Golf Club** (⊠ 3 Shadow Creek Dr., North Las Vegas, ☎ 702/791–7111) is owned by Mirage Resorts. One of the most exclusive golf courses in the country, it is a stomping ground for high-caliber celebrities and high rollers. Contrary to popular belief, mere mortals *can* get one of 6 to 12 daily tee times here. A round of 18 holes costs $1,000 and includes a personal caddie, a suite at the Mirage, and round-trip limo transfers. Call the Mirage to make arrangements. If you're staying at any of the MGM/Mirage properties you may qualify for a special $500 play and priority tee-times; check with your concierge at the following hotels: MGM, Mirage, Golden Nugget, The Bellagio, and Treasure Island.

In addition to the area's top courses, there are several other golfing options. **Calloway Golf Center** (✉ 6730 Las Vegas Blvd. S, South Strip, ☎ 702/896–4100) is a 42-acre golf training facility offering instruction, a 110-station driving range, and a 9-hole par-3 course. The PGA-managed **TPC/The Tournament Players Club at the Canyons** (✉ 9851 Canyon Dr., Summerlin, ☎ 702/256–2000) is an 18-hole championship lay-out complete with elevation changes, steep ravines, and a canyon lake. The **Desert Pines Golf Club** (✉ 315 E. Bonanza Rd., East Side, ☎ 702/366–1616) is an 18-hole traditional course with many trees and a good deal of water. With two large lakes and spectacular desert landscaping, the 40-year-old **Black Mountain Golf and Country Club** (✉ 500 Greenway Rd., Henderson, ☎ 702/565–7933) is a good place for beginners. The **Painted Desert Golf Course** (✉ 5555 Painted Mirage Rd., ☎ 702/645–2568) has a challenging eighth hole and a design by architect Jay Morrish.

Health Clubs

Most big hotels have health clubs, and they all charge hefty admission fees, even for guests. **Bally's, Caesars, Flamingo, Harrah's, Imperial Palace,** and the **Riviera** have separate facilities for men and women; the **Las Vegas Hilton, Luxor, Mandalay Bay, MGM Grand, Monte Carlo,** and **Tropicana** are coed. All of the above are open to the public; hotel guests and nonguests pay the same fee, generally $10–$25 per day. The health club at the Bellagio is for hotel guests only and even then the daily fee is $25.

Las Vegas Athletic Club. There are four facilities around the city. Each offers large and clean workout areas and plenty of equipment, along with racquetball courts, indoor pools, big Jacuzzis, coed steam rooms, saunas, Nautilus and free weights, aerobics classes, tanning, massage, and snack bars. The fee is $15 per day or $35 per week. ✉ 1070 E. Sahara Ave., East Side, ☎ 702/733–1919; ✉ 5090 S. Maryland Pkwy., East Side, ☎ 702/795–2582; ✉ 3830 E. Flamingo Rd., East Side, ☎ 702/451–2526; ✉ 5200 W. Sahara Ave., West Side, ☎ 702/364–5822.

Hiking and Walking

You do a lot of walking in Las Vegas. The distance from one end of the Strip to the other is deceptively long: it's 4 mi from Stratosphere at the north end to Mandalay Bay at the south end. Though the terrain is perfectly flat, often you're not wearing proper footwear, or the sun is more ferocious than you think, or the wind is whipping harder than you realize, and usually the distances are farther than you bargained for. Fatigue, overheating, and blisters are common on the Strip. Be prepared for walking more than you're used to during your Las Vegas visit: train a little before you arrive, bring comfortable walking shoes (and moleskin), and either carry water and snacks, or remember to buy them along the way.

For dyed-in-the-wool hikers and climbers, Las Vegas is a year-round draw. Within an hour of the city center are literally hundreds of trails, paths, and bouldering routes around Red Rock Canyon, Lake Mead National Recreation Area, Valley of Fire State Park, and Mt. Charleston Wilderness Area. Where you wind up hiking, bushwhacking, bouldering, and/or climbing usually depends on the season.

In summer, hikers escape the heat by traveling 45 minutes up to **Mt. Charleston,** where the U.S. Forest Service maintains more than 50 mi of marked hiking trails for all abilities. Trails range from ¼-mi long (the Robber's Roost and Bristlecone Loop trails) to the extremely strenuous 10-mi North Loop Trail, which reaches the Mt. Charleston summit at 11,918 ft; the elevation gain is 3,500 ft. There are also plenty of intermediate trails, along with marathon two-, three-, four-, and five-peak routes only for hikers who are highly advanced (and in peak physical condition). The Mt. Charleston Wilderness Area is part of the Toiyabe National Forest; for information, contact the **U.S. Forest Service** (⊠ 2881 S. Valley View Blvd., Suite 16, Las Vegas, NV 89103, ☎ 702/873–8800, WEB www.fs.fed.us).

In winter, when downhill and cross-country skiing are the outdoor activities of choice on Mt. Charleston, hikers head to **Red Rock Canyon Recreation Area** (⊠ W. Charleston Blvd., ☎ 702/363–1922, WEB www.redrockcanyon.blm.gov), which encompasses 83,100 acres of Bureau of Land Management recreation lands. Like Mt. Charleston hiking, Red Rock Canyon hiking runs the gamut from short discovery trails for children to all-day routes up the sandstone to various mountain peaks. Note that there are only 25 mi of maintained trails at Red Rock, and it's extremely easy to get lost; search-and-rescue teams, including helicopters, are dispatched regularly to find lost hikers. People are also hurt or killed occasionally in falls. It's imperative to know where you're going (and how to get back!) and what you're doing before you set out to conquer the Aztec sandstone of Red Rock Canyon. Make sure someone else knows where you're going, and when you're expected to return, as well. For guided group hikes in Red Rock Canyon, contact the local chapter of the **Sierra Club** (☎ 702/363–3267).

The best books on hiking in the area are *Hiking Las Vegas* and *Hiking Southern Nevada*, both by local mountain man Branch Whitney and both published by local publishing company **Huntington Press** (☎ 800/244–2224, WEB www.huntingtonpress.com). Each book contains 60 trails located within 60 minutes of the Las Vegas Strip; there are hikes for everyone from rank beginners to mountain goats.

Horseback Riding

Bonnie Springs Ranch. A little past Red Rock Canyon (18 mi from the Strip), Bonnie Springs offers one-hour guided rides at the base of the Spring Mountains, within the canyon. The rides cover 3–4 mi round-trip and cost $25. The ranch also offers a four-hour excursion to see wild horses for $130, including meal; and a sunset ride for $135, including meal. Note that no children under 6 are allowed. ⊠ *1 Bonnie Springs Ranch Rd.*, ☎ *702/875–4191.* ☉ *Rides set out at 9, 10:15, 11:30, 12:45, 2, and 3:15. Two rides are added during the summer months at 4:30 PM and 5:45PM.*

Sagebrush Ranch. Sagebrush offers one- and two-hour guided rides as well as breakfast and dinner trail rides. The one-hour ride is $25, the two-hour ride is $50. The breakfast ride includes a big hot meal cooked and served around a campfire ($99); dinner is an all-you-can-eat steak feast ($139). The ranch caters to families, and riding helmets are provided. The rides head up into the Spring Mountains, where the landscape looks like something straight out of a John Wayne movie. ⊠ *12000 West Ann Rd., North Las Vegas*, ☎ *702/645–9422.*

Jogging

You can spot many joggers at dusk on the wide sidewalks south of the Mandalay Bay, running parallel to the airport and the Bali Hai golf course. However, it gets noisy on the boulevard and somewhat polluted. A little calmer are the jogging trails that run around the **Las Vegas Hilton.** Your best bet for jogging in Las Vegas is the **University of Nevada–Las Vegas** (⊠ 4505 S. Maryland Pkwy., University District, ☎ 702/739–3011), where you'll find a regulation track (Bill Cosby's favorite hangout when in town), from which you can see the Strip in the distance as you run without inhaling exhaust fumes.

You can also jog at Red Rock Canyon: the 2-mi Moenkopi Loop begins and ends at the Visitors Center; the Willow Springs Trail is a 3-mi circuit. The most pleasant time to hit the streets of Las Vegas, especially in the hot months, is early in the morning.

Racquetball

Several places in Las Vegas have racquetball courts that are open to the public for a fee. **Las Vegas Athletic Clubs** (1070 E. Sahara Ave., East Side, ☎ 702/733–1919) has courts at this and its four other locations; the fee is $15 per day for non-members or you can pay a weekly fee of $35 if you plan to play more than once. This Athletic Club is open 24 hours a day and the other three are open 7 AM to 8 PM. The local **YMCA** (4141 Meadows La., ☎ 702/877–7200) issues daily passes for its facilities including a jogging track. Passes are $10.

Rafting

Black Canyon, just below Hoover Dam, is the place for river running near Las Vegas. You can launch a raft here on the Colorado River year-round. The 11-mi run to Willow Beach on the Arizona side is reminiscent of rafting the Grand Canyon, with its vertical canyon walls, bighorn sheep on the slopes, and feeder streams and waterfalls coming off the bluffs. The water flows at roughly 5 mph, but some rapids, eddies, and whirlpools can cause difficulties, as can head winds, especially for inexperienced rafters.

If you want to go rafting in Black Canyon on your own, you must apply for a permit from the **U.S. Bureau of Reclamation** (✉ Box 60400, Boulder City, NV 89006, ☎ 702/293–8204) for $5. Permits are issued immediately. The bureau will also send a list of guides and outfitters. Launches take place every morning at 8:30AM and 10AM.

Rock Climbing

The best places to climb in the area are among the Calico Hills in Red Rock Canyon. This is a year-round international rock-climbing destination, with more than 1,500 known routes up the sandstone-limestone escarpment (Todd Swain's *Red Rocks Select* details many of them).

For guided hikes and climbing instruction, contact **Sky's the Limit** (☎ 702/363–4533), run by Randall Grandstaff. He's been climbing at Red Rock for nearly 20 years and has pioneered many of the routes. Half-day ($180) and full-day ($280) private lessons or private guided hikes are available; Sky's the Limit also has two-day classes ($220). All equipment is provided.

Beginner to advanced rock climbers hone their climbing skills indoors on the simulated rock walls at **Powerhouse Climbing Center** (✉ 8201 W. Charleston Blvd., West Side, ☎ 702/254–5604). The **Desert Rocks Sports** (✉ 8201 W. Charleston Blvd., West Side, ☎ 702/254–1143) sells indoor and outdoor equipment and has knowledgeable salespeople who will happily advise you on routes.

Scuba Diving

Lake Mead offers many opportunities for scuba divers. Because the reservoir flooded so much land, sights of the deep abound. The yacht *Tortuga,* doomed and possibly haunted, rests at 50 ft near the Boulder Islands, and Hoover Dam's asphalt factory sits on the canyon floor nearby. The boat *Cold Duck,* in 35 ft of water, is an excellent training dive. The old Mormon town of St. Thomas, inundated by the lake in 1938, has many a watery story to tell. Wishing Well Cove has steep

canyon drop-offs, caves, and clear water. Ringbolt Rapids, an exhila-
rating drift dive, is for the advanced only, and the Tennis Shoe Graveyard, near Las Vegas Wash, is one of may footholds of watery treasures.
In the summer, Lake Mead is like a bathtub, reaching 85 degrees on
the surface and staying at about 80 degrees down to 50 ft below the
surface. Divers can actually wear bathing suits rather than wet suits
to do some of the shallower dives. Visibility averages 30 ft to 35 ft.
The National Park Service has designated an underwater trail at Boulder Beach, near the Pyramid Island Causeway; just follow the buoys.

Certified divers can rent masks, fins, boots, wet suits, tanks, and regu-
lators from **Desert Divers Supply** (⊠ 5720 E. Charleston Blvd., East Side,
☎ 702/438–1000). **Neptune Divers Scuba Center** (⊠ 3985 E. Sunset
Rd., East Side, ☎ 702/564–5253) rents scuba equipment and offers
lessons. The **American Cactus Divers** (⊠ 5831 E. Lake Mead Blvd., East
Side, ☎ 702/433–3483) has scuba diving courses and issues certificates.

Skating

Crystal Palace. There are four Crystal Palace roller- and ice-skating rinks
in the area. Each has a large skating floor, rentals (you can also bring
your own skates or blades), a snack bar, an arcade, a youth hockey
clinic, and plenty of public skating time. ⊠ *3901 N. Rancho Dr.,
North Las Vegas,* ☎ *702/645–4892;* ⊠ *4680 Boulder Hwy., Boulder
Strip,* ☎ *702/458–7107;* ⊠ *9295 W. Flamingo Rd., West Side,* ☎ *702/
253–9832;* ⊠ *1110 E. Lake Mead Dr., Boulder City,* ☎ *702/564–2790.*

☾ **Santa Fe Station Ice Arena.** This professional ice-skating arena has 17,000
square ft of ice and 2,500 seats. This is not only the one ice-skating
rink at a casino in the country, it's also the only professional-level indoor ice-skating rink in the state. Instruction, skate rentals, and public skating hours are all available here; Little League and semi-professional
hockey teams compete at the Santa Fe as well. There's even a typical
Las Vegas hotel-casino buffet, with one wall of booths in the dining
area overlooking the arena. ⊠ *4949 N. Rancho Dr., Rancho Strip,* ☎
702/658–4993.

Skiing and Snowboarding

☾ **Las Vegas Ski and Snowboard Resort** (⊠ Mt. Charleston, Hwy. 156,
☎ 702/646–0008) is southern Nevada's skiing headquarters. It's a mere
47 mi northwest of downtown Las Vegas; depending on traffic and conditions, it can take as little as an hour to go from a 70-degree February afternoon on the Strip to the top of a chairlift at an elevation of
9,500 ft. Las Vegas is probably the only city in the world where you
can hike in the desert in the morning, downhill ski in the afternoon,
get married in the evening, and shoot craps all night long! "Ski Lee,"
as it's affectionately known, is equipped with three double chairlifts,
a ski school, a ski shop, rental equipment, and a day lodge with a coffee shop and lounge. There are 40 acres of groomed slopes; 15% of
the trails are for beginners, 80% are intermediate, and 5% are advanced
runs. The longest run is 3,000 ft, with a vertical drop of more than
1,000 ft. To get here, take U.S. 95 north to the Lee Canyon exit (Hwy.
156), and head up the mountain. You'll know you're at the closest ski
resort to Las Vegas when you see the slope names: Blackjack, High Roller,
Keno, the Strip, Bimbo 1 and 2, and Slot Alley. The lifts are open Thanksgiving to Easter for skiing, and all summer for scenic rides. Ski-lift rates
are $28.For snow conditions, call ☎ 702/593–9500. For a local road
report, call ☎ 702/486–3116.

Swimming

Every hotel and most motels have outdoor pools that are open from
mid-March through October—but only until 6 or 7 PM even when it

stays light until late. Hotel managements maintain that they can't afford to hire lifeguards to work through the night; in fact, they can't afford to have you lounging in the water when you could be spending your time and your money in the casino. The best hotel pools are at Mandalay Bay, Flamingo, Tropicana, Bellagio, Mirage, MGM Grand, Monte Carlo, and Treasure Island casino-hotels. For lake swimming, make the 30-mi drive to Lake Mead.

There are several public pools in town; two are conveniently located for visitors. **Baker Swimming Pool** (✉ 1100 E. St. Louis Ave., East Side, ☎ 702/229–6395) is open Memorial Day through Labor Day. The **Municipal Pool** (✉ 430 E. Bonanza Rd., Downtown, ☎ 702/229–6309), built in the late '90s, is open year-round and is a reasonable walk from Fremont Street hotels. **YMCA of Southern Nevada** (✉ 4141 Meadows La., West Side, ☎ 702/877–7200) is across the street from the large Meadows Mall and has a full-size indoor pool with separate children's pool. It reciprocates with YMCA memberships in other cities.

Tennis

Las Vegas has an abundance of tennis courts, many of them lighted for evening play. The eight courts at **Bally's Casino Resort** (✉ 3645 Las Vegas Blvd. S, Center Strip, ☎ 702/739–4111) are open to the public for a $15–$18 court fee per person (good for the entire day). The Flamingo, New Frontier, MGM Grand, and Riviera also have tennis courts where the public is welcome, though hotel guests take priority. At the New Frontier, there is no charge for hotel guests.

The **University of Nevada–Las Vegas** (✉ 4505 S. Maryland Pkwy., University District, ☎ 702/895–4489) has a dozen lighted tennis courts available to the public for $5 per person per day; reservations are essential.

Spectator Sports

Baseball

The **Las Vegas 51s** used to be the Las Vegas Stars. But when the parent team switched from the San Diego Padres to the Los Angeles Stars, the team adopted a more distinctive and publicity-generating name, taken from Area 51, rumored home of UFO and mysterious military activity. The triple-A Pacific Coast League team plays at **Cashman Field** (✉ 850 Las Vegas Blvd. N, Downtown, ☎ 702/386–7200), north of downtown, where professional baseball made its Las Vegas debut in 1983.

Basketball

The hottest tickets in town during the school year were once the basketball games of NCAA champions the **Runnin' Rebels**, of the University of Nevada–Las Vegas. But since head coach Jerry Tarkanian was fired in the early 1990s, the Rebels—and their ticket sales—have cooled off considerably. Charlie Spoonhour coached the 2001-02 season. Games take place at the **Thomas & Mack Center** on the UNLV campus (✉ 4505 S. Maryland Pkwy., University District, ☎ 702/895–3900).

Bowling

Las Vegas is home to the **Castaways Invitational Bowling Tournament,** the Professional Bowling Association's oldest competition, which takes place at the Castaways Hotel and Casino (✉ 2800 Fremont St., Boulder Strip, ☎ 702/385–9153) and airs every January.

Boxing

Championship boxing came to Las Vegas in 1960, when Benny Paret took the welterweight title from Don Jordan at the Las Vegas Convention

Center. Since then most of boxing's superstars have fought here. A title match draws the well-heeled and the well-known from all fields—and brings out the high roller in everyone. Spectators willingly fork over $200 to $1,500 a seat to watch two guys pummel each other, then hang around the casinos laying down chips for the rest of the evening, sometimes for the rest of the week. Major fights are usually held at Mandalay Bay, the MGM Grand or the Thomas and Mack Center. To learn about upcoming boxing events, look for the fight odds posted in the race and sports book of any casino. For the most comprehensive fight listings, check at the **Caesars Palace** (⊠ 3570 Las Vegas Blvd. S, Center Strip, ☎ 702/731–7110, WEB www.caesarspalace.com).

Football

Spectator interest couldn't have been lower for the **Runnin' Rebels**, UNLV's Division 1A, Mountain West Conference football team, during the years when the men's basketball team was a national power. But spectator interest shifted somewhat to the football Rebels when John Robinson came on board as coach. Home games are held at **Sam Boyd Stadium** (⊠ 7000 E. Russell Rd., East Side, ☎ 702/895–4978).

Golf

October brings the annual **Las Vegas Invitational** golf tournament, with top PGA golfers competing for high stakes. Now that the Desert Inn is closed, the tournament will be held at the private Robert Trent Jones–designed course Southern Highlands, which is south of Las Vegas. Tournament-related events will be held at the **TPC/Tournament Players Club at the Canyons** (☎ 702/256–2500), from which you can obtain more information.

Rodeo

When the **National Finals of Rodeo** (☎ 702/895–3011) comes to town in December, the casinos showcase country stars and the fans sport Western gear. The NFR, said to be the Super Bowl of professional rodeo, offers more than $2 million in prize money. It is held at the Thomas and Mack Arena on the UNLV campus.

8 SHOPPING

Like most other experiences in Las Vegas, shopping here scales the heights and plumbs the depths. The square footage in the Forum Shops at Caesars is the most valuable retail real estate in the country; bring two credit cards to buy any one thing. On the other hand, all the Elvis clocks and gambling-chip toilet seats you never wanted to see are available in a hundred tacky gift shops. Vegas finds run the gamut from a couture ball gown in a vintage store to a fine pair of Tony Lamas in a Western store leftover from the town's cowboy days. You can bring home a vintage slot machine or Lenôtre chocolates from the only place in the United States where you can buy them (at Paris, Las Vegas in case you're salivating). After all, gambling is not the only way to spend your bankroll in this town.

W HERE YOU SHOP IN LAS VEGAS will depend more on how much you want to spend—and how far you want to drive—than on what you're looking for. The Strip offers a shopping extravaganza. You'll find rows and rows of stores that sell Las Vegas souvenirs and sundries. At most of the Strip hotels you can buy expensive dresses, swimsuits, jewelry, and menswear; almost all the hotels have shops offering logo merchandise for the hotel or its latest show. A few hotels offer more than just the usual stores, but several properties take their themes to extremes: you can stroll along a Venice canal at the Venetian, traverse North African trade routes at the Aladdin, and enter a kingdom of upscale shops and talking statues at Caesars Palace. Inside the casinos the gifts are elegant and expensive; outside, it's Tacky City. The endless gift shops along Las Vegas Boulevard all sell the same dice clocks, jack and queen playing-card earrings, decks of used casino cards, Vegas belt buckles, key chains, and bath towels. Some stores look so schlocky you'll be embarrassed to step inside. Shoppers looking for more practical items or for an excuse to drive around the greater metro area can head for neighborhood malls, supermarkets, shopping centers, and specialty stores. And those not averse to doing a bit of driving might find some of the same high-ticket items at lower prices at one of the town's factory outlet malls.

Revised and updated by Lenore Greiner

Shopping Neighborhoods

The Strip (South)

The south end of the Strip, from the famous and much-photographed WELCOME TO LAS VEGAS sign to the always traffic-filled Tropicana Avenue, offers fewer chances to max out your credit card than the Strip's center. However, like slot machines and free drinks, places to spend your money can be found just about anywhere in Vegas—if you know where to look. On the east side of this section of the Strip you'll find gas stations, tourist centers, specialty shops such as **Nevada Bob's Golf Store,** fast-food restaurants, and a few incidental motels and casinos. Prime examples of Vegas's themed and upscale resorts, **Luxor** and **Mandalay Bay,** inhabit the west side. At the intersection of Tropicana Avenue and Las Vegas Boulevard, informally known as the Four Corners, four major hotels are visual juxtapositions of old and new Vegas. The **Tropicana** and **Excalibur** refuse to yield to the encroachment of the newer, slicker properties; they face, respectively, the **MGM Grand,** with its emerald-green building and brass lion, and **New York–New York,** with its big-city spires and mini Brooklyn Bridge. Next to the MGM Grand, the **Showcase Mall** offers sweet temptations.

The hotels occupying the south end of the Strip offer the typical upscale shops found in most of the major hotels, albeit with different themes and ambiences. You can easily spend outrageous sums on clothes, jewelry, luggage, and other luxury items. The Tropicana offers very little shopping fun. New York–New York does not measure up to its namesake, but does have some places to shop and eat in **SoHo Village** and on the second floor mezzanine. The MGM Grand's cavernous **Studio Walk** includes more places to eat than places to shop, but more stores can be found at the lower-level **Star Lane Shops.** While most of the Excalibur's retail offerings aren't too noteworthy, it's worth a trip to the castle to visit **Merlin's Mystic Shoppe.** This store, just before the indoor walkway to the Luxor, has the benign (key chains) and the bizarre (a toilet-brush holder in the shape of a skull).

A walkway takes you from the medieval to the Mideast—the Luxor. Talking camels greet you at the entrance of the **Giza Galleria.** The galleria shops are worth a look-see, especially the **Treasure Chamber,** where you can purchase real Egyptian artifacts, and the **Cairo Bazaar,** designed to look like an open market with canvas-covered carts of merchandise. Upstairs from the Luxor casino is a faux minicity with the inevitable souvenir shops.

Mandalay Bay has stores, expensive restaurants, an art gallery, and a gourmet coffee shop. A must-see store is the **Bali Trading Company;** reminiscent of a market you might find on a South Seas island, it offers an assortment of unusual gifts. As long as you're at Mandalay Bay, don't miss the chance to see the **House of Blues.** The outside of the restaurant and bar is made up of eye-popping "garbage" art: everything from bottle caps to mirror shards has been used to create its eclectic exterior. Buy music, books, hot sauce, and T-shirts at the souvenir shop. A free tram runs between Mandalay Bay, Luxor, and Excalibur.

The Strip (Center)

The best shopping on the Strip can be found in its mid-section, from Harmon Avenue to Spring Mountain Road. Here are some of the most extravagant shopping experiences in the world. Where else on earth can you explore exotic North African bazaars, stroll through a Parisian shopping lane, cross the street to visit the elegant boutiques of international designers, then traverse the short distance to ancient Rome?

Occupying three corners of the intersection of Flamingo Road and Las Vegas Boulevard, **Bally's, Bellagio,** and **Caesars Palace** create a shopper's dream of shoes, handbags, evening wear, jewelry, art, and more—all within a two-block radius. Caesars rules the retail market with the **Forum Shops at Caesars** and **The Appian Way** that include everything from lingerie to linguine. The collection of **Avenue Shoppes** is Bally's offering, but not many Strip hotels can compete with the posh **Via Bellagio** promenade. Shoppers at Bellagio enjoy a nearly child-free spending spree: no children under the age of 18, except those of registered hotel guests, are allowed on the property.

Just south of this power trio, the battle for your gold card continues. The 13 shops of **Le Boulevard** at **Paris Las Vegas** mimic a Continental shopping excursion. However, Paris's next-door neighbor, the **Desert Passage at the Aladdin,** reigns as the supreme shopping experience, almost beating out the changing-sky ceiling and animatronic shows at the Forum Shops at Caesars. The **Desert Passage,** with over 130 retail shops and 12 restaurants, re-constructs the ancient trade routes through Spain, North Africa, India, a port on the Arabian Sea, and a mysterious Lost City.

A mile north, on the corner of Sands Avenue and Las Vegas Boulevard, are the sumptuous **Grand Canal Shoppes** at the **Venetian.** The usual assortment of stores can be found at **Harrah's,** but the hotel also has a nice outdoor mall with a Ghirardelli's chocolate store, a liquor store (one of the few on the Strip), a deli, and lots of places to sit. Concerts and other events are held on the covered stage.

Across the street, the **Mirage** and **Treasure Island** have a smattering of shops. Visiting Treasure Island is more fun; not only do you get to see a pirate battle, but the shops have names such as **The Candy Reef, Damsels,** and **Captain Kids.** On the corner of Spring Mountain Road and the Strip is the **Fashion Show Mall.** The two-story building contains 145 retail shops, including several department stores.

The Strip (North)

The Fashion Show Mall marks the end of serious mall shopping, but lots of little places along the last stretch of the Strip offer cheap and varied Las Vegas souvenirs such as key chains, shot glasses and magnets. For one-stop souvenir shopping, go to **Bonanza,** the "World's Largest Gift Shop," at the corner of Sahara Avenue. As for hotel shops, other than the regular logo gift stores and newspaper stands, choices are limited. The **Riviera** offers a few stores, including **Wine Street** (get customized labels for wine or champagne) and **Toni Cats and Company,** offering novelties and gifts featuring felines. **Circus Circus** has a 40,000-square-ft promenade with the usual eateries and souvenir shops.

Shopping opportunities grow sparse between Sahara Avenue and downtown LasVegas. Past the Stratosphere Hotel you'll end up among Vegas's seedier establishments: small motels, pawn shops, bail bond offices, and adult video stores. The older, stand-alone wedding chapels also populate this end of Las Vegas Boulevard. If you're close by and need film, money, or a quick meal, **Walgreens, Wells Fargo,** and fast food establishments are located just before Charleston Boulevard.

Paradise Road

The **Deep Space 9 Promenade** in the **Las Vegas Hilton's** *Star Trek Experience* has a collection of Star Trek souvenir shops, including the **Admiral Collection** where you can buy actual props from the Star Trek television shows. Pick up a Vulcan lute or the same phaser Captain Kirk screamed into. High-rollers take note—Klingon warrior uniforms cost only $12,000.

Maryland Parkway

Travel in either direction on any of the major streets that intersect Las Vegas Boulevard and you'll find a number of neighborhood strip malls with grocery, department, and specialty stores. However, a mile east of the Strip is a shopping destination popular with locals: Maryland Parkway. The best shopping areas are at the intersections of Maryland Parkway with Flamingo Road and with Tropicana Avenue, where there are numerous strip malls and lots and lots of stores, including national chains such as **Big & Tall, Best Buy, Marshalls, Target,** and **Tower Records.** There is also a diverse group of businesses across from the **University of Nevada–Las Vegas** campus, on Maryland Parkway between Flamingo Road and Tropicana Avenue. Most of these places appeal to young college students: you can pick up vintage fashions at **Buffalo Exchange,** buy gourmet coffee, grab a burger or taco, rent a video, make copies, drink beer, and even get a tattoo. One of Nevada's largest malls, **Boulevard Mall,** is at the corner of Maryland Parkway and Desert Inn Road.

Chinatown Plaza

On Spring Mountain Boulevard (about 2 mi west of the Fashion Show Mall), just off Valley View Boulevard, the two-story **Chinatown Plaza** shopping center is made up of restaurants, Asian food markets, gift shops, art stores, jewelers, and florists. Check out the **Snack House** for Asian delectables and unusual drink concoctions.

Fremont Street

The **Fremont Street Experience** is a four-block downtown pedestrian mall covered by a spectacular canopy featuring 2.1 million lights. Do a little shopping in hotel-casinos that line the street, or browse the kiosks scattered throughout the outdoor mall for trinkets, jewelry, T-shirts, and more. Depending on your beverage preferences, you can get gourmet coffee or a half-yard of beer (the beer is cheaper and it's served in a tall hard-plastic glass that makes a nifty souvenir). For a one-of-a-kind shopping experience, visit Fremont Street during the nightly light-and-sound shows. The shows begin at 6 PM and continue every hour on the hour until midnight. But don't expect to chat while you browse—the accompanying music reaches near-deafening volume.

Sunset Road and Green Valley Parkway, Henderson

Henderson is one of the fastest-growing cities in Nevada. Minutes away from the Strip, it offers big-time shopping in a small-town atmosphere. In the last three years the popularity of the area around the intersection of Sunset Road and Green Valley Parkway has resulted in the addition of two hotels, three restaurants, and a bank. To get to this trendy little spot, go south on Las Vegas Boulevard until you reach Sunset Road. Turn east and travel about 5 mi. Several shopping centers line either side of the street; stop and shop if you want, or keep driving until you reach Green Valley Parkway. Before the stoplight, on the left side, is a small shopping center with an **Albertson's** grocery store as well as an assortment of eating establishments and shops, including **Alligator Soup.** After the stoplight, on the right side of the street, is **Green Valley Plaza.** It has numerous stores, including **Agave,** which has hand-blown glass and other unique gifts; and **Natural Clothing Co.,** which sells imported clothing and jewelry. You'll also find **Trader Joe's,** a huge gourmet foods store, an inexpensive all-you-can-eat Chinese food buffet, and a discount shop where greeting cards are half the regular price.

On the left side of Sunset Road is **Town Center.** This complex includes a movie theater, several restaurants, a pet store, ice-cream parlors, and a grocery store. The front center of the complex has an outdoor seating area; in the summer, outdoor concerts and other events are held here. A fountain with dancing spigots of water entertains tired shoppers. Several fast-food chains dot both sides of Sunset Road. The street officially ends at the next stoplight, but if you travel through it you'll enter a series of business complexes. Turn left at the first "street" and then right at the stoplight to find **Ethel M. Chocolates Factory,** Henderson's most popular store.

Sunset Road and Stephanie Street

The corner of Sunset Road and Stephanie Street offers scads of shopping options in a fairly new area. On North Stephanie Street, you'll find lots of fast-food places and chain restaurants, but you can also get fresh bread and meats at **Wild Oats,** an upscale gourmet grocery. There's a nice **Barnes and Noble** bookstore sharing space with a **Starbuck's.** And you'll find many national chain stores such as **Petco, Ross Dress for Less, Old Navy, Circuit City,** and **Target. Galleria At Sunset,** a two-story mall with more than 130 stores, occupies the northeast corner of Sunset Road and Stephanie Street. Across the street from the mall is a favorite locals hotel-casino, Sunset Station, which has a movie theater, child care, and several eateries. If you continue east, you'll see delis, casinos, boutiques, pawn shops, clothing stores, and Highway 95 (take the highway north to return to the Strip). For a more unusual shopping experience, head for **Ron Lee's World of Clowns** (south on Stephanie Street to Warm Springs Road, turn left).

Malls and Department Stores

Appian Way at Caesars. Not to be confused with The Forum Shops at Caesars, these marble halls are centered around an exact replica of Michelangelo's David in Carrera marble. The upscale shops include **Cartier; Cottura,** the only Italian ceramics purveyor in town, with a grand selection of colorful ware; and **Cuzzens** for fine menswear. ⊠ *Caesars*

Palace, 3570 Las Vegas Blvd. S, Center Strip, ☎ *702/896–5599,* WEB *www.caesars.com.*

Belz Factory Outlet World. Just a few miles away from the Strip's most exclusive and expensive shopping areas is one of the country's largest discount malls. About 3 mi south of Tropicana Avenue on Las Vegas Boulevard South, you'll find 580,000 square ft of shopping choices. There are 155 different stores offering clothing, jewelry, toys, shoes, beauty products, housewares, accessories, sportswear, souvenirs, and much more at discount prices. You'll find **Jones New York, Esprit,** and **London Fog,** to name just a few. Belz has two food courts and a full-size carousel. **Off-5th Saks Fifth Avenue** occupies the majority of space at **Annex One,** a small separate building on Belz's south side. ✉ *7400 Las Vegas Blvd. S, South Las Vegas,* ☎ *702/896–5599,* WEB *www.belz.com.*

Boulevard Mall. You'll see places to shop all along Maryland Parkway, but this one, with 150 stores, has the greatest single concentration of retailers. Less expensive than its counterparts on the Strip, the mall is anchored by **Macy's, Sears, Dillards, Marshalls,** and **JCPenney** department stores. The food court offers mostly fast-food choices; for more leisurely meals away from the mall's hustle and bustle try **Applebee's** or the **International House of Pancakes,** both in separate buildings in the mall's parking lot. Stroller rentals are available; they're dispensed from automatic machines for $3. ✉ *3528 Maryland Pkwy., East Side,* ☎ *702/732–8949,* WEB *www.blvdmall.com.*

Desert Passage at the Aladdin. Inspired by the ancient trade routes through Spain, North Africa, and India, the 475,000-square-ft Desert Passage has more than 130 retail stores and 14 restaurants. The circular shopping center surrounds the 7,000-seat Aladdin Theatre of the Arts. Kiosks look like just-opened tents; watch belly dancers and other performers as you peruse the many fine shops. Be sure to watch the storm clouds gather every hour (and half hour Friday–Sunday) at the Merchant's Harbor. A gentle desert thunderstorm washes in and then passes quickly through the port as you sip espresso at the **Merchant's Harbor Coffee House** (sorry, no hookahs). The entrance to the **Endangered Species** store is guarded by a life-size stuffed gorilla. if you prefer your stuffed animals a bit more tame, you can create your own teddy bear at the **Build-A-Bear Workshop.** Other offerings include **bebe, Jhane Barnes, Tommy Bahama,** and **Eddie Bauer.** Desert Passage competes easily with the Forum Shops for upscale clothing boutiques: **Ann Taylor Loft, Hugo/Hugo Boss, Betsy Johnson,** and **White House/Black Market.** Buy shoes at **L'Idea** and handbags at **Jeanne,** then head over to **Sephora** for a make-over. Jewelry lovers have 16 fine stores to choose from, including **Clio Blue Paris, Joli-Joli,** and **Gioia.** For home accessories, check out **Chiasso, Illuminations, Sur La Table,** and **McGrail's of Erin.** Among the restaurants, the **Commander's Palace** is a branch of the Louisiana landmark in Sin City and the **Alakazam Food Court** serves Middle Eastern food. Las Vegas is one of only two U.S. cities that can claim the **Blue Note Jazz Club.** ✉ *3663 Las Vegas Blvd. S, Center Strip,* ☎ *702/866–0703 or 888/800–9474,* WEB *www.desertpassage.com.*

Fashion Outlets Las Vegas. This outlet mall is definitely worth a shopping safari to nearby Primm, about half an hour away on I-15. Here, you'll find many of the same superstars as on the Strip with prices as much as 75% less. And you often don't see these stores represented at an outlet mall: **Burberry's, Williams Sonoma Marketplace, St. John,** and **Versace Company Store. Last Call from Neiman Marcus** stocks Badgley Mischka and Armani as well as their private labels. And there are the usual outlet mall suspects: **DKNY, Banana Republic, Polo Ralph Lau-**

ren, Gap, Nike. A shuttle service runs daily from the MGM Grand and New York, New York, costing $13 each way. Call 702/874–1400 for reservations. ⊠ *32100 Las Vegas Blvd. S, Primm,* ☎ *702/874–1400,* WEB *www.fashionoutletslasvegas.com.*

Fashion Show Mall. Even though it's twice as large as Caesars' retail fantasyland (and in the process of growing even bigger), this mall is tame by comparison. Centrally located on Las Vegas Boulevard South next to the New Frontier, it's hard to miss, and thus often crowded. The place is very well maintained, and not everything is overpriced. The two-story building contains 145 shops, anchored by several large department stores: **Neiman Marcus, Saks Fifth Avenue, Macy's, Robinsons–May,** and **Dillards.** You'll find a lot of the same offerings at the casino malls such as **Louis Vuitton** and some different fare, such as a great shoe store, **Stiletto.** **Waldenbooks,** the only bookstore on the Strip, is also here. There's the usual assortment of fast-food choices in the food court but little else in terms of eateries. Stroller rentals are $5. ⊠ *3200 Las Vegas Blvd. S, North Strip,* ☎ *702/369–8382,* WEB *www.thefashionshow.com.*

Forum Shops at Caesars. This shopping extravaganza resembles an ancient Roman streetscape, replete with immense columns and arches, two central piazzas with fountains, and a cloud-filled ceiling displaying a sky that changes from sunrise to sunset over the course of three hours (perhaps inspiring shoppers to step up their pace of acquisition when it looks as if time is running out). The Festival Fountain (in the west wing of the mall) puts on its own show every hour on the hour starting at 10 AM: a robotic, pie-eyed Bacchus hosts a party for friends Apollo, Venus, and Mars, complete with lasers, music, and sound effects; at the end, the god of wine and merriment delivers a sales pitch for the mall. The "Atlantis" show (in the east wing) is even more amazing: Atlas, king of Atlantis, can't seem to pick between his son, Gadrius, and his daughter, Alia, to assume the throne; for eight minutes, the royal family struggles for control of the doomed kingdom amid flame and smoke. If you can tear yourself away from the animatronic wizardry, you'll find both familiar and unusual shops. The upscale and excellent include clothiers **Christian Dior, Gianni Versace, Gucci,** and **Bernini** and jewelers **Bulgari, Judith Leiber** (for jewel-like handbags), and **M. J. Christensen.** Shoppers will also find the **Planet Hollywood Superstore, Virgin Megastore,** and **Nike Town.** There's also a wide array of restaurants such as **Caviarteria, La Salsa, Spago,** and **Chinois.** You can glide into the Forum from the Strip on a moving sidewalk. The mall is open late (until 11 Sun.–Thurs., until midnight Fri.–Sat.). ⊠ *Caesars Palace, 3500 Las Vegas Blvd. S, Center Strip,* ☎ *702/893–4800,* WEB *www.caesars.com.*

Galleria at Sunset. This 130-store mall in Henderson, on the northeast corner of Sunset Road and Stephanie Street, sits directly across from the popular locals hotel-casino Sunset Station. Anchored by **Dillard's, Robinsons–May, JCPenney,** and **Mervyn's California** department stores, the two-level shopping complex has vaulted skylights, sparkling fountains, and huge palm trees. The floor-to-ceiling windows near the food court (second level) offer an astounding view of the surrounding mountains. The food court has mostly fast-food fare with two exceptions; **Edo Japan** stir-fries orders in view of customers, and the **Bourbon Street Grill** offers New Orleans–style edibles. Several restaurants can be found on the perimeter of the mall, but **Chevy's,** a Tex-Mex restaurant and bar, and **Red Robin,** a gourmet burger joint, are inside the Galleria. Strollers are available for $4; they must be returned within three hours. *1300 W. Sunset Rd., Henderson,* ☎ *702/ 434–0202,* WEB *www.galleriaatsunset.com.*

Grand Canal Shoppes at the Venetian. The most elegant shopping complex on the Strip is laid out along walkways bordering indoor recreations of Venice's Grand Canal and St. Mark's Square. For $12.50 per person, gondolas transport shoppers through the canals. Among the stores, **Bertone, Burberry, Lladró,** and **Pal Zileri** offer luxe shopping. Two must-see stores are **Il Prato,** which sells unique Venetian collectibles such as Carnevale masks, stationery sets, and glass pen and inkwell sets and **Ripa de Monti,** offering luminescent Venetian glass. **Canyon Ranch Living Essentials** has cookbooks, body products, and spa robes from Arizona's famous Canyon Ranch spa; its Las Vegas outpost, the Canyon Ranch Spa Club, is on the second floor of the Venetian. The elevator right next to the shop will take you to the Spa Club and its sophisticated, healthy restaurant. For another kind of refreshment, visit the food court, which has a **Krispy Kreme** and a **Carnevale Coffee** or choose from a variety of fine dining options, including Wolfgang Puck's **Postrio,** or the northern Italian fare of **Canaletto.** The mall is open late (until 11 Sun.–Thurs., until midnight Fri.–Sat.). ⊠ *The Venetian Resort-Hotel-Casino, 3355 Las Vegas Blvd. S, Center Strip,* ☎ *702/733–5000,* WEB *www.venetian.com.*

Le Boulevard at Paris Las Vegas. Petite by Vegas standards, this Parisian shopping lane has many Gallic delights. The **Lenôtre** café is the only place in the United States where the famous Lenôtre chocolates are sold. The café also has fresh French pastries and coffee. **La Boutique by Yokohama de Paris** has Parisian designer wear from Celine, among others, and Fendi watches. **Le Journal** is the place to pick up your jaunty French beret. ⊠ *Paris Las Vegas, 3655 Las Vegas Blvd. S, Center Strip,* ☎ *702/946–7000,* WEB *www.parislasvegas.com.*

Showcase Mall. Right next to the MGM Grand, this mall is worth a visit, especially for kids. **M&M's World** is a rollicking, four-story homage to the popular candy. There's logo merchandise from stuffed toys to sheets, and, of course, you can buy any type of M&M candy here. Better yet, create your own custom bag (all blue! only red! plain and peanut together!)—huge dispensers with every color and every type line one wall of the fourth level. There's the flagship store of **Ethel M. Chocolates,** the famous local gourmet chocolatier, and **Everything Coca-Cola,** offering collectibles; gifts; and, of course, Coke. You can sip a Coke float at an old-time soda fountain or buy a vintage Coke vending machine. Steven Spielberg had a hand in creating the high-tech **Gameworks** arcade. There's a multi-screen cinema and the **Grand Canyon Experience,** in case you can't make it to the real natural wonder. ⊠ *3785 Las Vegas Blvd. S, South Strip,* ☎ *702/740–2525.*

Via Bellagio. Steve Wynn spared no expense to create Bellagio, so be prepared to spare no expense shopping at its exclusive boutiques. Via Bellagio is a long passage lined with elegant stores such as **Prada, Chanel, Giorgio Armani, Gucci, Hermès, Moschino,** and **Tiffany and Co.** Bellagio's upscale restaurants include **Prime, Aqua,** and **Le Cirque.** Dine on the balcony at **Olives,** located right in the promenade, and get the best seat for watching the Fountains of Bellagio (otherwise known as the dancing waters). ⊠ *Bellagio, 3600 Las Vegas Blvd. S, Center Strip,* ☎ *702/693–7111,* WEB *www.bellagiolasvegas.com.*

Specialty Shops

Books

GENERAL

Las Vegas has a full complement of national bookstore chains, though only the Waldenbooks at the Fashion Show Mall is directly on the Strip.

Las Vegas Shopping

Bonanza Rd.
Bonanza Rd.
Fremont St.
Carson Ave.
Bridger Ave.
Clark Ave.
Bonneville Ave.
Garces Ave.
Gass Ave.
Main St.
Casino Center
4th St.
6th St.
Alta Dr.
Highland Dr.
Rancho Dr.
Palomino La.
Charleston Blvd.
Circle Park
Oakey Blvd.
Wyoming Ave.
St. Louis Ave.
6th St.
Las Vegas Blvd. S.
Sahara Ave.
Karen Ave.
THE STRIP
Industrial Rd.
Circus Circus La.
Riviera Blvd.
Las Vegas Country Club
Maryland Pkwy.
Stardust Rd.
Paradise Rd.
Desert Inn Rd.
Sierra Vista Dr.
Spring Mountain Rd.
Cambridge St.
Algonquin Dr.
Sands Ave.
Twain Ave.
Flamingo Rd.
Flamingo Rd.
Koval La.
University of Nevada Las Vegas
Harmon Ave.
Harmon Ave.
Paradise Rd.
THE STRIP
Las Vegas Blvd. S.
Tropicana Ave.
N
Hacienda Ave.
0 — 1 mile
0 — 1 km

Barnes & Noble. ⊠ *2191 N. Rainbow Blvd., North Las Vegas,* ☎ *702/ 631–1775;* ⊠ *3860 Maryland Pkwy., East Side,* ☎ *702/734–2900;* ⊠ *567 N. Stephanie St., Henderson,* ☎ *702/434–1533.*

B. Dalton. ⊠ *Boulevard Mall, 3860 S. Maryland Pkwy., East Side,* ☎ *702/735–0008;* ⊠ *Galleria at Sunset Mall, 1300 W. Sunset Rd., Henderson,* ☎ *702/434–1331.*

Borders Books and Music. ⊠ *2190 N. Rainbow Blvd., West Side,* ☎ *702/638–7866;* ⊠ *2323 S. Decatur Blvd., West Side,* ☎ *702/258–0999;* ⊠ *1445 W. Sunset Rd., Henderson,* ☎ *702/433–6222.*

Readmore Magazine and Book Store. ⊠ *2560 S. Maryland Pkwy., East Side,* ☎ *702/732–4453;* ⊠ *6154 W. Flamingo Rd., West Side,* ☎ *702/ 362–3762;* ⊠ *2250 E. Tropicana Ave., University District,* ☎ *702/798– 7863.*

Waldenbooks. ⊠ *Fashion Show Mall, 3200 Las Vegas Blvd. S, North Strip,* ☎ *702/733–1049.*

DISCOUNT

Used bookstores are as easy to find in Las Vegas as video-poker machines. If you venture out into the greater metro area, you'll inevitably find one stashed in among the many strip malls and neighborhood shopping centers. One of the best used bookstores can be found on Charleston Boulevard. **Book Magician** (⊠ 2202 W. Charleston Blvd. #2, West Side, ☎ 702/384–5838) has been in the book business for 20 years, making it one of the oldest bookstores in Las Vegas. With more than 150,000 in-stock titles, it's also one of the largest. The store carries a variety of genres, including a few comics, but its specialties are science fiction and metaphysics. A 10-minute drive from the Strip, in the Von's shopping center on the corner of Eastern Ave. and Desert Inn, is the **Albion Book Company** (⊠ 2466 E. Desert Inn Rd., East Side, ☎ 702/ 792–9554). The majority of space in the voluminous bookstore, which takes in about 6,000 books a month, is devoted to hardcovers on almost every possible topic in fiction and nonfiction. First-edition books and rare finds occupy a corner in the front of the store; mass-market paperbacks can be found in the back.

SPECIAL INTEREST

Gambler's Book Club. GBC is the world's largest distributor of books about 21, craps, poker, roulette, and all the other games, as well as novels about gambling, biographies of crime figures, used books and magazines, and anything else that relates to gambling and Las Vegas. Call for the jam-packed free catalog. ⊠ *630 S. 11th St., Downtown,* ☎ *702/382–7555 or 800/522–1777,* WEB *www.gamblersbook.com.*

Huntington Press. This small-press publisher produces some of the best books about gambling and Las Vegas. You can buy books, software, and hand-held games at its offices, just two blocks north of the Rio (less than 1 mi from the Strip). ⊠ *3867 S. Procyon Ave., West Side,* ☎ *702/252–0655,* WEB *www.huntingtonpress.com.*

Clothing for Children

Though the casino-hotel malls and area shopping centers have the usual children's clothing stores such as **Gap Kids** and **Gymboree,** you can find some great gifts for kids at the shops below.

Desert Brats. Little girls will find their inner showgirl in these frothy creations with feathers and sequins. ⊠ *Desert Passage at the Aladdin, 3663 Las Vegas Blvd. S, Center Strip,* ☎ *888/800–8284.*

Harley Davidson Café. The café's retail store is the spot to outfit kids with a Harley Hog Cap, flight jacket, or Captain American tee. ⊠ *3725 Las Vegas Blvd. S, Center Strip,* ☎ *702/740–4555.*

Les Enfants. This shop carries stylish French children's clothing. ⊠ *Paris Las Vegas, 3655 Las Vegas Blvd. S, Center Strip,* ☎ *702/946–7000.*

Clothing for Men

You can't walk into the shopping areas of the Strip's hotels without stumbling upon high-end men's clothiers. If the price tags on the Strip are too stratospheric, the outlet malls have brand names for less, such as Tommy Hilfiger, Eddie Bauer, and DKNY.

Bernini. This Rodeo Drive–based men's clothier has five branches in Las Vegas, three at Caesars Palace alone. You'll find a Bernini shop and a Bernini Collections in the Forum Shops and a Bernini Couture in The Appian Way shops inside the casino. All purvey the very best menswear and some even offer bespoke suits. There's a Bernini Collezioni located at the MGM Grand and a less expensive Bernini Sport at the Stratosphere. ⊠ *Forum Shops at Caesars, 3500 Las Vegas Blvd. S, Center Strip,* ☎ *702/893–7786;* ⊠ *MGM Grand, 3799 Las Vegas Blvd. S, South Strip,* ☎ *702/798–8786;* ⊠ *Stratosphere, 2000 Las Vegas Blvd. S, North Strip,* ☎ *702/471–7786.*

ESPN Zone SportsCenter Studio Store. Increase the cool quotient with official ESPN and ESPN Zone merchandise, including sportswear. ⊠ *New York–New York, 3790 Las Vegas Blvd. S, South Strip,* ☎ *702/ 933–3776.*

Giorgio Armani Boutique. This elegant store features the elegant simplicity of the Armani suit as well as signature sportswear, shoes, and accessories. ⊠ *Via Bellagio, 3600 Las Vegas Blvd. S, Center Strip,* ☎ *702/893–8327.*

Hugo Boss. Be prepared to be confused. Called Hugo/Hugo Boss at The Desert Passage and Boss/Hugo Boss at The Forum Shops, both have different owners and both carry styles off European and New York runways. ⊠ *The Forum Shops at Caesars, 3500 Las Vegas Blvd. S, Center Strip,* ☎ *702/696–9444;* ⊠ *Desert Passage at the Aladdin, 3663 Las Vegas Blvd. S, Center Strip,* ☎ *702/732–4272.*

Versace Jeans Couture. Casual and fashion-forward jeanswear. ⊠ *Forum Shops at Caesars, 3500 Las Vegas Blvd. S, Center Strip,* ☎ *702/ 796–7332.*

Clothing for Women

Vegas' shopping will send the most jaded shopper into ecstasy. Prepare to find the greatest selection of women's wear on the planet at area hotel-casino malls and outlet centers. Your favorite national chain store or designer boutique will have a Vegas outlet. In fact, name a designer and you'll find a signature shop in this town.

Ann Taylor Loft. The Loft offers value-price career and casual designs for women with more relaxed lifestyles. ⊠ *Desert Passage at the Aladdin, 3663 Las Vegas Blvd. S, Center Strip,* ☎ *702/732–3348.*

Burberry. The luxury British brand has its famous trench coat and rain gear as well as hot fashion accessories. ⊠ *Grand Canal Shoppes at the Venetian, 3355 Las Vegas Blvd. S, Center Strip,* ☎ *702/735–2600.*

bebe. Fashionistas will love this boutique's stock of dresses, jeans, and separates. ⊠ *Fashion Show Mall, 3200 Las Vegas Blvd. S, North Strip,* ☎ *702/892–8083;* ⊠ *Desert Passage at the Aladdin, 3663 Las Vegas Blvd. S, Center Strip,* ☎ *702/892–0406.*

DKNY. Up to the nano-second fashion from this New York designer collection is worth a test-drive. ⊠ *Desert Passage at the Aladdin, 3663 Las Vegas Blvd. S, Center Strip,* ☎ *702/732–3348.*

Gucci. If you must drop a grand on a pair of loafers, come here. Though the salespeople's noses are definitely turned up, the Gucci reputation prevails. ⊠ *Via Bellagio, 3600 Las Vegas Blvd. S, Center Strip,* ☎ *702/ 369–7333.*

Judith Leiber. These bejeweled handbags really qualify as fine jewelry with prices in the thousands of dollars to match. ⊠ *The Forum Shops at Caesars, 3500 Las Vegas Blvd. S, Center Strip,* ☎ *702/792–0661.*

Last Call from Neiman Marcus. Irresistible discounts on designer clothing as well as gifts, furniture, and men's clothing. ⊠ *Fashion Outlets Las Vegas, 32100 Las Vegas Blvd. S, Primm,* ☎ *702/874–2100.*

Marshall-Rousso on Park Avenue Collections. This shop has a fine selection of resortwear, shoes, and accessories. ⊠ *New York–New York, 3790 Las Vegas Blvd. S, South Strip,* ☎ *702/874–2100.*

Off 5th Saks 5th Avenue Outlet. Don't miss drop-dead low prices on a large selection of upscale casual and formal designerwear. ⊠ *Belz Factory Outlet, 7400 Las Vegas Blvd. S, South Las Vegas,* ☎ *702/263– 7692.*

Versace Jeans Couture. Trendy jeanswear and tops including sexy Italian leather jeans. ⊠ *The Forum Shops at Caesars, 3500 Las Vegas Blvd. S, Center Strip,* ☎ *702/796–7332.*

UNUSUAL SIZES

Rose of Sharon. There's a great selection of beautiful clothes sizes 14 and above here. ⊠ *The Forum Shops at Caesars, 3500 Las Vegas Blvd. S, Center Strip,* ☎ *702/791–0151.*

VINTAGE

The Attic. No other used-clothing store in the world compares. This vintage clothing shop is thick with incense and booming with club music. The two-story building is filled with an eclectic array of shirts, shoes, pants, hats, jewelry, halter tops, prom dresses, evening wear, and feather boas, as well as furniture and collectors' items. Fans of 1960s and '70s styles should especially love it. ⊠ *1018 S. Main St., Downtown,* ☎ *702/ 388–4088,* FAX *702/388–1047,* WEB *www.theatticlasvegas.com.*

Retro Vintage Couture. If you've dreamed of dressing like Sharon Stone in the film *Casino* you may find your treasure here. Retro's stylish owner, Melina Crisostomo, grew up here (her dad designed many of Vegas' famous neon-lit casino signs) and her boutique stocks mostly high-quality '60s and '70s fashions although she carries clothing from the '20s to the '80s. Finds include Pucci dresses, alligator bags, and beaded ball gowns. ⊠ *906 S. Valley View Blvd., West Side,* ☎ *702/877–8989,* WEB *www.retro-vintage.com.*

Food and Drink

Ethel M. Chocolates Factory and Cactus Garden. The "M" stands for Mars, the name of the family (headed by Ethel in the early days) that brings us Snickers, Milky Way, Mars Bars, Three Musketeers, and M&Ms. More than 1,000 people come daily to watch the candy-making at this fancy chocolate factory and taste free samples in the adjoining shop. A 2½-acre cactus garden contains more than 350 species of succulents and desert plants that are very colorful during spring flowering. You'll find nine other Ethel M. stores at casino-hotels and even at the airport. ⊠ *2 Cactus Garden Dr., Henderson,* ☎ *702/458–8864,* WEB *www.ethelm.com.*

Le Cave. After selecting your French imported wines, pâtés, and cheeses, you can buy the Limoges chinaware upon which to grandly dine. ✉ *Paris Las Vegas, 3655 Las Vegas Blvd. S, Center Strip,* ☎ *702/946–7000, Ext. 64339.*

M&M's World. On the Strip about a half block from the MGM Grand, this four-level candy store shares its complex with Gameworks, the Coca-Cola logo shop, and Ethel M's. This popular tourist attraction is usually crowded; it's not easy to maneuver strollers and wheelchairs around the displays. ✉ *Showcase Mall, 3785 Las Vegas Blvd. S, South Strip,* ☎ *702/458–8864.*

Rocky Mountain Chocolate Factory. This chocolate store and ice-cream parlor, in the Belz Factory Outlet, has a nice selection of boxed chocolates and assorted items that make ideal gifts for chocolate lovers. ✉ *Belz Factory Outlet, 7400 Las Vegas Blvd. S, South Las Vegas,* ☎ *702/361–7553.*

Snack House. Asian snack foods, dried fruit, and nuts make this Chinatown Plaza shop a popular stop. ✉ *Chinatown Plaza, 4215 Spring Mountain Blvd., West Side,* ☎ *702/247–9888.*

Teuscher's Chocolates. The tempting Swiss chocolates and a coffee bar make for a delightful way to gather energy for more shopping. ✉ *Desert Passage at the Aladdin, 3663 Las Vegas Blvd. S, Center Strip,* ☎ *702/866–6624.*

Wine Street. Your very own personalized wine label is yours for the asking at this wine shop. Labels are ready in 30 minutes. ✉ *Riviera Hotel and Casino, 2901 Las Vegas Blvd. S, North Strip,* ☎ *702/697–4444,* WEB *www.wineart2.com/Winestreet/Winestreet.htm.*

Gifts and Souvenirs

African & World Imports. This small shop tucked inside the Boulevard Mall has a wonderful selection of African art and cultural gift items. You'll also find music, incense, jewelry, and T-shirts. ✉ *Boulevard Mall, 3680 S. Maryland Pkwy., East Side,* ☎ *702/734–1900.*

Bali Trading Company. One of Mandalay Bay's most unusual stores, this is a good place to shop for such gifts as rain sticks and omnariums (semi-enclosed, self-sufficient aquariums), island-style clothing, and South Seas art. ✉ *Mandalay Bay Resort and Casino, 3950 Las Vegas Blvd. S, South Strip,* ☎ *702/632–6123.*

Bonanza "World's Largest Gift Shop." Across the street from the Sahara Hotel, Bonanza is the city's best souvenir store. It may not, in fact, be the world's largest, but it's the town's largest. And while it has most of the usual junk, it sells some unusual junk as well. It's so huge that you won't feel trapped, as you might in some of the smaller shops. And it's open until midnight. ✉ *2460 Las Vegas Blvd. S, North Strip,* ☎ *702/385–7359.*

Cairo Bazaar. Designed to look like an open market, this shop in the Luxor's Giza Galleria is filled with canvas-covered carts selling jewelry, scarves, and trinkets. ✉ *Luxor Hotel-Casino, 3900 Las Vegas Blvd. S, South Strip,* ☎ *702/632–6123.*

Canyonland. A big rock fountain gives this place at Belz Factory Outlet an "outdoor" feel. It offers decorative items, including Southwest-style accessories, ivory and jade statues, miniature fountains, wind chimes, and cedar trinket boxes. ✉ *Belz Factory Outlet, 7400 Las Vegas Blvd. S, South Las Vegas,* ☎ *702/361–6682.*

House of Blues. Buy music, books, hot sauce, and T-shirts at the souvenir shop in the popular bar/restaurant at the Mandalay Bay hotel. Rest for a bit in the comfortable chairs in the shop's alcove: read a book about the blues or look out the shop's windows into the restaurant. ⊠ *Mandalay Bay Resort and Casino, 3950 Las Vegas Blvd. S, South Strip,* ☎ 702/632–7600.

Il Prato. Il Prato saves you a shopping foray to Venice where the original pricey boutique stands. The Vegas outpost offers the same authentic gifts crafted by Italian artisans, tooled-leather journals and photo albums, glass-tip quills, wax seal kits, miniatures, and paintings. And, just as in Venice, you'll find a huge collection of traditional Carnevale masks here. ⊠ *Grand Canal Shoppes at the Venetian, 3377 Las Vegas Blvd. S, Center Strip,* ☎ 702/733–1201.

Les Memories. This shop stocking Diptyque candles, Provençal kitchenware, and French-milled soaps is a Francophile's fantasy. ⊠ *Le Boulevard at Paris, 3655 Las Vegas Blvd. S, Center Strip,* ☎ 702/946–7000, *Ext. 64329.*

McGrail's of Erin. This one-of-kind shop devoted to things Irish is found in an unlikely spot—the Desert Passage at the Aladdin. Buy a bit of the Blarney stone, Celtic jewelry, figurines, and apparel shipped all the way from Ireland. ⊠ *Desert Passage at the Aladdin, 3663 Las Vegas Blvd. S, Center Strip,* ☎ 702/732–8810.

Merlin's Mystic Shop. A life-size figure of Merlin hunched over a selection of crystal figurines sets the tone for this Excalibur gift shop. The eclectic collection includes glow-in-the-dark stickers, 3-D sand pictures, and a skull-shape toilet-brush holder. A palm reader can predict your gambling luck Thursday–Sunday. ⊠ *Excalibur Hotel and Casino, 3850 Las Vegas Blvd. S, South Strip,* ☎ 702/597–7251.

Ripa de Monti. Exquisite Venetian glass creations—everything from magnets and key chains to elaborate vases and figurines—are sold at this store, one of the Grand Canal Shoppes at the Venetian. It's one of Las Vegas's must-see shops. Buy glass-bead necklaces and earrings or a bowl of glass fruit for your dining-room table. ⊠ *Grand Canal Shoppes at the Venetian, 3377 Las Vegas Blvd. S, Center Strip,* ☎ 702/733–1004.

Toni Cats and Company. Looking for a gift for Fluffy? This shop has novelties and gifts for and about felines. ⊠ *Riviera Hotel and Casino, 2901 Las Vegas Blvd. S, North Strip,* ☎ 702/794–9612.

Treasure Chamber. Bring home a piece of Egypt (and a lighter wallet). This shop sells real and faux Egyptian artifacts, art, and jewelry in the Luxor's Giza Galleria. ⊠ *Luxor Hotel-Casino, 3900 Las Vegas Blvd. S, South Strip,* ☎ 702/730–5932.

Home Furnishings

National chains can be found in most Vegas malls, but be sure to hit Belz Factory Outlet World for reduced prices on brand names such as **Waterford, Springmaid, Corning-Revere, Mikasa, Pfaltzgraff, Lenox,** and a lot more.

Cottura Ceramic Art Imports. Las Vegas' only source for colorful ceramicware from Italy, Spain, and Portugal has a huge selection, even tabletops and fountains. ⊠ *Appian Way at Caesars, 3570 Las Vegas Blvd. S, Center Strip,* ☎ 702/892–9353.

Sur La Table. Culinary aficionados and home chefs will love the table linens, kitchen tools, and specialty foods here. ⊠ *Desert Passage at the Aladdin, 3663 Las Vegas Blvd. S, Center Strip,* ☎ 702/732–2706.

West of Santa Fe. One of The Forum Shops, it carries Southwestern home furnishings and accessories and also has a large selection of silver jewelry. ⊠ *The Forum Shops at Caesars, 3500 Las Vegas Blvd. S, Center Strip,* ☎ *702/737–1993.*

Williams Sonoma Marketplace. All the kitchen witchery of its catalog and stores are sold here at deep discounts. ⊠ *Fashion Outlets, 32100 Las Vegas Blvd. S, Primm,* ☎ *702/874–1780.*

Jewelry

Most malls and shopping centers on and off the Strip have a range of jewelry stores, including such national chains as **Ben Bridge, Gordon's, Lundstrom, Whitehall Co.,** and **Zales.** More exclusive jewelers can be found in several of the Strip hotels, most notably Bellagio and the Venetian.

Agatha. Clunky, hip, and affordable jewelry—gold and silver bracelets, necklaces, earrings, and even hair clips—is sold here. ⊠ *Grand Canal Shoppes at the Venetian, 3355 Las Vegas Blvd. S, Center Strip,* ☎ *702/ 369–0365.*

Ca' d'Oro. This is the premier jewelry shop on the Strip—perhaps in all of Las Vegas. Not surprisingly, it's one of the many unique, elegant stores in the Grand Canal Shoppes at the Venetian. The store is made up of several boutiques, among them the only Damiani boutique in the United States and one of only six Charriol boutiques in the country. UnoAerre, Charles Krypell, and Silvio Hidalgo offer jewel and enamel settings in platinum and 18-karat gold. Lovers of fine watches will find numerous brands, including Ebel, Omega, Tag Heuer, and Bertolucci. The Katherine Baumann purses, studded with Swarowski crystals and other gems, are carried by stars and celebrities to the Oscar and Emmy awards. ⊠ *Grand Canal Shoppes, 3355 Las Vegas Blvd. S, Center Strip,* ☎ *702/696–0080.*

Tiffany and Co. This branch of the world-renowned store in the Via Bellagio provides a full selection of Tiffany's timeless merchandise as well as the exclusive jewelry designs of Elsa Peretti, Paloma Picasso, and Jean Schlumberger. ⊠ *Via Bellagio, 3600 Las Vegas Blvd. S, Center Strip,* ☎ *702/693–7111.*

Only in Las Vegas

Dealers Room Casino Clothiers. If you've caught the gambling spirit and want to go home in a white shirt, black pants, and a big red bow tie, this place will be happy to sell you dealer's duds. ⊠ *4465 W. Flamingo Rd., West Side,* ☎ *702/362–7980;* ⊠ *3507 S. Maryland Pkwy., East Side,* ☎ *702/732–3932.*

Elvis-A-Rama Museum Store. You'll feel ecstatic shopping here if you're an Elvis fan; if not, you might wonder at the decline of our civilization. The store stocks such finds as an Elvis doll (the Army years), an Elvis lunchbox, aviator sunglasses, even a swatch of his pillowcase. There are many CDs, videos, and photos; even his old furniture is for sale. ⊠ *3401 Industrial Rd., West Side,* ☎ *702/309–7200.*

Gamblers General Store. There's a big collection of gambling books, such as "Craps for the Clueless," as well as poker chips, green-felt layouts, and slot and video-poker machines. Warning: the highly collectible vintage slots cost $2,000 and up. They'll make sure your state allows the type of slot machine you want before you buy. You can buy used casino card decks here but only after they've been re-sorted and repackaged by guests of the Nevada state penal system. It's eight blocks south of the Plaza Hotel on Main Street. ⊠ *800 S. Main St., Downtown,* ☎ *702/382–9903,* WEB *www.gamblersgeneralstore.com.*

Houdini's Magic Shop. Magicians are hot in Vegas and it's no surprise that Houdini's corporate headquarters is in town. You'll find seven branches, with its tricks and gags, in almost all the casino-malls. ✉ *Grand Canal Shoppes at the Venetian, 3355 Las Vegas Blvd. S, Center Strip,* ☏ *702/796–0301,* WEB *www.houdini.com.*

The Liberace Museum Store. The tiny store stocks the maestro's CDs and videos and, in case you're running low, his signature candelabras. ✉ *1775 E. Tropicana Ave., East Side,* ☏ *702/798–5595,* WEB *www.liberace.org.*

Paul-Son Dice & Card Inc. Want some authentic casino dice and chips? This store supplies the casinos and also sells retail. The company also designs and produces chips, gaming table layouts, and other tools of the trade—in case you're thinking of going into the business. ✉ *2121 Industrial Rd., West Side,* ☏ *702/384–2425.*

Ray's Beaver Bag. This place defies description as Vegas' most bizarre, and not to be missed, shop. As a supplier for pre-1840s mountain man re-enactors, it goes beyond moose milk, beeswax candles, black powder, and buffalo jerky. Even if you don't trap or fur trade, poke around the muzzle guns and bear skins and you may find a 1960s Indian trade blanket or a unique 4-ft-long beaded, fringed elk-skin pipe bag made by a Native American craftsman. ✉ *727 Las Vegas Blvd. S, Downtown,* ☏ *702/386–8746.*

Ron Lee's World of Clowns. Every kind of clown item known to man is sold at this bizarre shop. They also make clown figurines on the premises, and there's a self-guided factory tour. Clown clothing, accessories, and assorted other clown stuff line the walls in the tour area, which is touted as a Clown Museum. Children can ride the 30-ft carousel or take a gander at the Plexiglas-enclosed miniature carnival, complete with moving rides, in the front of the building. There's also a café. ✉ *330 Carousel Pkwy., Henderson,* ☏ *702/434–1700.* WEB *www.ronlee.com.*

Serge's Showgirl Wigs. If you always wished for the sleek tresses of those Vegas dancers (or female impersonators), head here. The largest wig store in the world can transform you into a Rennaisance angel or Priscilla Presley on her wedding day. After checking out Serge's celebrity wall of fame, head for their wig outlet directly across the parking lot. ✉ *953 E. Sahara Ave., East Side,* ☏ *702/732–1015.*

Vintage Slots. If taking home a classic slot machine would make your trip to Las Vegas complete, you might want to stop in this shop. But be warned: old slots can cost in the $2,000–$5,000 range, and in-home slots are legal in only 40 states. (The proprietors will let you know if they are legal where you live.) ✉ *3379 Industrial Rd., West Side,* ☏ *702/369–2323.*

Pawn Shops

Las Vegas is a great place to pick up cheap televisions, watches, and cameras pawned by locals feeding video poker habits or visitors who needed a little extra cash to get home.

Stoney's Loan and Jewelry. One of the oldest pawn shops in Las Vegas. ✉ *126 S. 1st St., Downtown,* ☏ *702/384–2686.*

Super Pawn. There are 25 locations around town, but the following is the most convenient for those staying on the Strip or downtown. ✉ *515 E. St. Louis St., East Side,* ☏ *702/792–2900.*

Sporting Goods and Clothing

Nike Town. This multi-level Nike theme park features booming 'Just Do It' videos and giant Swoosh symbols amid the latest cool technology in athletic shoes displayed in glass cases. Flashy and crowded, the salespeople run around with microphones and your purchase speeds through vacuum tubes from the warehouse below. On the first floor, the Swoosh info desk has the scoop on local sporting events, bike races and hiking spots. ⊠ *The Forum Shops at Caesars, 3500 Las Vegas Blvd. S, Center Strip,* ☎ *702/650–8888.*

Saint Andrew's Golf Shop. In the Callaway Golf Center at the south end of the Strip, this shop is part of a 45-acre state-of-the-art practice, instruction and learning center. ⊠ *Callaway Golf Center, 6730 Las Vegas Blvd. S, South Strip,* ☎ *702/897–9500.*

Toys and Games

Build-A-Bear Workshop. The store's motto is "Where Best Friends Are Made" . . . if your best friend is a soon-to-be stuffed animal. Choose a furry friend, take it to a stuffing machine (you work the pedals!), and pick out a cloth heart to put inside. An employee sews it up, then it's off for an air bath and brushing. If you don't want your new best friend to go out into the world naked, choose from a variety of tiny clothes, shoes, and accessories. Don't forget to fill out the stats for the birth certificate; all friends go home in a cardboard house. ⊠ *Desert Passage at the Aladdin, 3663 Las Vegas Blvd. S, Center Strip,* ☎ *702/836–0899,* WEB *www.buildabear.com.*

FAO Schwarz. No other toy store in Vegas can compare with this one. A two-story wooden Trojan horse, with moving head, whirling gears, and flashing lights, greets delighted shoppers as they enter this toy kingdom. You'll pay a pretty penny for brand-name toys, but you'll also have a lot of fun doling out those dollars. Full sections of the store are devoted to Barbie, Legos, Pokemon, Star Wars, Thomas the Tank Engine, and a multitude of other popular children's playthings. If playing with the action figures, game boards, models, and remote-control cars gives you the munchies, you can quench your thirst or snack at one of two cafés within the store. ⊠ *The Forum Shops at Caesars, 3500 Las Vegas Blvd. S, Center Strip,* ☎ *702/731–7110.*

Western Shops

Adams Western Store. This is the sort of traditional Western shop you might expect to find in Montana or Wyoming; the emphasis is on equestrian supplies and "wearing apparel." It's also the oldest Western shop in town (circa 1951), and the toughest one to get to. It's off Sahara Avenue, near the freeway, on a back street named (appropriately enough) Western Avenue. ⊠ *1415 Western Ave., West Side,* ☎ *702/384–6077.*

Shepler's. Cowboys (and cowgirls) can get their Wranglers and Stetsons here as well as western decor and accessories. ⊠ *4700 W. Sahara Ave., West Side,* ☎ *702/258–2000,* WEB *www.sheplers.com;* ⊠ *3025 E. Tropicana Ave., East Side,* ☎ *702/898–3000.*

Western Emporium. At 25,000 square ft, this is Nevada's largest western store. Located at Sam's Town Hotel and Gambling Hall in Henderson, you'll find cowpoke necessities such as boots and jeans as well as jewelry and original art. There's an old-time photo studio and a year-round Western Christmas shop. ⊠ *5111 Boulder Hwy., Boulder Strip,* ☎ *702/454–8017.*

9 SIDE TRIPS FROM LAS VEGAS

Although Las Vegas is one of the most remote cities in the United States, its surroundings are among its best assets. Stunning mountains of sandstone, in its many hues and shapes, are visible from any west-facing window on the Strip. The largest man-made lake in the Western Hemisphere is a mere 40 mi down the road. And the grandest canyon on the planet is just a hop, skip, and jump by plane or car.

Aᴺʸ ONE OF THE NATURAL and man-made scenic wonders a short drive away can add a memorable excursion to the unique experience that is Las Vegas. Strike out in any direction and within minutes you can enjoy the solace and serenity only the desert can provide. The most popular side trip is to Hoover Dam, 45 minutes away on the Arizona state line. Or why not fly to the Grand Canyon in an hour, or drive up to Death Valley National Park in three hours?

Updated by
Fred Couzens

Dining and lodging price ranges in this chapter refer to the charts in Chapters 4 and 5.

RED ROCK CANYON AREA

16 mi west of Las Vegas.

Look west from any vantage point in Las Vegas and your gaze will inevitably be drawn to the Spring Mountains, the big limestone and sandstone wall that hems in one side of the Las Vegas Valley. The centerpiece of the mighty Springs is **Red Rock Canyon,** with its scenic 13-mi loop road through red-rock formations and unusual high-desert scenery. A 30-minute drive west on West Charleston Boulevard (Highway 159) delivers you to natural vistas every bit as stunning as the unnatural ones found in the city.

Red Rock's **BLM Visitors Center** exhibits the flora and fauna of the Mojave Desert and the history of the various desert peoples. On Tuesdays, listen to "Cactus Jack" Ryan tell the story of Mojave Max, a real-life desert tortoise icon, that lives behind the visitors center with several other tortoises in a large, specially constructed habitat. The first stops

on the one-way loop road are the easy Calico Vistas 1 and 2 trails where even the most amateur rockclimber can safely get a feel of the red sandstone and have a "near-professional" experience. Farther on, 6½ mi past the Vistas pullouts, is a turnoff for Willow Springs/Lost Creek. Take this road to reach **Lost Creek Discovery Trail,** an easy ¾-mi loop trail that has been designated a children's trail. It starts in the valley, then climbs up into a wooded area, with rest stops and benches along Lost Creek. Native American pictographs and a seasonal waterfall also are on the trail. There are 20 tables and a great partly-shaded picnicking site next to the rocks, but arrive early to get a table at this popular stop. ⊠ *W. Charleston Blvd.,* ☎ *702/363–1922,* Ⓦᴇʙ *www.redrockcanyon. blm.gov.* 🚗 *$5 per car.* ☉ *Visitor Center daily 8–6; loop road daily 6 AM–8 PM.*

After completing the Red Rock Canyon scenic loop, you'll return to Highway 159. Turn right onto the highway and go 2½ mi to **Spring Mountain Ranch State Park.** This prime piece of property became a ranch in the 1860s, thanks to the abundant water that percolates down from the Spring Mountains (hence, the name of the range), and served as a working ranch through the 1950s. Past owners have included German actress Vera Krupp and eccentric millionaire Howard Hughes. The red ranch house, white picket fences, long green lawns, and colorful cliffs of the Wilson Range make this a perfect place for a picnic, and horseback rides are available year-round. **Super Summer Theater,** offered from June through August, transforms the sprawling grassy grounds into a playhouse under the stars. A volunteer organization has coordinated this highly successful theater-on-the-lawn for the past 26 years. ⊠ *Hwy. 159,* ☎ *Ranch, 702/875–4141; theater, 702/594–7529,* Ⓦᴇʙ *ranch www.state.nv.us/stparks/smr.htm; theater www.supersummertheatre. com.* 🚗 *Ranch, $5 per car; theater, prices vary/advanced purchase re-*

158

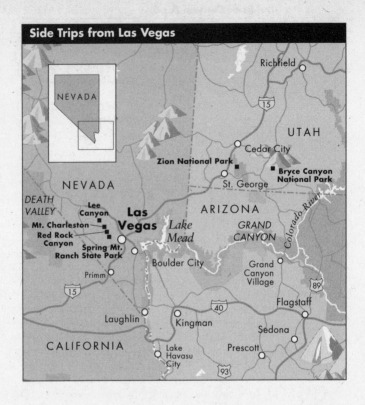

Side Trips from Las Vegas

quired. ⊙ *Daily 8–6; ranch house 10–4; walking tours of the old ranch at noon, 1, and 2 on weekdays, also 3 on weekends and holidays.*

From Spring Mountain Ranch State Park continue another mile on Highway 159 to **Bonnie Springs Ranch.** The duck pond, aviary, and large animal zoo are admission free. The ranch also has a rustic restaurant, a bar, and a 50-unit motel. Equestrians can rent horses from the large stable; one-hour guided trail rides take you past cacti, yucca, and Joshua trees.

Old Nevada, a Western-theme resort at Bonnie Springs Ranch (there's an admission charge), includes an opera house, two museums, a cemetery, a stamp mill, several stores, and a wedding chapel. Three times a day the Wild West comes to life here, with gunfights and hangings staged in the street. On weekends, you can ride the stagecoach or hop on a miniature train that chugs its way between the parking lot and the entrance. The stage costs $5, but train rides are free. ⊠ *1 Bonnie Springs Ranch Rd.,* ☎ *702/875–4191,* FAX *702/875–4424,* WEB *www. bonniesprings.com.* ⊠ *Ranch and petting zoo free, Old Nevada $6.50, horseback riding $25.* ⊙ *Labor Day–Memorial Day, daily 10:30–5; Memorial Day–Labor Day, 10:30–6.*

MT. CHARLESTON, AND KYLE AND LEE CANYONS

45 mi northwest of Las Vegas on U.S. 95.

For an alpine retreat, head to Mt. Charleston. In winter the upper elevations are used for cross-country and downhill skiing; in summer it's a welcome respite from the 115°F desert heat (temperatures are at least

20°F cooler than in the city), as well as a place to hike, picnic, and camp. For camping information in the Mt. Charleston area of the Toiyabe National Forest, contact the **U.S. Forest Service** (☎ 702/515–5400). For snow reports and wintertime road conditions, call the **Las Vegas Ski and Snowboard Resort** (☎ 702/593–9500).

At the intersection of U.S. 95 and Highway 157, turn left to Kyle Canyon. The first stop on Kyle Canyon Road (about 17 mi up) is the **Mount Charleston Hotel** (✉ 2 Kyle Canyon Rd., ☎ 702/872–5500 or 800/794–3456, WEB www.mtcharlestonhotel.com), built in 1984. The large, lodgelike lobby has a big hearth, bar, and spacious restaurant with a mountain view. If you take Highway 157 to its end you'll find the **Mt. Charleston Lodge** (✉ 1200 Old Park Rd., ☎ 702/872–5408 or 800/955–1314, FAX 702/872–5403, WEB www.mtcharlestonlodge.com). The lodge at 7,717 ft above sea level overlooks Kyle Canyon; it offers a fireside cocktail lounge, log cabin rentals, and nearby hiking trails.

From Mt. Charleston Lodge, take Highway 157 down the hill 4 mi to its intersection with Highway 158, then follow Highway 158 for 9 mi and turn left on Highway 156 toward **Las Vegas Ski and Snowboard Resort** (☎ 702/645–2754, WEB www.skilasvegas.com). Near the end of the road you'll find two campgrounds (at around 8,500 ft), a trail to a bristlecone pine forest (among the oldest living trees on Earth), and the **Lee Canyon** ski area. The resort's 10 ski trails cover 40 acres and, depending on snowfall, ski season can last from Thanksgiving to Easter. Lessons at the establishment's ski school also are available. Thanks to the 9,000-ft elevation, the area offers stunning views year-round.

BOULDER CITY, HOOVER DAM, AND THE LAKE MEAD AREA

Boulder City is an attractive and languid village, full of historic neighborhoods and businesses, parks and greenbelts, and not a single casino. Over the hill from town is the enormous Hoover Dam, which offers a popular tour. Behind it, backed up by mile after mile of rugged desert-canyon country, is incongruous and shimmering Lake Mead, the focal point of water-based recreation for all of southern Nevada and northwestern Arizona. All three are within an hour of Vegas.

Numbers in the margin correspond to numbers on the Boulder City, Hoover Dam, and Lake Mead Area map.

Boulder City

❶ *25 mi southeast of Las Vegas via Boulder Hwy. (U.S. 93/95) or I–515.*

In the city of Henderson you can stop at the **Clark County Heritage Museum.** A chronological history of southern Nevada includes exhibits on settler life, early gambling, and nuclear testing. Other museum attractions include a fully restored bungalow from the 1920s, built by a pioneer Las Vegas merchant; a replica of a 19th-century frontier print shop; and buildings and machinery dating from the turn of the 20th century. ✉ *1830 S. Boulder Hwy., Henderson,* ☎ *702/455–7955.* ⚏ *$1.50.* ☉ *Daily 9–4:30.*

More than 180 bird species have been spotted among the system of nine lagoons at the 200-acre **Bird Viewing Preserve.** Four dozen varieties are listed as resident including various ducks, hawks, cormorants and herons; many species are listed as migrant or winter visitors. ✉ *2400 B Moser Dr., Henderson,* ☎ *702/566–2939.* ⚏ *Free.* ☉ *Daily 6 AM–3 PM.*

Boulder City, Hoover Dam, and Lake Mead Area

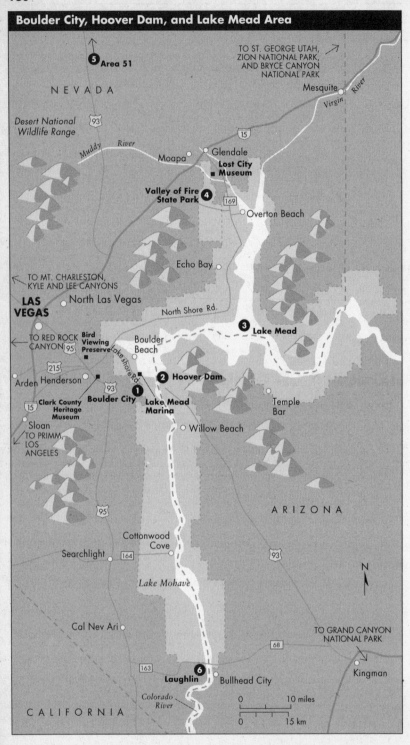

⑤ Area 51

TO ST. GEORGE UTAH,
ZION NATIONAL PARK,
AND BRYCE CANYON
NATIONAL PARK

N E V A D A

Mesquite

Virgin River

Desert National
Wildlife Range

93

Muddy   River

Moapa

Glendale

15

**Lost City
Museum**

**Valley of Fire
State Park ④**

169

Overton Beach

Echo Bay

TO MT. CHARLESTON,
KYLE AND LEE CANYONS

**LAS
VEGAS**

North Las Vegas

North Shore Rd.

③ Lake Mead

TO RED ROCK
CANYON

95

**Bird
Viewing
Preserve**

Boulder
Beach

215

Arden   Henderson

93

② Hoover Dam

Temple
Bar

15

**Clark County
Heritage
Museum**

Boulder City

**① Lake Mead
Marina**

Willow Beach

Sloan
TO PRIMM,
LOS
ANGELES

A R I Z O N A

95

Cottonwood
Cove

Searchlight

164

93

Lake Mohave

N

Cal Nev Ari

TO GRAND CANYON
NATIONAL PARK

68

163

**⑥
Laughlin**

Bullhead City

Kingman

*Colorado
River*

0   10 miles

0   15 km

C A L I F O R N I A

Continue past Henderson and desert terrain for 8 mi to reach Boulder City. In the early 1930s this town was built by the federal government to house 5,000 construction workers on the Hoover Dam project. A strict moral code was enforced, and to this day the model city is the only community in Nevada in which gambling is illegal. The two casinos at either end of Boulder City are just outside the city limits. After the dam was completed, the town shrank by more than half, kept alive by the management and maintenance crews of the dam and Lake Mead. But Boulder City slowly recovered and is now a vibrant little Southwest town. A tribute to the dam, a 34-ton water wheel once used to help generate electricity, is on display in Government Park.

Be sure to stop at the **Boulder City/Hoover Dam Museum** (⊠ 1305 Arizona St., ☎ 702/294–1988, www.accessnv.com/bcmha/index.htm), which preserves and displays artifacts relating to the workers and construction of Boulder City and Hoover Dam. It occupies the second floor of the historic **Boulder Dam Hotel** (☎ 702/293–5310, WEB www.BoulderDamHotel.com) built in 1932. Placed on the National Register of Historic Places in 1982, the 81-room hotel once was a favorite stopover for such notables as Will Rogers, Bette Davis, Shirley Temple, and the legendary Howard Hughes. The **Boulder City Chamber of Commerce** office (☎ 702/293–2034, WEB www.bouldercitychamber.com, ☉ weekdays 9–5), on the first floor of the Boulder Dam Hotel, is a good place to gather information on the history of Hoover Dam and historic sights around town. You can spend an enjoyable couple of hours strolling the main streets downtown, popping into Native American and Mexican gift shops, antiques and jewelry stores, and galleries.

Hoover Dam

★ ❷ *8 mi from Boulder City via U.S. 93.*

Congress authorized the funding of the $175-million dam in 1928 for two purposes: flood control and generating electricity. Named the Civil Engineering Monument of the Millennium by the American Society of Civil Engineers and one of the seven wonders of the world, the dam is 727 ft high (the equivalent of a 70-story building) and 660 ft thick at the base (about the length of two football fields). Construction required 4.4 million cubic yards of concrete—enough to build a two-lane highway from San Francisco to New York. Originally referred to as Boulder Dam, the structure was later officially named Hoover Dam in recognition of President Herbert Hoover's role in the project. Guided tours have been replaced by **The Discovery Tour,** which allows you to see the power plant generators, the Nevada Intake Tower, the visitors center, the old Exhibit Building and other vantage points at your own pace. Guide staff give talks every 15 minutes at each stopping point from 9:30 to 4:30. Be sure to stop at the street-level Winged Figures of the Republic statue and look down at the fascinating base, which is actually an astronomical star chart that pinpoints the location of the 200 brightest magnitude stars in the universe when the dam was dedicated on Sept. 30, 1935. Cameras, pagers, tote bags, and cell phones are subject to X-ray screening. The top of the dam is closed to visitors after 5:30 PM. Note: All specified hours are Pacific Time Zone. ⊠ *U.S. 93 east of Boulder City,* ☎ *Bureau of Reclamation 702/293–8000,* WEB *www.lc.usbr.gov.* ⬛ *Discovery Tour $10.* ☉ *Daily 9–5.*

Lake Mead

❸ *About 4 mi from Hoover Dam; travel west on U.S. 93 to the intersection with Lakeshore Dr. to reach the Alan Bible Visitors Center.*

Lake Mead, which is actually the Colorado River backed up behind the Hoover Dam, is the largest man-made reservoir in the country: it covers 229 square mi, and its irregular shoreline extends for 550 mi. You can get information on the lake's history, ecology, and recreational opportunities, as well as accommodations available along its shore at the **Alan Bible Visitors Center** (☎ 702/293–8990, WEB www.nps.gov/lame). The entrance fee (good for five days) is $5 per vehicle; watercraft charges are $10 for the first vessel and $5 for each additional vessel. Annual passes also are available.

People come to Lake Mead to swim: **Boulder Beach** is the closest to Las Vegas, only a mile or so from the visitors center; **Echo Bay,** roughly 40 mi beyond Boulder Beach, is the best place to swim in the lake because it has better sand and is less crowded than the other beaches. Anglers fish for largemouth bass, catfish, trout, and black crappie, but striped bass provide the most sport. Houseboating is a favorite pastime; you can rent houseboats, along with speedboats, ski boats, and Jet Skis at the various marinas strung along the Nevada shore. Divers have a fantastic choice of underwater sights to explore, including the entire town of St. Thomas, a farming community that was inundated by the lake in 1937. Other activities abound, such as waterskiing, sailboarding, and snorkeling.

At **Lake Mead Cruises** you can hop aboard a 57-ft, 50-passenger motorized catamaran that speeds its way (at 40 mph) to the mouth of the Grand Canyon. Or you can board the 300-passenger stern-wheeler that plies the lower portion of the lake; breakfast, cocktail, and dinner and dancing cruises are available. Sightseeing cruises are offered daily and last about an hour and a half. Dinner cruises are scheduled on weekends (or by charter) and last two to three hours. ⊠ *Lake Mead Marina,* ☎ *702/293–6180,* FAX *702/293–0343,* WEB *www.lakemeadcruises.com.* 🖃 *Catamaran, $165; Stern-wheeler, $19–$51; reservations strongly recommended.* ☉ *Stern-wheeler tours Oct.-Mar., daily at 10, noon, and 2; Apr.–Sept., daily at 10, noon, 2, and 4.*

You'll find boat rentals, a beach, camping facilities, a gift shop, and a restaurant at **Lake Mead Resort Marina** (☎ 702/293–3484). A drive of about an hour will take you along the north side of the lake, where you'll find three more marinas. When you reach the upper arm of the lake, about a mile past Overton Beach, look for the sign announcing the Valley of Fire. Turn left here, and go about 3 mi to reach the Valley of Fire Visitors Center.

Valley of Fire

55 mi northeast of Las Vegas; east on I-15, south on Hwy. 169; less than 2 mi west from upper arm of Lake Mead.

❹ The 56,000-acre **Valley of Fire State Park** was dedicated in 1935 as Nevada's first state park. Valley of Fire takes its name from its distinctive coloration, which ranges from lavender to tangerine to bright red, giving the vistas along the park road an otherworldly appearance. The incredible rock formations have been weathered into unusual shapes that suggest beehives, ducks, cobras, even pianos. You'll find petrified logs, Great Depression–era stone cabins, and the park's most photographed feature—Elephant Rock—just steps off the main road. Also found in the park are mysterious petroglyphs (carvings etched into the rock) and pictographs (pictures drawn or painted on the rock's surface) that are believed to be the work of the Basketmaker and ancestral Puebloan people, who lived along the nearby Muddy River between 300 BC and AD 1150. The most spectacular petroglyphs are found just off the park road, beyond the visitors center on a flat cliff face reached by a 100-step staircase.

The **Valley of Fire Visitors Center** has displays on the park's history, ecology, archaeology, and recreation, as well as slide shows and films, an art gallery, and information about the 50 campsites within the park. The park is open year-round; the best times to visit, especially during the heat of the summer, are sunrise and sunset, when the light is especially spectacular. ⊠ *Hwy. 169 (Box 515), Overton 89040,* ☎ *702/397–2088,* WEB *www.state.nv.us/stparks/vf.htm.* ⚐ *$5.* ◷ *Daily 8:30–4:30.*

OFF THE
BEATEN PATH

LOST CITY MUSEUM – The Overton area, along with the little bedroom community of Logandale, just north of it along the highway, has one of the finest collections of ancestral Puebloan artifacts in the American Southwest. Lost City was a major outpost of the ancient culture, which thrived during the early part of the last millennium and disappeared around 1150. The museum's immense collection of artifacts includes baskets, weapons, a restored Basketmaker pit house, and numerous black-and-white photographs of the excavation of Lost City in 1924. To get to the Lost City Museum from Valley of Fire, turn around on the park road and head back to the "T" intersection at the entrance to the Valley of Fire. Turn left and drive roughly 8 mi into Overton. Turn left at the sign for the museum and cross the railroad tracks into the parking lot. ⊠ *721 S. Moapa Valley Blvd.,* ☎ *702/397–2193,* WEB *www.comnett.net/~kolson.* ⚐ *$2.* ◷ *Daily 8:30–4:30.*

Area 51

❺ *143 mi northeast of Las Vegas, west of Hwy. 375.*

Area 51, found at Groom Lake, is a tiny nub in the northeast corner of the vast 3.5-million-acre Nellis Air Force Range. According to sketchy and unconfirmed media reports, Area 51, also dubbed Dreamland, has been a super-secret military installation since the 1950s, where the Air Force has tested top-secret aircraft (such as the U-2 spy plane; the Stealth bomber; and the Aurora, rumored to fly at 5,000 mph). Some people also believe that the government stores and does research on UFOs and even collects and studies extraterrestrial beings here. It's illegal to approach the installation; military police have complete authority (not only can they arrest you and take away your cameras, they have orders to use deadly force, if necessary) to prevent intrusions.

Highway 375, a 98-mi road that runs through southeast Nevada from U.S. 93 to U.S. 6, was named the "Extraterrestrial Highway" by the state's tourism office when public interest was piqued with the hit TV show "The X-Files." Signs along the road promote the eye-catching label—although they are frequently stolen. Thirty-six miles from the junction of U.S. 93 is the tiny town of Rachel, founded in the early 1980s as part of the aborted MX missile development. Today, thanks to its proximity to Area 51 and to the mysterious "Black Box" where the installation's mail was supposedly delivered, it is a pilgrimage site for UFO enthusiasts from around the world.

The main gathering spot in Rachel is the **Little A'Le'Inn** (⊠ Hwy. 375, HCR 61, Box 45, Rachel, NV 89001, ☎ 775/729–2515, FAX 775/729–2551, WEB www.dreamlandresort.com), which has a UFO theme. Spend a night or two under the stars near Rachel, and whether it's UFOs, military aircraft, meteors, or illusion, you'll start to think you've seen some pretty strange phenomena in the great big sky.

PRIMM, NEVADA

30 mi south of Las Vegas.

Las Vegas offers optimum shopping and gawking, but those looking for a less-crowded alternative to the Strip's shops and sights can head out to Primm, Nevada, a 30-minute drive south on I-15. Shop for bargains at Fashion Outlets Las Vegas or take a heart-pounding ride on Desperado, one of the world's tallest and fastest roller coasters. If you're in the mood to gamble or eat an inexpensive meal, stop by one of three casinos: Primm Valley Resort, Buffalo Bill's, or Whiskey Pete's. Primm also is the location for two challenging Tom Fazio–designed 18-hole championship golf courses. On the way to Primm from Vegas on I-15, stop in at the **Nevada Welcome Center** (☎ 702/874–1360, ☉ daily 8:30–5) in Jean for all your information needs.

Fashion Outlets Las Vegas is a circular building connected to the Primm Valley Resort & Casino. Designed like a cartoon city, complete with car kiosks and streetlights, the 360,000-square-ft mall is anchored by the outlet stores of Neiman Marcus, Polo Ralph Lauren, Calvin Klein, Williams Sonoma, and Banana Republic. Take time to see Bonnie and Clyde's shot-up car (yep, the real one) and the last shirt (blood stains and all) worn by Clyde. This mini-museum is up the escalators, just before you enter the casino. The arcade is also on this level. Catch a shuttle at New York–New York or MGM Grand, from which the round-trip ride costs $12.99. Shuttles leave six times each day (three times each from MGM and New York–New York); the first shuttle leaves at 9:15 AM and the last leaves at 3:15 PM. ⊠ *I–15, at Exit 1,* ☎ *702/ 874–1400; 888/424–6898 for shuttle reservations,* FAX *702/874–1560,* WEB *www.fashionoutletlasvegas.com.* ☉ *Mon.–Sat. 10–9; Sun. 10–8.*

Once you've shopped, you can drop, literally, by riding one of **Buffalo Bill's Rides.** The Desperado roller coaster promises G-forces of 4.0, near-zero gravity, and speeds of 90 mph in less than three minutes—two steep drops add even more thrills. Passengers board inside Buffalo Bill's Casino. Buffalo Bill's also offers the Venture Canyon Log Flume Ride (go splash, then travel the indoor river); the Turbo Drop (a 170 ft drop at 45 mph); a virtual roller coaster; and motion-simulator rides. ⊠ *31700 Las Vegas Boulevard S,* ☎ *702/386–7867 or 800/386–7867,* WEB *www.primadonna.com.* 🎟 *Rides $3–$6; half-day wristband $22, all-day wristband $30.* ☉ *Mon. and Thurs. noon–6, Fri. 11 AM–midnight, Sat. 10 AM–midnight, Sun. 10–7.*

Dining and Lodging

$–$$$ 🏨 **Gold Strike Hotel and Gambling Hall.** The Gold Strike has spacious rooms—with either two queen-size beds or one king and a pull-out sofa—that look out over the untamed Nevada desert for only $20 from Sunday through Thursday nights. The casino has a strong Old West vibe, although the weird white-and-orange facade has to be seen in full daylight to be appreciated. ⊠ *1 Main St., Jean 89019,* ☎ *702/477–5000 or 800/634–1359,* FAX *702/874–1355,* WEB *www.goldstrike-jean.com. 812 rooms. 3 restaurants, pool, lounge, casino. AE, D, DC, MC, V.*

$ 🏨 **Buffalo Bill's Hotel and Casino.** This is one of the three hotel-casinos right at the California border. Owned by the parent company of MGM-Mirage, the trio are a little world all their own, connected by a free monorail. To get people out here from Las Vegas, Bill's has to make it worth their while, and does so with $24.95 rooms, very inexpensive food, and excellent funbooks; a family of four could comfortably spend $100 for an overnight stay, enjoying much of everything there is to do. Rooms feel like the inside of a cabin, with log wallpaper and rustic furniture, and have great views of the surrounding mountains. An RV park has 199 75-ft pull-through lots with full hook-ups—cable and phone lines aren't available, however. ⊠ *I–15 S at state line, Primm 89019,* ☎ *702/386–7867 or 800/386–7867,* FAX *702/679–5424,* WEB *www.primadonna.com. 1,242 rooms. 4 restaurants, pool, spa, lounge, casino, comedy club/theater, showroom, meeting room. AE, D, DC, MC, V.*

$ ⊡ **Nevada Landing Hotel and Casino.** Right across I–15 from the Gold Strike (on the westbound side), Nevada Landing closely resembles its neighbor, except it's smaller and has a bright riverboat exterior. Both the Gold Strike and Nevada Landing are owned by Mandalay Resort Group. ⊠ *2 Goodsprings Rd., Jean 89019,* ☎ *702/387–5000 or 800/628–6682,* FAX *702/671–1407,* WEB *www.nevadalanding.com. 303 rooms. 3 restaurants, pool, lounge, casino. AE, D, DC, MC, V.*

$ ⊡ **Primm Valley Resort & Casino.** The new design, resembling a private country club, offers a classy touch normally not found in such distant locales. Faux ivy, latticework, and the green-and-white interior make for a comfortable, easy-going atmosphere. The property also provides a 21,000-square-ft conference center with the latest amenities. Top-notch lounge entertainment complements Buffalo Bill's 6,000-seat Star of the Desert Arena and Whiskey Pete's 700-seat showroom. There's also a major outlet mall not just next door, but accessible from the resort's casino. ⊠ *I–15 S at state line, Primm 89019,* ☎ *702/386–7867 or 800/ 386–7867,* FAX *702/679–5424,* WEB *www.primadonna.com. 624 rooms. 3 restaurants, pool, casino, meeting room. AE, D, DC, MC, V.*

$ ⊡ **Whiskey Pete's Casino and Hotel.** It's a noisy, surprisingly busy, state-line hotel-casino, with lounge bands, cheap food, and rooms for only $21–$49 a night. The rooms are large, with king-size beds, cable TV, and small bathrooms. When you're headed for Las Vegas from the west, an overnight stop at Pete's will leave you only 45 minutes of driving time in the morning. ⊠ *I–15 S at state line, Primm 89019,* ☎ *702/ 386–7867 or 800/386–7867,* FAX *702/679–5424,* WEB *www.primadonna. com. 777 rooms. 3 restaurants, pool, lounge, casino, showroom. AE, D, DC, MC, V.*

LAUGHLIN, NEVADA

❻ *90 mi south of Las Vegas; from Las Vegas, take Boulder Hwy. (U.S. 95/93) or I–515 east, then exit where U.S. 95 veers off to the south. Drive for an hour, almost to the California border. There, a left turn onto Hwy. 163 takes you east into Laughlin.*

Laughlin is a classic state-line city, separated from Arizona by the Colorado River. Its founder, Don Laughlin, bought an eight-room motel here in 1966 and basically built the town from scratch. By the early 1980s Laughlin's Riverside Hotel-Casino was drawing gamblers and river rats from northwestern Arizona, southeastern California, and even southern Nevada, and his success attracted other casino operators who took advantage of the affordable riverfront property. Today Laughlin is the state's third major resort area (Las Vegas and Reno/Lake Tahoe are the other two); it attracts almost 5 million visitors annually. The city fills up, especially in winter, with retired travelers who spend at least part of the winter in Arizona and a younger resort-loving crowd. Laughlin attracts folks who prefer low pressure, a slower pace, low-minimum tables, cheap food, and low-cost rooms. Take a stroll along the river walk, then make the return trip by water taxi ($3 round trip; $2 one way).

If you've been shuttered in Las Vegas casinos for a few days, you'll be amazed by the big picture windows overlooking the Colorado River

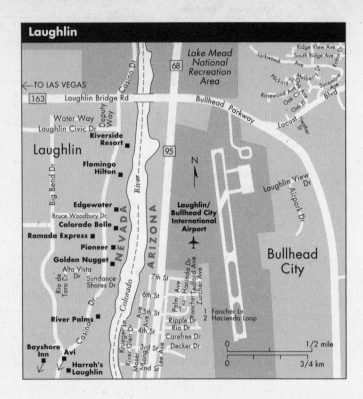

Laughlin

TO LAS VEGAS

Laughlin Bridge Rd

Lake Mead National Recreation Area

Bullhead Parkway

Water Way
Laughlin Civic Dr

Laughlin

Riverside Resort

Flamingo Hilton

Edgewater
Bruce Woodbury Dr
Colorado Belle
Ramada Express

Pioneer

Golden Nugget

Laughlin/ Bullhead City International Airport

Bullhead City

Alta Vista Dr
Rio de Toro Dr
Sundance Shores Dr

7th St

6th St

5th St
4th St

River Palms

Bayshore Inn
Avi

Harrah's Laughlin

3rd St
2nd St

Palm Ave
Hacinda Dr
Tedford Ave
Zurcher Ave

1 Fancher Ln
2 Hacienda Loop

Ripple Dr
Rio Dr
Carefree Dr
Decker Dr

1/2 mile

3/4 km

and the bright, airy, and open feeling they lend to the Laughlin casinos. The dealers are generally friendlier and the bettors more relaxed than in Las Vegas.

OFF THE BEATEN PATH

On the way to Laughlin, stop in at the **Searchlight Museum,** east of town, for the interesting display of artifacts, photos and "touch-me" tools for young hands. The modern, one-room exhibit area inside the town hall explains the area's rich mining history and extensively describes the lives of its most famous couple, legendary silent screen stars Rex Bell and Clara Bow. ⊠ *Hwy. 164 at Wendell Way,* ☎ *702/455–7955.* ⊠ *Free.* ⊗ *Weekdays 9–5, Sat. 9–1.*

Dining and Lodging

Note that Laughlin room tax is 9%.

$ ✕🏨 **Avi Hotel Casino.** This hotel-casino is owned by the Mohave tribe and is the only tribally owned casino in Nevada regulated by the Nevada Gaming Control Board. The 25,000-square-ft casino houses almost 800 slot and video-poker machines. There is also a 260-space RV park. The biggest draw, however, is the private white-sand beach; rent a Sea-Doo and cruise the Colorado River in style. ⊠ *10000 Aha Macav Pkwy., 89029,* ☎ *702/535–5555 or 800/284–2946,* 🌐 *www.avicasino.com. 300 rooms, 29 spa suites. 5 restaurants, 18-hole golf course, pool, gym, spa, beach, casino, baby-sitting. AE, D, DC, MC, V.*

$ ✕🏨 **Colorado Belle.** Owned by Mandalay Bay Resort Group, the Colorado Belle is a Nevada anomaly: a riverboat casino that's actually on a river. The 608-ft replica of a Mississippi paddle wheeler has nautical-theme rooms with views of the Colorado River. The Boiler Room Brew Pub (**$$–$$$**), the only brewery in Laughlin, is on-site, and you'll find live entertainment here on weekends. ⊠ *2100 S. Casino Dr., 89029,* ☎ *702/298–4000 or 800/477–4837,* 📠 *702/298–3697,* 🌐

www.coloradobelle.com. 1,201 rooms. 6 restaurants, 2 pools, hot tub, casino, dry cleaning, laundry service. AE, D, DC, MC, V.

$ ✕⚏ **Harrah's.** This is the classiest joint in Laughlin, and the only one with a private sand beach. It also has two casinos (one is no-smoking) and big-name entertainers perform in the Fiesta Showroom and at the Rio Vista Outdoor Amphitheater. William Fisk Steakhouse (**$$–$$$**) serves fine Continental fare. ✉ *2900 S. Casino Dr., 89029,* ☎ *702/ 298–4600 or 800/447–8700,* FAX *702/298–6855,* WEB *www.harrahs.com. 1,616 rooms. 5 restaurants, 2 pools, health club, hot tub, beach, lounge, casino, showroom, shop. AE, D, DC, MC, V.*

$ ✕⚏ **Pioneer Hotel and Gambling Hall.** You can spot this small (by casino standards) hotel by looking for the neon mascot, River Rick—he's Vegas Vic's brother. While other casinos stress the new, the Pioneer retains its laid-back western theme with checkered tablecloths and wagon-wheel light fixtures. Granny's Gourmet Room (**$$–$$$**) serves Continental and American cuisine. ✉ *2200 S. Casino Dr., 89029,* ☎ *702/298–2442 or 800/634–3469,* FAX *702/298–5256,* WEB *www.pioneerlaughlin.com. 416 rooms. 2 restaurants, pool, hot tub, lounge, casino. AE, D, DC, MC, V.*

$ ✕⚏ **Riverside Resort.** This is the original Laughlin joint, still owned by Don Laughlin himself. The Gourmet Room restaurant serves Continental and American cuisine. Check out the Loser's Lounge, with its graphic homage to famous losers, such as the *Hindenburg*, the *Titanic*, and the like. There's also a 900-space RV park. ✉ *1650 S. Casino Dr.,* ☎ *702/298–2535 or 800/227–3849,* FAX *702/298–2614,* WEB *www. riversideresort.com. 1,440 rooms. 6 restaurants, 2 pools, hot tub, bowling, lounge, casino, nightclub, showroom, theater. AE, D, DC, MC, V.*

$–$$ ⚏ **Golden Nugget Laughlin.** This miniversion of the Las Vegas Golden Nugget has a tropical atrium like the Nugget's big-sister casino, the Las Vegas Mirage. The 30-ft, glass-top atrium has two cascading waterfalls and more than 300 different types of plants from around the world. ✉ *2300 S. Casino Dr., 89029,* ☎ *702/298–7111 or 800/237– 1739,* FAX *702/298–7279,* WEB *www.gnlaughlin.com. 304 rooms. 4 restaurants, pool, hot tub, lounge, casino. AE, D, DC, MC, V.*

$–$$ ⚏ **Ramada Express.** For those seeking a refuge from children, this is the place. The Gamblers Tower in the railroad-theme hotel and casino is reserved for adults, and there are child-free restaurants and an adults-only pool. The 53,000-square-ft casino has state-of-the-art slots and a sports book. A museum focuses on the 1940s, and a miniature train takes you on a free ride around 27 landscaped acres. ✉ *2121 S. Casino Dr., 89029,* ☎ *702/298–4200 or 800/272–6232,* WEB *www. ramadaexpress.com. 1,501 rooms. 5 restaurants, pool, hot tub, lounge, casino, airport shuttle. AE, D, DC, MC, V.*

$ ⚏ **Bayshore Inn.** This small hotel has basic rooms with either a king-size or two double beds. It offers a picnic and barbecue area, video-poker machines, and watercraft available for rent. Complimentary coffee is available in the lobby in the morning. ✉ *1955 W. Casino Dr., 89028,* ☎ *702/299–9010. 100 rooms. Restaurant, picnic area, pool, boating, bar. D, MC, V.*

$ ⚏ **Edgewater Hotel Casino.** Like the Colorado Belle, this 26-story hotel is a property of the Mandalay Bay Resorts Group. The 60,000-square-ft casino includes nearly 1,400 machines. One-third of the rooms are reserved for nonsmokers. ✉ *2020 S. Casino Dr., 89029,* ☎ *702/298– 2453 or 800/677–4837,* FAX *702/298–8165,* WEB *www.edgewater-casino. com. 1,421 rooms. 4 restaurants, pool, hair salon, hot tub, lounge, casino, no-smoking rooms. AE, D, DC, MC, V.*

$ ⚏ **Flamingo Laughlin.** The casino at the largest resort in Laughlin has 1,500 slot and video-poker machines and a sports book. The Flamingo's

3,000-seat outdoor amphitheater, on the bank of the Colorado River, hosts big-name entertainers. Standard rooms have two double beds or a queen-size bed. Suites are larger (650–1,000 square ft) and equipped with coffeemakers, minibars, irons, and ironing boards. ☒ *1900 S. Casino Dr., 89029,* ☎ *702/298–5111 or 800/352–6464,* FAX *702/298–5116,* WEB *www.flamingo-laughlin.com. 1,824 rooms, 90 suites. 4 restaurants, 3 tennis courts, pool, casino, showroom, airport shuttle, car rental. AE, D, DC, MC, V.*

$ ☒ **River Palms Resort Casino.** A large balcony overlooks the table games in the 65,000-square-ft casino. For those seeking a quiet retreat, the hotel's south wing is adjacent to the outdoor pool and hot tub, away from the sizzling slots. ☒ *2700 S. Casino Dr., 89029,* ☎ *702/298–2242 or 877/787–7256,* FAX *702/298–2179,* WEB *www.rvrpalm.com. 1,003 rooms. 4 restaurants, pool, health club, hot tub, casino, showroom, airport shuttle. AE, D, DC, MC, V.*

Laughlin A to Z

To research prices, get advice from other travelers, and book travel arrangements, visit www.fodors.com.

AIR TRAVEL

Sun Country flies from Minneapolis, Denver, Dallas, San Antonio, Seattle, Portland (OR), and San Jose, CA. Air Laughlin offers service from three California cities: Ontario, San Jose, and San Diego. Several hotel-casinos also sponsor charter flights.

➤ AIRLINES: **Air Laughlin Tours** (☎ 800/633–4727, WEB www.airlaughlin.com). **Allegiant Charters** (☎ 800/221–1306). **Sun Country Airlines** (☎ 866/797–2537, WEB www.suncountry.com).

AIRPORTS

➤ CONTACTS: **Laughlin/Bullhead City International Airport** (☎ 928/754–2134).

BUS TRAVEL

Greyhound buses stop at the Airport Chevron at 600 Hwy. 95 in Bullhead City, Arizona. To get to Laughlin, walk to the boat dock across the highway and take a free ride to a Nevada hotel river landing. Individual hotel-casinos also sponsor bus trips from Las Vegas, Los Angeles, and other destinations.

➤ CONTACTS: **Greyhound** (☎ 800/231–2222, WEB www.greyhound.com).

CAR RENTALS

Avis, Enterprise, and Hertz vehicles are available at the Laughlin/Bullhead City International Airport. Other agencies can be found in Bullhead City; Avis also has a rental location in the Flamingo Hilton. All grades of gasoline can be as much as 40¢ per gallon less in Arizona than in Nevada.

➤ CONTACTS: **Avis-Airport** (☎ 928/754–4686, WEB www.avis.com). **Enterprise-Airport** (☎ 928/754–2700, WEB www.enterprise.com). **Hertz-Airport** (☎ 928/754–4111, WEB www.hertz.com).

TRAIN TRAVEL

Amtrak's *Southwest Chief* stops at Needles, California, which is 25 mi south of Laughlin. An Amtrak Thruway bus shuttles passengers to the Ramada Express in Laughlin.

➤ CONTACTS: **Amtrak** (☎ 800/872–7245, WEB www.amtrak.com).

VISITOR INFORMATION

➤ CONTACTS: **Laughlin Chamber of Commerce** (☒ 1585 S. Casino Dr., 89029, ☎ 702/298–7009 or 800/227–5245, WEB www.laughlinchamber.com). **Laughlin Visitor Information Center** (✉ 1555 Casino Dr., 89029, ☎ 702/298–3321 or 800/452–8445, WEB www.visitlaughlin.com).

GRAND CANYON NATIONAL PARK

240 mi east of Las Vegas; south on U.S. 93 to Kingman, east on I–40 to Williams, north on Hwy. 64.

Anyone who visits Las Vegas should seriously consider a side trip to the canyon, because it must be seen in person to be fully appreciated. Even the finest photographs fail to deliver a fraction of the impact of a personal glimpse into this vast, beautiful scar on the surface of our planet.

The canyon, eroded over aeons by the Colorado River, is 277 mi long, 17 mi across at its widest, and 1 mi deep at its lowest. The twisted and contorted layers of rock reveal a fascinating geological profile. Because this is one of the planet's greatest wonders, people from all across the country and around the world take advantage of Las Vegas's proximity to experience it.

There are two main access points to the canyon: the **South Rim** and the **North Rim,** both within the national park. But the vast polyglot of visitors converges primarily on the South Rim every summer, for good reason. Here travelers avail themselves of Grand Canyon Village, with most of the lodging and camping, restaurants and stores, and museums in the park, along with the airport, railroad depot, rim roads, scenic overlooks, and trailheads into the canyon. During these months you'll have a better chance at solitude and serenity at either the East or North rims, both of which are less accessible and have fewer, though comparable, tourist services. The geology and vistas of the East Rim closely resemble what you'll see from the South Rim, and the entrance is accessible from both the South Rim and Flagstaff. The South Rim is open year-round. The North Rim, by contrast, lies 1,000 ft higher than the South Rim and has a more alpine climate, with twice as much annual precipitation. The North Rim is relatively remote and secluded, set in the deep forest of the Kaibab Plateau. Here the crowds are thinner, the facilities fewer, and the views even more spectacular. The North Rim is closed to automobiles after the first heavy snowfall of the season (usually in late October or early November) through mid-May; due to severe winters, all North Rim facilities close between October 15 and May 15, though the park itself stays open for day use from October 15 through December 1, if heavy snows don't close the roads before then. The park has an entry fee of $20 per car, $10 per individual. ✉ *www.nps.gov/grca/index.htm*

Numbers in the margin correspond to numbers on the Grand Canyon National Park map.

South Rim

❶ **Mather Point,** approximately 4 mi north from the south entrance, gives you the first glimpse of the canyon from one of the most impressive and accessible vista points on the rim; from it, you can see nearly a fourth of the Grand Canyon. The **Canyon View Information Plaza,** in Grand Canyon Village at Mather Point, orients you to many facets of the site, and it's an excellent place for gathering information, whether you're interested in escapist treks or group tours. If you'd like a little exercise and great overlooks of the canyon, it's an easy hike from the back of the visitors center to the El Tovar Hotel. Walk through a pretty wooded area for about ½ mi; from there the path runs along the rim for another ½ mi or so.

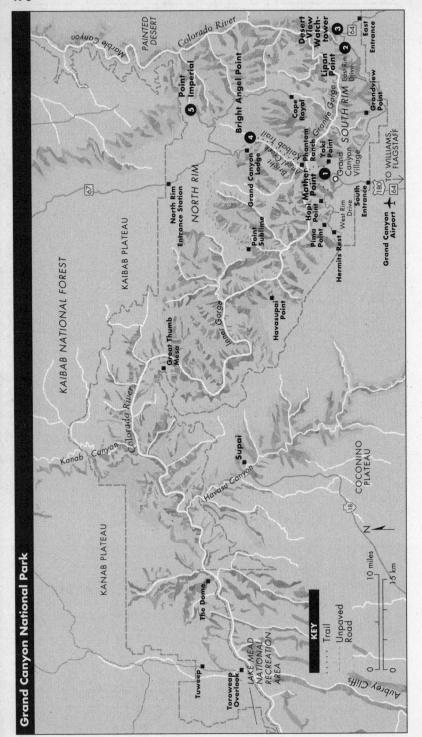

Grand Canyon National Park

The **East Rim Drive,** relatively uncluttered by cars and tour buses, also affords some beautiful views of the canyon and the raging river. The 23-mi, 45-minute (one-way) drive along the East Rim takes you past **②** **Lipan Point,** the widest and perhaps most spectacular part of the canyon, and continues to where you'll see partially intact ancient rock dwellings. On East Rim Drive, you'll find **Tusayan Ruin and Museum,** which has educational exhibits about various Native American tribes who have inhabited the region in the past 2,000 years. East Rim Drive **③** dead-ends at the East Rim Entrance Station and the 70-ft **Desert View Watchtower,** which clings precariously to the lip of the chasm.

The **West Rim Drive** runs 8 mi west from Grand Canyon Village to Hermits Rest. Along this tree-lined, two-lane drive are several scenic overlooks with panoramic views of the inner canyon—all of which are popular sunset destinations. The road is closed to automobile traffic from March through November, but you can catch the free shuttle bus at the West Rim Interchange near Bright Angel Lodge every 15 minutes 7:30 AM–sunset. The shuttle stops at all eight canyon overlooks on the 8-mi trip out to Hermits Rest, but only stops at Mohave and Hopi Points on the inbound leg. A complete round-trip takes 90 minutes.

Dining and Lodging

$$$–$$$$ ✕🏠 **El Tovar Hotel.** Built in 1905 of native stone and heavy pine logs, El Tovar is reminiscent of a grand European hunting lodge. Like all the lodges at the South Rim, the hotel is operated by Amfac Parks & Resorts Company. For decades the hotel's restaurant (**$$–$$$$**) has served fine food in a classic 19th-century room of hand-hewn logs and beamed ceilings. ✉ *Grand Canyon Village, AZ, 86023,* ☎ *303/297– 2757 (reservations only); 520/638–2631, Ext. 6384 (direct to hotel, no reservations),* FAX *303/297–3175 (reservations only); 520/638–9810 (direct to hotel, no reservations),* WEB *www.grandcanyonlodges.com. 70 rooms, 10 suites. Dining room, room service, bar. AE, D, DC, MC, V.*

$–$$$$ ✕🏠 **Bright Angel Lodge.** Built in 1936, this log-and-stone structure a few yards from the canyon rim has rooms in the main lodge or in quaint cabins (some with fireplaces) scattered among the pines. The informal steak house overlooks the abyss. ✉ *Grand Canyon Village, AZ 86023,* ☎ *303/ 297–2757 (reservations only); 520/638–2631, Ext. 6284 (direct to hotel, no reservations),* FAX *303/297–3175 (reservations only); 520/638–9810 (direct to hotel, no reservations),* WEB *www.grandcanyonlodges.com. 11 rooms with bath, 13 rooms with ½ bath, 6 rooms with shared bath, 42 cabins with bath. Restaurant, coffee shop, hair salon, bar. AE, D, DC, MC, V.*

$–$$$ 🏠 **Grand Canyon National Park Lodges.** The five Amfac properties— Maswik Lodge, Yavapai Lodge, Moqui Lodge, Kachina Lodge, and Thunderbird Lodge—on the South Rim are all comfortable, if not luxurious. The setting, rather than the amenities, is the draw here. Moqui is on U.S. 180, just outside the park, while the others are in Grand Canyon Village. Amfac also operates Phantom Ranch, 11 rustic wood-hewn cabins along Bright Angel Creek on the river's north side that are the only lodging facilities below the canyon's rim. ✉ *Grand Canyon Village, AZ 86023,* ☎ *303/297–2757 (reservations only),* FAX *303/ 297–3175 (reservations only),* WEB *www.grandcanyonlodges.com. 855 rooms. Restaurant, 2 cafeterias. AE, D, DC, MC, V.*

North Rim

④ At the North Rim, the trail to **Bright Angel Point,** one of the most awe-inspiring overlooks on either rim, starts on the grounds of the Grand Canyon Lodge and proceeds along the crest of a point of rocks that juts into the canyon for several hundred yards. The walk is only 1 mi round-trip, but it's an exciting trek because there are sheer drops just a few feet away on each side of the trail.

The road to Point Imperial and Cape Royal intersects Highway 67 about 3 mi north of Grand Canyon Lodge. The picture-perfect road winds 8 mi through stands of quaking aspen into a forest of unkempt conifers.

❺ When the road forks, continue 3 mi north to **Point Imperial**—the views of the eastern canyon and Painted Desert are spectacular at sunrise.

Dining and Lodging

$$–$$$ ✕🏠 **Grand Canyon Lodge.** This historic stone structure, built in 1928, has comfortable, though not luxurious, rooms. The lounge area, with hardwood floors and high, beamed ceilings, has a spectacular view of the canyon through massive plate-glass windows. Surprisingly sophisticated fare is served in the huge dining room. ✉ *North Rim, AZ 86052,* ☎ *303/297–2757 (reservations only); 520/638–2611 (direct to hotel, no reservations),* FAX *303/297–3175 (reservations only); 520/638–2554 (direct to hotel, no reservations),* WEB *www.grandcanyonnorthrim. com. 40 rooms, 161 cabins. Dining room, cafeteria, bar, store, laundry facilities, no-smoking rooms. AE, D, MC, V.*

$ 🏠 **Kaibab Lodge.** In a wooded setting just 5 mi from the North Rim entrance, this 1920s property contains rustic cabins with simple furnishings. When you're not out gazing into the abyss, you can sit around a stone fireplace (it can be chilly up here in spring and early fall). The lodge is open mid-May to mid-October. ✉ *AZ 67, HC 64, Box 30, Fredonia, AZ 86022,* ☎ *928/638–2389 (reservations for summer); 928/526–0924 (reservations for winter); 800/525–0924,* WEB *www. canyoneers.com. 29 cabin-style units; limited group quarters available. Restaurant, store. D, MC, V.*

Grand Canyon A to Z

To research prices, get advice from other travelers, and book travel arrangements, visit www.fodors.com.

CAR TRAVEL

It's a little less than 300 mi to the South Rim from Las Vegas. Take U.S. 93 to Kingman, Arizona; I–40 east from Kingman to Williams; then Highway 64 and U.S. 180 to the edge of the abyss. The South Rim is a long, 210-mi drive from the North Rim (if the Park Service were ever to build a bridge across the canyon, the North Rim would be a mere half-hour drive from the South Rim). The North Rim is about 275 mi from Las Vegas. Take I–15 east to Hurricane, Utah; Highways 59 and 389 to Fredonia; and U.S. 89 and Highway 67 to the North Rim.

TOURS

Air Vegas, Scenic Airlines and Grand Canyon Tour Company offer air tours of the Grand Canyon from Las Vegas; each provides ground transportation around the South Rim, stopping at spectacular scenic overlooks and Grand Canyon Village. You can also take a helicopter tour with any of the four Las Vegas–based companies that take you out over Hoover Dam and Lake Mead for a thrilling trip that can last from two to four hours. The chopper ride is a once-in-a-lifetime experience.

➤ AIR TOURS: **Air Vegas** (☎ 702/736–3599, 800/255–7474, WEB www. airvegas.com). **Grand Canyon Tour Company** (☎ 702/655–6060, 800/222–6966, WEB www.grandcanyontourcompany.com). **HeliUSA** (☎ 702/736–8787, 800/359–8727, WEB www.heliusa.net). **Maverick Helicopter Tours** (☎ 702/261–0007, 800/261–4414, WEB www.maverickhelicopter. com). **Papillon** (☎ 702/736–7243, 888/635–7272, WEB www.papillon. com). **Scenic Airlines** (☎ 702/638–3300, 800/634–6801, WEB www.

scenic.com). **Sundance Helicopter** (☎ 702/736–0606, 800/653–1881, WEB www.helicoptour.com).

VISITOR INFORMATION

➤ CONTACTS: **Grand Canyon Chamber of Commerce** (✉ Box 3007, Grand Canyon, AZ, 86023, ☎ 928/527–0359, WEB www.grandcanyonchamber.org). **Grand Canyon National Park Visitors Services** (✉ Box 129, Grand Canyon, AZ 86023, ☎ 928/638–7888 for recorded information, FAX 928/638–7797, WEB www.nps.gov/grca). **Kane County Office of Tourism** (✉ 78 S. 100 E, Kanab, UT 84741, ☎ 435/644–5033 or 800/733–5263, WEB www.kaneutah.com).

SOUTHWESTERN UTAH

This distant corner of Utah attracts people with the promise of warm weather—so much so that the largest city in the area, St. George, is also one of the state's fastest-growing communities. In addition to the enviable climate, the area offers a wealth of scenic wonders, from desert to sierra, and boundless opportunities to hike, bike, and tee off.

St. George, Utah

116 mi north of Las Vegas on I–15.

Three hundred Mormon families were sent from Salt Lake City to St. George in 1861 to grow cotton; the town was named after the group's leader, George A. Smith. The colony faced many hardships, among them disease, drought, and floods. After the completion of the transcontinental railroad in 1869 made their cotton farms insignificant, the settlers stayed on and built a red sandstone tabernacle.

In St. George you'll find an assortment of low-price motels, B&B inns, an old movie theater and a twinplex, souvenir shops, restaurants, Mormon historical sites, and red rocks. On a wintertime visit you might encounter snow, and in summer you can expect temperatures cooler than those in Las Vegas. An evening in St. George can be spent exploring the Victorian-style streets, climbing the red-rock cliffs, or looking out over the town.

The **St. George Temple** was completed in 1877 and is still in use today. From 1873 until his death five years later, Brigham Young spent his winters in a home he had built here. The visitors center offers free tours of the temple grounds and the winter home. ✉ *250 E. 400 S,* ☎ *435/673–5181.* ☉ *Daily 9–9.*

The **St. George Chamber of Commerce** is housed in the lovingly maintained Washington County Courthouse, built of adobe brick in 1876. The chamber's friendly and knowledgeable staff can help shape plans for touring the area.

Dining and Lodging

$ ✕ **Panama Grill.** The owners of Basilia's, a Greek and Italian restaurant, opted for a change of pace and a change of menu—to Mexican fare. Two of the most popular entrées are fish tacos and pork enchiladas. Dine indoors, amid exposed adobe brick walls, dark wood, and Mexican rugs, or outside, where the evening sun bathes the surrounding red cliffs. ✉ *Ancestor Sq., 2 W. St. George Blvd.,* ☎ *435/673–7671. MC, V.*

$–$$$ ⌂ **Greene Gate Village Historic Bed & Breakfast Inn.** This collection of nine vintage homes offers elegantly comfortable accommodations in historic downtown St. George, complete with such eclectic touches as massive antique beds and historic photographs mingled with the mod-

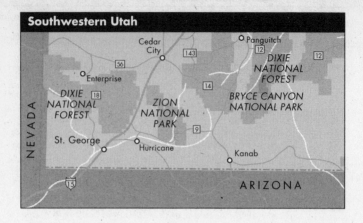

ern convenience of showers and whirlpool baths. There is no smoking in the rooms, and a full breakfast is included. ⊠ *76 W. Tabernacle St., 84770,* ☎ *435/628–6999 or 800/350–6999,* FAX *435/628–6989,* WEB *www.greengate.com. 20 rooms. Pool, hot tub; no smoking. AE, D, MC, V. BP.*

$$ ⌂ **Ramada Inn.** This hotel may very well be the nicest in St. George. The rooms and furnishings are up-to-date and comfortable. ⊠ *1440 E. St. George Blvd., 84770,* ☎ *435/628–2828 or 888/298–2054,* FAX *435/628–0505,* WEB *www.the.ramada.com/stgeorge00611. 136 rooms. Pool, hot tub, meeting room. AE, D, DC, V.*

Zion National Park

46 mi northeast of St. George; follow I–15 to first Hurricane exit, which will take you through the small town of that name. Driving up the mountain, you'll see signs directing you into the 6-mi park drive among mammoth red rocks.

The red rocks of St. George are only a preview of the wonderland of vividly hued canyons and monumental monoliths to be seen at Zion National Park. In 1863 the Mormons believed they had found God's country when they discovered the area, which was first established as Mukuntuweap National Monument in 1909. It became Zion National Park a decade later. Now the 229-square-mi park welcomes more than 2.5 million visitors annually. Most of these are accommodated in Springdale, at the park's main entrance on Highway 9 (30 mi from I–15). Although the road through town is lined with motels, restaurants, and shops, Springdale is still appealing, due mostly to the clearly visible formations of Zion in the background.

Inside the park, front and center is **Zion Canyon,** which contains the park's main road (a 6½-mi scenic drive), a historic lodge, and a visitor center. From March through September you must use the park's transportation system. (Guests staying at the park's lodge may use their own vehicles.) The bus makes one loop in the park with nine stops and a second loop in Springdale with six stops. You can also bike or hike into this section of the park. The east side of Zion is still accessible by private car. Some 2,500 ft deep, Zion Canyon is rimmed by such naturally sculpted landmarks as the **Sentinel, East Temple,** the **Temple of Sinawava,** and the **Great White Throne.** At road's end is the **Gateway to the Narrows.** As its name suggests, the Narrows is a slender passageway, in places only a couple of dozen feet wide, carved by the Virgin River. A paved, 1-mi-long trail heads into the abyss, but hikers often wade up the stream beyond. Hikes to the **Emerald Pools** are similarly worthwhile. The trailhead is across the road from the lodge. It is 1¼-mi round-trip on an easy trail to the lower Emerald Pools. The middle pools are reached by a moderately strenuous 2-mi loop. The upper pools are difficult to reach; inquire at the visitor center for specific directions. ⊠ *Zion National Park, Hwy. 9, Springdale, UT 84767,* ☎ *435/772–3256,* WEB *www.nps.gov/zion.* ⊑ *$20 per vehicle or $10 per individual for 7-day pass.* ⊘ *Visitor centers June–Aug., daily 8–7; Sept.–May, daily 8–5.*

Dining and Lodging

$$ ✕ **Bit and Spur Restaurant and Saloon.** This eatery serves innovative
★ and healthful southwestern-style Mexican food. Works by local artists fill the pine-panel interior, while the patio is awash in bright flowers and scents from the herb garden. ⊠ *1212 Zion Park Blvd., Springdale,* ☎ *435/772–3498. MC, V. No lunch.*

$$ ✕ **Bumbleberry Inn.** This combination motel-restaurant serves up a lodg-
★ ing-dining experience that can't be beat. Stumble on in and have any number of breakfast and pastry dishes featuring Springdale's world-famous bumbleberry. Legend has it the tasty burple and binkel berry comes from the giggle bush, which is why a piece of bumbleberry pie is something to relish (à la mode is even better). ⊠ *SR- 9, Springdale 84767,* ☎ *435/772–3611. D, MC, V. Closed Sun.*

$$$ ⊞ **Cliffrose Lodge and Gardens.** Acres of lawn, trees, and gardens surround the low, rambling stucco wings of this hotel on the banks of the Virgin River, ¼ mi from Zion. Desert hues decorate the ample rooms. ⊠ *281 Zion Park Blvd. (Box 510), Springdale 84767,* ☎ *435/772–3234 or 800/243–8824,* FAX *435/772–3900,* WEB *www.cliffroselodge.com. 36 rooms. Pool. AE, D, MC, V.*

$$ ⊞ **Novel House Inn at Zion.** Watchman Mountain overlooks this B&B inn just a mile from the Zion Canyon entrance. Each of the rooms is named after a noted novelist (Mark Twain, Louis L'Amour, and Jane Austen to name a few) and decorated accordingly. The Mark Twain Room includes a writing desk, riverboat queen bed, old-fashioned rocking chairs, and wash stand. Breakfast and English-style afternoon tea are served in the dining room every day. No smoking is allowed inside. ⊠ *73 Paradise Rd., Springdale 84767,* ☎ *435/772–3650 or 800/711–8400,* WEB *www.novelhouse.com. 10 rooms. Dining room, library; no smoking. AE, D, MC, V.*

Bryce Canyon National Park

From Zion National Park, head east on Hwy. 9 to Hwy. 89 and turn north. Drive about 40 mi to Hwy. 12, turn east, and another 17 mi will bring you into the park.

Bryce Canyon National Park may seem like the prehistoric world of the Flintstones. As at Zion, red is a dominant color here, but brilliant, iridescent hues of buff and tan also appear on the fantastically shaped rocks—resembling spires, cathedrals, goblins—sculpted by the waters and weather of several million years and visible from many overlooks along the park's 35 mi of paved road.

Not actually a canyon, Bryce Canyon is a set of amphitheaters carved into the eastern rim of the Paunsaugunt Plateau. Among the stunning sights are the **Silent City**, named for the eerie rock profiles and figures, and the "chessmen" of **Queen's Garden.** At dawn and dusk the sun casts an unusual glow on these rock formations, making Bryce many folks' favorite of Utah's national parks. Because it's nearly 8,000 ft above sea level, the area becomes a winter wonderland for cross-country skiers. The **Rim Trail** has nonstop scenery, while the **Fairyland Loop** and **Queen's Garden** trails lead hikers among the park's hoodoos.

Most of the activity at Bryce occurs below the trail entrances, at the foot of the canyons. The park's hiking trails can be explored in wintertime on snowshoes or cross-country skis. To ease the auto crunch, there are three shuttle lines—the Blue, Red, and Green—that provide service inside and outside the park on a voluntary basis from mid-May to late September. The Blue line starts outside at the Shuttle Parking Area and travels to the visitor center. Once inside, the Red line runs every 10 to 15 minutes and will ferry you throughout the highly popular park. The Green line travels to the south end of the park on a first-come, first-served basis and requires reservations one day in advance. Bryce officials anticipate starting a separate shuttle to Tropic (10 mi south from the park entrance on SR 12) where you'll find the closest concentration of lodging and restaurants outside the park. For the latest details, call the park. The $15 shuttle fare includes admission to the park (a $5 saving on the usually $20 entrance fee). ⊠ *Bryce Canyon National Park, Bryce Canyon, UT 84717,* ☎ *435/834–5322 or 888/ 362–2642,* WEB *www.nps.gov/brca.* ⌨ *$20 per vehicle for 7-day pass.* ⊙ *Visitor center daily 8–8, but seasonally variable.*

Dining and Lodging

$$–$$$ ✕☷ **Best Western Ruby's Inn.** Just north of the park entrance and housing a large restaurant and gift shop, this is Grand Central Terminal for visitors to Bryce. A nightly rodeo takes place nearby. Rooms vary in age, as sprawling wings were added to the hotel as the park gained popularity. All the guest rooms are comfortable and attractive, however, and there are camping and RV facilities available. The "southwestern chic" lobby, centered between the gift shop and restaurant, has roughhewn log beams and poles. ⊠ *Hwy. 63, Bryce Canyon, UT 84764,* ☎ *435/834–5341 or 866/866–6616,* FAX *435/834–5265,* WEB *www.rubysinn. com. 368 rooms, 2 suites. Restaurant, indoor pool, hot tub, shop, laundry facilities. AE, D, DC, MC, V.*

$$–$$$ ☷ **Bryce Canyon Lodge.** Inside the park, this historic property, designed by Stanley Gilbert Underwood for the Union Pacific Railroad and built in the mid-1920s, is a few feet from rim views. A National Historic Landmark, the lodge has been faithfully restored, right down to the lobby's huge limestone fireplace, log and wrought-iron chandelier, and bark-covered hickory furniture, which was built by the same company that produced the originals. There's a choice of motel-style rooms with balconies or porches; suites on the lodge's second level; or cozy lodgepole-pine cabins, some with cathedral ceilings and gas fireplaces. The place books up fast—try to reserve at least six months in advance. ⊠ *1 Bryce Canyon Lodge, Bryce Canyon, UT 84720,* ☎ *435/834– 5361 (direct to lodge); 303/297–2757 for reservations,* FAX *303/297– 3175,* WEB *www.amfac.com. 70 rooms, 40 cabins. Restaurant, hiking, laundry facilities, no smoking rooms. AE, D, MC, V. Closed Nov.–Mar..*

DEATH VALLEY, CALIFORNIA

With more than 3.3 million acres, **Death Valley National Park** is the largest national park outside Alaska. The topography of Death Valley is a mini geology lesson. Two hundred million years ago, seas covered the area, depositing layers of sediment and fossils. Between 35 million and 5 million years ago, faults in the Earth's crust and volcanic activity pushed and folded the ground, causing mountain ranges to rise and the valley floor to drop. The valley was then filled periodically by lakes, which eroded the surrounding rocks into fantastic formations and deposited the salts that now cover the floor of the basin. Today the area has 14 square mi of sand dunes, 200 square mi of crusty salt flats, hills, 11,000-ft mountains, and canyons of many colors. There are more than 1,000

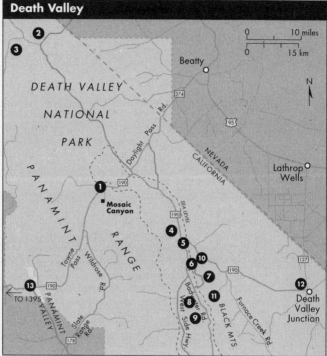

Death Valley

species of plants and trees—21 of which are unique to the valley, such as the yellow Panamint daisy and the blue-flowered Death Valley sage. Distances are deceiving here: some sights appear in clusters, but others require extensive travel. As with any desert travel, especially as the months get hotter, you should always carry plenty of water, sunblock, a hat, a mirror, and other potential lifesaving items—just in case. Fees of $10 per vehicle, collected at the park's entrance stations and at the visitor center at Furnace Creek, grant entrance for seven days.

Numbers in the margin correspond to numbers on the Death Valley map.

Stovepipe Wells Village

Stovepipe Wells Village was the first resort in Death Valley. The tiny town, which dates back to 1926, takes its name from the stovepipe that early prospectors left to indicate that they'd found water. The area contains a motel, a restaurant, a grocery store with unleaded fuel, a landing strip, and campgrounds. Located just minutes away are the world-famous sand dunes that "starred" in the *Star Wars* movies; Devil's Corn Field; Salt Creek, a brackish, salty year-round flow from underground springs that provides a breeding ground for the endangered pupfish; and colorful Mosaic Canyon.

Dining and Lodging

$$ ✕ Stovepipe Wells Village. An aircraft landing strip is an unusual touch for a motel, as is a heated mineral pool, but the rest is pretty standard. Still, this is the best lodging bargain inside the park, offering pleasant rooms at a reasonable rate, as well as a campground and RV park. The Old West—style Toll Road restaurant ($$) offers steakhouse fare—steaks, prime rib, salmon. The adjoining Badwater Saloon provides the park's only nightlife outside that in Furnace Creek. ⌧ *Hwy. 190, Death Valley National Park 92328,* ☎ *760/786–2387,* FAX *760/*

786–2389, WEB *www.stovepipewells.com. 83 rooms. Restaurant, tennis courts, pool, bar, shop, Internet. AE, D, MC, V.*

Scotty's Castle Area

2 *46 mi north of Stovepipe Wells Village; head east on Hwy. 190, then north at signs for castle.*

Scotty's Castle is an odd apparition rising out of a canyon. This $2.5-million Moorish mansion, begun in 1924 and never completed, is named after Walter Scott, better known as Death Valley Scotty. An ex-cowboy, prospector, and performer in Buffalo Bill's Wild West Show, Scotty always told people the castle was his, financed by gold from a secret mine. That secret mine was, in fact, a Chicago millionaire named Albert Johnson, who was advised by doctors to spend time in a warm, dry climate. The house, which functioned for a while as a hotel—guests included Bette Davis and Norman Rockwell—contains works of art, imported carpets, handmade European furniture, and a tremendous pipe organ. Costumed rangers portray life at the castle in 1939. Fifty-minute tours are conducted frequently, but waits of up to two hours are possible. Try to arrive for the first tour of the day, which will guarantee short lines following a traffic-free drive through desert country. ☏ 760/786–2392, WEB *www.nps.gov/deva/pphtml/facilities.html.* 🎫 *$8.* ☉ *Grounds daily 7:30–6, tours daily 9–5.*

3 The impressive **Ubehebe Crater,** 500 ft deep and ½ mi across, was created as a result of violent underground steam and gas explosions about 3,000 years ago; its volcanic ash spreads out over most of the area, and the cinders are as thick as 150 ft around the crater's rim. You'll get some superb views of the valley from here, and you can take a fairly easy hike around the rim at the west side to Little Hebe Crater, one of a smaller cluster of craters to the south and west. It's always a bit windy on this rise 8 mi northwest of Scotty's Castle; hold on to your hat.

Furnace Creek Area

54 mi south of Scotty's Castle, 25 mi southeast of Stovepipe Wells Village on Hwy. 190.

4 Renowned mule teams hauled borax from the **Harmony Borax Works** to the railroad town of Mojave, 165 mi away, and were truly a sight to behold: 20 mules hitched up to two massive wagons, each carrying a load of 10 tons of borax through burning desert. The teams plied the route between 1884 and 1907, when the railroad finally arrived in Zabriskie. The **Borax Museum,** 2 mi south of the borax works, houses original mining machinery and historical displays in a building that once served as a boardinghouse for miners; the adjacent structure is the original mule-team barn. ☒ *Harmony Borax Works Rd., west off Hwy. 190.* 🎫 *Free.* ☉ *Borax works daily, museum weekends.*

5 Exhibits on the desert, trail maps, and brochures can be found at the **Visitor Center at Furnace Creek.** ☒ *Hwy. 190,* ☏ *760/786–3200,* WEB *www.nps.gov/deva.* ☉ *Daily 8–5.*

6 **Golden Canyon** is named for the glowing color of its walls. A mild hike into this spacious landform affords some spectacular views of yellow and orange rock. Farther up the canyon, you'll encounter a colorful formation called Red Cathedral. ☒ *Badwater Rd., 3 mi south of Furnace Creek; turn left into parking lot.*

★ **7** The **Artists Palette,** named for the brilliant array of pigments created by volcanic deposits, is one of the most magnificent sights in Death Valley. Artists Drive, the approach to the area, heads one-way north off Badwater Road, so if you're visiting Badwater it's more efficient to come here on the way back. The drive winds through foothills composed of colorful sedimentary and volcanic rocks. ⊠ *8 mi north of Badwater, Badwater Rd. to Artists Dr.; 10 mi south of Furnace Creek, Hwy. 190 to Badwater Rd. to Artists Dr.*

8 Looking like peaks of whipped chocolate meringue, **Devil's Golf Course** actually is solid mud-color rock salt poking skyward. You don't want to venture off the road or turnaround because the jagged spires have been known to shred tennis shoes and produce severe scrapes and broken bones when you take a tumble. ⊠ *Badwater Rd., 5 mi north of Badwater, 14 mi south of visitor center at Furnace Creek.*

9 As you approach **Badwater,** you'll see a shallow pool lying almost lifeless against an expanse of desolate salt flats—a sharp contrast to the expansive canyons and elevation not too far away. Here's the legend: one of the early surveyors saw that his mule wouldn't drink from the pool and noted "badwater" on his map. Badwater is the lowest spot in the Western Hemisphere—282 ft below sea level—and also one of the hottest. The water contains mostly sodium chloride and is saltier than the sea. ⊠ *Badwater Rd., 19 mi south of visitor center at Furnace Creek.*

10 **Zabriskie Point** is one of Death Valley National Park's most scenic spots. Not particularly high—only about 710 ft—it overlooks a striking badlands panorama with wrinkled, multicolor hills. Film buffs of a certain vintage may recognize it (or at least its name) from the film *Zabriskie Point* by the Italian director Michelangelo Antonioni. ⊠ *Hwy. 190, 5 mi south of Furnace Creek.*

★ **11** **Dante's View** is more than 5,000 ft up in the Black Mountains. In the dry desert air you can see most of the valley's 110-mi expanse. The oasis of Furnace Creek is a green spot to the north. The view up and down is equally astounding: the tiny blackish patch far below is Badwater; on the western horizon is Mt. Whitney, the highest spot in the continental United States, at 14,494 ft. ⊠ *Dante's View Rd. off Hwy. 190, 21 mi south of Zabriskie Point.*

12 **Marta Beckett's Amargosa Opera House** is an unexpected pleasure in an unlikely place. Marta Beckett is an artist and dancer from New York who first saw the town of Amargosa while on tour in 1964. Three years later she came back and on impulse decided to buy a boarded-up theater amid a complex of run-down Spanish colonial buildings. Today the population is still in single digits (cats outnumber people here), but it swells when cars, motor homes, and buses roll in to catch the show Beckett has been presenting for nearly 30 years. To compensate for the sparse crowds her show attracted in the early days, Becket painted herself an audience, turning the walls and ceiling of the theater into a trompe l'oeil masterpiece. Now she often performs her blend of classical ballet, mime, and 19th-century melodrama to sell-out crowds, so advance reservations are strongly encouraged. After the show you can meet her in the adjacent art gallery, where she sells her paintings and autographs her posters and books. ⊠ *Hwy. 127, Death Valley Junction, California 92328,* ☎ *760/852–4441,* ℻ *760/852–4138,* 🕸 *www.amargosa-opera-house.com.* 🎫 *$15.* ☉ *Performances Oct.–May; 8:15 PM. MC, V.*

Dining and Lodging

$$$$ ✕🏨 **Furnace Creek Inn.** This historic stone structure tumbling down the side of a hill is something of a desert oasis; the creek meanders through its beautifully landscaped gardens, and the pool is spring-fed. All rooms have views of the lush grounds and scenic surroundings; fewer than half have balconies. Rates here drop in the summer. The Inn Din-

ing Room (**$$–$$$**), the best restaurant for miles, has white stucco walls, lace tablecloths, two fireplaces, and many windows with views of the Panamint Mountains. The seasonally changing menu has New American fare: seared *ahi* tuna and fire-roasted corn chowder might be available as starters; main-course options might include sesame-crusted salmon or medallions of veal; a few vegetarian entrées are usually available as well. The wine list is extensive. ✉ *Hwy. 190 (Box 1), Death Valley National Park 92328,* ☎ *760/786–2345 or 303/297–2757;* FAX *760/786–2514,* WEB *www.furnacecreekresort.com. 66 rooms. Restaurant, 4 tennis courts, pool, bar, meeting room. Energy surcharge. AE, DC, MC, V.*

$$–$$$$ 🏨 **Furnace Creek Ranch.** This was originally the crew headquarters for a borax company, the activities of which the on-site Borax Museum details. Four two-story buildings adjacent to the golf course have motel-type rooms that are good for families. The general store on the ranch sells supplies and gifts. The visitors center is a short walk away. At 218 ft below sea level, the Furnace Creek golf course guarantees you'll play your "lowest" round of golf there. ✉ *Hwy. 190 (Box 1), Death Valley National Park 92328,* ☎ *760/786–2345 or 303/297–2757,* FAX *760/786–2514,* WEB *www.furnacecreekresort.com. 224 rooms. Restaurant, coffee shop, 18-hole golf course, 2 tennis courts, pool, basketball, horseback riding, bar, playground, meeting room. Energy surcharge. AE, D, MC, V.*

Panamint Springs Area

🔟⃣③ *31 mi west of Stovepipe Wells Village on Hwy. 190, 48 miles east of Lone Pine, California on U.S. Hwy. 395.*

Added to the park in 1994, the remoteness of this quaint and quiet spot makes it a perfect stop for backcountry enthusiasts, especially if you have a high-clearance or four-wheel-drive vehicle. To the east and south on Emigrant Canyon Road is Skidoo, the remains of a once-thriving mining town, and Wildrose Charcoal Kilns, which produced fuel for silver ore processing more than 125 years ago, yet still faintly smells of smoke. To the west lies Father Crowley Point, a lava-filled landscape that looks out on the colorful Rainbow Canyon. Four miles farther west take a right turn on gravel-paved Saline Valley Road and head north about 6 mi to Lee Flat where the finest stands of tree-size yucca in the park grow. Just outside town is Darwin Falls, a rare water hole in the arid desert, which flows constantly 365 days a year.

Dining and Lodging

$–$$$ ✕🏨 **Panamint Springs Resort.** Though inside the park, this privately owned property is not associated with the National Park Service. It overlooks the nearby awesome geological formations as well as the Panamint Valley Sand Dunes. A campground and RV park are available. Chef Gil, a fixture at the resort, prepares great homemade food. Summertime barbecues are served outdoors on the porch overlooking a spectacular view of Panamint Valley. Breakfast, lunch, and dinner are served year round. ✉ *Hwy. 190, Box 395, Ridgecrest, CA 93556,* ☎ *775/482–7680,* FAX *775/482–7682,* WEB *www.deathvalley.com/reserve/reserve.shtml. 14 rooms, 1 cottage. Restaurant, bar, store. MC, V.*

10 PLAYING THE GAMES

To a gambler, luck is the ultimate authority. No guardian angel or guiding light; no god or goddess; no religion, science, or philosophy can sway the outcome of a chance event. Gambling is a means by which we strip away our orthodox certainties in order to summon up the deep human instinct to appeal to chance as the ultimate source of control. Strictly speaking, however, casinos don't offer pure games of chance because each gives itself a little edge. It's up to us players to counteract that edge whenever we can. Here's how.

By Deke
Castleman

Revised by Bill
Burton

O VER THE PAST 60 YEARS the name Las Vegas has become synonymous with gambling. Nine out of 10 visitors gamble while they're in town. It is almost perverse to visit Las Vegas and *not* gamble. But while unreasonable expectations can lead to disappointment or, worse still, the loss of a lot of money, the key to having a good time is to approach the casinos with the idea that, contrary to popular opinion, you *can* win or, at the very least, get much more than your money's worth of playing time. Your success depends less on being lucky than on being familiar with the rules of the games, being aware of the concepts *behind* the games, and being conversant with the strategies that enable you to play not only with confidence but also with a fair shot at walking away a winner.

CASINO STRATEGY

The House Advantage

The first important concept to understand about gambling in Las Vegas is that the odds for all the games provide an advantage for the casino ("house"), generally known, appropriately enough, as the "house advantage" (or "edge" or "vigorish"). The casino is a business, and wagering is its product. Because the house establishes the rules, procedures, and payoffs on every game, it builds an automatic commission into every bet to ensure a profit margin.

Here's how it works. Let's pretend that I'm the house and you're the customer and we're betting on a series of coin flips. The deal that I make with you is that every time the coin lands heads up, I win and you pay me a dollar. Every time the coin lands tails up, you win—but I only pay you 90¢. The law of averages maintains that out of every 100 coin tosses, heads will win 50 times and tails will win the other 50. If I take a dime out of every one of your winning payoffs, the longer you play, the more dimes will wind up in my pocket. If you started with a $50 bankroll, after 1,000 tosses, *even if you win half of them,* you'd be busted out. (Because it requires two trials—win one, lose one—for the house to make its 10¢ "commission," your "negative expectation," or house edge, in this example is 5%.)

The second important gambling concept is known as "fluctuation" (or "variance"). In plain English, we're talking about "luck." Looking at our coin-toss game through the lens of averages, if you and I flip a coin 1,000 times, it's reasonable to expect that the coin will land heads up and tails up close to 500 times each. However, if we flip the coin only 10 times, it's conceivable that the coin could land heads up only once or twice or as many as eight or even 10 times. Now let's say that we made the same betting deal as above but we limited the number of tosses to 10. This would largely eliminate your 5% disadvantage and leave it up to "the luck of the toss"—in other words, the fluctuation. Thus, a short-term fluctuation in the law of averages eliminates the long-term threat of the negative expectation.

How do these concepts—the house advantage and negative expectation, and the short-term fluctuation—apply to the choices that you make as a casino customer? Your decisions, based on these concepts, will determine not only what you play, but also how you play; how long you play; and, ultimately, how well you play.

Luck Versus the Edge

The average "bankroll" (cash carried for the sole purpose of gambling) of a Las Vegas visitor who plans to spend some time in the casino is roughly $500. This is a crucial statistic. The amount of your bankroll and your preferred style of "action" (how you risk your bankroll) define your relationship to luck and the house edge.

Basically, the parameters of gambling action are fast and slow. Some people, though they're in the minority, like their action fast and loose and high-risk; these are true "gamblers," in the old-fashioned sense of the word. The extreme version of this type of action is to take the whole $500 bankroll and lay it down on a single play—say, red or black on the roulette table. The odds are not quite even. The green 0 and 00 on the roulette table give the house an advantage of 5.26% (☞ Roulette). Still, even though the odds are less than fair, the immediate result will be the same: double or nothing.

Making one play eliminates both the law of averages and the long-term threat of the house advantage; here you rely solely on the luck of the draw. If you want to go on a roller-coaster ride of luck, with a minute or so of adrenaline-pumping, heart-pounding excitement, lay it all down at once. In a matter of moments, you'll either have twice the money you arrived with or none of it.

A less extreme version of this wild ride is to break your bankroll into two units, and make two bets. Here you can either double your money, lose it all, or break even. Similarly, if you separate your $500 bankroll into five units and make five bets, or 10 units and make 10 bets, your ride lasts a little longer and your outcome is a little less black and white: You can double, bust out, break even, or come out somewhat ahead or behind. Still, the cumulative danger of the house advantage barely comes into play.

Luck can supersede the house advantage, but only in the short run. And though luck accounts for winners big and small—such as the local cocktail waitress who, in January 2000, lined up three Megabucks symbols on the $3 payline to win $35 million, or the $2 dice shooter who parlays a hot hand into a couple of hundred bucks—the lack of luck can obliterate a bankroll faster than a crooked S&L.

Besides, most people who come to Las Vegas like to gamble for as long as they can without running out of money. These people take their $500 bankrolls and split them into 100 units to make $5 bets, 250 units for $2 bets, 500 units for $1 bets, or even 2,000 units for 25¢ bets. This guarantees plenty of time for the law of averages to even out the fluctuations. On the other hand, it puts the house advantage and the negative expectation right back into the game.

So how do you play as long as you like without the certainty of the house advantage grinding your bankroll into dust?

The Good Bets

The first part of any viable casino strategy is to risk the most money on wagers that present the lowest edge for the house. Blackjack, craps, video poker, and baccarat are the most advantageous to the bettor in this regard. The two types of bets at baccarat have a house advantage of a little more than 1%. The basic line bets at craps, if backed up with full odds, can have a house advantage of as low as 0.5%. Blackjack and video poker, at times, can not only put you even with the house (a true 50-50 proposition) but actually give you a slight long-term advantage.

How can a casino possibly provide you with a 50-50 or even a positive expectation at some of its games? First, because a vast number of suckers make the bad bets (those with a house advantage of 5%–35%, such as roulette, keno, and slots) day in and day out. Second, because the casino knows that very few people are aware of the opportunities to beat the odds. Third, because it takes skill—requiring study and practice—to be in a position to exploit these opportunities the casino presents. However, a mere hour or two spent learning strategies for the beatable games will put you light years ahead of the vast majority of visitors who give the gambling industry an average 12%–15% profit margin.

Comps, Clubs, and Coupons

Not only can you even out the odds to a certain extent, but you can also take advantage of the various attractive incentives casinos offer so that the suckers will stay and play—and, in the long run, lose, due either to house advantage or basic ignorance. These available, profitable, and somewhat prestigious incentives are known as "comps" (short for complimentaries) or "freebies." The most common comps are free parking in downtown parking structures (all you have to do is walk into the casino and validate your ticket at the cashier window) and free cocktails (all you have to do is play at any table or machine). Other comps range from a "line pass" (the right to proceed directly into a showroom or restaurant without having to wait in line) all the way to a penthouse suite complete with private swimming pool, butler, and chef, and round-trip airfare from anywhere in the world. It all depends on how much you're willing to risk: comps are calculated by multiplying your average bet by the amount of time you play by the house advantage.

Say, for example, that you play at a $25-a-hand blackjack table for eight hours. The casino expects you to participate in 60 hands an hour and lose at a rate of 2% (what the casino calculates as its average advantage). Sixty hands an hour times $25 a hand times eight hours times 2% equals $240. Of that anticipated profit, the house is prepared to return 30%–40% to you in complimentaries in order to "reward" you for your action. Thus, under the described circumstances, you'll qualify for $72–$96 worth of comps, whether you win, lose, or break even.

To be eligible for comps, you have to get "rated" as a player. When you sit down to play, have the dealer call over the pit boss—the person who supervises the action on the gaming tables—and tell him that you'd like to have your play rated. The pit boss will fill out a rating card with your name, average bet, and length of play. These data are input into the marketing department computer; based on your "comp equivalency" (for example, the $72–$96 you've qualified for), you'll be provided free food or room or perks. The kings of comps are the "high rollers," those willing to risk a lot of money at high-stakes games.

Slot clubs are another good way to reconcile the house advantage with playing for as long as you like. These clubs, introduced in the late 1980s to give slot and video poker players some high-roller status, are similar to frequent-flier programs offered by the airlines. It costs nothing to sign up for slot clubs and the benefits can be substantial. When you become a member, you're given a plastic card that you insert into the gaming machine you're using; the card tracks your play and you receive points based on the amount of money you risk. Slot-club points can be redeemed for free gifts, food, rooms, invitations to special parties and slot tournaments, VIP status, gift certificates at local stores, and cash. You can join slot clubs at as many casinos as you like, then play at the places that offer the best perks.

Finally, the best bet in any casino is one that is accompanied by a gambling coupon, known as a "lucky buck." These are most often found in hotel "funbooks," small coupon booklets given out free for the asking at casinos; generally all you need is a hotel room key and an out-of-state ID (this prevents locals from taking advantage of the valuable promotions). Most funbooks contain coupons that return 7 to 5, 3 to 2, even 2 to 1 on even-money wagers.

Playing with coupons gives you a decided advantage over the house. In our coin-toss example, you'd wager a dollar of your own and a coupon for another dollar. If you win, I'd pay you $2 (for a return of $3). That extra dollar, though it might not seem like much, would pay my commission on 10 additional coin tosses. Furthermore, because some of the major hotel-casinos and most of the smaller ones distribute free funbooks, you and a partner can collect a dozen of them and then go on a "coupon run." You make even-money bets backed up by coupons, touring a number of casinos while you're at it. Done properly, you could conceivably fill up an entire Las Vegas visit making positive plays with lucky bucks.

THE GAMES

Each of the casino games has its own rules, etiquette, odds, and strategies. When you've decided on the kind of action you wish to pursue, you can choose a game that best suits your style. Then, if you take the time to learn the basics and fine points thoroughly, you'll be adequately prepared to play with as much of an edge as the game, combined with comps and coupons if possible, provides. In the meantime, good short-term fluctuation can add to your winnings. Some of the casinos offer free lessons to teach you how to play the most popular casino games, including blackjack, craps, roulette, and mini-baccarat. These lessons are a good way to become familiar with the rules of the games and table etiquette.

 ## Baccarat

The most "glamorous" game in the casino, American baccarat (pronounced *bah*-kuh-rah), is a version of *chemin de fer,* popular in European gambling halls. The Italian word *baccara* means "zero"; this refers to the point value of 10s and picture cards. Most Las Vegas casinos like to surround baccarat with an aura of mystique: the game is played in a separate pit, supervised by personnel in tuxedos; the game's ritual is somewhat esoteric; and the minimum bet is usually $20–$100. Some casinos have forgone the larger baccarat pits in favor of the smaller mini-baccarat tables. Many players prefer mini-baccarat because it is less intimidating and can be played for lower limits. Mini-baccarat is essentially the same game, only it is played in the main blackjack pit, sans tuxedos and ritual, and with $5 minimums.

Up to 15 players can be seated around a baccarat table (six or seven at mini-baccarat). The game is run by four pit personnel. Two dealers sit side by side in the middle of the table; they handle the winning and losing bets and keep track of each player's "commission" (explained below). The "caller" stands in the middle of the other side of the table and dictates the action. A pit boss supervises the game and acts as final judge if any disputes arise.

Baccarat is played with eight decks of cards dealt from a large "shoe" (or card holder). Each player is offered a turn at handling the shoe and dealing the cards. Two two-card hands are dealt: the "player" and the "bank" hands. The player who deals the cards is called the banker,

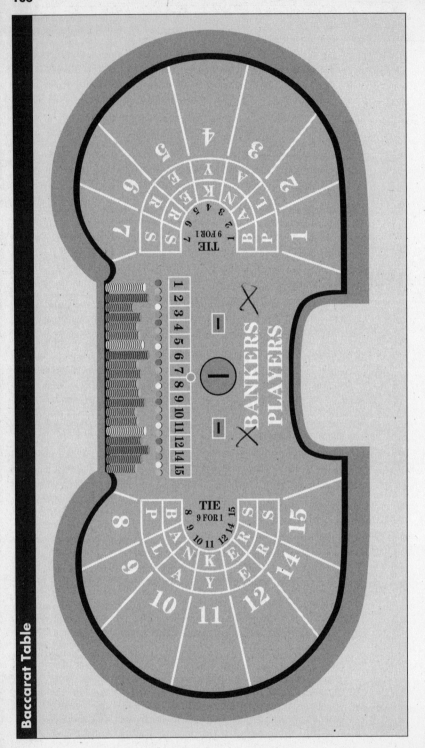

though the house, of course, banks both hands. The players bet on which hand, player or banker, will come closest to adding up to 9 (a "natural"). The cards are totaled as follows: Ace through 9 retain face value, while 10s and picture cards are worth zero. If you have a hand adding up to more than 10, the number 10 is subtracted from the total. For example, if one hand contains a 10 and a 4, the hand adds up to 4. If the other holds an ace and 6, it adds up to 7. If a hand has a 7 and 9, it adds up to 6.

Depending on the two hands, the caller either declares a winner and loser (if either hand actually adds up to 8 or 9), or calls for another card for the player hand (if it totals 1, 2, 3, 4, 5, or 10). The bank hand then either stands pat or draws a card, determined by a complex series of rules depending on what the player's total is and dictated by the caller. When one or the other hand is declared a winner, the dealers go into action to pay off the winning wagers, collect the losing wagers, and add up the commission (usually 5%) that the house collects on the bank hand. Both bets have a house advantage of slightly more than 1%.

The player-dealer (or banker) continues to hold the shoe as long as the bank hand wins. As soon as the player hand wins, the shoe moves counterclockwise around the table. Players are not required to deal; they can refuse the shoe and pass it to the next player. Most players bet on the bank hand when they deal, because they "represent" the bank, and to do otherwise would seem as if they were betting "against" themselves. This isn't really the case, but it seems that way.

Making a bet at baccarat is very simple. All you have to do is place your money in either the bank, player, or tie box on the layout (☞ Baccarat Table illustration), which appears directly in front of where you sit at the table. If you're betting that the bank hand will win, you put your chips in the bank box; bets for the player hand go in the player box. (Only real suckers bet on the tie, which has a house advantage of 14.4%.)

Because the caller dictates the action, the player responsibilities are minimal. It's not necessary to know any of the card-drawing rules, even if you're the banker. Playing baccarat is a simple matter of guessing whether the player or banker hand will come closest to 9, and deciding how much to bet on the outcome.

Bingo

Bingo is one of the world's best-known and best-loved games. It's also responsible for raising more money for charities, service organizations, religious institutions, and Native American tribes than any other fund-raiser.

One of the least profitable games for casinos, bingo was originally included in the roster of games for the same reason that extravaganzas were introduced to the showrooms, cheap steaks and breakfasts appeared in the restaurants, and coupons for free souvenirs began to be distributed via funbooks: to attract people into the casino. Simply by offering bingo, casinos can fill large halls with players, who have to pass by the pit and slots on the way in and out, where they'll drop a few bucks on a roulette wheel or in a slot machine.

Bingo is derived from the Italian game lotto but is similar to the original Chinese game keno. Both use numbered cards, numbered Ping-Pong balls blown from a cage, a caller, and a master board. There, however, the similarities pretty much dissolve. Bingo is played on paper cards marked with a "dauber" or on two-ply cardboard "boards" marked with little round plastic tabs. Bingo cards contain 25 squares. Five horizontal columns are topped with the letters B-I-N-G-O. Under the B are five boxes, with a number in each box between 1 and 15; under the I, five boxes with numbers between 16 and 30; under the N, four boxes numbered between 31 and 45; and a "free" box in the center of the card; under the G, five numbers between 46 and 60; and under the O, five numbers between 61 and 75.

The caller announces the letter and number of each ejected Ping-Pong ball and illuminates them on the master board. For example, if the caller announces "G-58" or "Number 58, under G," the players check their cards under the column topped by the G for the number 58. If it appears, they mark the number with the ink dauber or the plastic tabs. A winning card will have five numbers lined up in a row, either horizontally, vertically, or diagonally. The "free" square is always considered marked, so frequently you'll only need to match four numbers to win a game.

When a player lines up a card with the proper configuration of markings, he or she yells out "Bingo!" A floor person picks up the card and verifies the player's numbers by those on the big board, then declares the player the winner. The caller gives the other players a few moments to determine whether they, too, have won; if there's another winner, the two split the total prize money. Most of the time, however, there's only one winner per game, because great pains are taken to ensure that each card is unique. Prize money can range from $10 on a regular bingo game up to $50,000 for a progressive jackpot.

The variety of patterns for bingo games is vast, from the "no-number" card, where not a single number on the card has been called, to the "coverall" or "black-out," where every number on the card is marked. Configurations such as "inside corner," "outside corner," and shapes such as "diamond," "square," "picture frame," or the letters "L," "X," "T," "H," and "U" are announced by the caller at the start of each game, and the patterns illuminated on secondary boards around the room.

There are almost as many different buy-ins as there are patterns. Cards start at 25¢ and can go up to $500 and higher for special promotions and tournaments. Different-color cards have different buy-in denominations (for example, blue costs $3, green $6, orange $9, etc.); the prize money is determined by the card's worth. "Game packs" or "booklets" consist of a given number of paper cards stapled together and used up in a "session." A quick call to the bingo room can tell you which sessions are played when.

Each game moves fairly quickly. The numbers are called one right after the other, leaving the players just enough time to look for them on their cards. Old bingo hands can play dozens of cards simultaneously, but beginners should limit themselves to a half dozen at most. When you buy in, if it's a paper session (i.e., one played on paper cards), make sure you have a dauber on hand when the game starts; they're for sale at the bingo cashier for $1 or so. By watching, asking your neighbors or a floor person a quick question about something you don't quite understand, and playing, you'll be in the swing of things after the first few games of a session.

Though the pace of bingo can often be blistering, the games start out fairly relaxed—with empty cards and players gearing up for the pattern. Tension mounts as more numbers are called, cards fill up, and players await the magic number or two that will make them winners. Finally, someone yells, "Binnnnngooooo!" and for a brief moment the tension remains while the other players catch up on the last number or two. Then, as people realize they're not co-winners, the room deflates like a popped balloon. Quickly, the winner is verified and a new game starts the tension building all over again.

Blackjack

Blackjack is the most popular table game in the casino. It's easy to learn, fun to play, and it involves skill, and therefore presents varying levels of challenge. Blackjack also has one of the lowest house advantages. Furthermore, it's the game of choice when it comes to qualifying for comps: you can play for as long as you like, stand a real chance of breaking even or winning, *and* be treated like visiting royalty while you're at it.

Because blackjack is the only table game in the casino in which players can gain a long-term advantage over the house, it is the only table game in the casino (other than poker) that can be played professionally. And because blackjack can be played professionally, it is the most written-about and discussed casino game. Dozens of how-to books, trade journals, magazines, newsletters, computer programs, videos, theses, and novels are available on every aspect of blackjack, everything from how to add to 21 to when to stand or hit, how to play against a variety of shuffles, and the Level-Two Zen Count. Blackjack pros can spend hours debating whether the two-deck game at the Las Vegas Hilton has a starting house edge of 0.03 or 0.0275 because of the doubling-down-after-splitting option, or whether the Hi-Opt II count system's 88% betting efficiency correlation makes it stronger than the unbalanced count's perfect insurance indicator. Of course, training someone to play blackjack professionally is beyond the scope of this guide. Contact the **Gambler's Book Club** (☎ 702/382–7555) for a catalog of gambling books, software, and videotapes, including the largest selection on blackjack around.

The Rules

Basically, here's how it works: you play blackjack against a dealer, and whichever one of you comes closest to a card total of 21 without going over is the winner. Number cards are worth their face value, picture cards count as 10, and aces are worth either 1 or 11. (Hands with aces in them are known as "soft" hands. Always count the ace first as an 11; if you also have a 10, your total will be 21, not 11.) If the dealer has a 17 and you have a 16, you lose. If you have an 18 against a dealer's 17, you win (even money). If both you and the dealer have a 17, it's a tie (or "push") and no money changes hands. If you go over a total of 21 (or "bust"), you lose immediately, even if the dealer also busts later in the hand. If your first two cards add up to 21 (a "natural"), you're paid 3 to 2. However, if the dealer also has a natural, it's a push. A natural beats a total of 21 achieved with more than two cards.

You're dealt two cards, either face down or face up, depending on the custom of the particular casino. Two cards go to the dealer—one face down and one face up. Depending on your first two cards and the dealer's up card, you can:

stand, or refuse to take another card.

hit, or take as many cards as you need until you stand or bust.

double down, or double your bet and take one card.

split a like pair; if you're dealt two 8s, for example, you can double your bet and play the 8s as if they're two hands.

Blackjack Table

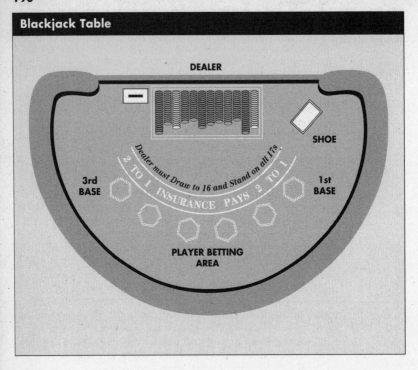

DEALER

SHOE

Dealer must Draw to 16 and Stand on all 17s.

2 TO 1 INSURANCE PAYS 2 TO 1

3rd
BASE

1st
BASE

PLAYER BETTING
AREA

buy insurance if the dealer is showing an ace. Here you're wagering half your initial bet that the dealer does have a natural; if so, you lose your initial bet but are paid 2 to 1 on the insurance (which means the whole thing is a push).

surrender half your initial bet if you're holding a bad hand (known as a "stiff") such as a 15 or 16 against a high up card like a 9 or 10.

Buying In and Playing 21

First you must select a table at which to play. A small sign in the left-hand corner of the "layout" (the diagram printed on the felt tabletop) indicates the table minimum and maximum and often displays the house rules. You can be sure that the $2-minimum tables will be packed, the $5-minimum tables will be crowded, and the $25 tables will have some empty seats. Look carefully before you sit, so as to avoid the embarrassment of parking yourself at a $25 table with $1 chips.

There are generally six or seven betting circles (or squares) on a black-jack layout. When you find an empty space at a table with your chosen minimum, you can join a game in progress between hands. Sometimes you'll have to squeeze in and the other players might not be too eager to make room for you for one reason or another (almost every one of them superstitious). The dealer should help make room for you. If everybody is particularly unfriendly, feel free to leave at any time, but it's to your advantage to spend as much time as possible playing at a crowded table, especially if your intention is to be rated for comps. The more crowded the table, the fewer hands will be played every hour, which reduces your risk. If everybody makes plenty of room for you to be comfortable and the dealer is friendly, you've got it made for hours.

Once you're settled, it's time to "buy in" (convert your cash to casino chips). Place your money on the layout between the betting circles or in the insurance space. If you lay cash *inside* the betting area, the dealer will say something like, "Money plays," and you might wind up betting your whole buy-in amount on the next hand! The dealer should exchange your cash for chips and deposit the bills in the drop slot, using a small plastic "pusher."

Now you can place your wager in the betting circle. You're dealt your two cards. If they're face down, you can pick them up, with one hand, and hold them. If they're face up, don't touch them. If you have a natural, turn them over and the dealer will pay you immediately and take your cards. Otherwise, everyone plays out his or her hand one at a time, from the right side of the table ("first base") to the left ("third base"). If you opt to stand, slide your two cards under your chips, then sit back and relax. If you want to hit, scratch the cards on the layout (seeing this done once will show you how). When you're ready to stand, slide the cards under the chips; if you bust, turn the cards over and the dealer will collect them and your bet. When everyone else has played, the dealer turns over her down (or "hole") card and plays out her hand, then settles up with all the players according to whether they won, lost, or pushed. Then the whole process starts all over again.

Playing blackjack is not only knowing the rules and etiquette, it's also knowing *how* to play. Many people devote a great deal of time to learning strategies, two of which are discussed in the sections that follow. However, if you don't have the time, energy, or inclination to get seriously involved, the following basic rules, which cover more than half the situations you'll face, should allow you to play the game with a modicum of skill and a paucity of humiliation:

1) When your hand is a stiff (a total of 12, 13, 14, 15, or 16) and the dealer shows a 2, 3, 4, 5, or 6, always stand.

2) When your hand is a stiff and the dealer shows a 7, 8, 9, 10, or ace, always hit.

3) When you hold a 17, 18, 19, or 20, always stand.

4) When you hold a 10 or 11 and the dealer shows a 2, 3, 4, 5, 6, 7, 8, or 9, always double down.

5) When you hold a pair of aces or a pair of 8s, always split.

6) Never buy insurance.

Basic Strategy

Available to anyone with an interest in the game, a system called "basic strategy" consists of a large set of exact decisions for optimum play at blackjack based on a player's hand versus the dealer's up card. These decisions have been developed via computer simulations of hundreds of millions of blackjack hands; they're not open to debate. You must spend several hours memorizing the basic strategy chart and then spend another several hours practicing basic strategy with playing cards. And then you must make the correct play on every hand, regardless of your "hunches" or what the person sitting next to you might recommend.

The accompanying Basic Strategy Chart lists all the possible combinations of blackjack hands against the dealer's up card. Here's how to read it. Say you're dealt a 7 and a 5 and the dealer is showing a 9. First look at the left-hand column, under YOUR HAND for the total, 12. Then follow the line across to the column under the number 9. The "H" stands for hit. So you would hit this hand. Now, suppose you're then dealt a 4. Look back at the left-hand column for the new total, 16. Then follow it across to the number-9 column again. Again you

Blackjack Basic Strategy Chart

Your Hand	2	3	4	5	6	7	8	9	10	A
5	H	H	H	H	H	H	H	H	H	H
6	H	H	H	H	H	H	H	H	H	H
7	H	H	H	H	H	H	H	H	H	H
8	H	H	H	H	H	H	H	H	H	H
9	D	D	D	D	D	H	H	H	H	H
10	D	D	D	D	D	D	D	D	H	H
11	D	D	D	D	D	D	D	D	D	D
12	H	H	S	S	S	H	H	H	H	H
13	S	S	S	S	S	H	H	H	H	H
14	S	S	S	S	S	H	H	H	H	H
15	S	S	S	S	S	H	H	H	H	H
16	S	S	S	S	S	H	H	H	H	H
17	S	S	S	S	S	S	S	S	S	S
18	S	S	S	S	S	S	S	S	S	S
19	S	S	S	S	S	S	S	S	S	S
20	S	S	S	S	S	S	S	S	S	S
21	S	S	S	S	S	S	S	S	S	S
A,2	H	H	D	D	D	H	H	H	H	H
A,3	H	H	D	D	D	H	H	H	H	H
A,4	H	H	D	D	D	H	H	H	H	H
A,5	H	H	D	D	D	H	H	H	H	H
A,6	D	D	D	D	D	H	H	H	H	H
A,7	S	D	D	D	D	S	S	H	H	H
A,8	S	S	S	S	S	S	S	S	S	S
A,9	S	S	S	S	S	S	S	S	S	S
A,A	SP	SP	SP	SP	SP	SP	SP	SP	SP	SP
2,2	H	SP	SP	SP	SP	SP	H	H	H	H
3,3	H	H	SP	SP	SP	SP	H	H	H	H
4,4	H	H	H	D	D	H	H	H	H	H
5,5	D	D	D	D	D	D	D	D	D	H
6,6	SP	SP	SP	SP	SP	H	H	H	H	H
7,7	SP	SP	SP	SP	SP	SP	H	H	H	H
8,8	SP	SP	SP	SP	SP	SP	SP	SP	SP	SP
9,9	SP	SP	SP	SP	SP	S	SP	SP	S	S
10,10	S	S	S	S	S	S	S	S	S	S

Dealer's up card

have to hit. (Pray for a 5 or less, your only way out of this worst-case blackjack scenario. Most of the time you'll bust.)

Say you're dealt, on the next hand, an ace and a 4 against the dealer's 3; counting the ace as 11, you have a total of 15. Find the A,4 listing in the YOUR HAND column and follow it across to the dealer's 3. According to basic strategy, you should hit. If you get a 6, you've got 21, not 12. If you get a 5, you've got 20; of course you should stand. (If you're in doubt, look up the A,9 listing.) If you get a 9, however, you'll have to count the ace as a 1, for a total of 14; otherwise you'd bust with 23. Now you look up the proper play for 14 against a dealer's 3; you'd stand.

Finally, suppose you're dealt a pair of 7s against a dealer's 7. The chart tells you to split the pair. Here you place both cards face up near your initial bet (don't worry about the exact position; no matter how close you place them, the dealer will *always* rearrange them slightly) and then place a second bet equivalent to the first. Then you play each 7 as its own hand. What if you're dealt a 4 on your first 7 for a total of 11? Some casinos will let you double down after splitting. Ask the dealer if she doesn't volunteer this information. What if you're dealt another 7? Again, some casinos will let you split the new pair and play out three hands.

Rules vary from house to house and city to city. In Las Vegas, some places allow you to surrender; some don't. At some places, dealers stand on soft 17; some places they don't. Basic strategy can get fairly advanced, and there are times when certain variations apply. But for most sets of rules at most Las Vegas joints, basic strategy will put you way ahead of the pikers who swell the casino coffers.

Card Counting

Card counting is an exacting technique for tracking the cards that have been played during a blackjack round and thereby determining whether the cards remaining to be played are favorable or unfavorable to the player. Card counters designate different plus or minus values for cards that are removed from the deck in play; based on the count, players can make better-informed decisions about playing and betting strategies. *Knock-Out Blackjack—The Easiest Card-Counting System Ever Devised* delivers what it promises in the subtitle: a card-counting system that takes only a few hours to learn and a few more to perfect, without sacrificing any of the power of the most complex and difficult counts. It's available from **Huntington Press** (✉ 3687 S. Procyon Ave., Las Vegas, NV 89103, ☎ 702/252–0655 or 800/244–2224).

Card counting is something the dealers, pit bosses, and video surveillance teams are constantly on the lookout for. In some casinos, if a player is suspected of card counting he will be asked to leave the table ("backed off") or, in some cases, to leave the premises ("barred"). However, some casinos don't sweat card counters too much. Others counter the card counters' edge by using "six-deck shoes"; that is, they combine six decks, which reduces the value of tracking the deck till deep into it. A common misconception is that counters keep track of more than 300 cards in a six-deck shoe; in fact, you're only counting the point totals (2s through 6s are worth +1, 7s and 8s are worth 0, 10s and aces are worth -1). Also, the casinos rarely deal all the way to the bottom of a single deck, two decks, or six decks, because it's easier to figure out what cards are left once you get towards the *bottom* of the pile. Using multideck shoes is just one of myriad countermeasures that casinos employ to foil card counters. Early and unbalanced shuffling, low table limits, and controlled betting spreads are among the many others. It's a tough business, and only a select few card counters are good enough to consistently win enough money to make a living at it.

Craps

Craps is a dice game played at a large rectangular table with rounded corners. Up to 12 players can crowd around the table, all standing. The layout (☞ Crap Table illustration) is mounted at the bottom of a surrounding "rail," which prevents the dice from being thrown off the table and provides an opposite wall against which to bounce the dice. It's important, when you're the "shooter," to roll the dice hard enough so that they bounce off the end wall of the table; this ensures a random bounce and shows that you're not trying to control the dice with a "soft roll." The layout grid is duplicated on the right and left side of the table, so players on either end will see exactly the same design. The top of the railing is grooved to hold the bettors' chips; as always, keep a close eye on your stash to prevent victimization by rail thieves.

It can require up to four pit personnel to run an action-packed, fast-paced game of craps. Two dealers handle the bets made on either side of the layout. A "stickman" wields the long wooden "stick," curved at one end, which is used to move the dice around the table; the stickman also calls the number that's rolled and books the proposition bets made in the middle of the layout. The "boxman" sits between the two dealers and oversees the game; he settles any disputes about rules, payoffs, mistakes, etc. A slow craps game is often handled by a single employee, who performs stick, box, and dealer functions. A portable end wall can be placed near the middle of the table so that only one side is functional.

To play, just join in, standing at the table wherever you can find an open space. You can start betting casino chips immediately, but you have to wait your turn to be the shooter. The dice move around the table in a clockwise fashion: the person to your right shoots before you, the one to the left after (the stickman will give you the dice at the appropriate time). If you don't want to roll the bones, motion your refusal to the stickman and he'll skip you.

Playing craps is fairly straightforward; it's betting on it that's complicated. The basic concepts are as follows: if the first roll turns up a 7 or 11, that's called a "natural"—an automatic win. If a 2, 3, or 12 comes up on the first throw (called the "come-out roll"), that's termed "crapping out"—an automatic lose. Each of the numbers 4, 5, 6, 8, 9, or 10 on a first roll is known as a "point": the shooter has to keep rolling the dice until that number comes up again. If a 7 turns up before the number does, that's another loser. When either the point (the original number thrown) or a 7 is rolled, this is known as a "decision"; one is made on average every 3.3 rolls.

But "winning" and "losing" rolls of the dice are entirely relative in this game, because there are two ways you can bet at craps: "for" the shooter or "against" the shooter. Betting "for" means that the shooter will "make his point" (win). Betting "against" means that the shooter will "seven out" (lose). (Either way, you're actually betting against the house, which books all wagers.) If you're betting "for" on the come-out, you place your chips on the layout's "pass line." If a 7 or 11 is rolled, you win even money. If a 2, 3, or 12 (craps) is rolled, you lose your bet. If you're betting "against" on the come-out, you place your chips in the "don't pass bar." A 7 or 11 loses; a 2 or 3 wins (a 12 is a push). A shooter can bet for or against himself or herself, as well as for or against the other players.

Crap Table

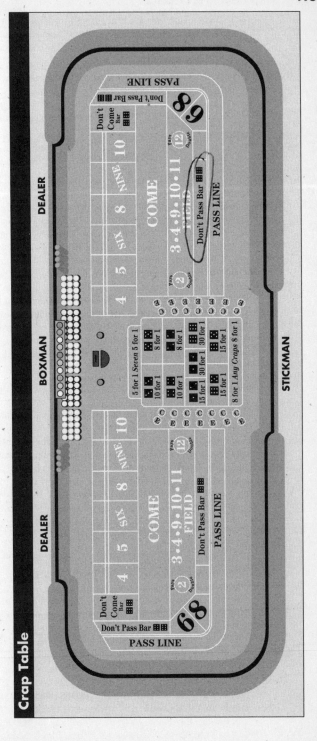

At the same time, you can make roughly two dozen wagers on any single roll of the dice. In addition to the "for" and "against" (pass and don't pass) bets, you can also make the following wagers at craps:

Come/Don't Come: After a pass-line point is established, the "come" bet renders every subsequent roll of the dice a come-out roll. When you place your chips in the come box, it's the same as a pass line bet. If a 7 or 11 is rolled, you win even money. If a 2, 3, or 12 is rolled, you've crapped out. If a 4, 5, 6, 8, 9, or 10 is rolled, it becomes another point, and the dealer moves your chips into the corresponding box on the layout. Now if that number comes up before the 7, you win the come bet. The opposite is true for the "don't come" box: 7 and 11 lose; 2, 3, and 12 win; and if the 7 is rolled before the point, you win.

Odds: The house allows you to take odds on whether or not the shooter will make his or her point, once it's established. The house pays off these bets at "true odds," rather than withholding a unit or two to its advantage, so these are the best bets in a crap game. Odds on the 6 and 8 pay off at 6 to 5, on the 5 and 9 at 3 to 2, and on the 4 and 10 at 2 to 1. "Back up" your pass line bets with single, double, triple, or up to 100 times odds (depending on the house rules) by placing your chips behind your line bet. For example, if the point is a 10 and your bet is $5, backing up your bet with single odds ($5) returns $25 ($5 + $5 on the line and $5 + $10 single odds); taking triple odds returns $55 ($5 + $5 on the line and $15 + $30). To take the odds on a come bet, toss your chips onto the layout and tell the dealer, "Odds on the come."

Place: Instead of waiting for a point to be rolled on the come, you can simply lay your bet on the number of your choice. Drop your chips on the layout in front of you and tell the dealer to "place" your number. The dealer puts your chips on the number; when it's rolled you win. The 6 and 8 pay 7 to 6, the 5 and 9 pay 7 to 5, and the 4 and 10 pay 9 to 5. In other words, if you place $6 on the 8 and it hits, you win $7. Place bets don't pay off at true odds, which is how the house maintains its edge (1.51% on the 6 and 8, 4% on the 5 and 9, and 6.66% on the 4 and 10). You can "call your place bet down" (take it back) at any time; otherwise the place bet will "stay up" until a 7 is rolled.

Buy: Buy bets are the same as place bets, except that the house pays off at true odds and takes a 5% commission if it wins. Buy bets have an edge of 4.7%, so you should only buy the 4 and 10 (rather than place them at a 6.6% disadvantage).

Big 6 and 8: Place your own chips in these boxes; you win if the 6 or 8 comes up, and lose on the 7. Because they pay off at even money, rather than true odds, the house edge is large—9.09%.

Field: This is a "one-roll" bet (a bet that's decided with each roll). Numbers 3, 4, 9, 10, and 11 pay even money, while 2 and 12 pay 2 to 1 (the 12 or "boxcars" pays 3 to 1 in Reno). The house edge on the field is 5.5%.

Proposition Bets: All the proposition bets are booked in the grid in the middle of the layout by the stickman. "Hardways" means a pair of numbers on the dice (two 3s for a hardways 6, two 4s for a hardways 8, etc.). A hardways 4 or 10 pays 7 to 1 (11.1% edge), and 6 or 8 pays 9 to 1 (9.09%). If a 7 or a 4, 6, 8, or 10 is rolled the "easy way," hardways bets lose. "Any seven" is a one-roll wager on the 7, paying 4 to 1 with a whopping 16.6% edge. "Yo'leven" is also a one-roll wonder paying 14 to 1 with a 16.6% edge. "Any craps" is a one-roll bet on the 2, 3, or 12, paying 7 to 1 (11.1%). Other bad proposition bets include the "horn" (one-roll bet on 2, 3, 11, or 12 separately; 16.6%), and "c and e" (craps or 11; 11.1%).

Note: the players place their own pass line, field, Big 6 and 8, and come bets. Players must drop their chips on the table in front of the dealers and instruct them to make their place and buy bets, and to take or lay the odds on their come bets. Chips are tossed to the stickman, who makes the hardways, any craps, any seven, and c and e bets in the middle of the layout.

Keno

Craps, blackjack, baccarat, and roulette arrived in Nevada casinos from Europe, but an early version of keno was brought over in the mid-1800s from China, where this bingo-type game was popular. It was rapidly Americanized in Reno casinos in the 1930s shortly after gambling was legalized.

Keno games are played once every seven or eight minutes. You participate by using a black crayon (provided) to mark a "ticket," imprinted with 80 boxes numbered 1 through 80, with 1 to 15 "spots" or numbers of your choice. You decide how many spots you want to mark based on how much money you're willing to bet. Eighty numbered Ping-Pong balls lying in a round plastic or wire bowl (the "goose") are mixed by an electric fan; the forced air blows the balls into two elongated tubes that hold 10 balls each. The numbers on the balls are announced over a public address system to the players in the keno "lounge" and are displayed on keno video monitors that hang all around the casino—in the coffee shop, restaurants, and bars. If enough of your numbers match the board's numbers, you win an amount enumerated in the keno payoff booklet (☞ Keno Payoffs chart).

You can bring your ticket to the central keno "counter," where a "writer" gives you a duplicate ticket and books your wager, or you can fill out a ticket at one of the casino's bars and restaurants, which are served by keno "runners," who collect tickets and bets and run them to the central counter where they are processed. The runners then deliver the duplicate tickets to you. After the game has been played and the winning numbers are displayed, the runner returns to check if there are any winners. If there are, the runner redeems the winning tickets for her customers—at which point it's customary to tip her.

There are six different types of keno tickets, the most common of which are the "straight," "replay," and "split" tickets. On a straight ticket, you mark off your chosen numbers—say, eight of them (remember, you're allowed to mark as many as 15). Looking at the payout chart, you can see that if four or fewer of your numbers match the called numbers, you lose. If five out of the eight match, you win $9 (on the $1 bet). If all eight match, you're an $18,000 winner. If you mark 15 spots and all 15 match (fat chance!), you win the big jackpot, usually $50,000.

A replay ticket uses the same numbers that you bet on with a previous ticket. Simply hand your bet (which doesn't have to be for the same amount) and the duplicate ticket from a prior game to the writer. A split ticket means that you're making two straight bets on a single ticket. Mark your numbers for the first straight bet and draw a line to separate them from the numbers for the second straight bet. Be sure to tell the writer that this is a split ticket.

Like the split ticket, "way" and "combination" wagers use one ticket to make what are often large and complex numbers of bets—a method

Keno Payoffs (for a bet of $1)

Numbers Marked	Winning Numbers	Pays $	Numbers Marked	Winning Numbers	Pays $
1	1 number	3			
			11	5 numbers	1
				6 numbers	8
2	2 numbers	12		7 numbers	72
				8 numbers	360
				9 numbers	1,800
3	2 numbers	1		10 numbers	12,000
	3 numbers	42		11 numbers	28,000
4	2 numbers	1	12	6 numbers	5
	3 numbers	4		7 numbers	32
	4 numbers	112		8 numbers	240
				9 numbers	600
5	3 numbers	2		10 numbers	1,480
	4 numbers	20		11 numbers	8,000
	5 numbers	480		12 numbers	36,000
			13	6 numbers	1
6	3 numbers	1		7 numbers	16
	4 numbers	4		8 numbers	80
	5 numbers	88		9 numbers	720
	6 numbers	1,480		10 numbers	4,000
				11 numbers	8,000
				12 numbers	20,000
7	4 numbers	2		13 numbers	40,000
	5 numbers	24			
	6 numbers	360	14	6 numbers	1
	7 numbers	5,000		7 numbers	10
				8 numbers	40
8	5 numbers	9		9 numbers	300
	6 numbers	92		10 numbers	1,000
	7 numbers	1,480		11 numbers	3,200
	8 numbers	18,000		12 numbers	16,000
				13 numbers	24,000
9	5 numbers	4		14 numbers	50,000
	6 numbers	44			
	7 numbers	300	15	7 numbers	8
	8 numbers	4,000		8 numbers	28
	9 numbers	20,000		9 numbers	132
				10 numbers	300
				11 numbers	2,600
10	5 numbers	2		12 numbers	8,000
	6 numbers	20		13 numbers	20,000
	7 numbers	132		14 numbers	32,000
	8 numbers	960		15 numbers	50,000
	9 numbers	3,800			
	10 numbers	25,000			

of reducing paperwork. But these bets are really just a fancier and faster way to lose money at keno. If you want to try them out, most keno lounges have a booklet explaining the way and combination bets.

Keno has the highest house advantage in the casino, but this doesn't seem to have much of an effect on its popularity. Even though you can expect to lose 25¢ to 40¢ on every dollar you wager, many people like keno. Why? It's easy to play and slow-paced; you can sit in the lounge, drink, and visit with your fellow suckers. You can also maintain a level of action while eating or drinking in a restaurant or bar. But mostly it's a long-shot game, at which you can win $25,000; $50,000; and, at some places, even $100,000 by risking only a few dollars.

Video keno is played similarly to "live" keno. You drop your nickel or quarter into the machine, then use the attached "pen" to touch your numbers of choice. When you press the button that says "play" or "start," the machine illuminates the winning numbers, usually accompanied by a beep. If enough of your numbers match the machine's, you're paid off either in coins or credits.

Poker Games

Over the last several years video poker has grown to be one of the most popular games in the casinos. Its no wonder that many of the newer table games that have made their way onto the casino floor are also based on poker. Let it Ride and Caribbean Stud are two of the fastest-growing table games, and Pai Gow Poker has been attracting new players to the tables. These games are fairly easy to learn; however, a player will need a general knowledge of the ranking of poker hands. From this, you'll understand what makes a winning hand and how to interpret the pay tables used for some of the bonus bets. Following is a hierarchy of poker hands, from strongest to weakest:

Royal Flush: This is the best poker hand, which is composed of a Ten (T), Jack (J), Queen (Q), King (K), and Ace (A) of the same suit.

Straight Flush: Five cards of the same suit that are in sequence.

Four-Of-A-Kind: Four cards of equal rank, one in each suit.

Full House: Three of a kind and a pair.

Flush: Any five cards of the same suit.

Straight: Five cards of any suit that are in sequence.

Three-Of-A-Kind: Any three cards of equal rank.

Two Pair: Two different pairs of the same rank.

One Pair: Two cards of the same rank.

Let It Ride

Let It Ride was first introduced to the casinos in 1993. The game is popular because it offers a potential for high payouts, but also because the players are not playing against each other or trying to beat the dealer, camaraderie develops among the players creating a fun atmosphere. The game and the correct playing strategy can be learned quickly. In essence, each player is trying to put together a winning poker hand.

The game is played on a blackjack-size table. There are three circles on the table in front of each player. The circles are marked with the numbers 1 and 2, and a dollar sign ($). To start the game a player places three equal bets in each circle. The Shuffle Master machine deals out cards three at a time.

The dealer distributes a three-card hand to each player and retains the last hand. The dealer looks at the dealer's hand, discarding one of the three cards; the two remaining dealer's cards—still face down at this point—become the "community cards" for all the players. More about those in a moment.

The machine counts out the remaining cards into the discard tray. When this is finished, the players are all allowed to look at their three-card hands. At this point each player has the option to take back the bet in circle number one or "let it ride." To take back your bet, you scrape your cards on the table toward you or make a brushing motion with your hand. If you let your bet ride, then it becomes part of your cumulative bet for the hand.

After all the players have made their decisions, the dealer will turn up the first of the two community cards. This card is used as the fourth card for all the players' hands. The players now have the option of taking down their second bet or letting it ride. You may take down the second bet even if you let the first bet ride, but you cannot take down the first bet if you passed on the last round or put it back up if your hand now has more promise than you originally expected.

After all the players make their decisions, the dealer will turn up the second community card. This card completes the five-card hand for all players. At this point, the dealer will pay all the winning bets according to the following pay-out schedule:

The "house edge" for the basic game is approximately 3.5% when you play the correct strategy. You must know which hands you should take down and when to "let it ride." Here is the proper strategy for the game:

Let It Ride Payout Schedule	
Hand	**Payout**
Pair of Tens or Better	1 to 1
Two Pairs	2 to 1
Three of a Kind	3 to 1
Straight	5 to 1
Flush	8 to 1
Full House	11 to 1
Four of a Kind	50 to 1
Straight Flush	200 to 1
Royal Flush	1,000 to 1

Let bet #1 ride if you have:

1) A winning hand—one pair of tens or better.

2) A three-card royal flush.

3) A three-card straight flush.

Let bet #2 ride if you have:

1) A winning hand—one pair of tens or better.

2) A four-card royal flush or straight flush.

3) A four-card flush.

4) Four high cards (ten or better).

5) A four-card open-ended straight (any four cards in sequence, where you could have a straight by adding a card at either end).

There is a dollar side bet that can be made for a bonus payoff when certain hands are made. The pay tables for the bonus vary from casino to casino. The house edge ranges from 15% to 30% on these bets. As with most side bets offered by the casino, these should be avoided.

Let It Ride can be a fun game for the recreational player. The game is slower than blackjack. You will be dealt about 40 hands per hour, and some casinos offer lower-limit games. If you take the time to learn the simple strategy, you can enjoy the excitement of this table game.

Caribbean Stud

Caribbean Stud is played on a blackjack-size table. It's another poker-based game, so you need to know the ranking of hands. You are playing against the dealer, and your hand must beat the dealer's hand. You do not have to worry about beating the other players' hands.

The game starts with each player making an ante bet equal to the table minimum. This is placed in the circle marked "ante" in front of the player. At this time the player also has the option of making an additional dollar side bet for the bonus jackpot. An automatic shuffler is used, and the dealer distributes a five-card hand to each player face down. The dealer retains a hand and turns one card face up.

Players look at their cards and decide to fold and forfeit their ante bet or call by making an additional bet, which is twice the size of the ante. For example, at a $5 table your ante bet would be $5 and your call bet would be $10.

After the players have made their decision to fold or call, the dealer's hand is turned over. The dealer must qualify by having a hand with ace plus king or better. If the dealer does not qualify, the players are paid even money for their original ante bet and the second call bet is a "push," which means it does not win or lose.

If the dealer qualifies and the player wins the hand, he or she is paid even money for the ante bet, and the call bet is paid based on the winning hand according to the table below:

Caribbean Stud Payout Schedule	
Hand	**Payout**
One Pair or Less	1 to 1
Two Pairs	2 to 1
Three of a Kind	3 to 1
Straight	4 to 1
Flush	5 to 1
Full House	7 to 1
Four of a Kind	20 to 1
Straight Flush	50 to 1
Royal Flush	100 to 1

The player must act before the dealer. This means there will be times when you fold a hand only to have the dealer not qualify. This does not mean you should play every hand. A simple strategy is to play your hand if it contains Ace-King or better, and fold anything else.

The house edge for the main game is about 5%, but the pace of the game is fairly slow. Because of this the house edge won't hurt your bankroll too much if you play for smaller stakes.

The same is not true of the side bet for the progressive jackpot. As with all so-called bonus bets, the bonus jackpot has a high house edge. You need a flush or higher to qualify for one of the bonus payouts, and the money you win when you receive one of these hands is not close to the odds of doing so. If you look at the chart below, you will see that you will make a flush once every 508 hands, and for this the casino will pay you $50 dollars. I think you can see why this is a bad bet.

Caribbean Stud Progressive Jackpot Payout Schedule		
Hand	**Dollar Jackpot**	**Odds Against**
Flush	$50	508 to 1
Full House	$75	693 to 1
Four of a Kind	$100	4,164 to 1
Straight Flush	10% of progressive jackpot	64,973 to 1
Royal Flush	100% of progressive jackpot	649,740 to 1

If for some reason you decide to make the side bet, you should know that you are eligible for the jackpot even if the dealer's hand does not qualify. You must inform the dealer immediately before they pick up the cards. Normally the dealer will pick up all the cards without turning them over. Make sure you speak up.

That is about all you need to know to play Caribbean Stud. Give it a try, but stay away from the side bet.

Caribbean Draw
The rules for Caribbean Draw are similar to those for Caribbean Stud. The payouts and betting strategies are the same. The difference is that after looking at their cards, the players have the option of discarding and drawing replacements for up to two cards.

The dealer must have a pair of eights or better to qualify. If not, only the ante bet will be paid. A simple strategy is to call with a pair of eights or better and fold all other hands.

Pai Gow Poker
Pai Gow is played with a standard 52-card deck and one joker, which can be used as an ace or a wild card to complete only a straight, flush, or straight flush. The game is played on a blackjack-size table with up to six players and a banker. The players are playing against the banker. In most cases the casino acts as the banker although players can choose to bank the game if they wish to. This would require having enough money to cover all of the other player's bets. The casino collects a 5% commission on all winning bets.

To start the game, the players make their bets according to the table minimum. The dealer shuffles the cards and deals out seven stacks containing seven cards. This is done no matter how many players there are. The banker shakes a cup containing three dice to determine who gets the first hand.

You look at your seven cards and set them into a two-card hand and a five-card hand. There is a place marked on the table to place your hands. The two-card hand is placed in front and the five-card hand is placed behind it. If both hands beat the banker's two hands you win. If one of your hands beats the banker's and one loses, it is a "push," and there are no winners. If either of your hands has the exact same value as the banker's hand it is a tie, which is called a "copy," and the banker wins.

When you are setting your hands, your five-card hand must be a higher value than your two-card hand (based on the values of poker hands). If you make a mistake and the two-card hand is higher it is a "foul," and you lose automatically. When the casino acts as the banker, the dealer must set the house hands according to certain rules, which is called the "House Way." If you are unsure of how to set your hand, you can ask the dealer to set it the "House Way." This will keep you from making a mistake.

Pai Gow is a slower-pace game than most table games. Since you must utilize only the seven cards dealt to you, there are many pushes. The banker has a slight edge because it wins the copies.

Here is a Pai Gow strategy:

The **Back** is the five-card hand; the **Front** is the two-card hand. A **complete hand** is a poker hand that requires all five cards to win (i.e., a straight, flush, or straight flush). A **set** is just a casino term for three of a kind.

No Pair: use the highest card in the Back and second- and third-highest in Front.

One Pair: place the pair in Back, the highest other two cards in Front.

Two Pair: if the "big" (i.e., higher-value) pair is **jack thru ace**, place the "small" pair in Front. If the big pair is **7s thru 10s**, place both pairs in Back if you can put Ace in Front. If the big pair is **2s thru 6s**, place both pairs in Back if you can put King in Front. Otherwise, **split** the pairs, always putting the bigger pair in Back.

Three Pair: place the big pair in Front.

Three of a kind: if you have **aces**, place an ace and the next-highest card in Front. If you have **kings and below,** place the three of a kind in Back, the two highest remaining cards in Front.

Two sets: place the pair from the higher set in Front; the remaining set goes in the Back.

Straight, flush, or straight flush: if you have **no pair,** place the two highest cards in Front that leave a complete hand in Back. If you have **one pair,** place the two highest cards possible (pair or no pair) in Front that leave a complete hand in Back. If you have **two pair,** use "two-pair" strategy above. If you have **three of a kind,** place a complete hand in Back, a pair in Front.

Full house: put the pair in Front, the set in Back.

Four of a kind: If you have **jacks thru aces,** always split the pairs, putting one in Front and one in Back. If you have **7s thru 10s,** place the four of a kind in Back if you can put ace or king in front; otherwise split into two pair. If you have **6s or below,** never split. If you **also have a pair,** play four of a kind in Back, the pair in Front. If you **also have three of a kind,** put the highest pair in Front, a full house in Back.

Five aces: Place a pair of aces in front.

Roulette ‍poison

Roulette is a casino game that utilizes a perfectly balanced wheel with 38 numbers (0, 00, and 1 through 36), a small white ball, a large layout with 11 different betting options (☞ Roulette Table illustration), and special "wheel chips." The layout organizes the 11 different bets into six "inside bets" (the single numbers, or those closest to the dealer) and five "outside bets" (the grouped bets, or those closest to the players).

The dealer stands between the layout and the roulette wheel, and chairs for five or six players are set around the roulette table. At crowded times, players also stand among and behind those seated, reaching over and

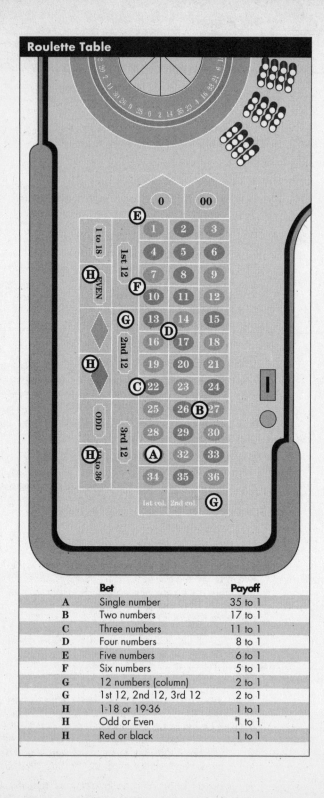

Roulette Table

	Bet	Payoff
A	Single number	35 to 1
B	Two numbers	17 to 1
C	Three numbers	11 to 1
D	Four numbers	8 to 1
E	Five numbers	6 to 1
F	Six numbers	5 to 1
G	12 numbers (column)	2 to 1
G	1st 12, 2nd 12, 3rd 12	2 to 1
H	1-18 or 19-36	1 to 1
H	Odd or Even	1 to 1
H	Red or black	1 to 1

around to place their bets. *Always* keep a close eye on your chips at these times to guard against "rack thieves," clever sleight-of-hand artists who can steal from your pile of chips right in front of your nose.

To buy in, place your cash on the layout near the wheel. Inform the dealer of the denomination of the individual unit you intend to play (usually 25¢ or $1, but it can go up as high as $500). Know the table limits (displayed on a sign in the dealer area); don't ask for a 25¢ denomination if the minimum is $1. The dealer gives you a stack of wheel chips of a different color from those of all the other players and places a chip marker atop one of your wheel chips on the rim of the wheel to identify its denomination. Note that you must cash in your wheel chips at the roulette table before you leave the game. Only the dealer can verify how much they're worth.

The dealer spins the wheel clockwise and the ball counterclockwise. When the ball slows, the dealer announces, "No more bets." The ball drops from the "back track" to the "bottom track," caroming off built-in brass barriers and bouncing in and out of the different cups in the wheel before settling into the cup of the winning number. Then the dealer, who knows the winning bettors by the color of their wheel chips, places a marker on the number and scoops all the losing chips into his or her corner. Depending on how crowded the game is, the casino can count on roughly 50 spins of the wheel per hour.

How to Place Inside Bets
You can lay any number of chips (depending on the table limits) on a single number, 1 through 36 or 0 or 00. If the number hits, your pay-off is 35 to 1, for a return of $36. You could, conceivably, place a $1 chip on all 38 numbers, but the return of $36 would leave you $2 short, which divides out to 5.26%, the house advantage.

If you place a chip on the line between two numbers and one of those numbers hits, you're paid 17 to 1 for a return of $18 (again, $2 short of the true odds).

Betting on three numbers returns 11 to 1, four numbers returns 8 to 1, five numbers pays 6 to 1 (this is the worst bet at roulette, with a 7.89% disadvantage), and six numbers pays 5 to 1.

How to Place Outside Bets
Lay a chip on one of three "columns" at the lower end of the layout next to numbers 34, 35, and 36; this pays 2 to 1. A bet placed in the first 12, second 12, or third 12 boxes also pays 2 to 1. A bet on red or black, odd or even, and 1 through 18 or 19 through 36 pays off at even money, 1 to 1. If you think you can bet on red *and* black, or odd *and* even, in order to play roulette and drink for free all night, think again: the green 0 or 00, which fall outside these two basic categories, will come up on average once every 19 spins of the wheel.

The house advantage of 5.26% on every roulette bet (except, as noted, the five-number bet) is five times the best bets at craps and five times less than the average bet at keno. European-style wheels, including those at Monte Carlo, have a single green 0, which slashes the house edge in half to 2.7%.

Slot Machines

Of all the games in the casino, slot machines are the most American: around the turn of the 20th century, Charlie Fey built the first mechanical slot in his San Francisco basement. Today, slot machines (along with video poker, keno, and blackjack machines) occupy more casino floor space and since 1992 have accounted for more gross casino winnings than all the table games combined. Once machine profits surpassed those of table games on the tony Las Vegas Strip, there's been no looking back. You'll soon realize that slot machines aren't confined to casinos, though. They're everywhere—in airports, supermarkets, bars, coin laundries, and minimarts.

Slot-machine technology has exploded in the past 20 years, and now there are hundreds of different models, which accept everything from pennies to specially minted $500 tokens. The old "mechanical" or "electromechanical" slots—all more than 30 years old—can still be found in some casinos, as antique or nostalgia pieces. They feature small skinny reels with fruit symbols; usually accept only one coin; don't have any lighting or sound effects; have a single pay line; and pay back minor amounts. "Multipliers" are machines that accept more than one coin (usually three to five, maximum) and are mostly electronically operated—with flashing lights, bells, and whistles, and spin, credit, and cash-out buttons. Multipliers frequently have a variety of pay lines: three horizontal for example, or five horizontal and diagonal.

One advance in the game, however, has been the progressive jackpot. Banks of slots within a particular casino are connected by computer, and the jackpot total is displayed on a digital meter above the machines. Generally, the total increases by 5% of the wager. If you're playing a dollar machine, each time you pull the handle (or press the spin button), a nickel is added to the jackpot. Progressive slots in many casinos are also connected by modem to other casinos throughout the state, and these jackpots often reach into the millions of dollars. The largest slot jackpot ever paid—$34.9 million, won by a 34-year-old cocktail waitress from the Monte Carlo Hotel-Casino at the Desert Inn in January 2000—was on a Megabucks progressive, which is competitive with surrounding state lotteries. (One form of gambling that is specifically illegal in Nevada is the lottery.) Nevada Nickels and Quartermania are lower-denomination versions of the statewide progressive. Lately, super high-tech slot machines have been emerging from manufacturers at a rapid clip, with large video screens and high-resolution graphics, games-within-a-game bonusing, and video clips (such as on the hot Elvis machines). Some of the new machines have such gimmicky themes as 1960s television programs ("I Dream of Jeannie," "The Addams Family"); a Chinese-theme machine features firecrackers, fortune cookies, and MSG symbols. In addition, some slots are beginning to resemble video-poker machines, in which you choose symbols to hold or discard.

An innovation has been the introduction of the multi-denomination machines. Players can choose to play for pennies, nickels, quarters, or dollars without having to switch machines. Instead of dropping coins in a tray, these machines pay out in vouchers that can be redeemed at the casino cage.

Insert your coins or dollar tokens—or slip your paper dollars into the bill receptor. Pull the handle or press the spin button, then wait for the reels to spin and stop one by one, and for the machine to determine whether you're a winner (occasionally) or a loser (most of the time). It's pretty simple—but because there are so many different types of machines, be sure you know exactly how the one you're playing operates. If it's a progressive machine, you must play the maximum number of coins to qualify for the jackpot. For example, the maximum bet at Megabucks is $3. You can play $1; this limits the action to the first-coin pay line (usually the middle line across the reels). The same goes for $2 and the second-coin pay line (the top line). But to win the progressive total, the three Megabucks symbols must be lined up on the third-coin pay line (not surprisingly, the bottom line). Can you imagine lining up three Megabucks symbols on the third pay line with only a dollar or two played? Instead of winning at least $5 million, you wind up with bupkis!

Slot candles: Many people have placed a quarter in a slot machine only to see it drop through into the tray below. At that point they realize it was a dollar machine that they were putting the quarter in. The denomination of the slot machine is posted on the machine, although many times it is hard to see. There is an easy way to determine the denomination of a slot machine. Look at the circular light on the top of the machine. This light is called a **candle.** The top half of the candle is white and lights up when you press the change button. The bottom half of the candle is colored. The color denotes the denomination of the machine. The candles are blue for the dollar machines, yellow for quarters, and red for nickel machines. By knowing the color of the candles, you can spot the denomination of the machine you want to play from across the casino floor. This little bit of knowledge will save you a lot of time when searching for a slot machine. The house advantage on slots varies widely from machine to machine, from 2% to 25%. Casinos that advertise a 97% payback are telling you that at least one of their slot machines has a house advantage of 3%. Which one? There's really no way of knowing. Generally, $1 machines pay back at a higher percentage than quarter or nickel machines. On the other hand, machines with smaller jackpots pay back more money more frequently, meaning that you'll be playing with more of your winnings. One good thing to keep in mind is this: in a recent nationwide study of slot-machine paybacks, a major gambling publication determined that downtown Las Vegas has the "loosest" slots. This means that from all the available data—specifically the ratio between the "handle" (total action wagered) and the "hold" (what the casino keeps) on slot machines (which is published by the Gaming Control Boards in most casino jurisdictions)—year after year downtown Las Vegas's is the lowest. In other words, they hold the smallest percentage of the total wagered.

One of the all-time great myths about slot machines is that they're "due" for a jackpot. Slots, like roulette, craps, keno, and the big six, are subject to the Law of Independent Trials, which means the odds are permanently and unalterably fixed. If the odds of lining up three sevens on a 25¢ slot machine have been set by the casino at 1 in 10,000, then those odds remain 1 in 10,000 whether the three 7s have been hit three times in a row or not hit for 90,000 plays. Don't waste a lot of time playing a machine that you suspect is "ready," and don't think that if someone hits a jackpot on a particular machine only minutes after you've finished playing on it that it was "yours."

If you have the hots for slots, remember to join as many slot clubs as you can. You're paying a pretty hefty commission for your romance with cherries, lemons, and 7s, so you might as well be rewarded with comps and perks.

Sports Betting

In Las Vegas, the word "book" rarely denotes a work of literature. More often than not, book isn't even used as a noun, but when it is, book almost always refers to the large room attached to the casino, where sports wagers are made and paid, the odds on sporting events are displayed, and sports bettors (often called "wise guys") watch the main events on large TV screens and video monitors. Bookmakers (or bookies) are people in the business of taking wagers. Book as a verb is the action of accepting and recording a wager, primarily on sporting and racing events, but also on casino games; the house books your blackjack, crap, and slot machine action.

Parlay Betting Odds

Number of Teams	Payout Odds	True Odds
2	13–5	3–1
3	6–1	7–1
4	10–1	15–1
5	20–1	31–1
6	35–1	63–1
7	50–1	127–1
8	100–1	225–1
9	200–1	511–1
10	400–1	1023–1

Teaser Betting Odds

Number of Teams	6 points	6½ points	7 points
2	even	10–11	1–12
3	9–5	8–5	3–2
4	3–1	5–2	2–1
5	9–2	4–1	7–2
6	7–1	6–1	5–1

The first race and sports book in a casino opened in 1975. Today nearly every major casino books race and sports bets. A book can be as small as a table with a clerk who quotes the odds and writes your receipt for a bet by hand, or as large as the Las Vegas Hilton's "super book," which boasts 46 video screens and 500 seats.

In Nevada you can bet on professional football, baseball, basketball, and hockey; college football and basketball; boxing matches; horse racing; and special events. But of all the sports, pro football draws the most action by far.

Football Betting

A wager made on a football game is one of the best gambling (and entertainment) bargains in the business. It costs you all of $1 in commission to the house to place a $10 bet on a team; the return is several hours of heightened excitement while the game is played. As anyone who's made a casual bet with a friend or group of coworkers knows, having a little money riding on a game introduces a whole new level of energy and interest to it.

There are four ways to bet on a football game: point spread, money line, parlay, and teaser. A wager based on the "point spread" (or a "straight bet") means that you're not only betting that one team will beat the other, but that it will win by a predetermined number of points. The point spreads are calculated for all pro football games by an outside "handicapper" (or oddsmaker) based on the relative strengths or weaknesses of the teams playing. For example, when a strong team, such as the Jacksonville Jaguars, plays a weak team, such as the New York Jets, the spread will favor the Jags by, say, 17 points. This means that the Jags have to beat the Jets by 18 points in order for a wager placed on Jacksonville to win. If the Jags beat the Jets by 10 points, they didn't "cover" the spread, so a bet on the Jets would win. If the

Jags win by 17 points exactly, it's a "push" or a tie, and the original bet (including the commission) is returned.

The "money line" bet on a pro football game uses odds instead of points and is determined simply by who wins and who loses. The money line for the Jacksonville-New York game might be a "minus 240 plus 180." This means you have to bet $24 to win $10 (for a total of $34) on the heavily favored Jags; conversely, a bet of $10 on the underdog Jets will win you $18 (for a total of $28).

A "parlay" is a bet on two, three, or four teams (sometimes more), all of which have to cover the point spread for you to win (☞ Parlay Betting Odds chart). If two out of the three teams cover and the third team wins but doesn't cover, you lose the whole bet. The payout on a two-team parlay is generally 13 to 5, on a three-team parlay 6 to 1, and on a four-team parlay 10 to 1.

A "teaser" is similar to a parlay, except that the point spreads are more variable than for a straight or parlay bet (☞ Teaser Betting Odds chart). If you win a three-team teaser after taking an additional 6 points on the spread, you're paid at 9 to 5; with 6½ additional points it's 8 to 5; and with 7 points, 3 to 2.

Football bets are usually made in denominations of $11, which includes the house's $1 commission for booking the bet. Winning bets pay off in denominations of $10. So, for example, you might bet $33 on the 49ers to cover the point spread. If the Jags cover, you win $30 (for a total payback of $63).

To make a football bet (or a bet on any sporting event), go to the sports book and step up to the counter. Study the board that lists all the games, and pick out the one(s) you want to put your money on. The teams are numbered. Give the team number, amount of the bet, and type of bet (points or money line) to the "writer," who inputs your bet into a computer and prints out your "ticket" or receipt. (Parlay and teaser cards are filled out and presented to the writer.) Check your ticket carefully to make sure the writer has given you the exact bet that you intended to make.

Then sit back and root for your money. If you lose, wallpaper your bathroom with the rest of your losing tickets. If you win, return to the casino where you made the bet, present the ticket to the sports book cashier, and receive your due.

Video Poker

Like blackjack, video poker is a game of strategy and skill, and at select times on select machines, the player actually holds the advantage, however slight, over the house. Unlike with slot machines, you can determine the exact edge of video-poker machines (or in gambler's lingo, "handicap" the machine). Like slots, however, video poker machines are often tied into a progressive meter; when the jackpot total reaches high enough, you can beat the casino at its own game.

The variety of video-poker machines is already large, and it's steadily growing larger. All the different machines are played in a similar fashion, but the strategies are different. This section deals only with straight-draw video poker.

You must first ascertain what denomination of coin a straight-draw video poker machine accepts. Thousands of penny, nickel, quarter, and dollar machines occupy casinos in Las Vegas. Five-dollar machines are becoming more popular around the state, and $25 and $100 machines

9/6 Video Poker Payout Schedule					
Royal Flush	250	500	750	1000	4000
Straight Flush	50	100	150	200	250
Four of a Kind	25	50	75	100	125
Full House	9	18	27	36	45
Flush	6	12	18	24	30
Straight	4	8	12	16	20
Three of a Kind	3	6	9	12	15
Two Pair	2	4	6	8	10
Jacks or Better	1	2	3	4	5

can be played at places such as the Mirage, Golden Nugget, and Caesars Palace. Then there are the new multigame machines, where you can play 3, 5, 10, even 50 hands of video poker at the same time.

The schedule for the payback on winning hands is posted on the machine, usually above the screen. It lists the returns for a high pair (generally jacks or better), two pair, three of a kind, a straight, flush, full house, straight flush, four of a kind, and royal flush, depending on the number of coins played—usually 1, 2, 3, 4, or 5. (The machine assumes you're familiar with poker and its terminology.) Look for machines that pay with a single coin played: 1 coin for "jacks or better" (meaning a pair of jacks, queens, kings, or aces; any other pair is a stiff), 2 coins for two pair, 3 for three of a kind, 4 for a straight, 6 for a flush, 9 for a full house, 25 for four of a kind, 50 for a straight flush, and 250 for a royal flush. This is known as a 9/6 machine: one that gives a nine-coin payback for the full house and a six-coin payback for the flush with one coin played (☞ 9/6 Video Poker Payout Schedule chart). Some machines pay a unit for a pair of 10s but get you back by returning only one unit for two pair. Other machines are known as 8/5 (8 for the full house, 5 for the flush), 7/5, and 6/5.

The return from a standard 9/6 straight-draw machine (with a 4,000-coin "flattop" or royal-flush jackpot) is 99.5%; you give up a half percent to the house. An 8/5 machine with a 4,000 flattop returns 97.3%. On 6/5 machines (such as those you find in supermarkets, 7-Elevens, and coin laundries around the city), the figure drops to 95.1%, slightly better than roulette. The return from a 25¢, 8/5 progressive machine doesn't reach 100% until the meter hits $2,200—a rare sight. (You can figure nickel, $1, and $5 progressives by the $2,200 figure. A 100% payback on nickels is $440; on $1 it's $8,800, and on $5 it's $44,000.) Machines with varying paybacks are scattered throughout the casinos. In some you'll see an 8/5 machine right next to a 9/6, and someone will be blithely playing the 8/5 machine!

As with slot machines, it's always optimal to play the maximum number of coins in order to qualify for the jackpot. You insert five coins into the slot and press the "deal" button. Five cards appear on the screen—say, 5, J, Q, 5, 9. To hold the pair of 5s, you press the "hold" buttons under the first and fourth cards. The word "hold" appears underneath the two 5s. You then press the "draw" button (always the same button as "deal") and three new cards appear on the screen— say, 10, J, 5. You have three 5s; with five coins bet, the machine will give you 15 credits. If you want to continue playing, press the "max bet" button: five units will be removed from your number of credits, and five new cards will appear on the screen. You repeat the hold and draw process; if you hit a winning hand, the proper payback will be added to your credits. Those who want coins rather than credit can hit the "cash out" button at any time. Some older machines don't have credit counters and automatically dispense coins for a winning hand.

Like blackjack, video poker has basic strategies that have been formulated by the computer simulation of hundreds of millions of hands. The most effective way to learn it is with a video poker computer program that deals the cards on your screen, then tutors you in how to play each hand properly. The best program is *WinPoker,* available from **Huntington Press** (⊠ 3687 S. Procyon Ave., Las Vegas, NV 89103, ☎ 702/252–0655 or 800/244–2444).

If you don't want to devote that much time to the study of video poker, memorizing these six rules will help you make the right decision for more than half the hands you'll be dealt:

1) If you're dealt a completely "stiff" hand (no like cards and no picture cards), draw five new cards.

2) If you're dealt a hand with no like cards but with one jack, queen, king, or ace, always hold on to the picture card; if you're dealt two different picture cards, hold both. But if you're dealt three different picture cards, only hold two (the two of the same suit, if that's an option).

3) If you're dealt a pair, always hold it, no matter what the face value.

4) Never hold a picture card or an ace ("kicker") with a pair of 2s through 10s.

5) Never draw two cards to try for a straight or flush.

6) Never draw one card to try for an inside straight.

Wheel of Fortune (Big Six)

Prize wheels are among the oldest games of chance and among the easiest to play and lose. Nevada-style big six is modeled after the old carnival wheels that attracted suckers on the midway. The standard wheel, usually 6 ft across, is divided into nine sections and 54 individual slots or stops. Fifty-two of the stops are marked by dollar denominations: 23 $1, 15 $2, 8 $5, 4 $10, and 2 $20 stops. The other two stops are marked by a joker or the casino logo. A leather "flapper" mounted at the top of the wheel clicks as it hits the wood or metal pegs that separate each slot. When the wheel stops, the flapper falls between two pegs and indicates the winning number.

You lay your bet on a glass-covered table in front of the wheel. The layout display consists of the actual currency, which matches the numbers on the wheel (a Washington, Lincoln, Hamilton, Jackson, etc.). To play, you simply place a chip or cash atop the bill you think will be the winner. The payoff is a multiple of the denomination: a $1 bet on the $1 bill pays a buck; a $1 bet on the $2 bill pays $2; a $5 bet on the $20 pays $100. The joker, casino logo, or other nonnumerical symbol on the wheel, however, pays 40 to 1: a successful $1 bet on one of these will get you back $40.

The house advantage starts at 11.1% on the $5 bet and rockets to 22.2% on the $20 bet and 24% on the joker. This isn't a game you'll want to play all night, or for more than a few spins. But the big six often draws a crowd. Even hardened gamblers like to stop and watch and listen to the wheel spin, with its hypnotic clicking of flapper against pegs, to see where it stops. They'd probably even lay down a buck or two, but they'd be too embarrassed in front of the dealer!

BOOKS AND MOVIES

Books

History and Biography

Learning from Las Vegas–The Forgotten Symbolism of Architectural Forms, by Robert Venturi et al., and *Viva Las Vegas—After Hours Architecture*, by Alan Hess, are readable analyses of the shapes, sizes, and placement of Las Vegas's signs, casinos, parking lots, and false fronts. *Literary Las Vegas*, edited by Mike Tronnes, is a superb collection of writings by well-known writers—Tom Wolfe, Joan Didion, Michael Herr, Hunter S. Thompson, among them—about the neon jungle. Of course, Hunter S. Thompson's *Fear and Loathing in Las Vegas* is the famous psychedelic account of the gonzo journalist's late-1960s trip to Las Vegas. For the most savage indictment of Las Vegas and its mobsters, payoffs, cheating, corruption, and prostitution, read *Green Felt Jungle*, by Ovid Demaris and Ed Reid. The book that Reid and Demaris used as their model to expose the seamy underside of Las Vegas was *The Great Las Vegas Fraud* by Sid Meyers, published in 1958, the first—and most vicious—in a long series of books that came to be called the Las Vegas Diatribe.

For the antidote to *Green Felt Jungle* and *The Great Las Vegas Fraud*, try to find *Playtown, U.S.A.*, by Katherine Best and Katherine Hillyer, a snapshot of Las Vegas written in 1955—one of the most insightful and colorful portraits of Sin City ever written. *Las Vegas—As It Began, As It Grew*, by Stanley Paher, covers in detail the popular early history of Las Vegas, from the Old Spanish Trail up through the building of Hoover Dam. *Resort City in the Sunbelt*, by Eugene Moehring, is a comprehensive, academic, and heavily footnoted history of Las Vegas's development since the 1930s. A more recent history of Las Vegas is *The Money and the Power: The Making of Las Vegas and Its Hold on America* by Sally Denton and Roger Morris. *Fly on the Wall—Recollections of Las Vegas' Good Old, Bad Old Days*, by Dick Odessky, is the personal account of a newspaper reporter turned casino publicist who lived through the transition from mob-run to corporate-owned Las Vegas. *Las Vegas—A Desert Paradise*, by Ralph Roske, is a large-format pictorial that covers Las Vegas's historical highlights. *Cult Vegas*, by *Las Vegas Review-Journal* entertainment columnist Mike Weatherford (a contributor to this book), delves into the offbeat entertainment history of the Entertainment Capital of the World. *Howard Hughes in Las Vegas*, by Omar Garrison, concerns the four years the enigmatic billionaire spent sequestered on the ninth floor of the Desert Inn. *No Limit—The Rise and Fall of Bob Stupak and the Stratosphere Tower*, by John L. Smith, is the fascinating biography of Las Vegas's most flamboyant modern casino operator. *Easy Street* is the sad and gripping autobiography of Susan Berman, only child of David Berman, one of the earliest mobsters to relocate in Las Vegas.

Fiction

Most of Mario Puzo's novels contain an enormous amount of inside dirt on Las Vegas, but *Fools Die* is centered on the city and contains some excellent descriptions of casino color and scams. *The Death of Frank Sinatra*, by L.A. novelist Michael Ventura, is a dark and disturbing but brilliant fictional look at the meaning of Las Vegas. Larry McMurtry's *Desert Rose*, conversely, is an affectionate and poignant character study of an aging showgirl and her ties to Las Vegas. *Last Call*, by Tim Powers, is a strange, suspenseful, violent tale about chaos and randomness, the patron saints of Las Vegas. *Devil's Hole*, by Las Vegas novelist Bill Branon, concerns a hit man hired by a Las Vegas casino to take out a wildly successful sports bettor. *Neon Mirage*, by Max Allan Collins, is a novel about Bugsy Siegel, as is *Las Vegas Strip*, by Morris Renek. *The Big Night* is a story about a notorious gambler who assembles a team of five women to beat Las Vegas out of a million bucks, by Ian Andersen, one of the world's most successful high-stakes blackjack players. Andersen's book is one of long list of pulp fiction based on "the great Las Vegas heist" theme: *The Vegas Trap*, by Hal Kantor; *Fortune Machine*, by Sam Ross; *Snake Eyes*, by Edwin Silberstang; and *Murder in Las Vegas*, by

Renaissance man Steve Allen, are other examples.

Gambling

Comp City—A Guide To Free Las Vegas Vacations, by Max Rubin, exposes the guarded world of the casino complimentary system. *Knock-Out Blackjack,* by Olaf Vancura and Ken Fuchs, is the easiest card-counting system ever devised. Ian Andersen, who's made his living at high-stakes blackjack for nearly three decades, tells all in two books, *Turning the Tables on Las Vegas* and *Burning the Tables in Las Vegas. The Man with the $100,000 Breasts and Other Gambling Stories,* by Michael Konik, takes readers deep inside the world of high rollers, hustlers, card counters, and poker champions. The best low-roller guide to gambling ever written is *The Frugal Gambler,* by Jean Scott. *Casino Secrets,* by Barney Vinson, is a gambling primer and Las Vegas guide.

Movies

Frank Sinatra made his feature-film debut in the 1941 picture *Las Vegas Nights.* Barbara Stanwyck loses house and husband after becoming a gambling addict in the melodrama *The Lady Gambles* (1949). Sinatra gangs up with the rest of the Rat Pack for a heist in the cornball *Ocean's Eleven* (1960). Elvis Presley plays a race-car driver on the loose in Las Vegas, meeting up with Ann-Margret, in the famous *Viva Las Vegas* (1964).

The James Bond film *Diamonds Are Forever* (1971) mixes footage of real-life casinos with shots from a fictional, studio-built casino. The main action in *The Electric Horseman* (1979) centers on Caesars Palace. *Melvin and Howard* (1980) tells the tale of Melvin Dummar, who presented for probate a will supposedly written by Howard Hughes. Much of the Albert Brooks comedy *Lost in America* (1985) takes place at the Desert Inn. Burt Reynolds stars as a Vegas private investigator in *Heat* (1987). On their way across the country in *Rain Man* (1988), Tom Cruise and Dustin Hoffman make a stop in Vegas to count cards.

Flying Elvii drop from the sky in the light comedy *Honeymoon in Las Vegas* (1992), part of which is set at Bally's casino. Robert Redford makes the titular *Indecent Proposal* (1993) to married couple Demi Moore and Woody Harrelson; some footage of the Las Vegas Hilton is included. Much of the campy schlocky *Showgirls* (1995) takes place at the Stardust. Nicholas Cage plays an unrepentant drunk in the bleak but moving *Leaving Las Vegas* (1995). Two of the better films about the role of organized crime in Las Vegas are *Bugsy* (1991), which traces the early days of mob involvement, and the Martin Scorcese movie *Casino* (1995), a look at how greed in the 1970s killed the goose that laid the Mafia's golden egg.

For scenes from present-day Las Vegas, check out *The Great White Hope* (1996), a satire about boxing that was shot at the MGM Grand; *Mars Attacks!* (1996), which incorporates real-life footage of the implosion of the Landmark Hotel-Casino (and also includes shots of the Luxor); *Con Air* (1997), whose closing action is set at the Sands Hotel; and *Austin Powers: International Man of Mystery* (1997), with Mike Meyers as a swingin' secret agent from the 1960s who was cryptogenetically frozen and defrosted in 1997, shagging his way through Las Vegas. The fountains of the Bellagio mesmerize George Clooney et al in Steven Soderbergh's 2001 remake of *Ocean's Eleven.*

INDEX

Icons and Symbols

★ Our special recommendations

✕ Restaurant

🔲 Lodging establishment

✕🔲 Lodging establishment whose restaurant warrants a special trip

☜ Good for kids (rubber duck)

☞ Sends you to another section of the guide for more information

⊠ Address

☎ Telephone number

☉ Opening and closing times

🎟 Admission prices

Numbers in white and black circles ③ ❸ that appear on the maps, in the margins, and within the tours correspond to one another.

A

A.J.'s Steakhouse ✕, *86*
A Taste of N'Awlins ✕, *70*
Air tours, *172*
Aladdin Hotel and Casino, *18, 20*
casino facilities, 45
dining in, 68, 69, 72
hotel facilities, 93
nightlife, 112
Aladdin Theatre for the Performing Arts, *112*
Alan Bible Visitor Center, *162*
Alexis Park Resort Hotel 🔲, *102*
Allied Arts Council, *126*
American Superstars (show), *119*
AmeriSuites 🔲, *103*
An Evening at La Cage (show), *119*
An Evening at the Improv (comedy club), *115*
Andre's French Restaurant ✕, *76*
Antonio's ✕, *79*
Appian Way at Caesars, *143–144*
Area 51, *163*
Arizona Charlie's Hotel and Casino West, *51–52*
Art galleries. ☞ *See Museums*
Artists Palette (view), *178–179*
Arts, *126–127*

ATMs, *xxviii*
Aureole ✕, *72*
Avi Hotel Casino, *166*

B

Baby's (dance club), *115*
Baccarat, *185, 187*
Badwater, *179*
Bahama Breeze ✕, *70*
Ballet, *126*
Ballooning, *129*
Bally's Casino Resort, *18, 20–21*
casino facilities, 45
dining in, 73, 86
hotel facilities, 93
nightlife, 120
Bally's Steakhouse ✕, *86*
Barbary Coast Hotel and Casino, *18, 21*
casino facilities, 45
hotel facilities, 97
nightlife, 114
Baseball, *137*
Basketball, *137*
Bayshore Inn 🔲, *167*
Beach (dance club), *115–116*
Beaches, *162*
Bellagio Las Vegas (casino hotel), *8, 21*
casino facilities, 45, 47
dining in, 68, 75, 77, 78, 82–83, 87
hotel facilities, 91
nightlife, 113, 116, 121
Belz Factory Outlet World, *144*
Bertolini's ✕, *80–81*
Best Western Ruby's Inn 🔲, *176*
Bicycling, *xiii, 129–130*
Big Six (Wheel of Fortune), *7, 211*
Bikini blackjack, *8*
Billy Bob's Steak House ✕, *87*
Bingo, *187–189*
Binion's Horseshoe Hotel and Casino, *34, 35*
casino facilities, 54
hotel facilities, 104–105
Bird Viewing Preserve (Boulder City), *159*
Bit and Spur Restaurant and Saloon ✕, *175*
Blackjack (twenty-one), *189–191, 193–194*
BLM Visitors Center, *157*
Blue Man Group: Live at Luxor (show), *119*
Blue Note, *118*
Boating, *130*
Bonanza Gift Shop, *8, 26, 27*
Bonjour Casual French ✕, *77*

Bonnie Springs Ranch, *134, 158*
Bookstores, *146, 148*
Border Grill ✕, *85*
Boston Grill & Bar (rock music), *118*
Bottom's Up (show), *118*
Boulder Beach, *162*
Boulder Lakes (RV park), *107*
Boulder Cinemas, *126*
Boulder City, Nevada, *6, 159, 161*
Boulder City/Hoover Dam Museum, *161*
Boulder Station Hotel and Casino
casinos, 56
dining in, 63
movies, 126
Boulder Strip
casinos, 56–57
nightlife, 113
Boulevard Mall, *144*
Bowling
facilities for, 130–131
Boxing, *137–138*
Brenden Theatres at the Palms (cinema), *126*
Bright Angel Lodge ✕🔲, *171*
Bright Angel Point, *171–172*
Broiler ✕, *63*
Brown Derby ✕, *62*
Bryce Canyon Lodge 🔲, *176*
Bryce Canyon National Park, *6, 175–176*
Buca di Beppo ✕, *81*
Budget Suites of America 🔲, *103*
Buffalo Bill's Hotel and Casino 🔲, *164–165*
Buffalo Bill's Rides, *164*
Buffet at Bellagio ✕, *68*
Bumbleberry Inn ✕, *175*
Bus travel, *xiv, 168*

C

C2K (dance club), *116*
Caeser's Magical Empire ✕, *76*
Caesars Palace (casino hotel), *18, 22*
casino facilities, 47
children, attractions for, 22
dining in, 71, 73, 76, 78, 80–81
hotel facilities, 93
night life, 114
California Hotel and Casino, *34, 35, 54*
Camping, *107–108*
Candlelight Wedding Chapel, *26, 27, 28*
Canyon View Information Plaza, *169*
Car rentals, *xv–xvi, 168*

Fodor's Key to the Guides

America's guidebook leader publishes guides for every kind of traveler.
Check out our many series and find your perfect match.

Fodor's Gold Guides
America's favorite travel-guide series
offers the most detailed insider reviews
of hotels, restaurants, and attractions
in all price ranges, plus great background information, smart tips, and
useful maps.

Fodor's Road Guide USA
Big guides for a big country—the
most comprehensive guides to
America's roads, packed with places
to stay, eat, and play across the
U.S.A. Just right for road warriors,
family vacationers, and cross-country
trekkers.

COMPASS AMERICAN GUIDES
Stunning guides from top local writers
and photographers, with gorgeous
photos, literary excerpts, and colorful
anecdotes. A must-have for culture
mavens, history buffs, and new residents.

Fodor's CITYPACKS
Concise city coverage with a foldout
map. The right choice for urban travelers
who want everything under one cover.

Fodor's EXPLORING GUIDES
Hundreds of color photos bring your
destination to life. Lively stories lend
insight into the culture, history, and
people.

Fodor's POCKET GUIDES
For travelers who need only the essentials. The best of Fodor's in pocket-size
packages for just $9.95.

Fodor's To Go
Credit-card–size, magnetized color
microguides that fit in the palm
of your hand—perfect for "stealth"
travelers or as gifts.

Fodor's FLASHMAPS
Every resident's map guide. 60 easy-
to-follow maps of public transit, parks,
museums, zip codes, and more.

Fodor's CITYGUIDES
Sourcebooks for living in the city:
Thousands of in-the-know listings for
restaurants, shops, sports, nightlife,
and other city resources.

**Fodor's AROUND THE CITY
WITH KIDS**
68 great ideas for family days,
recommended by resident parents.
Perfect for exploring in your own
backyard or on the road.

Fodor's ESCAPES
Fill your trip with once-in-a-lifetime
experiences, from ballooning in
Chianti to overnighting in the
Moroccan desert. These full-color
dream books point the way.

Fodor's FYI
Get tips from the pros on planning
the perfect trip. Learn how to pack,
fly hassle-free, plan a honeymoon
or cruise, stay healthy on the road,
and travel with your baby.

Fodor's Languages for Travelers
Practice the local language before
hitting the road. Available in phrase
books, cassette sets, and CD sets.

Karen Brown's Guides
Engaging guides to the most charming
inns and B&Bs in the U.S.A. and Europe,
with easy-to-follow inn-to-inn itineraries.

Baedeker's Guides
Comprehensive guides, trusted since
1829, packed with A–Z reviews and
star ratings.